*To the business and social sector leaders
who have had the vision, commitment, and
competency to combine resources to create
powerful partnerships that contribute to the
making of a better world.*

Contents

Tables and Figures

Tables

Figures

Contributors to SEKN Research

This book was made possible by the enthusiastic work of a large number of scholars and researchers from various institutions, who in different capacities contributed their efforts to the research that is crystallized in the following pages. We list all of them alphabetically below:

Luis Noel Alfaro Gramajo, Ph.D. in Agricultural Economy and Rural Sociology from Ohio State University, is a faculty member at INCAE, where he teaches MBA courses on Management Control, Finances, Micro-finances, Management Intervention Methods and Management Problem Analysis and Solving. He founded and chairs the consulting firm *Empresa y Desarrollo* (E&D). Gramajo has managed several strategic planning, turnaround and performance enhancement processes at various organizations, including BANRURAL S.A., one of the world's most successful financial institutions. He has authored and co-authored six books on finances for development and social organizations.

James Austin holds the Snider Professorship of Business Administration at the Harvard Business School and is the Faculty Chair of the School's Initiative on Social Enterprise. He has been a member of the Harvard University faculty since 1972. His Doctor of Business Administration and MBA degree with Distinction are from Harvard University. He has authored 16 books, dozens of articles, and over a hundred case studies on business and nonprofit organizations. His most recent book is the prize winning *The Collaboration Challenge: How Nonprofits and Businesses Succeed through Strategic Alliances*.

Julio Ayca, M.B.A. graduate from INCAE, works as a researcher at his alma mater. His research work focuses on operations and finances. He has conducted research and organization diagnosis surveys, and written several case studies on issues associated with Operations, Logistics, Finances, Management Control, Organization and Social Enterprise. In addition, he has worked for the Peruvian textile industry and the local tax collection agency, where he was involved in tax regulation projects dealing with cost reduction and service improvements.

Mónica Azofeifa graduated at the top of her MBA class at INCAE. Currently, she is a Senior Consultant at PriceWaterhouseCoopers, specializing in Human Resources. She worked at INCAE as a researcher for the Latin American Center for Competitiveness and Sustainable Development (*Centro Latinoamericano para la Competitividad y el Desarrollo Sostenible*, CLACDS), where she wrote teaching cases for faculty members. Additionally, she coordinated the SEKN project, representing Central America at the Social Enterprise Knowledge Network.

Gabriel Berger is an associate professor at Universidad de San Andrés, where he is in charge of the Graduate Program on Nonprofit Organizations (CEDES-UDESA-UTDT) and the Program on Social Responsibility. He coordinates the SEKN-Argentina team. He holds a Ph.D. in Social Policy and a Master's degree in Management of Human Services from the Heller School of Social Policy and Management (Brandeis University). His research interests and teaching focuses are Corporate Social Responsibility Strategies, Nonprofit Governance, and Strategic Management in Nonprofit Organizations.

Monica Bose graduated in Psychology and is currently pursuing her MBA studies at São Paulo University's School of Economics, Administration and Accounting. A researcher at CEATS—*Centro de Empreendedorismo Social e Administração em Terceiro Setor*—representing USP in the SEKN group, her research interests include topics concerning the third sector, Social Entrepreneurship and Management of Human Resources. Having published articles like "Human Resources Management on Nonprofit Organizations" (Balas Conference, April 2003), she is now working on her Master's Degree thesis on "People Management in Civil Society Organizations."

Tania Casado holds a Ph.D. in Business Administration from the School of Economics, Administration and Accounting at São Paulo University. A member of the SEKN group, she is part of the CEATS team—*Centro de Empreendedorismo Social e Administração em Terceiro Setor* (Center of Social Entrepreneurship and Administration on Third Sector), representing USP. She teaches for the Business Administration Department at /FEA/USP, where she also heads the Career Center. Her research work deals with Human Potential, Psychological Types, Self Assessment, Career Development, Organizational Behavior, and Social Entrepreneurship.

Forrest Colburn, Ph.D. in Government from Cornell University, is a visiting professor at INCAE. He was a faculty member at Princeton University for eight years and currently teaches at the City University of New York (CUNY). At INCAE, he has lectured on political analysis and public administration. He wrote *Latin America at the End of Politics* and *The Vogue of Revolution in Poor Countries*, both published by Princeton University Press. He co-authored (along with Fernando Sánchez) "Individuos versus Instituciones en las Democracias Centroamericanas" and "Empresarios Centroamericanos y Apertura Económica."

Arturo Condo, D.B.A. from Harvard University, teaches Business Strategy, International Business and Production and Operation Management at INCAE. He also serves as Associate Dean at the Latin American Center for Competitiveness and Sustainable Development (CLACDS). Professor Condo obtained his MBA degree at INCAE, where he graduated with the highest GPA in the history of the institution and was awarded the Distinguished Scholar title. He has led competitiveness programs for Latin American cluster development and strengthening. His research is primarily focused on the development of successful domestic and international strategies for Latin American companies.

Elidia Maria de Novaes Souza received her Master's degree in Social Communication at the Escola Superior de Propaganda e Marketing, São Paulo. She majored in Geography at São Paulo University's School of Geography and History. A member of the team at CEATS—*Centro de Empreendedorismo Social e Administração em Terceiro Setor*, representing USP in the SEKN group, Elidia works at the research, administration and communication areas. Her research focuses include Corporate Social Responsibility, Cross-Sector Strategic Alliances for social action, Social Entrepreneurship and Corporate Governance.

Alexandra de Royere holds an M.B.A. from Harvard Business School. After a decade of professional experience at the private sector in Europe and Latin America, she currently works as Senior Researcher at the Latin America Research Center (LARC) of Harvard Business School based in Buenos Aires. She has co-authored several case studies on business and nonprofit organizations in Latin America.

Guillermo S. Edelberg was the first Spanish-speaking national ever to obtain a D.B.A. degree from Harvard University, in 1963. Currently a professor at INCAE, his doctoral thesis was published in New York City. In Argentina, he chaired the Economic Research Center at Instituto Di Tella. He was also the first Director of IDEA's Administration School and an advisor to the Argentine Ministry of Economy and the Industry Secretary. In addition, he served as consultant for OAS' Economic Affairs Department. His book *Temas de Actualidad en Recursos Humanos* was published in 2002. He is a Fellow member of the International Academy of Management.

Diana Victoria Fernández, Industrial Engineer holding an M.A. in Organizational Communications, is in charge of the Communications Office at the Universidad Javeriana.

Rosa Maria Fischer is a Sociologist with a Master's and a Doctorate degrees from São Paulo University and a Ph.D. in Business Administration from the School of Economics, Administration and Accounting—FEA / USP, where she is now a Full Professor. She coordinates the CEATS (Center of Social Entrepreneurship and Administration on Third Sector) at the Foundation Institute of Administration—FIA, leading the team that represents USP in SEKN. Her research areas include Corporate Social Responsibility, Cross-Sector Strategic Alliances for social action, Social Entrepreneurship, Business and Third Sector Administration, Corporate Governance, Organizational Culture and Power, as well as HR Management.

Luz Marina García, M.Sc. in Industrial Engineering from the University of Wisconsin-Madison, is a consultant. She worked as a researcher for INCAE, where she wrote 30 case studies and 9 technical notes. She taught at marketing seminars, lectured on ISO 9000, and collaborated with Guillermo S. Edelberg in a chapter of his book *Temas de Actualidad en Recursos Humanos*. Her *Bembos* case will soon be published in the first issue of the *Journal of International Business*. This case was also published by INCAE's magazine in July 2003.

Gustavo González, Civil Engineer, holds a Ph.D. degree in Philosophy from the Universidad de Navarra. He served as Academic Deputy Dean at the Universidad de los Andes, where he now heads the Management Area and teaches Public Management and Social Responsibility.

Roberto Gutiérrez is an Associate Professor at the School of Administration of the Universidad de los Andes. He holds a Ph.D. in Sociology from Johns Hopkins University. For the past three years, he has been in charge of the *Program on Social Initiatives* and has received a "Distinction for Social Service" and an "Academic Excellence Award." He has published articles about education, alliances, and development in academic and informational journals.

Gustavo A. Herrero, HBS M.B.A. 1976, is the Executive Director of the Harvard Business School Latin America Research Center. Gustavo conducts Latin America-related research with/for every department at Harvard Business School. He has also been involved in the creation and coordination of various academic initiatives in the region, such as the Colloquium on Participant Centered Learning (CPCL), the Harvard Business School Publishing Latin American Case Consortium (LACC), and SEKN.

John Ickis, D.B.A. from Harvard University, is a Business Administration Full Professor at INCAE. His research work focuses on Strategic Processes in

Social Organizations. Dr. Ickis co-authored "Beyond Bureaucracy" and has published several articles at the Harvard Business Review and World Development. He has been listed at the Who's Who of Professionals, Who's Who in Finance and Industry, and Who's Who in the World. He was also awarded honorary citizenship in Soweto, South Africa.

Mladen Koljatic has been a faculty member of the School of Business Administration at the Pontificia Universidad Católica de Chile since 1974. He holds an M.B.A. from the University of Michigan and a doctorate in Education from Indiana University. He teaches courses on marketing research and advertising, and, more recently, on corporate social responsibility and management of nonprofit organizations. He has written several articles on higher education administration for prestigious international journals.

Francisco Leguizamón, D.B.A. from IESE, Universidad de Navarra, Spain, is a Full Professor at INCAE, where he has also served as Dean and Academic Director. Professor Leguizamón lectures at graduate programs and executive seminars on Organizational Behavior, Business Strategy, Negotiation and Small Company Management. He has authored two books on support programs for small and medium-sized companies. He has also written several articles and numerous case studies dealing with usual challenges in business administration.

Iván Darío Lobo Romero graduated as an Industrial Engineer at the Universidad de los Andes. He has been a SEKN member since April, 2002. As a research assistant for the Social Enterprise Initiative of the Universidad de los Andes' Administration School, he is interested in Social Ventures, Public Management, Planning and Development.

Gerardo Lozano, Ph.D. in Business Administration with a major in Marketing and International Business, is a professor at the Graduate School of Business Administration and Leadership (EGADE—Tec de Monterrey), where he leads the Mexican chapter of the Social Enterprise Knowledge Network (SEKN). Since 2001, he has taught at the Social Leaders' Program, an initiative undertaken by the Virtual University of Monterrey Tech, the Nature Conservancy, the World Bank, and the Mexican Center for Philanthropy (CEMEFI). This program provides distance capacity-building training to Civil Society Organizations in Latin America.

Angel Maass Villafranca is an Associate Researcher at the EGADE Tecnológico de Monterrey-Campus Monterrey SEKN team. He holds a B.A. degree in Economics (Tecnológico de Monterrey-Campus Monterrey, 2002). In addition, he has attended specialization courses in Banking and Finance

(ESC-Rouen, 2001). He is currently pursuing his M.Sc. in Finance (EGADE Tecnológico de Monterrey-Campus Monterrey). Among his recent research work, he co-authored the case studies "Let's Build their Dreams: Danone Mexico and the *Casa de la Amistad* para Niños con Cáncer" and "Recyclable by Nature," jointly with Harvard Business School.

Christopher Moxon, Associate Researcher for SEKN in Mexico, is a 2002 M.B.A. graduate from the Tecnológico de Monterrey's EGADE. Having a strong interest in the area of corporate social responsibility, he chose the "Let's Build their Dreams" case study as his final M.B.A. research project. Chris currently resides in Seattle, Wa., and is Vice President for Bank of America's Community Development Bank.

Enrique Ogliastri, Ph.D. from Northwestern University, leads the SEKN project at INCAE, where he teaches Negotiation, Organization, Strategy and Social Enterprise. A research professor at the Universidad de los Andes for 25 years and at Harvard University for four years, he has also been a visiting professor in Japan, France and Spain. He has conducted extensive research on inter-disciplinary areas, such as leading classes and regional power in Colombia, crises and stages in adult development, business history and strategy, culture and management relations, and cross-cultural negotiation processes. He has published 12 books.

Felipe Pérez Pineda, Ph.D. in Agricultural Economy from Purdue University, is an Associate Professor at INCAE. Pérez Pineda teaches several courses for the regular and executive M.B.A. program curricula, lecturing on Sustainable Development, Negotiation, Social Enterprise and Quantitative Methods. His research focuses on Valuation Methodologies for Environmental Goods, Environmental Legislation and Regulation, Economic Development and Growth in Emerging Countries, Competitiveness and Environmental Efficiency, as well as Agribusiness Updating. He participates actively in international endeavors such as SEKN and at academic events abroad, where he presents his research findings.

Andrea Prado, M.Sc. in International Economy from the University of Essex, works as a researcher at INCAE's Latin American Center for Competitiveness and Sustainable Development (CLACDS), where she is currently coordinating the Social Enterprise Knowledge Network (SEKN) project. She was granted the British Council's Oscar Arias scholarship to pursue her M.A. degree, which she obtained with honors. She worked as a CLACDS external consultant, contributing to the research conducted on tourist sector competitiveness in Central America. She has written several case studies and has been involved in Latin American competitiveness analysis.

Julio Sergio Ramírez, Ph.D. in Political Economy and Government from Harvard University, is a Full Professor at INCAE, where he teaches Political Analysis, Environmental Analysis, Managerial Decisions, Development Policies, Project Evaluation and Public Management, among other topics. His published works include "El Caballo Volador: Los Retos de la Gerencia General," "Negociar es Bailar: Conceptos y Guías para la Negociación Eficaz," and is currently working on a new approach to government and public agency strategy formulation and implementation.

Ezequiel Reficco holds a J.D. (Universidad de Buenos Aires, 1989), an M.A. in International Studies (Universitat Autònoma de Barcelona), and a Ph.D. in Law and Diplomacy (Tufts University, 2002). He joined the Harvard Business School faculty in 2002 as a Post-Doctoral Fellow in the school's Initiative on Social Enterprise. His HBS work has focused on Collaborations between Nonprofits and Businesses, Corporate Social Responsibility, and Corporate Social Entrepreneurship. He played a pivotal role in the launching of the SEKN. He has been published in newspapers and scholarly journals in the United States, Argentina, Spain, Italy and Venezuela.

Ricardo Reisen de Pinho has been a Senior Researcher at the Harvard Business School Latin America Research Center since 2002. He holds a P.M.D. from Harvard, an A.M.P. from Wharton, an M.Sc. in Finance and an Engineering degree from the Pontificia Universidade Catolica of Rio de Janeiro. He has contributed to several case studies on business and developed a career as an executive in banking through different assignments and positions within ABN Amro Bank, Garantia Bank and Itaú Bank.

Jesús Revilla de Taboada holds an M.B.A. from INCAE, where he graduated with honors. Currently, he is the Andean Region and Southern Cone Marketing Manager at RTC Industries, a multinational company that specializes in point of sale. After completing his M.B.A. studies, Jesús stayed on at INCAE as researcher and wrote 18 case studies, some of which have been published by academic journals and included in the book *Marketing* (Latin American Edition), written by Philip Kotler in 2001. In addition, he was in charge of Panama's Competitive Balance project, which served as the basis for a document used to support competitive development in that country.

Luciana Rocha de Mendonça has completed her M.B.A. studies and is currently pursuing a doctorate at São Paulo University's School of Economics, Administration and Accounting. As a researcher at CEATS—*Centro de Empreendedorismo Social e Administração em Terceiro Setor*, representing USP in the SEKN group, she has worked on Corporate Social Responsibility in

Nonprofit Organizations, Corporate Governance and Cross-Sector Alliances. Among her publications are "*O desafio das alianças intersetoriais para o desenvolvimento social,*" with R. M. Fischer and T. Dutra (CLADEA 2002) and "The Constitution of Cross-Sector Alliances," with R. M .Fischer (BALAS 2003).

Wendy Rodríguez, M.BA. from INCAE, is a researcher at INCAE's Latin American Center for Competitiveness and Sustainable Development. She has been a consultant in the field of Strategy, focusing on Financial, Economic, Social and Environmental Sustainability at indigenous communities in Mexico and the Galapagos Islands. Within the SEKN Program, she has studied the sustainability of social enterprises in Central America. Wendy is currently involved in Digital Nations, a research project launched by the Media Laboratory at the Massachusetts Technological Institute and several international corporations.

Mario M. Roitter is an economist (Universidad Nacional de Cuyo) and holds an M.B.A. (IESA-Caracas). He has worked as a local associate for Argentina in the International Comparative Project on the Nonprofit Sector, coordinated by the Johns Hopkins University. He is a Senior Researcher at the Center for Studies of State and Society (CEDES). He teaches at the Graduate Program on Non-profit Organizations (CEDES-UDESA-UTDT) and is a member of the SEKN-Argentina research team. His focuses for research and teaching include Corporate Social Responsibility and Nonprofit Sector studies.

Carlos Romero-Uscanga is a professor at the Graduate School of Business Administration and Leadership (EGADE) of the Tecnológico de Monterrey, Campus Monterrey. He has been a Professor since 1992. He holds a Ph.D. in Management from the Instituto Tecnológico y de Estudios Superiores de Monterrey (ITESM) and the University of Texas at Austin, and an M.B.A. degree from ITAM in Mexico City. He has authored several cases for books, articles, and three case studies on business and nonprofit organizations. His research topics are E-Strategy, Decision-Making Process, Social Enterprise and Environmental Management.

Jaime Alberto Ruiz, Industrial Engineer, holds a doctorate degree in Mathematics applied to Social Sciences from the École des Haûtes Études en Sciences Sociales in Paris. He teaches in the organizations area.

Alejandro Sanz de Santamaría, Industrial Engineer with a Ph.D. in Economics from the University of Massachusetts at Amherst, is a professor in the organizations area.

Loretta Serrano is a Research Associate and Project Manager of SEKN-EGADE. She holds an M.Sc. in Development Management from the London School of Economics and has been awarded fellowships from the Luis Donaldo Colosio Fund in Mexico and the U.N. University in Tokyo, among others. Her research interests include the distinct roles of the public, private, and third sectors in economic and social development. She has recently concluded her thesis *"Development Partners ... for Business?"* and has consulted for the Department for International Development's *Business Linkages Challenge Fund* in the United Kingdom.

Mónica Silva has been an associate researcher of the School of Business Administration at the Pontificia Universidad Católica de Chile since 1999. Her undergraduate training focused on Clinical and Educational Psychology, and she holds an M.S. degree and a Ph.D. in Educational Psychology from Indiana University. Her areas of expertise are educational assessment and research methods in the social sciences. She has authored books in adolescence and sex education, and several articles in evaluative research that have been published by prestigious international journals.

João Teixeira Pires graduated in Mechanical Engineering at POLI/USP —Escola Politécnica, at São Paulo University. He has completed his M.B.A. in Human Resources and is now pursuing an M.A. in Business Administration at FEA/USP—School of Economics, Administration and Accounting. João is a Researcher for CEATS (*Centro de Empreendedorismo Social e Administração em Terceiro Setor),* institution that represents USP at SEKN. His research areas involve Corporate Social Responsibility and Cross-Sector Strategic Alliances for social action. His published articles include "Evaluation of Social Projects and Programs"—VI SEMEAD (Seminários em Administração—FEA/USP) (2003).

Diana Trujillo is a Researcher at Social Enterprise Initiative (IESO) of the Universidad de los Andes. She graduated as an Industrial Engineer at the Universidad Javeriana and specialized in Human Resources Management at the Universidad de los Andes, where she is now pursuing an M.A. in Education. Her research interests focus on social enterprise, especially on issues related to individual and corporate social responsibility and cross-sector alliances.

Foreword

Much of what Professor James Austin and his excellent collaborators have written here reflects my business and my non-business approaches and philosophy. *Social Partnering in Latin America*, and the partnerships that it describes echo many of my own experiences, and enable me to more deeply understand partnerships between businesses and civil organizations. I had nothing to do directly with producing the book, but I certainly could have used a book like this ten years ago.

I have been a fairly successful entrepreneur over a 30-year career. In 1991, I took time out to establish the World Business Council for Sustainable Development, to offer a business perspective to the 1992 Rio 'Earth Summit' and to try to get the sustainable development message into companies. This was really an early attempt to create stronger links between companies and the wider society in which they operate.

In 1994, I established the AVINA Foundation, to support and encourage leadership for sustainable development in Latin America and the Iberian Peninsula. A problem immediately arose. If I live by and promote a certain vision and values, and my Latin American conglomerate, GrupoNueva, acts upon its own different vision and values, and the Foundation follows yet another set, then what does that say about my own integrity? Shouldn't I be able to integrate my values into any organization I create? Shouldn't my own company and foundation share my own vision? Is such integration possible, or is it naïve to expect organizations in different sectors to share core values?

For more than a decade now I have been using various strategies to cause AVINA and GrupoNueva to be motivated by the same 'VIVA' (vision and values). Thus it was with great interest that I read in *Social Partnering in Latin America* of various forms of 'alignment' between the values, strategies, and goals of Civil Society Organizations (CSOs) and companies—broad alignment, deep alignment, and ways of developing and maintaining alignments.

This book proves the significance of creating business-CSO partnerships as an innovative approach to harnessing the power of both sectors for the betterment of society. It shows companies that engaging with nonprofits can make eminent business sense. And the book represents a major contribution to our knowledge about the importance and feasibility of these cross-sector alliances.

As AVINA worked with both business and societal leaders, we noticed a disconnect. The CSO leaders knew their society and its troubles intimately and had some remedies to offer, but many lacked basic skills in managing money and projects—that is, business skills. Business leaders tended to know their businesses intimately, but knew less well the threats and opportunities lurking in the societies around them.

So AVINA began a bridge-building exercise to bring CSOs and companies together. In some countries, we started by simply offering CSO leaders a 'bonus grant' if they could match that bonus with money raised from the private sector—companies and individuals. This was financially successful. In Brazil, partners raised more than the total challenge grants we had offered.

But what are the more intangible benefits of such collaboration, and what are the obstacles, and how can these be overcome? It was with such questions in mind that AVINA partnered with the Harvard Business School and Professor James Austin to establish and fund in 2001 the Social Enterprise Knowledge Network (SEKN) to advance in Latin America the frontiers of knowledge and practice in social enterprise through collaborative research, shared learning, case-based teaching, and the strengthening of management education institutions' capabilities to serve their communities. Harvard started with six of the best institutions of management education in Latin America as its partners.

This book is an early, tangible result of that collaboration. It is not a sweet tome celebrating the wonders of business-CSO partnerships. It is instead a very tough book analyzing strengths and weaknesses, opportunities and threats. It notes at one point: "There is no such thing as a free collaboration. Partnering costs. When the benefits do not exceed those costs, the partnership is not sustainable. Nor should it be continued."

It divides CSOs into five levels, from ill-organized to mature and sustainable. It examines three stages of collaboration: the Philanthropic (exactly what it sounds like); the Transactional, where the business and CSOs collaborate on projects such as cause-related marketing or employee volunteerism, but with a circumscribed joining of forces; and the Integrative, where the project becomes more of a joint venture with highly aligned missions, values, and strategy and staff of both organizations mingling.

Such integrative projects are still the exception in Latin America, but I particularly enjoyed the description of one. The Argentine newspaper *La Nación* entered into a partnership with the Solidarity Network

(RS) to connect individuals or groups with specific needs to those who could provide the necessary help. One of the products developed by the alliance was the "solidarity classified ads," a regular section in the newspaper that listed unsatisfied social needs. The collaboration involved core business staff at both organizations: RS staff and writers from several of *La Nación*'s sections. It became hard to tell them apart. As a newspaper editor said, "Our relationship with the RS is more intense because it is an everyday deal."

The SEKN authors have identified some intriguing areas for further research. How do companies and CSOs partner with governments, particularly the local ones that often should be involved in these alliances? How does one overcome what the authors call "the apparent ambivalence that some business people and others feel about companies capturing commercial benefits while also producing social benefits"?

That latter question is crucial, because until companies can be a part of the development process as businesses, providing poor people with necessities such as water, food, healthcare, education, transportation, communications, and jobs in ways that benefit these customers and are profitable for the companies, then corporate efforts at development will always be marginal.

GrupoNueva is seeking ways of doing business with the poor. The WBCSD has organized a working group on such 'pro-poor business' and is amassing examples and working on a 'how-to' guide. In many of these examples, it is the CSOs that provide a link, a sort of honest broker function, between the companies and the poor neighborhoods they are serving.

As for me, I have taken the concept of alignment to something of an extreme, one which I hope will inspire other business owners. I have put the stock of the holding company GrupoNueva and other stocks into a trust to be managed by an entity called VIVA. This essentially represents the donation of my personal business holdings to the cause of the foundation. In simple terms, I want VIVA to play the role that I personally have been playing in the past. I no longer own the company, so VIVA will represent an owner's interest, giving fundamental strategic guidance to the board of GrupoNueva, and defining minimum standards of performance at the economic, social, and environmental levels. At the same time, the dividends that VIVA will receive from the company will allow it to fund AVINA. This is both a very deep and very broad alignment.

I congratulate the Social Enterprise Knowledge Network co-authors on *Social Partnering in Latin America*. It is sound analysis and an excellent read. Its contents add important intellectual advances, but these have been translated into very useable lessons and guidance for business and social leaders. I shall continue to use it and to recommend it to all business leaders, social leaders, politicians, and anyone devoted to a better future for Latin America. It shows the way forward.

Stephan Schmidheiny
Founder, AVINA Foundation

Preface

This book is the product of a major collaborative research effort by a group of leading business schools in Latin America and the Harvard Business School. In 2001 the following schools joined together with AVINA to create the Social Enterprise Knowledge Network (SEKN):

- Argentina: Universidad de San Andrés—Universidad Torcuato Di Tella—CEDES
- Brazil: *Universidade de São Paulo*—CEATS
- Central America: Instituto Centroamericano de Administración de Empresas (INCAE)
- Chile: Pontificia Universidad Católica de Chile
- Colombia: Universidad de los Andes
- Mexico: Instituto Tecnológico y de Estudios Superiores de Monterrey—Escuela de Graduados en Administración y Dirección de Empresas (EGADE)
- United States: Harvard University Graduate School of Business Administration (HBS)

SEKN schools and AVINA saw a pressing need to deepen knowledge of and managerial training for social purpose organizations or activities that we call *social enterprise*. That term encompasses any kind of organization or undertaking engaged in activities of significant social value, or in the production of goods or services with an embedded social purpose, regardless of legal form (for-profit, nonprofit or public). As professional schools of management, SEKN members have a strong orientation toward the world of practice. The research undertaken is aimed at generating new intellectual capital so as to enhance management practice in any type of social enterprise. SEKN's initial research project, presented in this book, has focused on the strategic collaboration between businesses and nonprofit organizations, which we viewed as an activity highly relevant to achieving social progress in Latin America and one for which there was a pressing need for new research.

The specific mission of SEKN is:

> *To advance the frontiers of knowledge and practice in social enterprise through collaborative research, shared learning, case-*

> *based teaching, and the strengthening of management education institutions' capabilities to serve their communities.*

This mission and the focus on social enterprise are considered an integral part of the basic purposes of each of the SEKN member schools. They are all committed to allocating significant resources to carry out social enterprise research and develop training courses for MBA students and practicing executives. There is also a deep belief in and commitment to working with other schools to achieve this collective mission.

SEKN's ability to engage in these activities has been fundamentally enhanced by the generous financial support and intellectual and experiential inputs from the AVINA Foundation. AVINA's mission is "to partner with leaders of civil society and business in their initiatives for sustainable development in IberoAmerica." AVINA demonstrated its entrepreneurial spirit by its willingness to partner with the SEKN schools in creating an unprecedented hemispheric alliance that itself is a manifestation of social enterprise. We are especially fortunate to have AVINA as our partner.

The applied nature of SEKN's research and case writing requires significant cooperation from businesses and NGOs. We are deeply indebted to the collaborating enterprises and their leaders for allowing us to learn from their experiences. Their generosity enabled the creation of this book and the related teaching case studies, which in turn will allow others to strengthen further their social enterprise activities. The business and NGO leaders are to be commended not only for their organizations' excellent social purpose activities but also their willingness to share with the larger community.

SEKN is also grateful to the deans, rectors, and presidents of each of the member schools for their unswerving support of this effort. Gratitude is also expressed to the multitude of administrative and research staff who have provided the essential support for our activities.

We also express our appreciation to Harvard University's David Rockefeller Center for Latin American Studies for considering our manuscript for inclusion in their special book series published by the Harvard University Press. We also thank the reviewers of the manuscript for their constructive inputs that further strengthened the book.

Finally, a very special thanks goes to each of the contributing authors, not only for their great professional and academic care in carrying out the complex field research and communicating the results, but also for their willingness and skill in collaborating with colleagues in different institutions and countries. This book is a product of the extraordinary collective effort of the research teams from each of the SEKN member schools. Great teams have great leaders. The book could not have been produced without their superb leadership: Gabriel Berger, Universidad de San Andres; Rosa Maria Fischer, Universidade de São Paulo; Roberto Gutíerrez, Universidad de los Andes; Mladen Koljatic, Pontificia Universidad Católica de Chile; Gerardo Lozano, EGADE; Enrique Ogliastri, INCAE. Lastly, special commendation goes to Ezequiel Reficco, who demonstrated exceptional skill, energy, and patience in carrying out the complex task of integrating the research findings from across the member country studies. Similarly critical to the realization of the multi-country effort was the exceptional effort and leadership of Gustavo Herrero, Director of the HBS Latin America Research Center, which served a vital coordinating role for the Network's collective endeavor.

Studies that are hemispheric in scale, involve dozens of researchers, a multitude of field institutions, and utilize a common research framework and methodology, are very difficult—which is why they are so rarely done. They therefore constitute a valuable opportunity to produce significant new knowledge that advances management practice. We hope that this book has made good use of that opportunity by shedding new light on this important arena of collaborations between Civil Society Organizations and businesses. While this work cannot produce final answers, we do believe that it advances our collective understanding significantly and also points to productive avenues for further research by other researchers. More than a book, *Social Partnering in Latin America* is a step on a continual journey of learning together for the well-being of our societies.

James E. Austin
Snider Professor of Business Administration
Chair of Initiative on Social Enterprise
Harvard Business School
Boston, Massachusetts

Acronyms

AEC	American Express Company
AEMA	*Aprender a Emprender en el Medio Ambiente*
AID	United States Agency for International Development
AMCHAM	American Chamber of Commerce
AUSOL	*Autopistas del Sol*
BAM	*Banco de Alimentos de Monterrey*
BCI	*Banco de Crédito e Inversiones*
CCA	*Coca-Cola de Argentina*
CCM	*Corporación de Crédito al Menor*
CdA	*Casa de la Amistad*
CEATS	*Centro de Empreendedorismo Social e Administração em Terceiro Setor*
CEDES	*Centro de Estudios de Estado y Sociedad*
CENPEC	*Centro de Estudos e Pesquisas em Educação, Cultura e Ação Comunitária*
CGH	*Centro de Gestión Hospitalaria*
CI	Conservation International
CMM	*Corporación Municipal de Melpilla*
COANIQUEM	*Corporación de Ayuda al Niño Quemado*
CPF	Canadian-Peruvian Fund
CRM	Cause Related Marketing
CSGs	Community Study Groups
CSOs	Civil Society Organizations
CSR	Corporate Social Responsibility
DJSGI	Dow Jones Sustainability Group Index
EGADE	*Escuela de Graduados en Administración y Dirección de Empresas*
EINC	*Ese'eja de Infierno Native Community*
EJN	*Emprendedores Juveniles de Nicaragua*
EPS	*Entidad Promotora de Salud*
FASA	*Farmacias Ahumada S.A.*
FIEMG	*Federação das Indústrias do Estado de Minas Gerais*
FIERJ	*Federação das Indústrias do Estado do Rio de Janeiro*
FLR	*Fundación Las Rosas*
FRP	*Fundación Rafael Pombo*
FSC	The Forest Stewardship Council
FUNAI	*Fundação Nacional do Índio*

FUPROVI	*Fundación Promotora para la Vivienda*
GEM	Global Entrepreneurship Monitor
GIFE	*Grupo de Institutos, Fundações e Empresas*
HBS	Harvard Business School
IMAFLORA	*Instituto de Manejo e Certificação Florestal e Agrícola*
INCAE	*Instituto Centroamericano de Administración de Empresas*
INDE	*Instituto Nicaragüense de Desarrollo*
ISE	Initiative on Social Enterprise
JAA	Junior Achievement Argentina
JAI	Junior Achievement International
JLCM	Mexico City Junior League Environmental Committee
KC	Kimberly-Clark
LARC	Latin America Research Center
MC	Management Committee
MD	*Corporación Minuto de Dios*
MECD	*Ministerio de Educación, Cultura y Deportes*
NGOs	Non-Governmental Organizations
NPOs	Nonprofit Organizations
PA	*Posada Amazonas*
PCF	Peru-Canada Fund
PROAC	*Programa de Apoio Comunitário*
REPRETEL	*Representaciones Televisivas*
RFE	Rainforest Expeditions
RS	*Red Solidaria*
SEKN	Social Enterprise Knowledge Network
SES	Sustainability, Education and Solidarity
TP	Tetra Pak
TRC	Tambopata Research Center
UNIANDES	*Universidad de los Andes*

PART

I

The Partnering Process

1

The Key Collaboration Questions

James Austin, Ezequiel Reficco, and SEKN Research Team

The Collaboration Phenomenon

Can businesses and nonprofit organizations work together? Many generally think of these two sectors as having quite distinct roles and very different characteristics. In fact, they are opposites in many regards. Minimal or no interaction would be quite understandable. Yet, increasingly they have been coming together to collaborate in social purpose activities. Such cross-sector collaboration has been documented in the United States.[1] The purpose of this book is to provide business and nonprofit managers as well as scholars of alliances a deeper understanding of such collaborations in Latin America, where this phenomenon has not been widely studied.

There is a long history in the U.S. of corporate philanthropy, of businesses making donations to charity. Most of today's leading foundations arose from the beneficence of business leaders and their corporate wealth: Rockefeller, Mellon, Ford, Gates, Kellogg, Packard, etc. All major companies engage in giving to nonprofit organizations. In 2002, corporations in the United States gave $12.2 billion in cash and in-kind donations to charitable organizations, an increase of 8.8 percent in real terms over the previous year.[2] But a significant shift is underway that has been transforming traditional "check-writing" relationships to broader and deeper forms of interaction.[3] These emerging forms of collaboration involve more and different types of bilateral resource flows and generate greater value to businesses, nonprofits, and society than the traditional approach. Of course, there are other important types of social purpose collaborations: between nonprofits,[4] between businesses,[5] between nonprofits and government,[6] between businesses and government[7] and among the three sectors.[8] Despite the significance of these varied kinds of collaborations, in this book we limit our inquiry to partnering relationships between corporations and nonprofit organizations (NPOs), which are often also referred to as Non Governmental Organizations (NGOs) or Civil Society Organizations (CSOs). While one might draw some organizational distinctions between these terms, we use them interchangeably in this book. For the purpose of our study, we will define those partnerships, or collaborations, as relationships entered into by two or more organizations from the business and nonprofit sectors, to achieve respective or common goals.[9]

Research on collaborations in the United States revealed a "Collaboration Continuum" (Figure 1) that depicts different types or stages of relationships between businesses and nonprofits ranging from Philanthropic to Transactional to Integrative.[10] Because we have used this framework as a starting reference point in conducting our research in Latin America, we will elaborate it here.

- **Philanthropic Stage.** This is the traditional and most common type of relationship between nonprofits and businesses. In somewhat oversimplified terms, it largely consists of corporations donating money or goods in response to requests from nonprofits. The level of engagement and resources is relatively low, infrequent, administratively simple, and nonstrategic. The corporate giver has a benefactor mindset and the nonprofit recipient a grateful attitude. The relationship is valuable to the nonprofit as a source of funds, which is how most nonprofits look at companies. It also has value to the company as a way of promoting an image and living up to company values as a caring, responsible institution.

- **Transactional Stage.** Significant numbers of firms and nonprofits are migrating into this second stage, in which the interaction tends to focus on more specific activities in which there is a significant two-way value exchange. The benefits are as perceived by each party rather than necessarily being the same, and in fact are almost always different. Both organizations begin to deploy their core capabilities; it is no longer simply a transfer of funds. The partnership becomes more important to each other's missions and strategies. This stage would encompass such activities as cause-related marketing programs, event sponsorships, special projects, and employee volunteer activities. Cause-related marketing activities, in particular, have grown rapidly and become a salient element in many companies' marketing mix. They generate about $1.5 billion annually for nonprofit organizations.[11]

- **Integrative Stage.** A smaller but growing number of collaborations evolve into strategic alliances that involve a meshing of missions, a synchronization of strategies, and compatibility of values. The organizations begin to interact with greater frequency and they undertake many more kinds of joint activities. The types and amounts of institutional resources used multiply. Core competencies are not simply deployed but joined to create unique and high value combinations. The degree of organizational integration begins to take on the appearance of a joint venture rather than a transaction. In some instances the partners have actually created new, jointly governed entities to carry out their collaboration.

Figure 1: Cross-Sector Collaboration Continuum

Some forms of value are common to all collaborations, but those with higher alignment generate additional forms of value to participating companies.			
	Stage I	Stage I	Stage I
NATURE OF RELATIONSHIP	Philanthropic	Transactional	Integrative
Level of Engagement	Low - →High		
Importance to Mission	Peripheral - - - - - - - - - - - - - - - - - - - →Central		
Magnitude of Resources	Small - → Big		
Scope of Activities	Narrow - → Broad		
Interaction Frequency	Infrequent - - - - - - - - - - - - - - - - - - →Intensive		
Managerial Complexity	Simple - →Complex		
Strategic Value	Minor - → Major		

Source: James E. Austin, *The Collaboration Challenge*, (San Francisco: Jossey-Bass, 2000).

In practice, the Collaboration Continuum has proven particularly useful to managers and scholars as a way to understand systematically the nature of a relationship. It is important to note that the three stages are not put forth as unique or discrete points. Collaborations can fall at any point on this Continuum for any of the descriptive parameters. There may be elements of the Philanthropic and Transactional stages, for example, coexisting in a relationship and these can change as the partnership evolves, because partnering should be seen as a dynamic phenomenon. This framework is not rigid; collaborations can have many permutations under these categories. Nor is progression along the Continuum automatic; it is the result of partner decisions and actions. And movement can be in either direction. The Continuum is also helpful in mapping out the different types of collaborations one has when there are several.[12] What is important for practitioners and researchers is to identify and analyze systematically the multiple characteristics of the alliances to be better able to decide how to manage or change them so as to generate greater benefits.

This growth in more robust forms of collaboration is not simply a U.S. phenomenon. It has emerged in other nations around the globe. For example, in the Republic of South Africa, 48 percent of the corporations surveyed had partnerships with nonprofit organizations (and 30 percent with government). It is also occurring in many European countries[13] and Japan.[14]

But What about Latin America?

Intersectoral collaboration in the developed nations is clear, but one might understandably doubt that this phenomenon would hold in Latin America. Personal and institutional philanthropy in Latin America are not as well developed as in the wealthier nations of the North. Governments have traditionally played a much larger role in the provision of social services. On the social institutions side, churches have similarly played a disproportionately important role in charity.[15] At the individual level, extended families have served as the societal mechanism for mutual care. Businesses were seen as having to do with business, full stop. In fact, in many countries the business sector has been looked on with suspicion and concern about self-interest and exploitation rather than as sources of beneficence and caring about the well being of the larger community. In contrast to this image, research has revealed that there are vigorous, social purpose collaborations between businesses and NGOs throughout Latin America.

In Brazil a survey of 385 companies found that they increasingly fulfill their social responsibility in partnership with other institutions, as opposed to doing it unilaterally.[16] That same study found that companies looked to the third sector as a valuable partner to carry out their social initiatives more often than they sought the support of government or the private sector. Among the companies surveyed, 85 percent had social action alliances, of which 80 percent incorporated NGOs, 56 percent included government entities, and 47 percent encompassed other companies. Another study carried out in Colombia identified over 300 cross-sector alliances.[17] In Mexico, a recent survey of the third sector found that 61 percent of the 44 NGOs covered in the study had maintained some kind of collaboration with the private sector, and among this group 87 percent expressed that as a result of the experience their institutions had been strengthened. More generally, the World Bank surveyed 210 partnerships between businesses, nonprofits, and governments in Argentina, Bolivia, Colombia, El Salvador, Jamaica, and Venezuela.[18]

Clearly, many businesses and nonprofits in Latin America are collaborating and there is a rising interest in such engagements. Multiple forces are propelling this shift. There is a growing recognition that the increasing complexity of social and economic problems transcends the capacity of any single sector. In many countries national governments have engaged in processes of privatization and devolution. Many goods and services that were once produced and delivered by the state have been privatized and are now being handled by businesses either through outright ownership or under contract to companies or Civil Society Organizations. Federal governments have decentralized and enabled local governments to assume responsibility for a variety of services, which has created opportunities for many more cross-sectoral activities at the local level. There is a movement away from a state-centric model of development, but there is a growing recognition that market forces alone will not alleviate the gamut of social problems. Business leaders increasingly are seeing the improvement of those conditions as vital to the development of more vibrant and sustainable business environments. And there is a growing expectation in the larger society that businesses will play a broader and more significant social role than in the past. It is important to recognize that partnerships are not a panacea for Latin America's social ills. There are many important actions that businesses, NGOs, and governments must take on their own independent of any collaboration. Furthermore, there are costs and risks in collaborations; partnering is not appropriate for every business and NGO. Nonetheless, the aforementioned World Bank study on collaborations concluded that "the payoff from partnerships is very large... [and]...there is a growing awareness in the region of that potential....[Furthermore] there is a great need among members of existing and new partnerships for guidance on the "how-tos" for partnership building."[19]

Sample Cases and Methodology

This book responds directly to that cited need. There is a paucity of detailed analyses of actual collaboration practice in Latin America and this book will help fill that empirical void. Our purpose is to enable practitioners and scholars to understand more deeply the nature of the partnering process in multiple countries in Latin America, and the factors that contribute to developing effective alliances. The book will provide nonprofit and business leaders with practical insights and advice. While the application of the existing conceptual framework on collaborations to new contexts is valuable, this research will also extend and refine those frameworks for analyzing cross-sectoral collaborations. These extensions and refinements are subsequently highlighted in the corresponding chapters as well as in the final chapter. Lastly, the comparative analysis will enable us to explore the question: What is the same and what is different about these collaborations in Latin America compared to the United States and across different Latin American countries?

To do this, research teams from the member schools of the Social Enterprise Knowledge Network, (SEKN, see Preface for description and www.SEKN.org) analyzed in-depth 24 alliances between businesses and nonprofit organizations; four each in Argentina, Brazil, Chile, Colombia, and Mexico, three in Central America, and one in Peru, thus giving us coverage of North, Central, and South America. To provide richer diversity and applicability, the studies cover a broad range of collaborations in terms of kinds of businesses and NGOs as well as types of collaborations that encompass the entire span of the Collaboration Continuum discussed above.

These field-based case studies used a common research protocol so as to be able to study this phenomenon in a structured and focused way that would permit cross-country comparative analysis. Each alliance was analyzed via in-depth interviews with the key actors from both the businesses and NGOs. Relevant documentation regarding the collaboration was reviewed. Thus, the findings presented in the following chapters enable a broader hemispheric view of cross-sector partnering both among Latin American countries as well as in comparison to the United States, which will be capsulated in the final chapter of the book.

Case study research is limited in its scale and scope and so does not pretend to be representative necessarily of an entire population. Rather, it puts a reduced number of cases under the microscope to enable an in-depth look so as to provide deeper understanding of the phenomena. The alliances studied intentionally involve a wide range of institutions. The companies are national and multinational corporations, family-owned and publicly-owned businesses, and operate in many different sectors such as supermarkets, banking, agribusiness, media, energy, and tourism. The nonprofits are also diverse, being engaged in, for example, health, education, environment, youth development, and housing. Our focus is on partnering between businesses and nonprofits in general, across a broad range of industries and types. Most of the alliances are between a single company and a single nonprofit, but in some cases we examine multiparty collaborations involving several businesses and nonprofits. We explicitly exclude from this study alliances with the government, either by businesses or nonprofits or both, not because they are unimportant but rather to retain a clear focus within the feasible limits of this research. In some instances, however, we have included as partners autonomous government entities that operate on a similar institutional basis as NGOs as a deliverer of goods or services, for example, a public school or a public-private municipal corporation, rather than in a superior regulatory or legislating capacity.

In the following chapters we will make reiterated references to the alliances we have studied to illustrate the findings. Table 1 lists the main participants in our sample of collaborations and the SEKN members that carried out the field research. In addition to being the core input in our cross-section collaboration process analysis for this book, each alliance was separately written up as a teaching case to reproduce the challenges faced by these organizations during their cross-sector collaborations for teaching purposes. Copies of these cases are distributed worldwide and available through Harvard Business School Publishing (www.hbsp.harvard.edu).[20]

As in a complex play, we would like to introduce the reader to the cast of characters. We offer the following brief descriptions to provide a richer flavor of the institutional protagonists in these illuminating alliances. In the chapters you will also meet the social and business entrepreneurs who crafted these collaborations.

ARGENTINA

- *Autopistas del Sol* **and Alberto Croce.** In 1994, *Autopistas del Sol* (AUSOL) won the contract to build and manage two highways into the city of Buenos Aires. Early in the project, the company had faced the opposition of the mayors and residents of some upscale towns adjacent to the highway. This opposition threatened to converge with the emerging unrest of low-income families who had settled in the lands to be

Table 1: SEKN Members and Sample Cases

Argentina Universidad de San Andrés – Universidad Torcuato Di Tella – CEDES	• Autopistas del Sol — Alberto Croce • Coca-Cola de Argentina – Junior Achievement Argentina • La Nación – Red Solidaria • Techint Group *Fundación Proa*
Brazil Universidade de São Paulo	• Banco Itaú – Centro de Estudos e Pesquisas em Educação, Cultura e Ação Comunitária • Natura – Matilde Maria Cremm School • Natura – Imaflora – communities • Telemig Celular – Grupos de Apoio de Voluntários
Central America (and Peru) Instituto Centroamericano de Administración de Empresas (INCAE)	• Nicaragua's American Chamber of Commerce – Nicaragua's Ministry of Education, Culture and Sports – schools • Rainforest Expeditions – Ese'eja Native Community • Representaciones Televisivas Fundación Promotora para la Vivienda • Texaco – Emprendedores Juveniles de Nicaragua
Chile Pontificia Universidad Católica de Chile	• Agrícola Ariztía – Corporación Municipal de Melipilla • Banco de Crédito e Inversiones – Corporación de Crédito al Menor • Esso Chile – Corporación de Ayuda al Niño Quemado • Farmacias Ahumada – Fundación Las Rosas
Colombia Universidad de Los Andes	• Centro de Gestión Hospitalaria – Fundación Corona – Johnson & Johnson – General Médica de Colombia • Foro de Presidentes de la Cámara de Comercio de Bogotá – schools • Indupalma – Fundación Rafael Pombo • Manuelita – Corporación Minuto de Dios
Mexico Instituto Tecnológico y de Estudios Superiores de Monterrey – Escuela de Graduados en Administración y Dirección de Empresas (EGADE)	• Danone de México – Casa de la Amistad • H-E-B – Banco de Alimentos de Monterrey • Grupo Bimbo – Papalote Museo del Niño • Tetrapak – Mexico City Junior League

crossed by the new road layout, and were facing the prospect of being evicted. The situation, potentially conflictive, was overcome by means of a collaboration between the company and social leader Alberto Croce, who had been working at the grass-roots level in some of the areas affected by the project. In this partnership, the company found a new way to relate to the community, which was maintained even after the pressing circumstances in which they had come about subsided. AUSOL's commitment to Croce and his team grew over time; when in 1999, he created the SES Foundation to develop informal education programs for low-income youths, the company provided the newly created CSO strong support. In time, the SES Foundation became an essential vehicle for AUSOL's social activities.

- **Coca-Cola de Argentina and Junior Achievement Argentina.**
The Argentine chapter of Junior Achievement Inc. had been
founded in 1990 to spread the values of individual responsibility, entrepreneurship and free enterprise through education.
In its first years of operation it grew rapidly, working with the
best private schools in the country. In 1999, this CSO underwent some substantial changes: its mission was expanded to
include social entrepreneurship and personal responsibility in
community and environmental issues; at the same time, the
organization became willing to work with public schools in
order to gain scale. Coca-Cola de Argentina was the local affiliate of the Coca-Cola Company. For more than four decades,
the company's community relations policy had been based on
cash and in-kind donations. In the 1990s, the company shifted
towards a focus on programs associated with waste recycling,
environmental protection, and education. One of these programs was "Learning Environmental Entrepreneurship,"
launched jointly with Junior Achievement Argentina in 1999
for public schools in the city of Buenos Aires and its surroundings. The program viewed the city as an urban ecosystem and
taught children to identify those social agents who bear responsibility for the well-being of that environment. Due to its
initial success, the program was replicated in other Argentine
provinces between 2000 and 2002.

- *La Nación and La Red Solidaria. La Nación*, the second largest
circulation and one of the most influential newspapers in Argentina, started to include articles about the social sector and
to cover innovations from community based organizations in
dealing with pressing social needs. In this process *La Nación*
journalists and management have worked with the Solidarity Network (*Red Solidaria*, hence RS) a grassroots group that
emerged in 1995 with the mission of spreading the culture of
solidarity in Argentina society by connecting those who experience a need with those who can help. Through this relationship, they have identified cases and examples to report in the
newspaper, have developed sections for the newspaper and the
weekly magazine, and since September of 2000 have launched
a section—which uses at least half a page per day—in its
classified advertising insert called "Solidarity Classifieds." In
this section nonprofits publish free ads communicating their

needs for goods, equipment, and volunteers, and volunteers
can publish their offer for services to nonprofits. This joint
project has proven to be a very powerful tool to connect donors and social sector organizations.

- **The Techint Group and the *Fundación Proa*.** Techint was
  founded in 1945 in Italy, and expanded its engineering and
  construction and steel activities in Latin America, in particular in Argentina. During the 1990s, the Techint Group also
  expanded its non-steel activities by successfully participating
  in the privatization of a number of enterprises. In late 1996,
  the Techint Group supported the creation of the *Fundación
  Proa* (Proa), a contemporary art center located in the La Boca
  neighborhood, a southern needy district in the city of Buenos Aires. In the same year Techint continued its international
  expansion through the acquisition of the steel manufacturing
  plant of Dalmine in Italy. As a result of the ongoing process
  regarding the steel area of the Techint Group, a new global
  company called Tenaris was created in 2002, gathering steel
  manufacturers in seven nations (Canada, Brazil, Italy, Japan,
  Argentina, Mexico and Venezuela) and a commercial network
  linking over 20 countries. The creation of Tenaris imposed on
  Techint's management the challenge of building a coherent
  corporate identity for it. In that context, the company's relationship with the foundation acquired a new dimension: on
  one hand, by supporting Proa, Tenaris followed its 'multilo-
  cal' approach; on the other hand, art represented a powerful
  communication tool for Tenaris to connect culturally with its
  diverse internal and external stakeholders.

BRAZIL

- **Itaú Bank and CENPEC.** Itaú Bank, founded in 1945, is the
  second largest private bank in Brazil. As part of its social responsibility strategy, it created a Community Assistance Program aimed at projects in education and health. To carry out
  this program, the bank established cross-sector alliances with
  partners selected for their technical expertise to operate these
  programs and to establish relations with the .communities.
  Education and Participation, one of these programs, helped
  Civil Society Organizations to assist needy students with sup-

plementary schooling programs. Itaú's partners included the Ministry of Education, UNICEF, and CENPEC, a nonprofit organization dedicated to research and strengthening public education. CENPEC provides technical direction and establishes contacts with community organizations. One of the most important actions inside the Education and Participation Program is the giving of an award to outstanding projects developed by NGOs every other year since 1995.

- **Natura and the Matilde Maria Cremm School.** Natura is a company in the personal care, health, and cosmetic industry in Brazil. In the early 1990s, the company started to make sporadic contributions to the communities surrounding its manufacturing plants and office premises, as part of its "good corporate neighbor" policy. Natura's relationship with the Matilde Maria Cremm public school, located near its Iapecerica da Serra plant, followed that pattern: by 1992, it had all the characteristics of a traditional philanthropic collaboration, consisting of cash and in-kind donations made by the company to respond to specific school needs. However, Natura's management was not satisfied with this type of relationship, which they regarded as patronizing. They approached their school counterparts to propose a new kind of relationship that would yield deeper and more sustainable results. Through dialogue, both partners crystallized a shared vision in which the school would become a transformation agent in its community. To accomplish this goal, they sought the assistance of the above mentioned CENPEC. As a result of this partnership, Matilde, a school located in an outer section of a county surrounding the state capital, managed to turn into the one of the top five schools in that region of the state of São Paulo.

- **Natura, Imaflora, and Various Communities.** As mentioned in the previous paragraph, by the year 2000 Natura had been carrying out social initiatives with communities surrounding its plants and offices. With the launching of the Ekos product line, however, Natura drove social responsibility to the core of its business. Ekos' distinctive feature was its rooting in Brazilian biodiversity, incorporating several substances that had only been used by traditional indigenous communities in the hinterlands. Instead of simply buying the raw materials from them, Natura built a partnership with these communities to share with them the economic benefits resulting from responsible resource exploitation. Coincidentally, the communities that had the key know-how needed to develop Ekos products lived in remote locations in extremely primitive conditions. Thus, Ekos success had the potential of improving their lives in profound ways. The CSO Imaflora also participated in the alliance to ensure that this natural resource exploitation was socially, economically, and environmentally sustainable.

- **Telemig Celular and the Volunteer Support Groups.** In 2002, Telemig Celular was a mobile telephone company operating in the Brazilian state of Minas Gerais. The company had founded its operations on the "capillarity" principle: reaching to consumers spread throughout the state to effectively cater to their needs. This principle also applied to the Telemig Celular Institute, the company's social division, which focused on children's and teenagers' rights. To uphold this mission, the Institute decided to work for the creation and strengthening of Tutoring Councils (local government bodies in charge of guaranteeing children's rights) and Municipal Councils for Children's and Youths' Rights (organs that elaborated local public policies regarding children and youth) in the Minas Gerais state. For its Pro-Council Program, the Institute gathered CSOs from every one of the 12 regions in the state to build the so-called Volunteer Support Groups. Under the Institute's leadership and counseling, these groups worked with local administrations and provided operational support for council creation.

CENTRAL AMERICA (AND PERU)

- **Nicaragua's American Chamber of Commerce, Nicaragua's Ministry of Education, Culture and Sports, and Public Schools in Nicaragua.** In 2000, Nicaragua's American Chamber of Commerce (AMCHAM), under the leadership of its education committee, promoted a school sponsorship program for private companies, supported by the Ministry of Education (MECD), to provide assistance to needy public schools in Nicaragua. AMCHAM's promoter role focused on raising the business community's interest in supporting education, motivating companies to join and staying in the program, and serving as an information and support channel between the companies and the MECD. The characteristics of individual relationships varied, but, in general terms, they were limited to financial or in-kind donations by private companies, who tried to the best of their possibilities to contribute to the solution of the shortcomings described by their school partners. The collaboration did not have any impact in the strategy or internal operations of participating companies. Neither were schools expected to change their internal policies or management practices. The scheme involved no common support systems or minimum standards. The degree of support in each individual partnership was mainly a function of the sponsor's available resources, the initiative shown by the recipient in engaging its private partner, and the personal commitment of the interlocutors involved.

- *Representaciones Televisivas* **and** *Fundación Promotora para la Vivienda*. This alliance in Costa Rica between *Representaciones Televisivas* (REPRETEL), one of the major television companies that had recently been acquired by Mexican investors, and the *Fundación Promotora para la Vivienda* (FUPROVI), a nonprofit developer on low income housing, emerged in response to the damage caused by a hurricane. The collaboration mounted a television fundraising campaign and rebuilt houses for victims of the hurricane. This collaboration centered on this particular project and did not continue after it was completed.

- **Texaco and** *Emprendedores Juveniles de Nicaragua*. Texaco was part of the Chevron Texaco business holding and was assigned an annual budget for social contributions. Nicaragua's Young Entrepreneurs (*Emprendedores Juveniles de Nicaragua*, hence EJN) had been founded in 1991 as the local chapter of Junior Achievement International, with the support of Nicaragua's Institute for Development. The purpose of EJN was to promote the values of free enterprise and market economy among national youths. Since its inception EJN engaged in a philanthropic relationship with Texaco, in which the company contributed funds and volunteers who acted as teachers and tutors in the CSO's programs. In 1997, EJN adopted a new approach which departed from the the established Junior

Achievement programs, originally developed in the United States. Considering that the school drop-out rate in the U.S. was 5 percent while Nicaragua's was 50 percent, EJN adjusted and started to target at-risk youths in its programs. That same year, Texaco built a primary and secondary school near one of its plants, to offer job training for low-income students. In 1999, EJN started delivering several of its training programs at Texaco's educational facilities.

- *Rainforest Expeditions* **and the Ese'eja Native Community.** In 1997, an ecotourism company called Rainforest Expeditions (RFE) entered into a partnership with the *Ese'eja de Infierno* Native Community from the Peruvian Amazonia. As a result of this agreement, the Amazonia Lodge (*Posada Amazonas*) was built in the Tambopata-Candamo Reservation area. The agreement was signed for a period of 20 years, and it involved mutual obligations. The native community provided the rights for tourism usage in 4,940 acres of extraordinary environmental wealth that had been granted to the community by the government. In addition, it agreed to work exclusively for RFE in tourism-related activities and to protect environmental and touristic resources in the area. In turn, RFE agreed to get the necessary funding to build the lodge, to manage it, and to hire community members for its operation. The company received 40 percent of the profits, while the community kept the rest; both parties had 50 percent voting shares in the lodge governance. Once the term of the agreement was over, the community would have the option to continue or terminate the partnership.

Chile

- *Empresas Ariztía* **and** *Corporación Municipal de Melipilla.* *Empresas Ariztía*, one of Chile's leading poultry producers, engaged in a partnership with the Melipilla Municipal Corporation (*Corporación Municipal de Melpilla*, hence CMM), a nonprofit entity that managed the public health and education system of this municipality of 100,000 inhabitants south of Santiago. The company viewed the community as one of its central stakeholders. The head of this family-owned company played a leadership role on the board of the CMM and brought a managerial mindset to its administration. By 2002 CMM was one of the few financially healthy municipal corporations. The leaders of both the company and the CMM faced succession issues with the corresponding challenges for the continuity of the partnership.

- *Banco de Crédito e Inversiones* **and the** ***Corporación de Crédito al Menor.*** The *Banco de Crédito e Inversiones* (BCI) was one of the few domestic banks in Chile and, traditionally, among the most profitable in that market. In 1990, some of the bank's executives and its controller decided to found the nonprofit Corporation for Children's Credit (*Corporación de Crédito al Menor*, hence CCM) to protect girls at risk due to abandonment, poverty, abuse, or dysfunctional families. The new organization started to operate under BCI's tutoring. Eventually, the relationship between both institutions deepened, once it gained the support of the bank's general manager and board members. Although both organizations were formally independent, CCM's board was made up of current or former bank employees. The partnership came to embrace not only the bank's executives and staff, but also its customers, who participated in this relationship by means of monthly contributions deducted from their accounts. CCM grew and became an exemplary organization in at-risk-youth protection, to a large extent due to the support provided by BCI.

- **Esso Chile and the** *Corporación de Ayuda al Niño Quemado.* *Esso Chile*, a company controlled by the global ExxonMobil corporation, was the main fuel dealer in the country. The Burned Children Assistance Corporation (*Corporación de Ayuda al Niño Quemado*, hence COANIQUEM) was a nonprofit organization founded in 1979 to provide free treatment for burned children. Shortly after its creation, COANIQUEM entered into a partnership with Esso, which has endured for more than two decades. Through the years, the collaboration consolidated and deepened. The company support was instrumental to making COANIQUEM visible and renowned, both in Chile and abroad. At the same time, this partnership became a source of benefits for the company as well.

- ***Farmacias Ahumada*** **and** ***Fundación Las Rosas.*** By 1997, *Farmacias Ahumada S.A.* (FASA) was the leading drugstore chain in Chile. The *Fundación Las Rosas* (FLR) was an NGO devoted to caring for needy old people. Encouraged by a FASA top executive, both organizations started a collaboration relationship that year. Company cashiers were trained to request a small monetary contribution from drugstore customers before they paid for their purchase. The company discovered that, as its employees improved their fund-raising skills, they also became better salespeople—in other words, as the collaboration consolidated, both organizations benefited. By 2002, FASA contributions accounted for 5 percent of the Foundation's operating costs, and actors involved were optimistic as to the chances of increasing their share through human resource training and motivation.

COLOMBIA

* *Centro de Gestión Hospitalaria*, **Corona Foundation, Johnson & Johnson** and *General Médica de Colombia.* The Hospital Management Center (*Centro de Gestión Hospitalaria*, hence CGH) started operating in March 1992 as a nonprofit mixed corporation. Its sponsors were five foundations, three of which represented the social arm of a Colombian holding company and none of them related to the health sector; six companies, all of them in the health industry; seven hospitals; the government's National Planning Department and the Social Security Institute. Among the sponsoring foundations was the Corona Foundation, the social division of the Corona organization—a business group mainly engaged in manufacturing and marketing ceramic products. CGH's mission was to "promote and lead health management transformation through innovative projects and programs in order to contribute to overall social development of the country." Private sector sponsors included Johnson & Johnson Medical, a local affiliate of the multinational Johnson & Johnson Corporation. This company produced equipment for injury treatment, infection prevention, vascular access, and patient monitoring. Another private sponsor was *General Médica de Colombia*, local representative of General Electric Medical Systems, specializing in image diagnosis equipment sales and maintenance. All sponsoring members were committed

to developing the health sector through providing advice and financial support to the CGH. In addition to sponsors, other organizations joined in as active and institutional members. In its ten years of existence, the CGH's yearly forum has been attended by approximately 600 representatives from around 130 institutions. In counseling and training, the CGH worked with 125 hospitals that accounted for 25 percent of the total Colombian hospital capacity, 10 health insurance organizations representing 35 percent of all health system and social security members, 5 Health Secretaries covering 34 percent of the total Colombian population, and 35 walk-in health service suppliers.

- *Foro de Presidentes* and Colombian Schools. The Twenty-First Century Leaders project (*Líderes Siglo XXI*, hence *Líderes*) was born in 1994 from the initiative of a group of business leaders from Presidents' Forum of Bogotá's Chamber of Commerce (*Foro de Presidentes de la Cámara de Comercio de Bogotá*). Ten companies and private schools found a common goal in improving the quality of education in Colombia. Today, 189 private and public schools have partnered with 109 companies in nine cities to strengthen their organizations, benefiting over 100,000 children. The project helps schools adopt best practices in management and in 2002 they held the Second Meeting on Quality of Educational Management to highlight the experience of the schools that had made the most progress. In addition to quality themes, they also have worked on planning and policy implementation.

- **Indupalma and the Rafael Pombo Foundation**. Indupalma was a Colombian company producing and marketing palm oil since 1961. The Rafael Pombo Foundation was a CSO devoted to "contributing to boys' and girls' education by integrating creativity and culture into informal educational activities promoting the development of an awareness of their rights and obligations." In 2000, both organizations signed the Good Manners Agreement (Convenio del Buen Trato), by which they delivered open enrollment workshops for the whole San Alberto community to improve interpersonal relationships and promote closer ties among generations and genders. After that first positive experience, they decided to continue working to "build peace." To that end, in 2001, they implemented the "Hands for Peace" program (*Manos a la Paz*), consisting of a series of workshops. The program closed with a public fair in October that year, where San Alberto's children discussed their needs with the community and the local government, and made a number of proposals to address them that were later included in the county's development plan.

- **Manuelita and the *Corporación Minuto de Dios*.** Manuelita S.A. was a Colombian agribusiness group which had originated in a sugar plantation established in the mid-nineteenth century. Over time, it diversified its operations to other industries, especially to the food business. One Minute for God (*Corporación Minuto de Dios*, hence MD) was a nonprofit organization devoted to promoting comprehensive development for human beings and poor communities according to the Gospel. It focused on social housing projects: between 1956 and 1995, it had built more than 15,000 housing solutions in 17 Colombian cities and more than 40,000 houses in disaster relief projects. These two organizations had established an alliance in 1955, which, by the time this study was undertaken, had lasted over five decades and gone through various stages. At times the alliance was restricted to a transaction, where Manuelita provided funds and in return MD publicly acknowledged its sponsorship. At other times, Manuelita also contributed its marketing capabilities to advise MD on corporate image design. Also, the collaboration sometimes involved the combination of core competencies from both partners to create new projects; for example, when neighborhoods for plantation workers were built with the contributions of both organizations.

MEXICO

- **Danone México and the *Casa de la Amistad*.** In 1997, the Mexican subsidiary of the Groupe Danone, a global actor in the food industry, decided to launch a cause-related marketing campaign jointly with a CSO. The chosen partner was the Friendship Home (*Casa de la Amistad*), an organization engaged in providing free medical treatment to low-income children suffering from cancer. Through the campaign, called

"Let's Build Their Dreams," the company donated a fraction of the price of each yoghurt product sold over a period of time. The campaign had been repeated annually for several years.

- **H-E-B Supermarkets and *El Banco de Alimentos de Monterrey.*** HEB, a family-owned Texan retailer is the twelfth largest supermarket chain in the U.S. In expanding its operations into Mexico in 1997, the company transferred not only its products and services but also its social strategy of working with food banks. The Monterrey Food Bank (*Banco de Alimentos de Monterrey*), one of Caritas' social service programs, began in 1989 with the purpose of providing nutritional assistance to needy families regardless of religious affiliation. The collaboration of HEB with the Monterrey Food Bank enabled this operation to move from a basic to a world class level in terms of new storage and handling facilities and administrative systems. The partners perceived significant benefits for each other and the community. Strong leadership and interpersonal relationships contributed to the development of considerable mutual trust that has fostered a vigorous and growing partnership.

- **Bimbo Group and the *Papalote Museo del Niño.*** In the early 1990s, the Mexican *Grupo Bimbo* was a leader in the world food industry, operating in 16 countries. In November 1993, the Papalote Children's Museum (*Papalote Museo del Niño*) was created in Mexico City. This CSO intended to contribute to children's intellectual and emotional development through interactive and educational games and experiments. Shortly after its creation, the museum entered into a collaboration agreement with Bimbo, and the company agreed to sponsor several exhibitions in exchange for brand exposure on museum premises. Eventually, both parties jointly developed new activities such as the Public School Sponsorship Program, which covered the expenses for low-income children's visits to the Papalote. Through sponsorships, the company contributed to several museum programs, such as the "Mobile Papalote"—a traveling version of the museum touring other regions in the country.

- **Tetrapak and Mexico City's Junior League.** The latter was the Mexican chapter of the Junior League International, an NGO founded to promote volunteer work, women's potential, and community enhancement. Tetra Pak was the world's leader in multi-layer packaging production. In the mid 1990s, parts of the urban waste were not recycled in Mexico, such as multi-layer packaging containers. Mexico City alone disposed of 35 million containers of this kind every month, which took 35 years to disintegrate. In 1995, both organizations entered into a partnership to recycle these containers. They jointly launched a program called "Naturally Recyclable" and invited all parties that benefited from multi-layer packaging to join in, thus sharing the responsibility for their final disposal. Therefore, the program included manufacturers, marketers, consumers, and even the local government.

Overview of the Contents

Although every case of collaboration between a nonprofit organization and a private company is distinctive, there are some dimensions that are common to them all. We conceptualize the partnering process as having four components: starting and building the relationship; achieving alignment between the organizations' missions, strategies, and values; generating value to the partners and the larger society; and managing the partner interface. We set forth these partnering components as distinct elements to facilitate analysis but it is important to remember that they are highly interrelated and interactive.

The subsequent chapters will explore some key questions in each of these areas. In answering these questions, our goal is both descriptive and analytical. There is a paucity of detailed documentation of collaborations, so seeing various examples of how businesses and non-profits work together in actuality in Latin America will illuminate the partnering possibilities for readers. However, too many trees can block the view of the forest, so it is also important for practitioners to be able to conceive of the partnering process in a systematic and analytical way. Thus, we also will provide conceptual frameworks that allow the reader to see the broader phenomenon, examine it systematically, and derive useful guidelines. Part I of the book encompasses chapters two to five, and draws on and integrates the findings from the 24 case studies to examine the following key components and questions in the partnering process.

- *Building the Bridge*
  - Why do businesses and nonprofits collaborate?
  - What are the critical barriers to such collaborations?

  – How can these barriers be overcome?

- *Achieving Alignment*
  – What is the nature and significance of aligning missions, strategy, and values between businesses and NGOs?
  – What are the barriers to achieving this fit?
  – How can alignment be achieved, maintained, and increased over time?

- *Generating Value*
  – How do businesses and NGOs view value creation?
  – What are the factors that contribute to the creation and preservation of value?
  – How can a cross-sector partnership create value for NGO's, private companies, and communities?

- *Managing the Alliance*
  – What appear to be the most critical factors in managing partner relations?
  – How can partners deal with those factors most effectively?

Part II of the book, encompassing chapters six through eleven, focuses on specific countries and probes in more detail some important dimensions of the partnering process that were especially salient in a particular country context. These chapters will allow the readers to understand more deeply the contextual realities in specific country settings and how these affect alliance actors, processes, structures, and dynamics.

- *Argentina: Identifying the Role of Alliance Social Entrepreneurs*
  – How have forces in the larger country context contributed to the emergence of social entrepreneurs?
  – What are the salient characteristics of the social entrepreneurs that push them toward alliance creation?

- *Brazil: Understanding the Influence of Organizational Culture on Alliances*
  – How does organizational culture influence the social action strategy and partner selection?

- How do organizational values and beliefs shape the evolution of an alliance and the perceived worth of the partnership?

- **Central America and Peru: Analyzing Possible Barriers and Enablers to Alliance Integration**
  - What factors hinder the evolution of a partnership into an integrative alliance?
  - What factors enable integration?

- **Chile: Building Trust in Alliances**
  - How does the national culture affect the trust-building process?
  - What mechanisms contribute to trust-building at different stages of alliance development?

- **Colombia: Managing Multi-Party Alliances**
  - Why do multiparty alliances emerge?
  - What complexities arise in managing such alliances and how can they be best dealt with?

- **Mexico: Making Business Sense of Inter-Sectoral Alliances**
  - How do alliances with nonprofits benefit businesses?
  - How do social and economic motivations interact and change during the evolution of a partnering relationship?

These country chapters, like the earlier ones, in addition to describing and analyzing partnering practices, will also distill out apparent lessons that should be useful to managers from nonprofits and businesses for the effective development of their alliances.

Whereas Part I of the book integrates the findings across the countries and Part II focuses on specific countries, the final chapter revisits the comparative question of salient similarities and differences between the United States and Latin America and across the various Latin American countries. That chapter will also highlight some of the conceptual advances emanating from the research as well as some of the discovered avenues for productive future research. The Epilogue provides an additional perspective on partnering based on the collaboration experience of the Social Enterprise Knowledge Network itself.

Notes

1   Alan R. Andreasen, "Profits for Nonprofits: Find a Corporate Partner," *Harvard Business Review*, November 1996; James E. Austin, *The Collaboration Challenge: How Nonprofits and Businesses Succeed through Strategic Alliances*, 1st ed. (San Francisco: Jossey-Bass Publishers, 2000); James E. Austin, "Marketing's Role in Cross-Sector Collaboration," *Journal of Nonprofit and Public Sector Marketing* 11, no. 1 (Spring 2003); James E. Austin, *Meeting the Collaboration Challenge Workbook: Developing Strategic Alliances Between Nonprofit Organizations and Businesses* (San Francisco: Jossey-Bass Publishers and Peter Drucker Foundation, 2002); James E. Austin, "Principles for Partnership," *Leader to Leader*, no. 18 (2000); James E. Austin, "Strategic Collaboration between Nonprofits and Business," *Nonprofit and Voluntary Sector Quarterly* 29 (supplemental 2000); Dwight Burlingame and Dennis R. Young, eds., *Corporate Philanthropy at the Crossroads, Philanthropic Studies* (Bloomington: Indiana University Press, 1996); Cone Communications and Roper Starch Worldwide, "Cause-Related Marketing Trends Report," (Boston: Cone Communications and Roper Starch Worldwide, 1997); Peter Frumkin and Alice Andre-Clark, "When Missions, Markets, and Politics Collide: Values and Strategy in the Nonprofit Human Services," *Nonprofit and Voluntary Sector Quarterly* 29, no. 1 (Supplement 2000); Joseph Galaskiewicz and Michelle Sinclair Coleman, "Corporate-Nonprofit Relations," in *The Nonprofit Sector: A Research Handbook*, ed. Richard Steinberg and Walter W. Powell (New Haven, CT: Yale University Press, 2002); Joseph Galaskiewicz and Akbar Zaheer, "Networks of Competitive Advantage," in *Research in the Sociology of Organizations* (Greenwich, Conn. and London, England: Jai Press, 1999); Rosabeth Moss Kanter, "From Spare Change to Real Change: The Social Sector as Beta Site for Business Innovation," *Harvard Business Review* (May 1999); Hamish Pringle and Marjorie Thompson, *Brand Spirit: how Cause Related Marketing Builds Brands* (Chichester; New York: Wiley, 1999); Shirley Sagawa and Eli Segal, *Common Interest, Common Good: Creating Value through Business and Social Sector Partnerships* (Boston, Mass.: Harvard Business School Press, 2000); Craig Smith, "The New Corporate Philanthropy," *Harvard Business Review*, May-June 1994; Roxanne Spillett, "Strategies for Win-Win Alliances," in *Leading beyond the Walls: How High-Performing Organizations Collaborate for Shared Success*, ed. Frances Hesselbein, Marshall Goldsmith, and Iain Somerville (San Francisco: Jossey-Bass Publishers and The Peter F. Drucker Foundation, 1999); Sandra A Waddock and Samuel B Graves, "The Corporate Social Performance-Financial Link," *Strategic Management Journal* 18, no. 4 (April 1997).

2   American Association Fundraising Council, *Giving USA 2003* (Bloomington, IN: AAFRC Trust for Philanthropy, 2003).

3   The following publications are particularly useful in documenting the shifting nature of corporate philanthropy and business relations with nonprofit organizations: Austin, *The Collaboration Challenge: How Non-profits and Businesses Succeed through Strategic Alliances* (workbook may be downloaded free from www.pfdf.org); Edmund M. Burke, *Corporate Community Relations: the Principle of the Neighbor of Choice* (Westport, Conn.: Quorum Books, 1999); Burlingame and Young, eds., *Corporate Philanthropy at the Crossroads*; Kanter, "From Spare Change to Real Change: The Social Sector as Beta Site for Business Innovation"; Peggy H. Cunningham Minette E. Drumwright, Ida E. Berger, *Social Alliances: Company/Nonprofit Collaboration* (Cambridge, Mass.: Marketing Science Institute, 2000); Michael E. Porter and Mark R. Kramer, "The Competitive Advantage of Corporate Philanthropy," *Harvard Business Review* 80, no. 12 (2002); Sagawa and Segal, *Common Interest, Common Good: Creating Value through Business and Social Sector Partnerships*; Michelle Sinclair And Joseph Galaskiewicz, "Corporate-Nonprofit Partnerships: Varieties and Covariates," *New York Law School Review* XLI, no. 3 and 4 (1997); Smith, "The New Corporate Philanthropy."

4   For studies on collaborations between nonprofits, see: Jane Arsenault, *Forging Nonprofit Alliances: A Comprehensive Guide to Enhancing Your Mission Through Joint Ventures and Partnerships, Management Service Organizations, Parent Corporations, and Mergers* (San Francisco: Jossey-Bass, 1998); Charles E. Bartling, *Strategic Alliances for Nonprofit Organizations* (Washington, D.C.: American Society of Association Executives, 1998); Karen Ray, *The Nimble Collaboration: Fine-Tuning Collaboration for Lasting Success* (St. Paul, MN: Amherst Wilder Foundation, 2002).

5   For business to business collaborations with a social purpose see: James E. Austin, "Business Leadership Coalitions," *Business and Society Review* 105, no. 3 (2000); Austin, "Principles for Partnership." For business to business partnerships more generally see: Rosabeth Moss Kanter, "Collaborative Advantage: The art of alliances," *Harvard Business Review* (1994); Rosabeth Moss Kanter, *World Class: Thriving Locally in the Global Economy* (New York: Simon & Schuster, 1995).

6   For nonprofit and government collaborations see: Elizabeth T. Boris and C. Eugene Steuerle, eds., *Nonprofits and Government: Collaboration and Conflict* (Washington, DC: Urban Institute Press, 1999); Arthur C. Brooks, "Is There a Dark Side to Government Support for Nonprofits?," *Public Administration Review* 60, no. 3 (2000); James M. Ferris, "The Double-Edged Sword of Social Service Contracting: Public Accountability Versus Nonprofit Autonomy," *Nonprofit Management and Leadership* 3, no. 4 (1993); Peter Frumkin, "After Partnership: Rethinking Public-Nonprofit Relations," in *Who Will Provide?: The Changing Role of Religion in American Social Welfare*, ed. Mary Jo Bane, Brent Coffin, and Ronald F. Thiemann (Boulder, Colo.: Westview Press, 2000).

7   For businesses and government collaborations see: Austin, "Business Leadership Coalitions"; James E. Austin, "Business Leadership Lessons from the Cleveland Turnaround," *California Management Review* 40, no. 1 (1998); James E. Austin, "The Cleveland turnaround case studies (A) 9-796-151, (B) 9-796-152, (C) 9-796-153, (D) 9-796-154," *Harvard Business School Publishing* (1996); Michael Keating, *Comparative Urban Politics: Power and the City in the United States, Canada, Britain, and France* (Aldershot, England: E. Elgar, 1991); J. Pierre, "Models of Urban Governance: The Institutional Dimension of Urban Politics," *Urban Affairs Review* 34 (1999); Clarence N. Stone, *Regime politics : Governing Atlanta, 1946–1988, Studies in Government and Public Policy* (Lawrence, Kan.: University Press of Kansas, 1989); Clarence N. Stone, "Summing up: Urban regimes, development policy and political arrangements," in *The Politics of Urban Development*, ed. Clarence N. Stone and Heywood T. Sanders (Lawrence, Kan.: University Press of Kansas, 1987); Clarence N. Stone, M. Orr, and D. Imbroscio, "The Reshaping of Urban Leadership in U.S. cities: A Regime Analysis," in *Urban Life in Transition*, ed. Mark Gottdiener and C. G. Pickvance (Newbury Park, CA: Sage Publications, 1991).

8   For three sector partnering see: Austin, "Business Leadership Lessons from the Cleveland Turnaround"; James E. Austin and Arthur McCaffrey, "Business Leadership Coalitions and Public-Private Partnerships in American Cities: A Business Perspective on Regime Theory," *Journal of Urban Affairs* 24, no. 1 (2002); Barbara Gray, "Cross-Sectoral Partners: Collaborative Alliances among Business, Government and Communities," in *Creating Collaborative Advantage*, ed. Chris Huxham (Thousand Oaks, CA: Sage Publications, 1996); Independent Sector, "Crossing the Borders: Collaboration and Competition among Nonprofits, Business and Government," (Washington, D.C.: Independent Sector, 2000); Paul W. Mattessich, Marta Murray-Close, and Barbara R. Monsey, *Collaboration: What Makes It Work*, 2nd ed. (St. Paul, MN: Amherst H. Wilder Foundation, 2001).

9   This working definition was adapted from Mattessich, Murray-Close, and Monsey, *Collaboration: What Makes It Work 4*. Some of the partnerships included in our sample cases challenge that definition, as they did not involve two formally structured organizations. Those were the "community partnerships," a form of collaboration where local communities partner with private companies represented by traditional or informal leaders. This point is further discussed in Chapter 2.

10 Austin, *The Collaboration Challenge: How Nonprofits and Businesses Succeed through Strategic Alliances* 19–39.

11 Andreasen, "Profits for Nonprofits: Find a Corporate Partner"; Austin, "Marketing's role in cross-sector collaboration"; Cone Communications and Roper Starch Worldwide, "Cause-Related Marketing Trends Report"; Susan Gray and Holly Hall, "Cashing in on Charity's Good Name," *The*

Chronicle of Philanthropy (1998); Pringle and Thompson, *Brand Spirit: How Cause Related Marketing Builds Brands;* Walter W. Wymer Jr. and Sridhar Samu, "Dimensions of Business and Nonprofit Collaborative Relationships," *Journal of Nonprofit and Public Sector Marketing* 11, no. 1 (2003).

12   James E. Austin, "Managing the Collaboration Portfolio," *Stanford Social Innovation Review* 1, no. 1 (2003).

13   Sue Adkins, *Cause Related Marketing: Who Cares Wins* (Oxford; Boston: Butterworth-Heinemann, 1999).

14   For example, in Japan The Partnership Support Center gives an annual award for the most outstanding nonprofit-business collaboration.

15   Andrés A. Thompson and Leilah Landim, "Culture and Philanthropy in Latin America: From Religious Charity to the Search of Citizenship," (World Bank, mimeo, n.d.).

16   Rosa Maria Fischer, "Alianças estratégicas intersetoriais para atuação social: pesquisa descritiva," (São Paulo: Centro de Empreendedorismo Social e Administração em Terceiro Setor, forthcoming).

17   Diana Trujillo Cárdenas, "Informe de análisis de 142 casos de alianzas en Colombia recopilados durante 1997, 1998 y 1999," (Bogotá, Colombia: Banco Mundial—Fundación Corona, DFID, Universidades y Centros Regionales de Investigación, 2000).

18   Ariel Fiszbein and Pamela Lowden, *Working Together for a Change: Government, Business and Civic Partnerships for Poverty Reduction in Latin America and the Caribbean* (Washington, DC: 1999). Fifty of the partnerships have case study descriptions that are available at www.alianzas.org.

19   Ibid. 94–95.

20   To order copies of the case or request permission to reproduce materials, call 1-800-545-7685 if in the U.S. or 617-783-7500 from abroad, write Harvard Business School Publishing, Boston MA 02163, or go to http://www.hbsp.harvard.edu.

2

Building Cross-Sector Bridges

James Austin, Ezequiel Reficco, and SEKN Research Team

The research results analyzed in the previous chapter seem to suggest that collaboration efforts in Latin America between private companies and the third sector have been more widespread and effective than we often tend to think. If we take into account the fact that such cross-sector collaboration represents a break in a long-lasting inertia for the region, an initial and most appropriate starting point is an exploration of the motivating forces driving companies and Civil Society Organizations (CSOs) to come together in these joint efforts. Furthermore, reaching a decision to engage in collaborations entails overcoming certain hurdles. The first part of this chapter deals with those motivating forces, while the final section draws lessons from how the surveyed organizations managed to build bridges to overcome those barriers.

What Motivates Organizations to Collaborate?

It is important to understand the motivating forces behind the decisions of businesses and CSOs to enter collaborations, because they form the cornerstone upon which alliances are built. By motivations, we mean the conscious values and explicit purposes that initially drive individuals and organizations to explore the possibility of working across sectors. It is vital that each partner have clarity regarding their own motivations so that they can shape the relationships to attain the desired outcome. Of comparable importance is an understanding of why the other partner wishes to engage in the collaboration so that the participant can be responsive to those goals and needs.

In thinking about motivations systematically, it is helpful to have a framework, and we have derived one from our examinations of cross-sector collaborations in the Americas. A basic element is the recognition that there can exist a wide range of motivations across the partners and a mix of motivations for each partner. We conceptualize this as the Partnering Motivation Spectrum. At one end are the Altruistic Motives aimed at benefiting others rather than the partners themselves. At the other extreme are the Utilitarian Motives that focus on the benefit to the partner rather than others.[1] In either case, there is the potential for benefits to accrue to the partners or to others, but in the Partnering Motivation Spectrum, the focus is simply on the partners' motivations rather than the ultimate outcomes.

Altruistic motives are centered, for example, on helping individuals in need, solving community problems, or making other general contributions to the well-being of society. Such motives spring from the humanitarian values possessed by the organizations or individuals involved. Utilitarian motives, on the other hand, cater to the partners' organizational needs, focusing on issues like risk management or the creation of competitive advantages. These motives are rooted in serving the particular institutional interests of the partners. Since NPO's missions are generally imbued with social purpose, their general motives tend to be predominantly altruistic in nature, but collaborating with businesses can also meet specific CSO institutional needs. The basic focus of businesses is to generate economic returns, so it makes sense that some motives would tend toward the utilitarian, coexisting with altruistic motivations of business leaders and manifesting themselves in the collaborative undertakings. Thus, motives can be idealistic or utilitarian, altruistic or self-interested.

Our cases show that regardless of the precise motivational starting point, as long as cross-sector collaborations continue to serve the interests of all partners, their motivations are likely to evolve. In most real life cases, organizations are motivated by a mix of altruistic and utilitarian motivations that differs from case to case. As Figure 2 below shows, any kind of motivation, or combination of them, can trigger a sustainable partnership as long as it is intense. When the intensity is lacking, depicted as the darker zone in the *southwest* corner of that figure's quadrant, that represents the area of lowest sustainability for the partnership. Our research suggests that as the collaboration progresses, motivations *gain intensity* (represented with arrow #1 in Figure 2 below) and *become more blended* (represented with arrows 2a and 2b). In principle, we should expect to see more sustainable ventures when motivations are placed higher and closer to either end of the spectrum (utilitarian or altruistic drives), becoming most sustainable when they become strong and blended, as represented in the *northeast* corner. Chapters 3 and 4 explore the proposition that strong, blended motivations tend to generate richer, fuller relationships capable of producing intense value for participants in different dimensions. Figure 2 can help collaborators gain clarity about their motivations by plotting them on the two axes. The resulting location is a qualitative self-assessment and judgment of what is the driving behavior rather than a precise calculation.

Figure 2: Cross-Sector Collaboration Motivational Spectrum

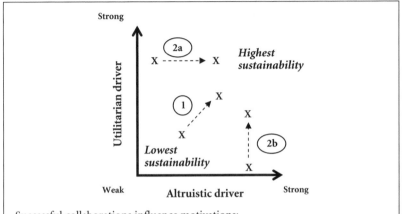

Successful collaborations influence motivations:
(1) Even if mix of original motivations remains constant (50%–50% in example), intensity may increase.
(2) Even if intensity of original motivation remains constant, it may become more blended:
    2a Generating a value-oriented and emotional connection in the ultra-pragmatic actor
    2b Generating a utilitarian connection in the purely-altruistic and idealist actor

Before undertaking any sort of substantial motivation analysis, it is worthwhile to focus on two different but related questions: what drives organizations to engage in cross-sector collaborations, and what do they expect to gain from them? The first question focuses on motivations, while the second one has more to do with the benefits sought in interactions with future partners. This chapter will only tackle the first question, leaving the second for Chapter 4 when we will discuss value creation in collaborations.

Altruism

As a general rule, collaboration efforts between companies and CSOs have an inherent social dimension. While the main objective of the private business sector is economic value creation, the altruistic dimension prevails in the third sector. In our cases, social leaders approached companies for a variety of reasons that most certainly included accruing some organizational advantages, thus giving their approach a utilitarian component. However, these social leaders viewed those advantages as a vehicle for contributing to solutions of certain social problems. According to Juan Carr, founder of the Solidarity Network (*Red Solidaria*, hence RS), the institution's mission "to improve life conditions for needy individuals" could only be achieved if the Argentine society underwent a cultural transformation, setting solidarity as a core shared value. Its association with the prestigious newspaper *La Nación* served as a valuable tool in attaining such an objective; it was a utilitarian means used to attain an altruistic goal.

Altruism and solidarity were also significant drivers in the private sector, resulting in large part from the long-standing tradition of charity and civil commitment derived from the region's powerful Catholic background.[2] For some business leaders, participation in the solution of social problems is simply a question of "doing the right thing" from an ethical standpoint. In the opinion of Manuel Ariztía, renowned Chilean businessman and owner of *Empresas Ariztía*, his company's responsibility to collaborate in solving community problems, regardless of any potential organizational advantage, arises from an ethical imperative that falls on the shoulders of the individuals that lead it.

In addition to this tradition, in the 1990s there emerged a new vision regarding the role of private companies in society, by a new generation of leaders who took over some of the region's most important business holdings. The traditional Argentine newspaper *La Nación* provides an example of such a shift, when in 1996 a change in ownership of the controlling stake led to the appointment of Julio Saguier as board chairman. Saguier was intent on committing the company to the development of a different society through a cultural change that had solidarity as its core value.

In our sample alliances, this motivation was associated with a specific company type: *family-owned businesses*. These are companies controlled by an individual or a family, despite the existence of a sophisticated corporate structure with management and ownership formally represented in different organs. In the case of *La Nación*, the newspaper is owned by a corporation (*La Nación* S.A.), but the Saguier family, descending from its founder, controls both its board and top management.

Family-owned businesses usually highlighted altruism as the main motivation driving them to engage in cross-sector collaborations.[3] According to Norma Treviño, public relations manager of H-E-B Supermarkets Mexico, "We are not doing this to increase our sales... or our profits." Our sample cases have exhibited remarkable correlation between altruistic drives and family companies. From an ethical point of view, it is to be expected that individuals acting out of pure altruism would do so with their own resources and not those of third parties. Michael Porter points out that when social activities lack a strategic dimension, Milton Friedman's well-known criticism that philanthropy has no place in business, suddenly seems to take on more credibility.[4] From an administrative point of view, when management is a mere agent for shareholders, it will likely find it hard to justify significant resource allocations resulting from decisions based primarily on altruistic motives rather than company-related needs.

Several of these companies were founded by individuals with a strong personal inclination towards philanthropy, later incorporating such ideas into their organizational vision and values. Mexico's Bimbo Group provides a clear example; this world leader in the food industry, a multinational corporation with operations in 16 countries, was founded more than five decades ago by Lorenzo Servitje, a distinguished philanthropist well-known for his social commitment.[5] Despite the expansion and level of sophistication of operations achieved by the corporation over the years, its founder's vision and values remain rooted in the group's organizational identity. According to Martha Eugenia Hernández, Bimbo's institutional relations manager, "Over time, Don Lorenzo's personal values have permeated Bimbo's philosophy."

Utilitarianism

Collaborations may also fulfill a very practical function: to satisfy partners' organizational needs, both in the private and third sector. It is important to clarify upfront that the dichotomy between altruistic and utilitarian drivers does not carry with it any implicit value judgment, of the "good" vs. "bad" type. While it is clear that helping the community is a socially desirable value, serving an organization's legitimate needs is an equally genuine goal. Self-interest should not be confused with exploitation or opportunism, as both are very different things. One of the arguments put forward in this book, which we develop later, is that there is no inherent tension between altruism and enlightened self-interest; on the contrary, both can reinforce each other.

Moving on to the specific drivers at play in our sample cases, we identified two powerful utilitarian motivations: risk-management and competitive advantage creation.

Risk Management

A common reason for engaging in cross-sector collaboration has been to make use of it as an effective risk-management tool, whether for minimizing the occurrence of previously identified risks, or for being prepared to face their consequences, were they to occur. In the third sector, these collaborations contributed to the diversification of revenue sources and a reduction of their dependence on public funding. For the Monterrey Food Bank (*Banco de Alimentos de Monterrey,* hence BAM), the collaboration with H-E-B Supermarkets (HEB) served to reduce its exposure to political instability. BAM's director Blanca Castillo believed that when an OSC relies to a large extent on public funding, there is always the political risk that "when their term is over, so is the program. A new administration will step in with new programs."

Our sample cases also registered such motivation in the private sector. Cross-sector ventures served some companies to meet an objective explicitly present in their strategy. Among these cases were some companies with structural vulnerabilities built into their business models, thus forcing management to create the necessary tools to face difficult times.

In the case of *Autopistas del Sol* (AUSOL), a company responsible for managing one of the Greater Buenos Aires area privately managed highway networks, its business largely depended on good relationships with the communities surrounding the new highway layout. Thus, community goodwill became a crucial "operating license" for the company. In poverty-stricken and disjointed societies, as is all too frequently the case in Latin America, such a license should not be taken for granted, especially when collection of tolls appears to be a rather unpopular means of funding, as revealed from several of our interviews.[6] Another example along these lines would be a company that commercialized products potentially hazardous for human health or the environment. In this scenario, it would make sense for such a company to become part of the solution, and engage in programs aimed at solving these issues, thus the interest of the beverage and packaging companies we studied in environmental recycling collaborations.

Another characteristic shared by this group of businesses was that they were all *multinational corporations,* a fact that helps us to understand many of their decisions. Sample cases show that subsidiaries' top executives engaged in cross-sector collaborations to respond to parent company instructions to work with the community. This is an interesting dimension of globalization that calls for further study: multinationals transfer not only their technology, but also their values and social policies. María Marta Llosa, external relations manager of Coca-Cola de Argentina, explained that "we have a worldwide mission: to become leading corporate citizens."

In several cases, this mandate was the result of traumatic experiences or scandals that required huge efforts on the part of companies to repair damaged reputations. The 1989 Exxon Valdez tanker oil spill in Alaska was a haunting benchmark not only for Exxon-Mobil but for global corporations at large, which have since become keenly aware of their exposure to this type of episode. Shell was also deeply affected by the 1995 dispute with Greenpeace over Shell's disposal of its Brent Spar off-shore oil platform, as well as its operations in Nigeria.[7] These disturbing experiences forced companies to create a strategic tool for managing risks at a global level. Mariale Álvarez, environmental technical coordinator of Coca-Cola de Argentina, explained just how her company underwent such a change:

> For many years, the company had focused on its internal operations and paid little attention to external communications about its social activities. However, this changed in the late 1990s, partly due to external pressures. There were some confrontations with NGOs, not in Argentina. Also, there was an awareness shift in consumers and in the communities where we operated.

Contrary to competitive motives that seek to improve companies' market share, the risk management motivation mainly attempted to preserve a favorable status quo. Very often these were companies which enjoyed a position of leadership in their industries, with great public exposure. For example, Coca-Cola de Argentina and Tetra Pak Mexico both confronted similar challenges: as a result of the widespread success of their products, their disposable containers inevitably attracted the attention of government and public opinion concerned with environmental degradation, generating a weak flank that had to be covered. Both companies resorted to alliances with CSOs in order to convey the message that responsibility for discarded containers was shared by several stakeholders, not just manufacturers.

The case of Tetra Pak illustrates particularly well how this type of motivation seeks the maintenance of a favorable state of affairs. When the company perceived on the horizon the emergence of potential threats looming from public authorities and the third sector, it strove to change its vision and find a way to manage these risks. Lorena Mañón, member of the Mexico City Junior League Environmental Committee (JLCM), explained that in the early 1990s "radical environmental groups arrived [at Tetra Pak] with a trailer full of empty containers and piled them up outside the plant. This type of action opened the company's eyes to civil society." Mañón added, "It also opened their eyes to the stir that government was creating" in order to regulate the industry. Company spokesmen have confirmed that they are aware of the ever present risk of government regulation. Environmental manager Sergio Escalera stated, "The government blames the industrial sector, thus holding manufacturers responsible. The upcoming period of legislative meetings will tackle the new law on containers and packages. There are several proposals, and the last version I have heard is rather scary."

Contrary to what was the case in most other partnerships in our sample, Tetra Pak strove to restrict exposure of its efforts and prevent a close association of its brand with the "Recyclable by Nature" (*Reciclable por Naturaleza*) program undertaken with the JLCM, despite the project's success and prestige. The characteristics of the industry and the company itself may help us understand this decision. If their intended message was that several institutional stakeholders shared responsibility in waste disposal, then over-identification of its brand with the effort would have proven counterproductive. Of course, an alternative course of action would have been the one chosen by Shell, which from the experiences in the above mentioned negative events, strove to assume leadership of the environmental cause in its industry, and turned it into a competitive advantage.[8] However, unlike Shell, Tetra Pak had no competitive incentives to do that. At the time of entering the collaboration with the JLCM, it held an oligopolistic leading position in its industry on a global level, reaching almost 80 percent of the Mexican market. Moreover, increasing its market share would have entailed the risk of triggering Mexican anti-trust laws. Thus, the collaboration with the JLCM sought to maintain a state of affairs almost ideal for the company, with a market share high enough to dissuade potential competitors but low enough to keep the government undisturbed.

The Quest for Competitive Advantage

Cross-sector collaborations can provide a powerful leverage for optimizing the competitive positioning of an organization, both from the private and the third sectors. While risk-management is not necessarily absent in this group, what these organizations sought was to go beyond that defensive dimension and leverage their cross-sector partnerships in order to improve market positioning. The companies started off with the following question: what are the obstacles hindering corporate performance and how can cross-sector collaborations contribute to overcoming them? The competitive dimension of cross-sector collaborations, with a special focus on the Mexican context, is explored further in Chapter 11.

The Chilean *Farmacias Ahumada S.A.* (FASA), Latin America's largest drugstore chain, faced a significant challenge in 1997. In the words of Jaime Sinay, general manager at the time, "the company intended to establish a closer relationship with the community. Our business carries a complex connotation. It is a fact of life that people dislike buying medicines. Furthermore, Chile offers no reimbursements for pharmaceutical expenses, so this tends to add to customers' negative disposition." To respond to this situation, FASA considered a possible collaboration with the *Fundación Las Rosas* (FLR), a home devoted to caring for elderly in need. According to some analysts who had been monitoring the evolution of FASA, the decision was a step in the right direction, as "promoting customers' goodwill was important to strengthen the company."

In Colombia, President Cesar Gaviría's so-called "*revolcón*"—his plan of economic modernization and structural adjustment, implemented in the early 1990s—exerted a significant impact on the health sector. Budgetary cutbacks forced hospitals to become much more conservative in their procurement policies. *General Médica,* a vendor of high-complexity medical equipment, knew that their products were competitive, but it was also aware that they could not compete on price. A demanding market would reward *General Médica,* but that would require educating hospitals to familiarize them with the latest technological developments in the field, so they could make adequate purchasing decisions. Only a highly educated buyer would appreciate the advantages of a sophisticated product. Therefore, from the outset the company sought involvement with the Hospital Management Center (*Centro de Gestión Hospitalaria,* hence CGH), a permanent forum that gathered actors from different sectors to contribute to improving the Colombian health sector. Johnson & Johnson, on the other hand, joined CGH not to educate the market about the available supply, but to learn about its demand. Its objective was "to gain insight into hospital problems in order to serve them better," in a market where service would make the difference since price disparities were rapidly vanishing due to increasing competition.

The candid involvement of companies like Johnson & Johnson and *General Médica* in organizations like the CGH, places them in the paradoxical situation of being partners and competitors at the same time. One way to understand this apparent contradiction is to consider their participation as a case of "coopetition," a dynamic combining cooperation and competition dimensions.[9] Actors cooperate to *develop* the market, expanding and strengthening it, while at the same time, they compete among themselves to *divide* it.[10] This is also an example of what Porter and Kramer call strategic philanthropy, in which a company makes a contribution (sometimes in collaboration with competitors) to a social cause related to its core business, altering the context in such a way that it produces a positive impact on its business.[11]

In looking at the organizational structures of companies in this group, we can identify two patterns. The first and largest subgroup is made up of multinational corporations that "export" this practice to their subsidiaries. The Danone Group provides a good example, as their corporate mission is to create economic and social value, and hence they do not perceive any incompatibility in using one dimension in favor of the other. Aminta Ocampo, public relations manager of Danone Mexico, explained how "Danone's social policy consists of what we call the 'double project': our social and economic objectives cannot be separated."

A challenge that these multinational companies usually face is obtaining local credentials; that is, overcoming the emotional distance between its brands and local consumers. By 1997, Danone Mexico had its first run-in with this problem when marketing research revealed that the general public held the company in high regard, but perceived it as somewhat detached from consumers. Ultimately, management's search for a solution led the company to collaborate with a local CSO, the Friendship Home (*Casa de la Amistad,* hence CdA). In Costa Rica, the television corporation *Representaciones Televisivas* (REPRETEL) met a similar challenge. This company, owned by Mexican businessmen, managed three of the six existing channels in Costa Rica, and by 1996, ranked second in the Costa Rican television industry, trailing only Teletica, a long-standing, locally-owned network. René Barboza, REPRETEL reporter, elaborates,

We needed a more popular positioning since the REPRETEL brand was frowned upon for being foreign, for its foreign capital. Besides, our competitor had skillfully used the concept of *"we are Costa Rican; we think like you; Teletica Channel 7 has always been with you."* People were scared because REPRETEL had bought several networks in Costa Rica, and they didn't know what those channels would do, what kind of mindset they would foster for children.

To enhance its brand, REPRETEL resorted to a partnership with the *Fundación Promotora para la Vivienda* (FUPROVI), an NGO devoted to the development of public housing and community strengthening programs.

It is interesting to note the absence of family-owned companies in this group. If we take into consideration the fact that the use of social ventures as a competitive tool is not entirely legitimized within the Latin American business community, it is not surprising that this reluctance may surface stronger where ownership is concentrated in a few individuals. In contrast, those multinational corporations surveyed, where ownership is diversified and anonymous, had no misgivings about the link between social policy and financial return. According to Guillermo García, public relations manager of Esso Chile, "The motivation that drives us to collaborate in community projects is quite simple: it's good for our business." Esso believed that collaborations generated a win-win situation both for the company and society. In a similar vein, the contrast between two sample cases with multiple similarities also illustrates this point: both Danone and HEB are foreign companies belonging to the food industry, which at the time of initiating cross-sector collaborations did not enjoy long-established reputations in Mexico. The main difference between the two companies lies in their ownership structure: publicly held in Danone, family-based in HEB. Accordingly, while the former explicitly leveraged the collaboration in support of its business operations, the latter chose to maintain both spheres separately.

In addition to multinational corporations, a few large local companies engaged in cross-sector collaborations driven by competitive motivations. Since they constitute real success stories in terms of their economic and social impact, it is worth discussing these experiences in greater detail. One of the companies was Indupalma S.A., a Colombian company engaged in African palm oil production and marketing.

Rubén Darío Lizarralde, Indupalma's general manager, is conclusive about the fact that social investments are not triggered by altruism but by potential profitability. The notion that "social aid pays back" is a concept deeply rooted in his vision, also serving as the title of a presentation in which Lizarralde describes the company's experience, *Lo Social Paga*. In order to understand this vision, not widespread within the Latin American business leaders, we need to relate it to the particular context of Indupalma and Colombia.

The political unrest and social violence prevailing in Colombia in the past decades had affected the company, creating dysfunctions that, by 1991, put Indupalma on the verge of bankruptcy.[12] Its management soon realized that, to remain viable, the company would need to become involved in the pacification of its environment. The depth of the crisis forced Indupalma to completely review its organizational identity. From this process, a new vision emerged; one in which Indupalma viewed itself at the center of what it called a "business community," which was to be the basis of a sustainable economic and social development model. This strategy was based on four axes, which included: (a) alliances with labor cooperatives to generate income opportunities for the regional population; (b) educational development of neighboring communities to promote individual growth and technical training associated with palm oil production; (c) development of peaceful interpersonal relations; and (d) education of committed and solidarity-conscious citizens. The first axis was implemented through alliances with labor cooperatives, while the remaining three were based on alliances with local CSOs.

The notion that "social aid pays back" is embedded in Indupalma's competitive strategy, but it also serves its risk management, since one of the company's primary objectives is to reduce the threat of armed groups affecting their operations. This kind of double motivation derived from a very particular context does not fit the general pattern described in the previous section, where we analyzed how some organizations made use of cross-sector collaborations for risk management purposes.

The second case in this sub-group is that of Natura, a leading cosmetic company in Brazil that placed social responsibility at the core of its competitive strategy. The company defined itself as a "dynamic set of relations" with its stakeholders, and viewed each of those relations as an asset. One of those assets was the strong connection with its consumers, mostly women, based on personal relationships with a direct sales force totaling 270,000 saleswomen—that the company called "associates" (*colaboradoras*). The "power of relationships," grounded on the emotional link with its brand, was the essence of Natura's organizational culture and competitive strategy. In the words of Phillipe Pomez, business innovation and development vice-president, "All Natura product lines *must have a cause and a story to tell,* so as to strengthen and consolidate the identification of our *colaboradoras* with the company."

In line with this rationale, Natura launched an innovative product line called Ekos. The "story to tell" behind this new line was the preservation of Brazilian natural biodiversity. "Natura intends to help the country take advantage of its biodiversity, thus transforming it into a source of social wealth. We need to turn that cause into a tangible object," explained Pedro Passos, operations president. The "tangible object" was a product line based on plant and vegetable oils traditionally used by indigenous communities in the hinterlands.[13] The communities that possessed the key knowledge of how to produce, extract, and apply the components of their traditional crops lived in primitive conditions; thus, incorporating them into the company value chain would have a significant impact on their lives. This was accomplished through a cross-sector partnership, to be discussed at length in subsequent sections.[14]

In the last case of this sub-group, the use of a cross-sector collaboration as a competitive leverage came about through the incentives provided by an international development agency. Rainforest Expeditions (RFE) was a small Peruvian ecotourism company that detected the opportunity to open an *eco-lodge* in the Tambopata-Candamo Reservation area, in the Peruvian Amazonia. When the traditional funding sources turned their backs on the company, RFE appealed to the Canadian-Peruvian Fund (CPF), a technical cooperation entity that promoted innovative sustainable development projects. The CPF welcomed the proposal, but imposed one condition: instead of employing local natives, RFE would need to partner with the community and train its members in order to qualify them for a future takeover of the joint-venture. This case is discussed later on in more detail;[15] for our purposes here suffice it to say that when faced with the CPF proposal, the company realized that it could obtain competitive advantages from its association with the community.

This competitive drive is also relevant for the third sector. The Forest Stewardship Council (FSC) is a global CSO, until recently headquartered in Oaxaca (Mexico), which supports the sustainable management of the world's forests. In this task, the FSC faced the competition of other CSOs that were sponsored and funded by large industrial groups. To improve its competitive position, the FSC engaged in an alliance with the some of the largest retail chains in the "do-it-yourself" industry, by which the latter gave preference in their procurement to those suppliers certified as complying with FSC standards. These alliances created a strong incentive for producers to join the FSC certification scheme.[16]

Colombia's Hospital Management Center (CGH) is also a good example of this point. The CGH's mission was "to promote and lead health management transformation in order to contribute to overall industry development," which was carried out through advisory services to health sector organizations. Among CGH's key competitive strengths vis-à-vis professional service firms offering similar advice, were its multiple alliances with private companies, universities, and other institutions, which supplied the center with a deep knowledge of the sector hardly available to its competitors.

Overcoming Barriers to Collaboration

Whatever the motivations behind collaborations, embarking on a new course of action usually demands overcoming hurdles and breaking inertias. It is highly probable that any organization considering the possibility of launching a cross-sector collaboration will, sooner or later, confront several obstacles. In this regard, the experience accumulated in our sample cases constitutes a valuable resource to readers, offering takeaways and information that will allow them to analyze the strengths and weaknesses associated with the building of a cross-sector partnership. This section will discuss the nature of those obstacles and the means used by the surveyed organizations to overcome them. These include the search for an interlocutor, the importance of preexisting relationships among future partners, the impact of shortcomings in institutional capacity, the effect of differences in organizational cultures, the importance of communicating effectively, and the value of being proactive and persistent. Chapter 8 will also analyze the overcoming of collaboration barriers, with a special focus on the Central America and Peru cases provided by the *Instituto Centroamericano de Administración de Empresas* (INCAE).

The Search for an Interlocutor

Who leads the initial collaboration process? Sometimes, choosing an interlocutor is almost as important as choosing the message. Therefore, it is useful to take a close look at our sample cases to check on "who did what" in the initial stages of collaboration. Bilateral alliances exhibited two distinct approach patterns: one from CSOs to companies, and another from companies to CSOs.

From CSOs to Companies

In most of the bilateral alliances surveyed, the initiative of "crossing the bridge" to propose joint-work was taken by third-sector representatives. The dynamics displayed followed a similar pattern that consisted of initially "getting a foot in the door" of the companies,[17] and then working to "sell the project" to top management. The first stage consisted of CSOs looking for the point of least resistance within a company in order to awaken the curiosity and interest of an interlocutor. As a general rule, this task was carried out by the CSO's top officials,[18] which reinforced the credibility and quality of the message. The counterpart in the private sector tended to be its middle management, particularly those responsible for marketing and/or public relations. Table 2 below lists the key actors in alliances adhering to this pattern.

Table 2: The Search for an Interlocutor

	CSO head →	*Private company middle management*
Bimbo-Papalote	Marinela Servitje de Lerdo de Tejada, Papalote Children's Museum general director.	Sergio Montalvo, Bimbo Group marketing director.
Danone-CdA	Amalia García Moreno, Casa de la Amistad (CdA) founder and life-long patron.	Aminta Ocampo, Danone Mexico public relations manager and public relations and communications director.
Esso-COANIQUEM	Jorge Rojas, COANIQUEM founder and head.	Christian Storaker, Esso Chile public relations head.
H-E-B – BAM	Blanca Castillo, Banco de Alimentos de Monterrey head.	Eddie García, Texas Food Banks program head, Lola Landa, H-E-B Monterrey public relations manager.
LN-RS	Juan Carr, Red Solidaria leader.	La Nación newspaper's General Information editors, Sunday magazine editors, special section reporters.
RFE – Comunidad Ese'ja	Ese'eja Native Community leaders.	Kurt Holle, Rainforest Expeditions marketing director.
TP – JLCM	Martha Rangel, Mexico City Junior League president.	Salvador Alanís, Tetra Pak Mexico marketing director.
Techint – Proa	Adriana Rosenberg, Fundación Proa president.	Techint corporate communications Dept.
Texaco – EJN	Maritza Morales, EJN's founder and executive director.	Texaco brand, advertising and customer service coordinator.
CCA – JAA	Eduardo Marty, Junior Achievement Argentina founder and executive director.	María Marta Llosa, internal relations head of Coca-Cola Argentina

However, no project can move forward without the support of to-anagement. Therefore, after outlining a shared vision on a potential joint collaboration, those who led the initial contacts strove to commit the company's senior managers to the project. Usually, social leaders had to meet this challenge without having had the benefit of a prior acquaintance with those individuals. Thus, in order to achieve a strong effect in short time, they aimed at generating an emotional response to spark attachment and loyalty to the cause. This was mainly accomplished through field visits that allowed companies' management to experience direct contact with the organizations' beneficiaries.

For example, after agreeing on general partnership guidelines, García Moreno, Friendship Home's (CdA) founder, and Ocampo, Danone's public relations manager, set out to involve Danone's CEO in the project. Both officials organized a visit to the CdA, where the general manager saw the work carried out by the organization and met the children afflicted with cancer that would benefit from the campaign. The visit deeply moved Danone's CEO and translated into his substantial support of the collaboration. Something similar happened during the early stages of the collaboration between Esso Chile and the Burned Children Assistance Corporation (*Corporación de Ayuda al Niño Quemado,* hence COANIQUEM). In describing their initial encounter with COANIQUEM, Esso Chile officials ventured away from usual business rhetoric; in their own words, "they fell in love."

At times, those responsible for initial negotiations become internal *champions* of the initiative, as they develop a strong identification with it and work intensely within their organizations to get it off the ground. This dynamic may lead champions in each partnering organization to engage in a joint effort *across* organizational boundaries.

This was true in the above described case with Danone Mexico, whose public relations manager worked in close association with the CdA founder to arrange the visit of Danone's general manager to the organization site. The visit succeeded in drawing the general manager's commitment, and became a standard practice systematically repeated with every change in senior management, an issue which we will later address in Chapter 5. In the case of *La Nación* and the Solidarity Network (RS), rather than generating an individual champion inside the newspaper, what Juan Carr accomplished was to win over all the journalists with whom he established initial contacts. They proudly alleged that the partnership with the RS "started right here with us, journalists, and that won our deep commitment to the cause." The support of those journalists proved useful later on, when Carr approached newspaper president Julio Saguier to ensure his commitment to the partnership.

From Companies to CSOs

Companies that decided to contact CSOs followed two different patterns. In the first one, a middle management executive bonded with a cause, not with an organization, and set out on a personal crusade to engage top management's commitment. Once he secured that support, he then contacted a CSO. This dynamic includes all the components of the pattern described in the previous section, though the sequence of events is in reverse order; the contact with the future partner comes after having obtained top management's support. The most difficult part of the persuasion process takes place at an early phase within the company. In these cases, CSOs were approached by already motivated and committed partners submitting a proposal for joint work. To maximize the chances of success for this internal persuasion process, efforts were aimed strategically, as we will see next.

The partnership between *Farmacias Ahumada S.A* (FASA) and the *Fundación Las Rosas* (FLR), a home for needy elders, provides a good example of the first pattern explained. Alex Fernández, FASA board member, had become acquainted with the FLR's work during his experience as manager of another company. Moved by his deep emotional bond to the cause, Fernández decided to become the organization's champion within FASA and to work towards building an alliance between the company and the FLR. The question was where to start. Fernández chose to focus his efforts on a key player, after whom it all should fall into place: José Codner, FLR board chairman. He explained, "Codner was the man to convince; the rest of the board members would go along with his decision." His efforts proved fruitful. Codner welcomed Fernández's arguments, and under the shared leadership of the Fernández-Codner tandem, the rest of the board members committed themselves to the initiative.

Renato Ferretti, marketing manager of Chilean Credit and Investment Bank (*Banco de Crédito e Inversiones de Chile*, hence BCI), used a similar strategy. Moved by poverty-stricken children, Ferretti decided to mobilize support within the bank to contribute to alleviating that social issue. As in the previous case, Ferretti aimed his efforts at a strategic actor: Héctor Pozo, bank comptroller. Pozo was also a key figure within the BCI; he had worked in the institution for forty years, and he was deeply trusted by both the president and the board. Ferretti anticipated that gaining Pozzo's support would greatly facilitate the selling of the idea to the other managers. He recalls, "I first approached the bank comptroller, Hector Pozo, who offered his support and agreed to open a joint account for fund raising purposes. With his support, I went door-to-door and received approval from the remaining managers." Only after securing this general approval did Ferretti turn his attention to the "hardest nut to crack," the bank's CEO. "The last person I approached was Enrique Yarur, general manager at the time, because of course, should I have gone to him first, it would have been very difficult for me to convince him. It was a lot easier to submit an idea already endorsed by many. And so Yarur also approved the project."

Another case in this group was the collaboration between the television company REPRETEL and FUPROVI, a nonprofit organization engaged in public housing projects. René Barboza, REPRETEL journalist, felt the need to help Costa Ricans who had lost their homes to Hurricane César in July 1996. Barboza managed to convince board members to launch a campaign with a CSO to offer relief to this emergency, and he assumed the position of project leader.

As for the second pattern, companies got in touch with CSOs through their top executives. The fact that these collaborations were handled on such a high level can be explained by the strategic importance that these ventures had to the companies involved. This is clearly illustrated in the case of *Telemig Celular*, a mobile telephone company operating in the Brazilian state of Minas Gerais. In 2001, Telemig Celular launched its Pro-Council program (*Programa Pró-Conselho*), an effort aimed at strengthening municipal institutions (the councils, or *Conselhos*) that guaranteed children's rights. To carry out this program, Francisco Azevedo, president of Telemig Celular Institute, sought the support of leaders of several local CSOs. Thus, the Volunteer Support Groups were formed, building up a vast network that worked at city administrations to achieve the program objectives.

The strategic dimension of the collaboration accounts for the involvement of Telemig Celular's top executives. The company supplied a service that had until recently been provided by the government. By 2001, Telemig Celular was in the process of consolidating a transition to a new organizational culture that revolved around consumers, and was based on "capillarity:" the capacity of reaching consumers and effectively serving their needs, wherever they happened to be. The company's social arm, the Telemig Celular Institute, operated on the same rationale. Thus, the Pro-Council program allowed Telemig Celular to manage an efficient statewide operation through the articulated activities of local players.

Collaborations also drew the attention of top business leaders when they became a leading case towards the redefinition of the company's social enterprises. For example, the partnership between the Brazilian Itaú Bank and the Center for the Study and Research of Education, Culture and Community Action (*Centro de Estudos e Pesquisas em Educação, Cultura e Ação Comunitária,* hence CENPEC), a CSO devoted to improving public education, arose as part of a soul searching process undergone by the company's board of directors. In 1993, Roberto Setúbal took over the bank from his father Olavo. Since that changeover, the board had been discussing a deep reform of the bank's social policy to make it more strategic and systematic. To this purpose, Roberto Setúbal approached CENPEC as part of a paradigm change that was to set the tone for the bank's social activities for years to come.

Something similar happened with Natura, the Brazilian cosmetic company. As part of its "good corporate neighbor" policy, Natura had been making sporadic donations to the Matilde Maria Cremm public school. According to Irineu Cintra, teaching staff member, "whenever we needed anything, we would knock on Natura's door and always got an answer." But Guilherme Leal, Natura's president, was not satisfied with the relationship, which he saw as patronizing. "I knew we had to change. People viewed the company as synonymous with power and resources, and I wanted to build a different kind of relationship." What Leal had in mind was a more strategic and sustainable social policy that would have a lasting impact, in which Natura would operate as a change agent to help Matilde rediscover itself. Driven by this purpose, Natura recreated its partnership with the school, and summoned CENPEC as an expert in education. As in the previous case, the collaboration with Matilde was a landmark that signaled a change in the company's future social policy.

The same applies to the relationship between *Autopistas del Sol* (AUSOL), the highway construction and management company, and Alberto Croce, community leader. This collaboration, handled at a top corporate level because of its strategic importance, also introduced a permanent shift in the company's social policy.[19] In the case of Indupalma S.A., the Colombian oil palm producer, the collaboration with the Rafael Pombo Foundation was also managed at top executive levels. Rubén Darío Lizarralde, Indupalma general manager, took the initiative of approaching an old acquaintance, Clara Teresa Arbeláez, director of the Rafael Pombo Foundation, a renowned CSO dedicated to the informal education of Colombian children. Here the collaboration did not bring about a cultural change in the company, but rather emerged as a result of it. As we have already mentioned, Indupalma had undergone a terminal crisis in 1991 that had given birth to a new corporate culture that had social policy at the core of its competitive strategy. Within this pattern, contributions to the pacification of this region, torn by tensions between guerrillas and paramilitary groups, were considered strategically paramount for the company's survival.

The Power of Pre-Existing Relations

Our study validates the importance of social networks as a critical resource for organizations. The existence of prior links between parties had a substantial impact on the way initial contacts unfolded. In most of the cases surveyed these pre-existing relationships provided the seed capital that was to serve as the basis for future partnerships. Our sample encompassed different kinds of prior links, summarized in Figure 3 below, which influenced the unfolding dialogue in diverse ways. Preexisting relationships can include emotional ties with individuals, such as family or friends, or they can emerge from direct or indirect professional interactions with fellow employees or colleagues. Both of these types of relationships can serve to create credibility in the potential partner. In their absence, one still might be able to connect to potential partners through their emotional affinity to the social

Figure 3: The Power of Pre-Existing Relations

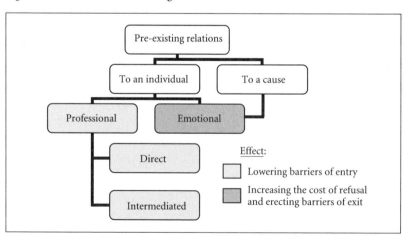

cause of the collaboration. We will illustrate these various connections below; the impact of pre-existing relations and its effect on trust building is analyzed again later on, in Chapter 9, with special emphasis on the Chilean context and cases.

Lowering Barriers of Entry

Plunging into a joint project with a different sector often involves taking an uncertain path. Therefore, any resource that may help in reducing such uncertainty performs a key function. Usually, social relationships are useful in tracing back an individual's background, identifying his/her personal values and professional reliability; in that way, they, lower perceived risks and provide a smooth path for potential communication. In our cases, professional relationships performed that task.

In that light, a first-hand and long-time acquaintance with the future partner will constitute the best guarantee to the individual in charge of initial contacts (Relationship with an individual, in Figure 3). Initial conversations between Danone Mexico and the Friendship Home (CdA), a CSO that provided free assistance to low-income children suffering from cancer, profited greatly from the existence of a sound professional relationship between those who led the initial contacts between organizations. Amalia García Moreno, CdA founder and life-long patron, Aminta Ocampo, Danone's public relations manager, and its director of communications and public relations, had long known each other, from the time when they held executive positions in first-tier private companies. The three women fully trusted each other's professionalism (Direct professional relationship, in Figure 3).

In order to have a positive impact, the pre-existing relationship need not be imbued with positive feelings, as it happened with Danone and CdA, where mutual admiration prevailed. Ultimately, for a prior link to perform its risk control function, it only needs to project itself towards the past, casting light into it and dispelling the uncertainty. The alliance between the Ese'eja native community and the RFE eco tourism makes a good example. In this association, the community provided an area with an extraordinary environmental wealth, while the company agreed, among other things, to hire community members to work in an eco-lodge and train them to the point that they would be qualified enough to take over lodge management in 20 years.

Since 1992, RFE had been managing another lodge, the Tambopata Research Center (TRC), accessible only by an eight-hour boat ride from Puerto Maldonado. In order to take tourists to the TRC, the company had been hiring six Ese'eja commoners on a regular basis.

By 1995, when commoners approached the company to request the hiring of more community members, both parties had developed a trusting relationship. Management was aware that an association with the locals would present certain challenges, but they knew exactly what these challenges could look like. In turn, the community knew RFE and was familiar with their commitment to environmental preservation, a fact that encouraged their decision to entrust them with reservation management.

When there was no personal knowledge available, actors often resorted to a second-best alternative: by transitive character, they extended their trust to the acquaintances of people they trusted. If A trusts B, and B trusts C, A can safely trust C (Intermediated link, in Figure 3).[20] Extended family networks that included in-law relatives fell into this category. After spending two frustrating years in search of funding to start his foundation, Dr. Jorge Rojas got an opportunity through in-law relatives. "It all started with a social event, as is usual in Chile. My wife and I went to my mother-in-law's birthday party, and we happened to share a table with one of my wife's cousins and her husband, Christian Storaker, Esso public relations manager." This dinner conversation, in a reliable, extended-family context, paved the way for the alliance between Esso Chile and the Burned Children Assistance Corporation (*Corporación de Ayuda al Niño Quemado,* hence COANIQUEM). Rojas himself was emphatic in acknowledging the importance of this pre-existing relationship, as he admitted that had it not existed, he never would have dared to knock on Esso's door. He asks rhetorically, "Why would they have trusted me, a perfect stranger to them?" Chapter 9 expands on the significance of the trust variable in Chile.

As our cases studied were in predominantly Catholic societies, the Catholic Church surfaces as a significant social reference institution, embodying widely shared values.[21] When no direct relationship existed between the parties, the intervention of Church sometimes provided "guarantees" of the reliability of individuals and organizations, thus dismissing uncertainties and easing initial contacts between future partners. The Greater Buenos Aires highway management company AUSOL needed to initiate conversations with the communities that would be affected by the future highway layout. Initial efforts, however, proved futile for a lack of valid counterparts. Community relations were a sensitive area for the company, because of its undeniable political connotations. This impasse was eventually overcome when members of the San Isidro Diocese strongly endorsed the name of community leader Alberto Croce. A similar impact was felt in the initial conversations between the Monterrey Food Bank (BAM) and H-E-B supermarkets. The fact that the BAM was affiliated with Cáritas, a Catholic institution widely perceived as trustworthy, with an impeccable reputation and long-time presence in Mexico, spurred the development of a working relationship between both organizations. The role of the Church in facilitating dialogue also emerges prominently in the Chilean cases, which are covered in greater detail in Chapter 9.

The desire of potential partners to get to know the other's personalities and values, may account for the low willingness on the part of surveyed organizations to use data bases or other objective selection mechanisms. Very few of the sample alliances resorted to a systematic search to choose collaboration partners, and even in those cases, previously established personal relationships made a difference. Among these cases was Danone Mexico. Upon deciding to enter into an alliance with a CSO, that company initiated a systematic search through the data base maintained by the Private Assistance Institutions Board, the public agency that oversees the Mexican third sector. The query was guided by two key criteria: potential candidates had to work with children and enjoy a reputation for professionalism. After filtering the data, the company invited those in the reduced candidate pool to submit their projects for evaluation. CdA's proposal was the one selected, as both the project and the organization complied with the selection criteria set by Danone. However, in addition to this seemingly objective and rational choice, and without discounting CdA's institutional capability, our interviewees suggested that the preexisting bond between managers in both organizations was a decisive factor in the final selection.

This tension between objective and subjective criteria in partner selection also emerged in the collaboration between the drugstore chain FASA and the *Fundación Las Rosas* (FLR). In 1988, FASA began their search for the most adequate third-sector organization with which to associate. Several board members felt that the target institution's mission should complement that of the company, focusing primarily on solving health-related problems. Thus, the initial round of candidates was primarily focused on foundations devoted to fighting diseases such as AIDS or blindness. However, in reaching their decision, the board took another route: selecting FLR, a home for needy elders. The selection was far from arbitrary: some objective and rational factors

were paramount, such as the OSC's transparency in resource allocation and the professionalism of its management. At the same time,
leading participants were quick to point out that the intervention of
Alex Fernández, FASA director, was ultimately decisive. Fernández
was very familiar with FLR operations as a result of previous interactions with the organization before joining FASA. In the words of Jaime
Sinay, FASA general manager, "Fernández's lobbying turned the scales
in favor of the FLR."

On account of their structure, multilateral collaborations involving
multiple parties have different characteristics that will be dealt with in
Chapter 8. By definition, they involve a large number of actors who
rarely share pre-existing relationships among all of them. Regardless,
pre-existing relationships also played a significant role in these associations, as trust relations among a few served as seed capital for the later
incorporation of other actors. One example was the project Twenty-
First Century Leaders (*Líderes Siglo XXI*, hence *Líderes*), created in Colombia in 1994 to apply popular private sector quality techniques to
education. The program was the result of an initiative started at the
Presidents' Forum, whose members had been working since 1989 under the motto "learning, communicating, growing together." According to Hugo Valderrama, NCR Colombia's board chairman, "In order
to improve, we shared what we were doing, our failures, our successes,
our progress. We visited one another and we simply copied what was
good. That legitimate imitation propelled incredibly fast progress."

Such a generous openness is only possible when there is trust based
on mutual knowledge. When this organizational culture was trans-
ported to a wider setting, and expanded to encompass other social actors, it became a key asset in collaboration building at the multilateral
level. Also, it is to be noted that when the business community decided
to approach the educational sector, businessmen contacted "only the
schools we knew," in the words of one of the protagonists; that is, the
educational institutions attended by their children or whose principals
they knew personally.

Increasing the Cost of Refusal and Erecting Barriers of Exit
When the nature of a prior relationship is more than a mere acquaintance, and entails more intimacy and an emotional dimension, their
impact is even greater (Emotional relationship, in Figure 3). Not only
do they remove obstacles; they turn into a magnet for winning people
over, making rejection far more difficult. It is not the same to turn down

a proposal submitted by an anonymous counterpart, as doing so with someone we care for. The emotional commitment to the person easily spills over to the initiative, and translates into an enthusiasm that, once rooted, tends to be lasting. This dynamic could be summed up in the colloquial expressions "I can't refuse you and I won't let you down."

In 1982, when Manuel Ariztía was summoned to join the newly created Melipilla Municipal Corporation (*Corporación Municipal de Melipilla*, hence CMM), his company, *Empresas Ariztía*, was undergoing a difficult financial situation. It was not an ideal moment to divert his time and attention towards new projects, no matter how important. However, since the request had come from Álvaro Gutiérrez, city mayor, with whom he felt a close affinity, and because the matter at hand held his deepest interest, Ariztía himself admitted that "he just couldn't refuse."

This effect also emerges in the recently mentioned *Líderes*. With the intellectual capital on quality issues accrued at the Presidents' Forum, businessmen and school principals worked in pairs to download those concepts to the specific reality of educational institutions, with input from relevant stakeholders of participating schools. These pairs were organized in different groups (advanced, intermediate, and new), all operating under the program's broad umbrella.

The co-existence of different groups enables a comparative analysis. In the so-called "intermediate" and "new" groups, from the outset, the group's operating rules are clearly communicated to new entrants. During group operation, if the expectations of newly admitted members' go in a different direction, the group tries to adjust the incoming partner to conform to standard practice; if that does not happen, the dissenting member is invited to leave. In the "advanced" group, things are different: when the parties' expectations exceed program proposals, they become inputs for new projects. This is why it is considered the most innovative group, the one that forges the path to be followed by the rest. The contrast is sharp. What is the difference between these groups? While the intermediate groups were created in 1999 and the new ones in 2000, the advanced groups have been working since 1994. Years of joint work allow the advanced groups to assimilate high expectations and create value. In addition to this greater productivity, close relationships developed by school-company pairs also have an important role. This bond makes rejection difficult, as it would involve rejecting not only an expectation, but an individual or group with whom they have developed personal and professional relationships.

However, bonding occurs not just with people, but also with causes. When a social cause has been part of one's history, it holds a place in one's heart, and it will not be easily evicted (Link to a cause in Figure 3). This ultimately has a powerful influence when building a cross-sector collaboration, as seen in the case of the alliance between the Azúcar Manuelita sugar company and the Minute of God Corporation (*Corporación Minuto de Dios,* hence MD). The MD was a Colombian holding made up of eight nonprofit companies, originated in the social work carried out in the 1950s by Eudist Father Rafael García Herrero. Álvaro Galeano, Manuelita's marketing manager, had participated in García Herreros' teenage programs; he knew the MD well and held a deep affection for it. Driven by this emotional bond, he sought joint work opportunities to strengthen the partnership:

> Since I joined Manuelita in 1973, I always sought opportunities to work with MD, but the possibilities were limited. Nearing 1990, I became marketing director and the number two man in the company. It was then that I started toying again with the idea of working with MD. In 1990, a friend of mine who had been my boss for a long time was elected president, and I told him. "Look, I'm in marketing. Why don't we improve our alliance with MD? From the marketing point of view, I'm certain it will benefit the company."

While Galeano kept his position at Azúcar Manuelita, the partnership with the MD grew stronger. Interestingly enough, when he moved on to another organization belonging to the same business group, his successors lost interest and the collaboration shrank to a minimal level. This reveals a weakness in the alliance, since it proves that bonds and benefits did not go beyond an individual's personal relationship and commitment.

The alliance between FASA, the Chilean drugstore chain, and the Fundación Las Rosas (FLR) provides another powerful example of an emotional bond to a cause. Alex Fernández, who served as liaison between the two organizations, initially approached that CSO driven by a strong utilitarian motivation, which was enriched emotionally when he personally met the organization's leaders and its beneficiaries. Fernández himself provided a moving account,

The original idea was to take some pictures to get a commercial value out of this gesture, with advertising purposes in mind. But the appalling conditions of the home and the sight of the old people sitting there really moved me... most were very neat and tidy, dressed in raggedy coats and old ties. I asked the Father: "Did you dress them up on our account?" He answered, "No son, they are waiting for their families to come and fetch them. But they never do. They have abandoned them." With a lump in my throat, I said good-bye and added, "This check is not enough. You need more. I'll see what else we can do."

That night, Fernández and his wife Gloria decided that they would work to help that elderly group. Years later, that commitment led him on a personal crusade to convince his fellow board members of the need to collaborate with FLR.

The emotional connection was particularly strong when the bond to both person and cause overlapped. This was the case in the collaboration between the Brazilian Itaú Bank and the Center for the Study and Research of Education, Culture and Community Action (CENPEC), a CSO with the mission of improving the quality of Brazilian public education. Both organizations entered into an alliance in 1993 to implement projects to improve primary school teachers' training, an unusual focus in Brazil at the time. In addition to the impeccable professional credentials of the CENPEC staff, the profound emotional bond between organization leaders could not be ignored. On the one hand, Roberto Setúbal, the bank's president, was the brother of Maria Alice Setúbal, CENPEC board chairman. But at the same time, both protagonists shared a very special commitment to the cause of public education. Their deceased mother, Matilde "Tide" Setúbal, had devoted her life to the cause, so much so that she had become nationally renowned for her efforts.

Table 3 below shows how the cases of our sample fell within the different conceptual categories analyzed in the preceding paragraphs. To wrap up this section, it is worth pointing out that in the few cases where at the outset there was no pre-existing link with the potential partner, social leaders set about building personal relations or emotional bonds during the collaboration, thus producing a similar effect. This process will be discussed later, while discussing the management of the collaboration.

Table 3: Origin and Nature of Pre-Existing Relationships

Source of trust	Nature of link	Case
Individual	Close relative	Itaú Bank-CENPEC-UNICEF Bimbo-Papalote
	Prior personal relationship	FASA-FLR CMM-Agr. Ariztía Indupalma-FRP
	Prior professional relationship	CdA – Danone RFE-Ese'ja community AMCHAM LSXXI CGH Techint-Proa CCA–JAA Natura-Matilde CCM – BCI Telemig Celular – Volunteer Support Groups
Family	In-law relative	COANIQUEM-ESSO
Church	Backing of Catholic Church	AUSOL – Croce H-E-B – BAM Minuto de Dios – Manuelita

Imbalances in Partners' Institutional Capabilities

Among the factors that conditioned the initial dialogue between future partners, the institutional capabilities of third-sector partners' surface as one of the most influential and widespread. Our research findings suggest that, all other aspects being equal, the lower CSOs' institutional capabilities were, the higher the barriers for cross-sector dialogue. In our sample, as the institutional capabilities of CSOs decreased, private-sector partners seemed to need more powerful incentives to consider them as potential partners. This is not to say that this factor was determinant: the level of the OSC's institutional capacity was not the only variable at play, and in any case, weaknesses there could be compensated by other strengths evaluated later in this chapter. Moreover, our sample does feature some exceptions to this rule. However, even acknowledging those constraints, the fact that this tendency showed up in most surveyed cases seems suggestive. It is important for companies to dig early on into the institutional capabilities of potential partners in order to decide whether alliances will prove effective, or to envision the steps that should be taken to boost partners' capabilities in order to achieve a productive collaboration.

Table 4 below shows this dynamic with some brief examples that are discussed in the ensuing pages. The upper line of the sample provides a simple typology of the CSOs encompassed in our sample, highlighting their level of institutional capacity, from low (left) to high (right). It should be noted that this typology does not purport to be representative of the entire Latin American third sector. Categories 1 and 2 do not fit easily into our definition of collaboration, as they do not involve two formal organizations. These are "community collaborations," a form of partnership that generates community involvement through the informal representation of a group.[22] Inversely, the lower line of the table represents the magnitude of the barriers faced by prospective partners, from low (right) to high (left). In short, the lower the institutional capacity, the higher the barrier to collaboration.

Community, Devoid of Organizational Structure

In an extreme case, the private-sector actor did not find a counterpart to engage, not even a social leader with the necessary skills to align the community's interest with those of the company, so as to weave an al-

Table 4: Institutional Capacity and Barriers to Collaboration

− INSTITUTIONAL CAPACITY +				
(1) Community, devoid of organizational structure	(2) Individual (community leader)	(3) Individual, surrounded by weak organization	(4) Individual or group, backed by an established organization	(5) Mature organization, with strong executive leadership and highly specialized staff
Ese'eja Native Community	Alberto Croce	Juan Carr and the Solidarity Network (*Red Solidaria*)	Amalia García Moreno and the Friendship Home (*Casa de la Amistad*)	CENPEC
Partnering was not in the company's original plans; only "employing" natives. The company only came to consider an alliance as a result of an imposition by a third party.	Partnering was not in the company's original plans; only "negotiating." The company came to consider partnering with communities in response to powerful contextual incentives.	The social leader took the initiative to approach the company. He found slight initial resistance, overcome by his professionalism and personal charm. The company agreed to collaborate philanthropically once the social leadr managed to "set foot in the door."	The company approached the CSO. Their original idea was to create a business foundation, but, as a result of a visit to the CSO, the company was pleasantly impressed by its professionalism and proposed that OSC start a collaboration.	The company decidedly sought the CSO. Building a collaboration with it did not come about as a second best, but was considered the most efficient strategy from the outset.

BARRIERS TO CROSS–SECTOR COLLABORATION

liance. Faced with this obstacle, the company was forced to "create" its partner and to train the next generation of leaders. Such a colossal task required powerful incentives for the private sector.

Such was the situation in the case of the previously mentioned alliance between Rainforest Expeditions (RFE) and the *Ese'eja de Infierno* Native Community. This community certainly had sound and inveterate social institutions, but lacked the organizational structures and leadership to perform as an equal partner in a cross-sector collaboration involving the operation of an enterprise. It was only through the interaction with RFE that a new generation of leaders was trained and given the necessary skills to represent community interests before the private and public sectors.

In response to a proposal presented by the local settlers, RFE came to consider the possibility of opening an eco-lodge in the Tambopata area. But partnering with the community was not in the company's plans at that time; they initially envisioned only investing the necessary capital and hiring locals, as had been the case so far. However, carrying out the original plan proved to be more difficult than anticipated. Venture capitalists and traditional banks turned their backs on the project, which they regarded as uncertain and too risky. After a fruitless search, RFE contacted the Peruvian-Canada Fund (PCF), a Canadian technical cooperation state agency that encouraged innovative projects promoting sustainable development.

As previously explained, the PCF made its support of the project contingent on the launching of a cross-sector alliance between RFE and the community. For PCF to fund the initiative, the company would need to partner with the community and train its members to a level that would allow them to take over the project at some point in the future. From this "take it or leave it" situation, the company came to see that partnering with community would afford everyone significant benefits, to be discussed at length in later chapters.[23] It took the extremely powerful incentive of conditioned funding that was imposed upon the company for this alliance to take shape.

Individuals

In the second category, when the private company considered a collaboration with the third sector, it encountered a skilled social leader, who enjoyed broad legitimacy in the eyes of the community and had the skills to aptly represent its interests. Building on the relationship with these key individuals, a company may start a constructive dialogue with the community. These leaders are willing and able to mediate between the private sector and civil society, aligning the company's needs with the solution of social problems. Such a relationship can be a valuable asset upon which a company can build, entering into alliances with other existing CSOs or helping the leader create his own formally structured organization.

This was the dynamic of the relationship between community leader Alberto Croce and *Autopistas del Sol* (AUSOL), the company that had won a contract to build and manage toll roads into the city of Buenos Aires. In 1994, the company was experiencing a critical situation. Portions of the future highway layout, which crossed conflictive neighborhoods in the Greater Buenos Aires area, had been illegally occupied by squatter families. Highway privatizations had been ill-received by public opinion, particularly the middle-class neighbors that would be affected by highway construction in particular. At first, the company considered the obvious alternative: to enforce its rights and evict the occupants through police power, since the contract specified that the area would be cleared before construction work began. But such an alternative was very risky. If poor and middle-class sectors converged to confront the highway construction, the situation could become politically explosive. Building a highway involves a sizable upfront investment of capital that, upon completing construction, generates a substantial cash flow. Should AUSOL's international investors experience a change in risk perception, the cost of capital could have increased, potentially hurting the viability of the project. Thus, the company realized that navigating the construction stage smoothly was an absolute necessity.

Taking all of these into account, AUSOL decided to put confrontations aside and approach the affected Malaver and Villafate communities. The idea was to seek a local leader with whom to "negotiate." That "negotiation" turned out to be a profound learning experience for the company. Eventually, AUSOL learned that the relationship had far greater potential than it had originally anticipated. As we will see, the collaboration between AUSOL and Croce grew steadily, leading to the eventual creation of the SES Foundation. Here, too, it took strong contextual pressures for the company to engage in cross-sector collaboration. However, once this initial reluctance was overcome Croce's apt leadership eased the transition towards more structured forms of partnership.

An Individual Surrounded by a Weak Organization

In other cases, the private sector dealt with an individual with strong personal leadership, around whom gravitated a weak CSO. In these cases, the leader's personal traits had a strong impact on the alliance. Despite the existence of formal relationship with an organization, the company placed its trust in *that individual* as the primary resource for value creation. In these situations, the question of long-term sustainability of the partnerships inevitably becomes a challenge, as the leader's charisma proves difficult to replace.

An example of this dynamic was the relationship between the Argentine newspaper *La Nación* and Juan Carr, the Solidarity Network (RS) leader. As already explained, Carr realized that *La Nación* had certain features that would significantly enhance the impact of his work. In 1995, he decided to contact *La Nación*'s editorial department to request the publication of solidarity ads. After several unsuccessful attempts, the editors finally agreed to provide RS with some free space. In order to "get his foot in the door," Carr leveraged two assets: his personal charm and the impact of his work. RS was still unknown to the general public and lacked a well known brand; it was an emerging organization with neither legal status nor formal incorporation. However, during their short time of operation (just one year), Carr and his small team of collaborators had already produced visible results. RS's initial contact in the newspaper, journalist Marta García Terans, recalls that Carr's first requests always focused on communicating the organization's activities.

The emergence of this partnership met little resistance. There were no contextual pressures, nor powerful incentives; just a leader with outstanding communication skills, supported by a volunteer team. When organizations are weak or still in their initial stages, the personal talents of their leaders are essential for alliance building. This concept will be further discussed in a later section.

An Individual or Group Backed by an Established Organization

In other cases, the role of the social leader was limited to building bridges with private and public sector organizations. When approaching a potential partner, these leaders leveraged their personal charm, but also the credentials and goodwill built into the name of the organization they represented, which facilitated the initial contacts. Contrary to the previously discussed categories, once the leader managed to "get a foot in the door," the organization's staff stepped in to occupy center stage in the partnership. Though still acknowledging the importance of personal leadership, in this group, companies placed their trust in *organizations'* capabilities as value creation resources.

The partnership between the Friendship Home (CdA) and Danone Mexico offers a clear example of this relationship dynamic. Founded in 1990 by Amalia García Moreno, the CdA is a CSO, located in one of the outskirts of Mexico City, that provides assistance to children suffering from cancer. When Danone Mexico decided in 1997 to launch a social program, it initially sought to create a corporate foundation. Its communication and public relations manager got in touch with García Moreno, whom she had known and respected professionally for a long time. The idea was to visit the CdA premises in order to get acquainted with the operation of a CSO.

This visit ultimately had an enormous impact on Danone's representative, and completely changed her perspective. She realized that implementing social projects was more complex than she had ever imagined, and at the same time, she was very impressed with the CdA's institutional capacity. This CSO had a highly qualified senior management, a sizable volunteer force, a qualified staff, and a group of widely respected patrons committed to its governance. Thus, the company decided that a collaboration with the CdA would prove to be a more effective instrument in carrying out its social initiative. García Moreno's professionalism and CdA's institutional capacity played a pivotal role in Danone's decision to change course and engage in a cross-sector collaboration.

Mature Organization with Strong Executive Leadership and Highly Specialized Staff

At the opposite end of our typology, companies found a mature counterpart in the third sector. In these relationships, key individuals still made a difference, but their leadership was at the service of a sound organizational dynamic that ultimately exceeded them. In this category, CSOs had a vast and proven ability to create value for potential partners, regardless of the specific individuals involved. They commanded a specialized technical knowledge highly appreciated and sought after by private companies and the public sector. The institutional capacity of these CSOs was such that they could conceive, design, and implement large scale programs, often at a national level.

The collaboration between the Center for the Study and Research of Education, Culture and Community Action (CENPEC), run by Maria

Alice Setúbal, and the Itaú Bank constitutes an example of this type of dynamic. When Roberto Setúbal became president of the bank's board of directors in 1992, he decided it was time to systematize the company's social initiatives. In spite of the numerous donations that the bank was making, a common uneasiness prevailed among top executives on account of what was perceived as low impact and lack of direction in the bank's social initiatives. To change that state of affairs, the board summoned CENPEC, the most prestigious educational research center in Brazil. Over the years, CENPEC had acquired substantial intellectual capital through a highly qualified technical team. Its activities included research, consulting, training, and the dissemination of research findings within the academic community and the general public. In response to the bank's request, CENPEC devised an ambitious nationwide action plan that incorporated UNICEF,[24] in which each actor would contribute according to its key competencies.

This case represents the opposite extreme of our typology. In those collaborations where participating CSOs displayed high institutional capacity, a renowned brand, and a tested operational model, the a priori barriers to cross-sector collaboration were negligible. However, even in these cases, differences in organizational cultures remained as potentially relevant obstacles.

Differences in Organizational Cultures

All organizations operate based on norms, either tacit or explicit, shared values, and beliefs, which define their profile and behavior. This organizational culture conditions not only their internal activities but also the interaction with their environment. When two potential partners operate on the basis of incompatible organizational cultures, it is hard to develop shared visions. Our sample provides a rich array of possibilities for evaluating the impact of this factor, portraying collaboration cases with compatible organizational cultures, others with different cultures, and even cases in which organizational cultures changed during the process. Chapter 7 will analyze in greater detail the relevance of organizational cultures as collaboration barriers, placing a particular emphasis on the Brazilian context.

Early conversations between Danone Mexico and the Friendship Home (CdA) representatives exemplify the positive effect brought about by matching organizational cultures. The three protagonists who led the initial contacts, CdA's founder, Danone's public relations manager, and its public relations director, had previously been professionally socialized by the same corporate culture in their capacity as private sector executives, before engaging in social enterprises. Therefore, when the time came to analyze the prospect of collaborative work, the three women were concerned with the same issues, and brainstormed solutions along similar lines, despite the fact that they belonged to different sectors. Another interesting example is the partnership between Coca-Cola de Argentina and Junior Achievement Argentina, whose representatives also found common ground quickly to work together on an environmental education program. Interestingly enough, both parties shared similar organizational cultures: a business model based on franchising, with heavy emphasis on marketing, and a focus on brand positioning. Both parent organizations had originated in the United States and promoted free enterprise and individual initiative values.

In contrast, when faced with disparate organizational cultures, partners had to invest time and energy in building the communication bridge. This comes across clearly in the previously mentioned Twenty-First Century Leaders (*Líderes*) program, the result of the collaboration between the Presidents' Forum of Bogotá's Chamber of Commerce and several public schools. The lack of a *common language* was the first hurdle that the alliance had to overcome. While businessmen naturally considered their consumers and suppliers as "clients," this term was shocking for educators. The education community, generally indisposed to consumerism, viewed students as "young citizens" and passionately rejected applying business terminology to them. As one actor explained, "We had to carry out a very hard preaching mission because we spoke different languages. And the lack of a common language was killing us."

Peruvian Rainforest Expeditions executives faced a similar challenge during the initial negotiation stages with the Amazonia Ese'eja Native Community. On account of the community's total lack of formal education or previous business management experience, there was no basic terminology to even "name" the problems before moving on to discuss possible solutions. Implementing a functional alliance required a laborious educational process. The solutions to these challenges will be dealt with later on when we analyze trust building in collaborations.

The gap in organizational cultures can create negative *stereotypes* distorting the perception of "the other party," leading one actor to construct conspiracy ridden explanations of the other side's motivations, dictated by supposed "hidden agendas." In the early stages of *Líderes*, many educators found it hard to believe that a business executive would be willing to devote his or her time and efforts to a cause without having ulterior profit-making objectives. This bias did not go unnoticed to the participating business leaders, and it became an impairing factor during the initial dialogues. One of them commented on this point, "Educators are convinced that they contribute to society, while businessmen exploit people in their relentless search for profits and benefits. It's certainly a very short-sighted vision of the Colombian business community."

Another dimension of this problem is the clash of "*the culture of austerity versus the culture of opulence.*" In the *Líderes* project, many school teachers who served poverty-stricken sectors identified management excellence with the resource rich world of business, finding it hard to see how that approach could possibly be relevant for their resource poor world of education. According to a teaching staff member, "Whenever they came to us saying 'we are going to implement this quality process,' we replied, 'What's all this talk about quality? Children here are hungry!'" Similar cultural differences also hindered the initial dialogue between the H-E-B supermarket chain and the Monterrey Food Bank (BAM). On the one hand, the former came from the American business culture, where excellence and efficiency are paramount. On the other hand, the latter's mindset was, in the words of its director Blanca Castillo, dictated by the "culture of austerity:"

> We can't have a new truck because we are a social aid institution; we can't buy a computer because that's only for private companies; we can't use new hydraulic cargo lifts for the warehouse... We could only use manual dollies; all other devices were meant for corporate warehouses.

These cultural discrepancies proved dysfunctional during initial conversations, though BAM top management's willingness to learn greatly helped overcome many of the early difficulties. Castillo added, "We took it as a consulting engagement; we realized HEB had a lot of experience in food banks, and we were interested in their opinion." What makes this case particularly interesting is that it shows the effects produced by a cultural change within an institution. Until then BAM's controlling entity, Cáritas, had been governed by a board deeply embedded with the traditional vision of what a social organization should be like. However, while BAM and HEB were in the process of building their alliance, Castillo recalled, "there was a change in the board chairmanship," and a new leader coming from the private sector took over. "New people came onboard, who shared HEB's vision in terms of institutional quality and professionalization. That allowed us to start speaking a common language, and to develop a kind of empathy," Castillo explained. This new vision allowed BAM to adopt practices previously considered inappropriate to social activities, such as hiring food experts or acquiring cutting-edge technology to optimize its operations.

Cultural dissonance also emerged in the *different time frameworks* of the business sector's expectations and those of the third sector. Businessmen tend to demand short-term, measurable results, something in principle alien to the culture prevalent in the third sector. For example, in the *Líderes* project between public schools and Bogotá's Chamber of Commerce Presidents' Forum, educators placed their expectations in the future generation of citizens. As a participating businessman put it, "schools have a different speed. Companies operate on an immediate basis. At schools, results are expected to be seen in 15 years; a company expects them in a one-year period."

Similar problems arose when the television company REPRETEL entered into an alliance with FUPROVI, a Costa Rican CSO specialized in social housing, with the goal of helping those who had lost their homes in July 1996 as a result of Hurricane César. Dissimilar time frameworks constantly generated frictions, which each party interpreted according to its own organizational cultures. Again, the private sector focused its expectations on visible short-term results. "There were times when I despaired because progress was very slow," admitted René Barboza, REPRETEL's alliance representative. Its partner had a different vision. As stated by Carmen González, FUPROVI development manager and official in charge of the collaboration, "Our working styles were very different. Reporters (…) are more impulsive. They want things *now!*" This cultural incompatibility is analyzed in more detail in Chapter 8.

Communicating Effectively

An effective message demands a skilled communicator. Leaders with good communication skills are important during the whole collaboration process. However, their role is most vital during initial contacts, particularly when the time comes to answer the key question: "how can a cross-sector collaboration benefit my organization?" As we have already seen, this task was usually handled by CSOs top officials, who engaged in initial conversations with private-sector middle management executives. Our research suggests that the most effective tool for generating enthusiasm and persuading future partners is a passionate leader, able to tailor the message according to the targeted audience.

Social leader Juan Carr provides a clear example of this type of leadership. In the interviews carried out as part of our study, his interlocutors at *La Nación* highlighted his modesty, honesty, and the deep conviction that came across in his message as the outstanding features of his communication style. What makes this trait essential at this early stage of the relationship is that it may offset other weaknesses. We have already mentioned that at the time of the initial contact between Carr and *La Nación*, the former had no sound organization behind him, as the Solidarity Network (*Red Solidaria*) had neither legal status nor a renowned brand to support it. Thus, his ability to communicate his vision and his general enthusiasm proved critical in "getting a foot in the door" of *La Nación*, winning over converts to his cause through the newspaper, and eclipsing potential weaknesses.

Dr. Jorge Rojas, COANIQUEM director, is another good example. According to Guillermo García, public relations manager of Esso Chile and his chief contact in the collaboration process, Rojas is an "extraordinary and charming human being and a great communicator." As in the previous case, when Rojas first contacted Esso Chile, he lacked the support of a prestigious CSO and had no proven model to show. In spite of his impeccable medical background, he even lacked credentials as an effective social leader. Once again, his skillful communication ability made up for those shortcomings.

However, communication capability was a relevant factor for others outside of the third-sector as well. Previous sections in this book have shown that, in some cases, the initiative came from the private sector, usually through a middle management executive who had to "sell" his idea to top management.

That was the case with the collaboration partnership between the Chilean Credit and Investment Bank (*Banco de Crédito e Inversiones,* hence BCI) and the Corporation for Children's Credit (*Corporación de Crédito al Menor,* hence CCM), a CSO devoted to providing temporary care for homeless girls. This association was the result of the vision of Renato Ferretti, BCI marketing manager. Upon embarking on his personal crusade, Ferretti had nothing to show but his personal vision, for potential partners did not even exist. Again, his ability to communicate effectively offset this deficit. Juan Esteban Musalem, BCI general manager, defined him as "a creative guy, full of crazy ideas." We have already mentioned that Héctor Pozo, bank comptroller, was the first convert to the cause and a key figure in the campaign to persuade top management. In describing Ferretti's communication style, Pozo underlines the two features that seem to be essential for an effective social entrepreneur: the ability to communicate his vision and to transmit his enthusiasm.

> In the beginning, he talked about his project and I listened with little faith. But in the end, you couldn't help but give in to his enthusiasm. It was a crazy idea, but Ferretti managed to convince other "crazy" bank executives to follow him....

The Importance of Being Proactive and Persistent

Connecting successfully with another organization entails an alignment of several factors. Since this may be an instant occurrence, it is best to be adequately prepared to seize this window of opportunity. Initial contacts were smoother when social leaders and their organizations had been working hard to answer effectively and convincingly the question of "how can your organization benefit mine?" For example, once AUSOL executives decided to initiate conversations with the communities affected by the highway layout, the task was largely facilitated by the existence of grass-roots organizations that had been working under the leadership of Alberto Croce. According to Croce,

> Immediately after they made the announcement of the highway construction, we decided that we needed to come up with a proposal. We were most interested in finding a solution to the housing situation in the communities, because people had nowhere to go. We carried out a neighborhood census, we organized every little detail: we developed a project, and came up with different possible alternatives to find a solution to the situation.

A proactive attitude based on consensus, oftentimes may offset weaknesses in a social actor's institutional capacity. In this regard, the case of Croce is enlightening, as he managed to carry out a successful collaboration operating as an individual. Yet, the experience of the Peruvian Amazonia Ese'eja Community, which even lacked a Croce-like leader, is even more illustrative. The successful joint-venture that made possible the emergence of Posada Amazonas was the result of an initiative triggered by community leaders concerned with the lack of labor opportunities in the region. Though several other factors intervened to make the project viable, nothing would have happened without the drive of the community. The case is particularly interesting because, as already discussed, the community lacked the necessary organizational and management tools to become a partner.

Even for those well prepared to seize emerging opportunities, success may prove elusive. Several of the alliances studied would not have existed without the sheer determination of their social leaders. It should be noted that determination crops up as a relevant factor in those few sample cases in which there was no pre-existing relationship before initial contacts. This suggests that persistence may be a useful tool for making up for the lack of a pre-existing direct link between the parties: if you cannot get the door opened from the inside, you will need to be patient and ring the bell until it does open. In spite of his personal charm, social leader Juan Carr had to cope with several failures before persuading the editors of *La Nación* to provide him with free newspaper space for his solidarity ads. Likewise, Blanca Castillo, BAM director, had to toil patiently and persistently in her attempt to convince Eddie García, H-E-B's executive responsible for food banks. Despite a favorable first contact, it took BAM months, through both letters and phone calls, to get an interview with García. Eventually, García visited Monterrey, and Castillo seized the opportunity. It was at this point that the alliance finally gathered momentum.

However, the significance of determination surfaces with utmost clarity in the experience of the Mexico City Junior League (JLCM). In the early 1990s, this organization began focusing on environmental issues, the recycling of urban waste in particular. JLCM management decided to focus on a potentially high-impact market niche: the multi-layer packaging treatment. This extremely contaminating product was not recycled in Mexico at the time, since the process involved very complex technical procedures. Moreover, multi-layer containers took some 35 years to disintegrate and be reabsorbed by the environment. Since the Tetra Pak company produced around 80 percent of these containers, its involvement was considered critical in tackling the problem.

JLCM approached Tetra Pak in 1993, but received a rather cold welcome. In spite of numerous attempts, the organization was unable to persuade the company of the potential benefits of a joint collaboration to handle multi-layer container recycling. JLCM relentlessly pursued its efforts and tried to persuade other organizations to join in, so as to gather momentum. Its first step was to procure the support of a plant in the Mexican city of Celaya, one of the few with the technical capacity to reprocess multi-layer containers. With this asset in hand, it won over other environmental groups who joined the initiative: the Mexican Environmental Group, the Education and Sustainable Development Promotion Group, and the Environmental Education Foundation, among others. However, just when their efforts seemed to be about to materialize, the organization received a shocking blow. In the words of Martha Rangel, JLCM president at the time, "We had woven an alliance with several environmental groups under JLCM leadership, and as soon as we had the project ready to go, we found out that the Celaya recycling plant had gone bankrupt…"

Far from discouraged, JLCM rekindled its attempts to get the project going. Personal connections allowed the organization to reach Kimberly-Clark's (KC) top management, who agreed to join the initiative. This incorporation ultimately proved paradoxical in nature, for though some observers considered the company's material contributions to be relatively insignificant, KC's participation actually proved crucial to the project. According to Rangel,

> We had spent over a year and a half trying to convince Tetra Pak to no avail. But when the company found out that Kimberley had joined in, it suddenly became very eager to participate. All we did was mention KC; when you drop that name, all of a sudden everything starts to fall into place. Its incorporation was essential to getting other companies' collaboration, especially Tetra Pak's.

After *a year and a half* of tenacious, focused work, JLCM leaders managed to convince its private sector partner of the advantages of entering a collaboration. Tetra Pak's social networks enabled JLCM to recruit another plant that was technically capable of recycling multi-layer containers, thus securing the project's launching. In addition to illustrating the importance of pursuing a specific objective, this case also displays the unexpected ways in which social capital may operate. The lack of a pre-existing relationship hindered direct access to Tetra Pak, but a contact with KC ultimately opened that door in indirect fashion, finally giving them access to the desired company.

Key Points to Consider

This chapter has shown that those who engage in building a cross-sector collaboration should not be surprised if their path does not turn out to be completely obstacle-free. However, it has also shown that these obstacles can be overcome. Organizations need to be well prepared to face those hurdles successfully in their efforts to achieve an effective partnership. The following questions seek to contribute to that task, offering some clues meant to guide the process of self-assessment.

A good start would be to reflect on the motivations that bring my organization to a cross-sector collaboration. It is neither necessary, nor desirable, that all answers fit into a single category. On the contrary, it will be useful to remember from the precedent analysis that altruistic motivations *are not necessarily in tension* with utilitarian purposes, and that both may co-exist, in different proportions and intensities, even reinforcing each other. The key point to consider regarding altruistic drives is probably intensity: Which is my most powerful motivation, the one that myself or my organization is most passionate about? In considering utilitarian motivations, it should be useful to analyze how collaborations may contribute to the handling of risk management or the creation of competitive advantages for my organization.

Once an organization has spelled out its motivations and needs, the following step would be to tackle the question of where to start. We have learned that an organization's portfolio of social networks is a very valuable asset during the initial contact stage. How can an organization or an individual leverage their professional and personal relations to capture the attention of potential cross-sector partners? Does my organization possess an institutional memory that may help to leverage old-time relationships with individuals who may currently hold positions of leadership? If no direct relationship with the target person exists, would it be feasible to gain access to him/her through the intervention of an acquaintance? Is it possible to think of a related institution, in which shared membership may be a common reference point with a future partner? And finally, even if there is no personal relationship, the potential partner may have a connection with or affinity toward the social cause.

In the search for this initial contact, sample cases have shown that being proactive is a key factor to success. How may that contact be facilitated? What can the organization offer to a potential partner? What institutional assets may it lay on the negotiation table? What key points should it clearly convey to potential partners? How can it effectively communicate its needs?

Answering these questions will be crucial in tackling the challenge discussed in the following chapter: how to develop a deep and committed bond between organizations, which generates value to both partners on various dimensions.

Notes

1   Here we are not using the term Utilitarianism as it is sometimes used in moral philosophy as referring to a decision rule for resolving ethical dilemmas by weighing the relative costs and benefits from a moral perspective, but rather we are using it to focus on the practical costs and benefits to the individual partners as they consider their self-interest.

2   Cynthia A. Sanborn, "Philanthropy and Civil Society in Latin America" (John F. Kennedy School of Government, Harvard University, 2001) 2. The Catholic tradition also had two additional effects—which are later discussed again. First, it provided a common set of values for third and private-sector leaders, which served as the basis for a common diagnosis and, later, joint actions. Second, it supplied a legitimate validation reference for "others," thus reducing initial uncertainty and mistrust. This last aspect is also discussed in depth in Chapter 9, "Chile: Building Trust in Alliances."

3   In some cases, alliance dynamics led to a revision of this stance, as discussed later.

4   "Those areas where the company neither creates value nor derives benefit, should appropriately be left—as Friedman asserts—to individual donors following their charitable impulses." Michael E. Porter and Mark R. Kramer, "The Competitive Advantage of Corporate Philanthropy," *Harvard Business Review* 80, no. 12 (2002): 68.

5   In 1995, Lorenzo Servitje received the Eugenio Garza Sada Award for his social commitment.

6   In the specific case of AUSOL, this built-in vulnerability was stressed by contextual factors that are analyzed in another section.

7   The organizational value transformation undergone by Shell after the Brent Spar incident and the events in Nigeria is reported in Lynn Sharp Paine, "Royal Dutch/Shell in Transition (A)," HBS Case No. 9-300-039, (Boston: Harvard Business School Publishing, 1999); and "Royal Dutch/Shell in Transition (B)," HBS Case No. 9-300-040, (Boston: Harvard Business School Publishing, 1999).

8   The challenges faced by this company when it incorporated corporate so-
    cial responsibility and sustainable development principles into its strategy
    are discussed in Jane Wei-Skillern, "Sustainable Development at Shell (A),"
    HBS Case No. 9-303-005, (Boston: Harvard Business School Publishing,
    2003); and "Sustainable Development at Shell (B)," HBS Case No. 9-303-
    072, (Boston: Harvard Business School Publishing, 2003).

9   Adam Brandenburger and Barry Nalebuff, *Co-opetition*, 1st ed. (New York:
    Currency/Doubleday, 1996).

10 Chapter 10 deals again with this dynamic.

11 Porter and Kramer, "The Competitive Advantage of Corporate Philan-
    thropy."

12 These included the 1997 kidnapping of Hugo Ferreira Neira, general man-
    ager, and the ensuing collective labor negotiations carried out under the
    threat to put an end to his life. The events that led to Indupalma's terminal
    crisis are reviewed in Diana V. Fernández, Diana M. Trujillo and Roberto
    Gutiérrez, "Indupalma: 1961–1991 Chronicle of a Foretold Crisis (A),"
    SEKN Case No. SKE006, (Boston: Harvard Business School Publishing,
    2003); and Diana V. Fernández, Diana M. Trujillo and Roberto Gutié-
    rrez, "Indupalma: 1961–1991 Chronicle of A Foretold Crisis (B)," SEKN
    Case No. SKE025 (Boston: Harvard Business School Publishing, 2003).
    The comeback of the company is discussed in Diana M. Trujillo and
    Roberto Gutiérrez, "Indupalma and the Associated Labor Cooperatives,
    1991–2002," SEKN Case No. SKE026 (Boston: Harvard Business School
    Publishing, 2003).

13 In 2002, Ekos line inputs came from the Amazonas, Amapá, Pará, Rondô-
    nia, Piauí, Minas Gerais, Bahia, São Paulo, Paraná and Rio Grande do Sul
    states.

14 The alliance structured around the Ekos line is discussed at greater length
    on p. 82, and is also the subject of an in-depth analysis in Chapter 7.

15 The case is discussed under the headings "Community, Devoid of Organi-
    zational Structure" (p. 57) and "Broad Alignment" (p. 82). The case is also
    discussed in greater detail in Chapter 8.

16 The competitive challenges faced by FSC are reviewed in James E. Austin
    and Ezequiel A. Reficco, "Forest Stewardship Council," HBS Case No. 9-
    303-047 (Boston: Harvard Business School Publishing, 2002).

17 A two-phase conformity technique in which an influential actor manages
    to obtain a response for his/her request by asking, first, for a lesser contri-
    bution. Jonathan L. Freedman and Scott C. Fraser, "Compliance without
    pressure: The foot-in-the-door technique," *Journal of Personality and So-
    cial Psychology* 4 (1966).

18 By "top officials" we are referring to those individuals in charge of day to day operations, such as CEOs in private companies, or executive directors in CSOs. This definition excludes those responsible for the organization's governance, such as board members. "Middle management" is a residual category embracing all individuals with management responsibility behind the previously mentioned top layer.

19 A brief summary of that relationship was offered in Chapter 1 (p. 9). For a more in-depth description readers may consult the discussions under the headings "Individuals" (p. 58), and "Cross Fertilization" (p. 94.)

20 Russell Hardin, *Trust and Trustworthiness* (New York: Russell Sage Foundation, 2002).

21 Chapter 9, "Chile: Trust Building in Alliances," dwells again on the Catholic Church capacity as a moral role model in Latin American societies, legitimized by social sectors with very disparate visions.

22 "Barr and Huxham have pointed out that the so-called community collaborations in their study were far from being cross-organization collaborations. These groups seem to consider collaborations as a form of community involvement (however defined) in a shared-risk venture. The fact that involvement must entail organizations' joint work seems to be relatively (or totally) unimportant." Chris Huxham, "Collaboration and collaborative advantage," in *Creating Collaborative Advantage*, ed. Chris Huxham (Thousand Oaks, CA: Sage Publications, 1996), 9.

23 The value generated in this alliance is discussed under the headings "Value Created for Companies" (p. 132) and "Value Created for Communities" (p. 146). For an in-depth description of the alliance, see "Posada Amazonas" (p. 258), in Chapter 8.

24 UNICEF is a hybrid organization, which has a mandate from the United Nations General Assembly but raises its own funding from non UN sources. It also has national committees that are separately incorporated NGOs. See John A. Quelch and Nathalie Laidler, "UNICEF," HBS Case No. 9-503-032 (Boston: Harvard Business School Publishing, 2003).

3

Building Alignment

James Austin, Ezequiel Reficco, and SEKN Research Team

The Alignment Concept

Once the barriers that prevent connections and hinder communications are overcome, future partners should focus on searching for agreement areas from which to build a common project. Early on, they should collectively articulate a shared set of expectations upon which a partnership can be built. It is important that in these early discussions all participants express clearly what they expect to obtain from each other and as results of the collective effort. At the same time, it is essential that each partner individually examines how this potential collaboration fits into its organizational reality. The key question should be, "How suitable is this collaboration for our mission, our values, and our strategy?"

This chapter focuses on alignment and the factors that shaped it in our sample cases. In general terms, the closer collaborations fit with organizational missions, values and strategies, the more chances they will have for success.[1] Although it is impossible to foresee the problems arising in specific collaborations, companies and organizations that are highly aligned in their causes will tend to experience fewer incompatibilities throughout their partnerships.[2] Finally, the strength of the alignment will influence the resources to be allocated and the value to be created. This topic will be discussed again in the next chapter, when value generation is analyzed in more detail.

Conceptually the degree of alignment between two organizations can be understood in terms of two dimensions: *breadth* and *depth*. Breadth contemplates some key variables for any organization—mission, values, and strategy—and examines how many are related to the collaboration, thus determining whether alignment will be *broad* or *narrow*. Depth relates to the strength of the alignment between partners along any dimension, which may be *superficial* or *profound*.

By considering both depth and breadth, potential partners can better assess and manage relevant linking factors that contribute to strong alignment. The following section illustrates these notions with examples from our sample cases. In addition to enlightening these concepts, the examples will be useful in analyzing how partnering organizations managed to build alignment.

Alignment Breadth

All organizations have a *mission* that captures their core aim, *values* that guide their behavior and a *strategy* to make it all happen. As Figure 4 below shows, all of them may become the links for collaborations between companies and CSOs. An intense connection in only one category may be enough to build a solid and enriching bond between them. However, as in interpersonal relationships, bonds are stronger when they encompass several dimensions. Moreover, if the collaboration is structured around a single point of connection, any change in the motivations or context in one of the partners might throw the entire relation out of alignment, as there would be no other point of alignment to fall back on—this point is discussed in more detail further below. Other things being equal, collaborations will tend to be more sustainable when connections are broader.

Alignment does not mean being identical in terms of needs or objectives, but rather that there is some degree of fit between their distinct yet complementary goals. In any given collaboration, the partnership may hold different relevance for each member. While for one of them the project may fit in with its strategy and organizational values, it may turn out to be totally irrelevant for the other partner's strategy but tightly aligned with its values. Alignment is a relational attribute: it will result from what partners have in common, and will be determined by their shared minimum common denominator.

In our sample cases, values emerged as the most common point of contact between partnering organizations, either alone or in cojunction with strategy. Only in a few cases did the partners manage to align all three dimensions. Below we review the collected data.

Narrow Alignment

This group includes collaborations built by organizations which only manage to align one out of the three key variables—either mission, values or strategy. According to recent research, business leaders in Latin America and the rest of the world are increasingly paying atten-

Figure 4: Alignment Breadth

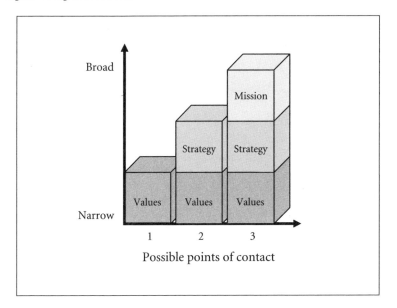

tion to organizational values.[3] Since the promotion of certain values is also the main focus for the third sector, it should not be surprising that some of the collaborations studied were exclusively based on the strong consistency of **values** among participating organizations.

As we have said, among our sample cases the companies involved were often family businesses, and their owners worked to materialize their values through projects that lacked a strategic dimension for their organizations. One of them was the collaboration between the Chilean company *Empresas Ariztía* and the Melipilla Municipal Corporation (*Corporación Municipal de Melpilla,* hence CMM), a decentralized local government agency devoted mainly to public education. The company owner, Manuel Ariztía, a renowned philanthropist with deep religious principles, was especially interested in education. Since the creation of CMM in 1982, Ariztía was thoroughly committed to the cause and worked very hard to ensure its success. *Empresas Ariztía* and the CMM came together because of their mutual interest in education. There was an alignment of values, but because of *Empresas Ariztía's* business characteristics, a collaboration focusing on public education lacked any significant alignment with the company's strategy.

The company's deep roots in Melipilla (14,000 acres and 24,000 employees) made it appealing to become a good corporate citizen and to generate goodwill among the local population. However, the company never announced its commitment to the CMM because, according to its president, referring to a religious tenet, "Your left hand should not know what your right hand is doing." What about future benefits? The company's work on local education could produce a more trained labor force or a better environment for its employees by improving their children's education. Still, the link to its strategy is weak and indirect: as Ariztía himself admitted, the company's commitment to the CMM lacked a strategic dimension. Thus, although Ariztía's vision includes a "shared mission" between both organizations, the fact is that the collaboration has tended to be restricted to the company president, while operating departments have been somewhat distant.

In other cases, the connection among partners resulted from the collaboration's alignment with their **strategy**. In these collaborations, partners' organizational values, though not conflicting, were only an inconspicuous backdrop to the relationship and did not serve as links. A cross-sector partnership can be aligned with an organization's strategy in three different ways: by connecting with the organization's *internal stakeholders* (human resources), its *external stakeholders* (customers or followers), or by adding value to or contributing to repositioning its *products*. The following examples illustrate these alternatives.

When company employees relate emotionally to the collaboration's cause, they often identify more with the company and come to perceive they are accruing an additional, non-monetary form of compensation for their work. At the same time, when company customers (or CSO followers) identify with the collaboration, the organization obtains a point of differentiation from competitors, and its name generates goodwill. The collaboration between *Farmacias Ahumada S.A.* (FASA) and the *Fundación Las Rosas* (FLR) proves both points. By 2001, FASA had become the largest drugstore chain in Latin America and the sixth largest worldwide. It targeted a market segment mostly made up of senior citizens, who had never had an emotional connection to the company. As we have pointed out in the previous chapter, "medicines are never a pleasant buy." That same year, FASA entered into a collaboration with FLR, a CSO created in 1967 by the Santiago Archdiocese to manage homes for disadvantaged elders. The collaboration was clearly aligned with FASA's need to reach out to its consumers, mostly older people. At the same time, it also helped motivate its sales force and increase their loyalty to the company. As FASA's human resources manager explained, "When employees participate in a collaboration of this kind, they feel they are contributing to the common good. Collaborators share the company's mission and vision; they 'wear the company colors,' as we say in Chile."

The case of *Autopistas del Sol* (AUSOL) exemplifies a different twist: collaborations may serve your organization's strategy by building a connection with *your partner's* external stakeholders. For example, if the followers of a CSO can impact your product or service, establishing an emotional connection with them by means of a collaboration may bear a significant impact on your strategy. As we have said before, in 1994, AUSOL faced a potentially dangerous situation.[4] A portion of the lands that the new highway would cross had been illegally occupied and the settlers were poised to resist eviction. Considering highway privatization was far from unanimously approved by society, an increase in tension threatened to unite several social sectors against the company. The external risk was too large to be ignored.

To respond to this situation, the company entered into a partnership with community leader Alberto Croce, who had been involved with grass-roots organizations in those neighborhoods. Croce would act as a liaison between the company and the affected families; the idea was to get the approval of that community in order to generate goodwill in other social sectors that could actually exercise their implicit veto power on company plans. Thus, the collaboration aligned the interests of several communities with the company's strategic needs. The case also shows how successful collaborations may be built exclusively on the basis of the alignment of the partners' strategies, since in those exchanges the value connection between the parties was extremely weak.[5] AUSOL initially reacted to the community complaints by sending over its security staff, which speaks to the company's initial diagnosis. Regardless of the formally proclaimed values, it is clear that at that point the company had not developed the concept of social responsibility in its "organizational DNA."[6]

Finally, collaborations may contribute to organizational strategy by building a link to product needs. This happens when a specific product, either belonging to a company or to a CSO, becomes differentiated or somehow enriched as a result of a cross-sector collaboration. In the mid 1990s *Representaciones Televisivas* (REPRETEL), a Mexican-owned television corporation, was prominent in the Costa Rican market, but faced a significant challenge that was detailed in the previous chapter. Basically, the company had to cope with a serious image problem "because the REPRETEL brand was frowned upon for being foreign," as René Barboza, one of its most popular reporters, asserted. Its broadcasting content, mostly Mexican, was mistrusted by some in its target audience.

In July 1996, Hurricane César caused great damage in Costa Rica, leaving hundreds of families homeless. REPRETEL joined *Fundación Promotora para la Vivienda* (FUPROVI), a CSO engaged in social housing and community strengthening, to launch a campaign to provide homes for those families. Again, this collaboration was clearly aligned with the company's strategic needs. REPRETEL's efforts to address the Costa Rican citizens' misfortune through its alliance with FUPROVI, served to shore up its local credentials and commitment to that community. Most of the company's target audience belonged to middle and low-income sectors, who were also the groups that had been most affected by the hurricane.

Medium Alignment

Other organizations accomplished greater breadth of alignment in their collaborations. These companies built a strong connection with CSOs on the basis of organizational values, and they managed to materialize those values by serving their organizational strategies. In these collaborations, partners tended to incorporate some of their core competencies and to involve some of their functional managers.

One of these cases involves the collaboration built in 1996 between the H-E-B supermarket chain (HEB) and the Monterrey Food Bank (*Banco de Alimentos de Monterrey*, hence BAM) in Mexico. Social involvement had been a company trait since its founding at the turn of the century by Charles and Florence Butt in Texas. In 1996, the chain was managed by their descendant, Charles C. Butt, also a renowned philanthropist. As part of this philanthropic commitment, the company supported dozens of food banks in the cities in which it operated in the United States. At the same time, its social responsibility actions had a strategic dimension, since its partnerships with food banks were aligned to its disposal of cosmetically damaged products and to the need for relating emotionally to customers and employees.

HEB targets a very demanding consumer segment that only purchases top quality products. Therefore, the company has resorted to excellence as its differentiating factor. As part of this strategy, HEB rejects a large number of products that meet sanitation standards but are unfit for store sale because they do not comply to its appearance standards—for example, goods with damaged packaging. As opposed to some competitors, the company does not sell these products at discount prices in second or third-class markets. Through its collaboration with food banks, the BAM among them, HEB maintains its brand top-quality image, and, at the same time, helps the needy. Finally, since collaboration beneficiaries belonged to the same community as HEB customers and employees, the grounds were laid for a deeper affinity. Although the company was known in Northern Mexico before its actual arrival, undoubtedly, this link to the local community is highly valuable when a foreign company such as HEB enters a new market.

Indupalma is another example of a company approaching collaborations as a result of value motivations, while at the same time keeping a close alignment to its business strategy. As we have seen before, Indupalma bounced back from a terminal crisis with a new corporate culture, in which the company saw itself at the core of a "business community," surrounded by a series of stakeholders it needs to serve. It is worth recalling that during the crisis, the company was trapped in the severe socio-political contradictions at play in the Colombian environment, including clashes between left and right-wing guerrillas. The company has chosen alliances as the instrument to relate to those stakeholders, building collaborations with both labor cooperatives and CSOs. Indupalma and the Rafael Pombo Foundation (FRP) collaborated in working for peace at the San Alberto area. Both organizations joined efforts to create workshops for children and youths in order to "generate peaceful living conditions, focused on human and children's rights," as a FRP official put it.

On the one hand, this collaboration was built on the basis of strongly convergent values. The company's belief that "one can accrue greater economic capital when social capital grows, and economic and social factors come together" favored this closeness. This CSO had never worked with the private sector before, and the social commitment it found in Indupalma took them by surprise. According to the FRP's project director, "We had mostly worked with international organizations, such as UNICEF, Save the Children, Christian Children, etc. Our relationship with Indupalma was our first experience in peace work with the private sector." In FRP's view, Indupalma was one of the few companies that truly lived up to its social responsibility commitment.

At the same time, this partnership was aligned with two of Indupalma's strategic objectives: its need to build a "culture of peace and peaceful living conditions" and its desire to "develop the necessary capabilities for citizen involvement and solidarity."[7] As opposed to the cases previously discussed in this section, this collaboration was not primarily aimed at the company's customers or personnel. It was community-oriented, seeking to facilitate the necessary conditions for the company to operate. In other words, it was a company's attempt to change the context through strategic philanthropy.[8]

Broad Alignment

In a few cases, organizations sought partners who, though belonging to a different sector, shared the same **mission**. The concept of organizational "mission" may be interpreted in different ways. We have adopted a restrictive definition: "the primary objective toward which the organization's plans and programs should be aimed;"[9] that is to say, its reason for being, or its *core business*. This congruency of objectives yields a powerful dynamic: working together, partners are simultaneously serving their values, strategies, and organizational missions. These collaborations were structured around what participating organizations do best, strengthening the means at the disposal of each partner to attain its ultimate purpose. The rationale underlying these partnerships is that by pooling their efforts together, participants create synergies, pursuing their organizational goals more effectively than they would do separately. At the same time, having broad alignment of mission, values and strategy as partners does not mean that the organizations become identical; in fact, they preserve their separate identities, which remain a source of strength for the alliance, even in integrative stage collaborations where the organizations have fused their resources and structures to capture operating synergies and efficiencies.

Broad alignments appeared in two collaborations of our SEKN sample cases,[10] as well as in two other cases the authors have recently worked on involving Latin America.[11] When there is mission overlap between parties, both interact intimately in their core businesses. These collaborations tended to operate like a joint venture and to revolve around a common product, which was the visible result of the alliance. Since these partnerships are less frequent and have greater impact potential, we will examine them in greater detail.

The first case is the collaboration built around the Brazilian cosmetic company Natura's Ekos product line. The company had been involved in social aid through cross-sector collaborations since its inception. However, with the launching of this innovative line, Natura decided to drive its social responsibility to the heart of its business. As we have said,[12] through the Ekos line, the company intended to transform the cause of Brazilian biodiversity into a "tangible object" that would turn into "a source of economic and social wealth," according to Pedro Passos, Natura's operations manager. In other words, Ekos' essence lay in aligning a social cause to Natura's commercial strategy. The new products would be based on plants and vegetable oils extracted from Brazil's vast countryside. The project held enormous potential because the communities that had the knowledge on how to produce, extract and apply those ingredients had many unfulfilled needs. A cross-sector alliance offered the chance to produce a remarkable impact on local living conditions while contributing to the company's strategy of generating wealth in a socially responsible fashion and differentiating its products.

To carry out this project, Natura built partnerships with a large number of small traditional communities, such as the *ribeirinhos, sertanejos, caboclos,* and several indigenous groups scattered across the national territory in extreme isolation.[13] In order to join this venture, these groups adopted various organizational formats, including labor cooperatives, or simply keeping their social structures and choosing a community leader to represent them. The partnership also included Cognis, an industrial material supplier, in charge of processing delivered natural ingredients and preparing them for industrial use. This company adhered to values that were highly consistent with Natura's. The partners benefited from the participation of Imaflora, a São Paulo-based CSO associated with the global CSO Forest Stewardship Council (FSC).[14] Its role was to certify that natural resources were extracted in an economically, socially, and environmentally sustainable fashion as per the criteria set by the FSC. Even though Imaflora's involvement in the collaboration was limited to certification activities, it was nonetheless important for Natura and Cognis, as it ensured that the companies' names would not be associated with practices that were inconsistent with their values and detrimental to their brands.

The alignment of values, strategies and missions is high in this collaboration. All organizations involved shared the need to preserve traditional lifestyles and to extract resources in a sustainable manner—although these values may have been perceived differently by the members of the many indigenous communities involved. The collaboration's alignment to Natura's strategy is direct and immediate: it provides a unique positioning for company products that is difficult for competitors to replicate. The strategic alignment in the case of Cognis and Imaflora is equally clear, since their contributions to the cross-sector collaboration are intrinsic parts of their core businesses, as opposed to an ad hoc public relations or social responsibility program. Even though participating communities lacked a formally designed strategy, the collaboration was a means to attain widely shared goals: creating employment opportunities and fighting social exclusion.

The second case in our sample featuring broad alignment was the collaboration built around the Peruvian eco-tourism Amazon Lodge (*Posada Amazonas*) developed jointly by the Rainforest Expeditions (RFE) Company and the native Ese'eja community. As we mentioned in the previous chapter, the Peruvian government had granted some 24,700 acres to the native community, which it had turned into a natural reserve of extraordinary environmental richness—the Tambopata-Candamo Reservation. RFE was a Peruvian company engaged in sustainable ecotourism, promoting natural preservation of all the locations where it operated. Company operations combined tourism, research, and educational activities. The collaboration resulted in the Amazon Lodge, inaugurated in 1997, a 20-year joint venture to which the community contributed with the reservation land and labor, while RFE provided funding and management expertise. At the end of the 20-year period covered by the contract, the community would keep the lodge.

This cross-sector collaboration was clearly aligned with RFE's strategy. For an ecotourism lodge, essential assets include access to an outstandingly rich ecosystem, as a competitive advantage over alternative destinations, and qualified guides, as a point of differentiation vis-à-vis other local suppliers of similar services. RFE's alliance with the native community supplied both. Moreover, by assuring that the Amazon Lodge accrued those resources from the community in exclusivity, it erected a barrier of entry toward potential new competitors, which sustained good profit margins. At the same time, the collaboration was indeed a suitable mechanism to accomplish the community's goal of preventing the disintegration of the Ese'ejas. As in the previous case, this joint venture was based on the alignment of three dimensions: the *mission* or purpose of each of the partners, centered on the generation of economic value and the protection of the local environment; their *strategy*, in which they pulled together their resources to jointly profit from the lodge located at the Tambopata-Candamo Reservation; and their *values*, convergent on the need to ensure a sustainable use of the local environmental resources.

Finally, the collaboration built around the Chiapas Project by Starbucks, Conservation International (CI), and a series of small coffee producing cooperatives also featured high alignment. As in the previously discussed cases, Starbucks had driven the concept of social responsibility to the heart of its core business, turning it into a strategic point of differentiation. CI was a global CSO devoted to environmental protection, operating through partnerships with private, public and third-sector organizations. In the mid 1990s, CI and other environmental CSOs realized that coffee production had critical implications for global biodiversity. Traditionally, coffee had been planted in the shade to protect plants from direct sunlight. However, in the 1980s, new high-yielding sun-resistant, fertilizer-responsive varieties were developed, allowing for massive low-cost production. In the ensuing years, large forests that were critically essential for global biodiversity were cleared. By the mid 1990s, "Almost 25 million acres of natural jungle had been replaced by coffee plantations throughout the world," explained Glenn Prickett, CI vice president.[15]

In 1996, CI launched the Chiapas Project in Southern Mexico, and Starbucks joined in the following year. The program intended to create incentives for local producers to return to the traditional method of growing coffee under shaded conditions, in order to preserve a buffer zone surrounding the *El Triunfo* Biosphere Reserve, an area of extraordinary environmental wealth. CI offered technical assistance for local cooperatives to produce top-quality organic coffee, which traded at a premium over regular coffee, and also facilitated access to international distribution channels. Starbucks would purchase the coffee produced—although the company never agreed to any fixed or minimum amounts—and would provide funds and technical assistance so that producers could comply with its high quality standards.

To describe Starbucks' social investments, Orin Smith, company president, explained, "We want to create an important difference in the lives of our stakeholders, and shareholders are not our only stakeholders." This cross-sector collaboration proves this intention because it was aligned with Starbucks' core strategy of providing value to internal and external stakeholders. One of these groups is the company's 54,000 employees, with whom it seeks to establish a strong emotional connection. Starbucks wants its employees to be "proud of the company we work for. It's more than a paycheck. You're proud to tell your peers, or your parents, or whomever, where you work. That's a pretty powerful factor in your loyalty, how long you're going to stay with us, what kind of job you're going to try to do for us. So it's an integral part of the whole business strategy."

At the same time, Starbucks' involvement in the Chiapas Project enables the company to reach out to its consumers. The brand's strong association to social projects is a significant component of the "Starbucks experience" that the company promotes. These values have become a competitive advantage over other chains that "just sell coffee," providing Starbucks with sizeable benefits.[16] Finally, the collaboration is also aligned to product needs, since it builds long-term relationships with producers, ensuring the steady provision of the company's key input, high quality coffee. In addition, selling a differentiated product—shade grown organic Mexican coffee—adds value to its offering.

Here again, this collaboration was built on the convergence around sustainable development values, and it involved both partners' core missions and strategies, all aligned towards an economic and social value creation project.

Alignment Depth

In analyzing collaborations, we may be tempted to follow a simple mathematic logic and believe that three links are worth more than a single one. This rationale would be tricky: these dimensions are not constant value units, allowing for simple arithmetic comparisons. A sole but strong connection in any given dimension can structure a solid and stable partnership. This is why we also need to look at the *depth* of the connection.

The organizational characteristics of partners can be aligned in different degrees. The connection may be such that the missions, strategies or values of both will coexist comfortably—in other words, they could be merely *compatible*. They could even reinforce each other, which make them *convergent*; finally, if the fit is absolute, they would be *congruent*. In these cases of deepest connection, even a single point of contact can be the source of intense value creation, the reason being that, at least theoretically, in a case of complete congruence, an organization would be advancing all of its partner's goals—as it pertains its mission, values or strategy—through alternative means.

The depth of the alignment is a relational attribute: if the values promoted in a collaboration are central to one of the partners but peripheral to the other, the connection will only be superficial. Here, as with alignment breadth, we need to focus on the minimum common denominator.

The impact produced by the connection depth becomes clear when we compare the collaborations built by the manufacturing company Danone Mexico and the Argentine newspaper *La Nación*. In the mid 1990s, both organizations entered into cross-sector alliances that were aligned with their organizational values and eventually became directly linked to their business strategies. After a brief description of each of these cases, we will discuss the role played by connection depth in their collaborations.

A core value for Danone is its so-called *dual project*: the company seeks investments that strengthen its business strategy and create economic value for its shareholders while also generating social value.[17] In 1997, its Mexican affiliate faced an image problem, to be analyzed in depth later,[18] resulting from a lack of emotional connection between the general public and the company brands. Quality had ceased to be a differentiating factor in the Mexican dairy industry: all top brand products offered comparable traits in terms of flavor, nutrition, and other attributes appreciated by consumers—thus tending to become commodities. For this reason, Danone needed to rely on brand attributes, such as proximity and caring, to differentiate its products. To tackle this problem, the company decided to join in a cause-related marketing campaign with the Friendship Home (*Casa de la Amistad,* hence CdA), a local CSO devoted to "providing comprehensive support for Mexican low-income children who suffered from cancer." In spite of some initial difficulties, the campaign turned out to be a complete success. The positive results obtained drove the company to renew this annual campaign for six years (1997–2002).

Since his joining *La Nación* newspaper's management in 1996, Julio Saguier worked to update the company's social initiatives, systematizing donations to enhance their impact. That same year, the newspaper entered into a partnership with the Solidarity Network (*Red Solidaria,* hence RS), an organization focused on linking individuals with unsatisfied social needs and those willing to help. Its founder, Juan Carr, describes the RS' primary purpose in these terms,

> The underprivileged and the children suffering from malnutrition have a cultural rather than a feeding problem. They are removed from our daily sight, so we don't actually see them. Since we don't see them, we don't have them incorporated in our culture. Thus, *the first thing to do is make them visible,* and then people will automatically respond.

The RS had a very small structure and based its work on a large volunteer network. In 1998, the newspaper created the *La Nación* Foundation. Its board chairman, Julio Saguier, summed up the foundation's mission. "Its main purpose will be to promote volunteer work as a cultural phenomenon in our society where we feel it is still underdeveloped. Our motto will be 'helping those who want to help.' We will contribute our capability to communicate, to inform and to teach in order to reach this goal."

A rapid review of both descriptions show several similarities between RS and *La Nación*. They both relied on communications as a means to produce a cultural change in Argentina, moving away from paternalism and focusing on solidarity. The RS model, based on volunteer work, was exactly what the newspaper management intended to promote and support. It does not seem farfetched to conclude that the RS embodied the newspaper's values. For *La Nación*, RS was not a mere alternative among others, but a partner advancing its own values through different means.

It is interesting to compare the depth of this alignment to the connection existing between Danone and the CdA. To serve its *dual project,* the company was firmly committed to social value creation, in part through cross-sector collaborations. Its values were aligned with those of its partner, but not as deeply as in the previous case: while both were compatible, there was no congruency between them. Treating cancer-afflicted children was just one of the many possible ways in which Danone could live up to its values. For that reason, before engaging CdA, Danone considered partnering with a wide array of other organizations—which *La Nación* never did.

The Danone-CdA partnership involved a series of promotion campaigns, reviewed yearly. By 2002, the collaboration had proven to be long-lasting, but only through market incentives: when the campaigns turned out to effectively arouse the interest of Danone's internal and external stakeholders, the company did not hesitate to repeat them year after year. However, if the impact were to dwindle due to customers' fatigue, Danone could very well discontinue its partnership and seek other, more effective ways to pursue its two-fold purpose. For *La Nación*, instead, the partnership constituted a stable alliance. As with any relationship, it is subject to change, but the value match between both is so deep and intense that in all likelihood it would cement the alliance *despite* unfavorable market conditions. Different values have different weights for each organization. When collaborations involve organizational values that are absolutely crucial for both partners, in and of itself that link will serve as a foundation for long and fruitful alliances.

Though convenient as a diagnosis and analytical tool, alignment depth may not be measured accurately by external observers. It can only emerge from an introspective self-assessment. In this regard, a good start would be to consider which elements of a potential collaboration at hand are *incompatible* with the organization's mission, values or strategy. This list may serve, inversely, to review the depth of the connection between one's own organization and a potential partner. If it is very short, there probably will be a match in any of those dimensions; if it is long, there will be only superficial contact—or possibly up-front conflict.

Putting It All Together: Breadth and Depth

Ideally, one would like the fit with a potential partner to be complete and absolute, featuring both broad and deep levels of alignment. In the real world, however, it is unlikely that an organization will be lucky enough to find itself in that partnering nirvana of "total alignment"— Figure 5 below depicts such a perfect and comprehensive fit.

Figure 5: Total Alignment

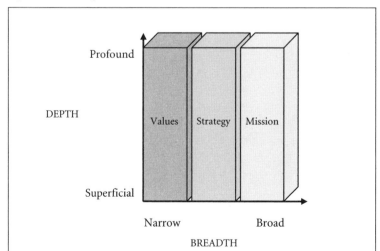

As explained earlier, in principle it will be advisable to seek connection in all three dimensions, since other things being equal, the broader the fit, the richer the value that the relationship will create. At the same time, it is important to keep in mind that the depth of the alignment is critical, as it can make up for lack of breadth. A deep connection in any one of the three key organizational dimensions can be the cornerstone of a fruitful and solid relationship—as exemplified in Figure 6 (a) below. On the other hand, a collaboration built around a weak connection in all three dimensions—like the one depicted in Figure 6 (b)—is likely to be unstable. However, either narrow or superficial connections are fragile in that disruptions in the circumstances of a partner might readily dislodge these links. Consequently, broadening and deepening the connections are highly desirable to achieve collaboration sustainability.

While there is no intrinsic tension between breadth and depth, most organizations looking for a prospective partner may find themselves facing the predicament of having to choose between candidates, in order to maximize one or the other. There are not set rules here: the key will consist in thinking along both dimensions at once, trying to establish which mix will yield more value for one's own organization.

Figure 6: Depth vs. Breadth

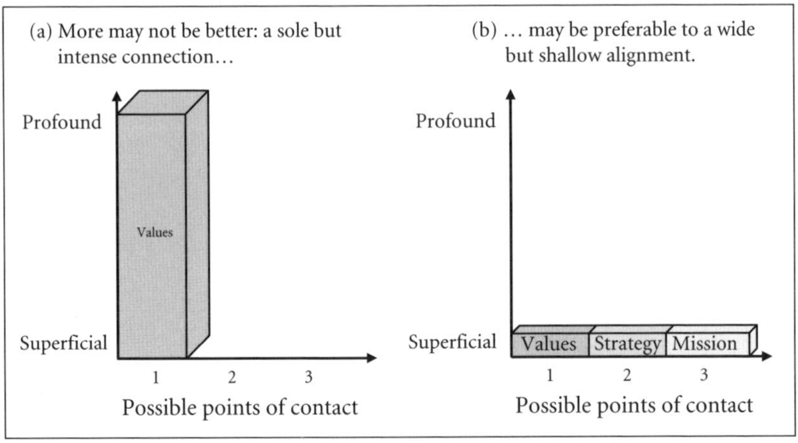

| (a) More may not be better: a sole but intense connection… | (b) … may be preferable to a wide but shallow alignment. |

Alignment's Personal Dimension

So far, we have discussed how collaborations are built around a connection in the values, strategies and/or missions of partnering organizations. Individuals may do little to manage cross-sector collaborations on the basis of their own individual values if these values are not shared by their organizations, or if they are conflicting. The value or strategy alignment among organizations is necessary, but is not enough. Oftentimes, organizational values and strategies really *are* what key individuals *say they are*. Our sample cases prove we also need to pay attention to what's in the minds of those individuals, since this last link may facilitate or hinder connections.[19]

Alignment to organizational values, though apparently obvious in hindsight, is often not as clear for actors looking for common ground. Frequently, collaborations kick off when individuals feel their own values match those of potential partners. Then, in promoting their idea up the ranks they try to articulate their message according to their organizations' values and interests so as to foster support. This gap between personal and organizational alignment does not usually surface, but some cases can help to exemplify the point.

The collaboration between REPRETEL and FUPROVI is one of those. At the beginning of the chapter, we discussed the challenge faced by this Mexican television company in its Costa Rican operations. Essentially, "REPRETEL needed to gain a popular position because our brand was frowned upon for being foreign," as René Barboza, collaboration promoter, asserted. The Caesar hurricane of 1996 provided a good opportunity to meet that challenge. Why not build a partnership with FUPROVI, a CSO specializing in social housing projects, to remedy the housing shortage caused by the hurricane? The message Barboza presented before company board members was that leading a high-profile campaign would, in his view, help reposition their brand.

In objective terms, the collaboration was clearly aligned to company strategy. REPRETEL's target audience and the hurricane victims shared several socio-economic characteristics; thus it was highly probable for the collaboration to generate the market's goodwill for the company. However, that was not Barboza's personal agenda; behind the discourse that he had articulated with his superiors, there was a different kind of alignment with a more personal vision:

> I had a personal interest in that project. I was doing it because it was a personal goal. True enough, it would benefit REPRETEL's image and all, but there was something deep inside of me that pushed me to work in getting the job done to benefit those needy people.

The collaboration between the Manuelita company and the Minute of God Corporation (*Corporación Minuto de Dios,* hence MD) also shows a similar situation. As we have mentioned before, this collaboration dates back to the 1950s, when it crystallized around a cause-related marketing campaign. Both organizations shared a strong connection in terms of organizational values and strategy. MD was a CSO, founded by Father García Herreros to, "Organize a Christian community to try to provide comprehensive solutions for their affiliates' social problems." Manuelita was a business group, founded by a renowned Colombian philanthropist, Harold Eder, which had remained a family-owned business. Integrity, respect for others, social responsibility, and austerity were among the company's core values, and its management was strongly committed to living up to them.

The collaboration's alignment to company strategy was clear. Since 1955, Manuelita had sponsored an MD micro-show on television, which was enormously popular in Colombia. When Álvaro Galeano became the company's marketing corporate director in early 1990, he carried out several market research surveys to measure Manuelita's brand awareness among Colombians. The company ranked first in the local market, and the mention of Manuelita Sugar on MD's television show was the reason. As he remembered, "Most people remembered our sugar from the Minuto de Dios time slot. All surveys reported, 'Manuelita is sugar,' even if the interviewees did not use sugar. This top of mind business is something else!!"

The survey results did not surprise Galeano; he had anticipated them. He was actually looking for a way to prove that the partnership with MD was providing an economic return for the company. In other words, moved by his own personal values, Galeano was trying to prove the collaboration matched the company's interests. He explained, "We can't tell our marketing people to put up some money to help the poor, because, on the spot, they'd say, 'Who do you think we are? Mother Teresa?' But, it's different if we tell them, 'hey, let's do social marketing because we'll earn more while helping people!'"

For the purpose of our analysis, it is most interesting to review what happened after Galeano left the company, at the end of the 1990s. Even though the alignment between the organizations' values and strategies did not change, and although the collaboration had proven once and again that it could create value for stakeholders, the collaboration intensity dwindled. Galeano points out:

> I left Manuelita two years ago. Now, the partnership with MD is handled by a marketing person, *who doesn't seem to be interested in it.* Maybe I'll return to Manuelita this year or the next

and, in charge of this issue, *I'll take it up again; I'll get Manuel-ita to make a more serious investment* on better programs with MD that will benefit the company.

In spite of a strong alignment in partners' organizational values and strategies, the lack of alignment in key individuals' personal values can hinder the connection. In cross-sector partnerships, market signals are usually weaker than in same sector alliances. Sometimes, a strong personal alignment is necessary to expose the benefits that may accrue to organizations through cross-sector engagement. We will retake this point in Chapter 5, where we will discuss the role of champions within each organization to energize the relationship.

The Dynamic Construction of Alignment

Even if future partners initially invest time and energy in finding common ground, often cross-sector collaboration alignment evolves during its lifetime. Several factors may contribute to add breadth to the connection between partners' values, strategies, or missions, or increase its depth. It may happen as a result of unilateral learning on the part of any one partner, cross fertilization among them, a change in one partner's strategy, and/or pressures in the competitive environment. Next, we will discuss each one of these dynamics.

Unilateral Learning

The previous chapter explained how from the initial contact between organizations mutual learning takes place. For example, when future partners lack a common language, they have to resort to ad hoc conceptual tools devised to be able to work together. As collaborations grow and expand, the learning process continues and reaches new dimensions that may impact on the partnership's level of alignment. Very often, one of the organizations "discovers" that the relation with its partner offers more connection links than it originally envisioned. For example, a company may decide to collaborate with CSOs exclusively as a way of living up to its organizational values, only to realize later that its partnership also holds the potential of having a beneficial impact on strategy. Understanding partners better leads to the discovery of new possible alignments to enrich collaborations; when this happens, alignment gains in *breadth*.

The involvement of *Meals de Colombia S.A.* (Meals) in the Twenty-First Century Leaders (*Líderes Siglo XXI*, hence *Líderes*) program serves to illustrate this concept. This frozen food marketing company was a very enthusiastic participant in this program to improve schools' educational management in Bogotá and other cities. The company's initial commitment was driven only by the strong connection of its organizational values with the initiative. According to Meals president Alberto Espinosa,

> Our corporate philosophy is highly related to our work on education. We believe people are the most important factor in the organization, our employees are the company, and our success depends on the success of our people. We consider successful people to be those who constantly accomplish their improvement goals and fully grow as human beings.[20]

However, through its joint work with schools, Meals came to realize that the collaboration had an unexpected impact on its business strategy. Adriana Hoyos, human resources and quality manager, points out that the company "has found an unsought benefit for its image. People get to know Meals through the project." Most importantly, the company also spotted advantages in human resources management, adding a new dimension to the collaboration. As Espinosa put it,

> Our human resources' profile largely arose from the definition of quality individuals developed with schools (...) Basically, what happens is that students' motivational processes are similar to those used to motivate workers. Then, it all comes down to understanding what really motivates people.

On account of this greater alignment, Meals commitment to the initiative grew. Of course, these dynamics are deeply linked to value creation in the partnership, since these "discoveries" are essentially triggered by the value the company obtains from the alliance. We will discuss this topic at length in the next chapter.

Cross Fertilization

Through mutual interaction and discovery, learning may be taken to even more profound levels, to the point of influencing partners' own organizational identity. If communications are intense and deep, the collaboration may alter the way in which each partner views itself and defines its interests, thus reshaping missions, values or strategies. In this process the partners' organizational identities are reshaped: they become more alike. Higher congruency in missions, values or strategies determines that the collaboration alignment gains in *depth*, and becomes more profound.

The experience of the Argentine road-building company AUSOL provides a good example of this process. When AUSOL started its partnership with Alberto Croce in 1994, community service was formally a part of its mission, but social responsibility actually held a peripheral position among the company's organizational values. In the previous chapter, we described the challenge this company faced in 1994.[21] Essentially, the company had to determine how to handle conflicting interests with some of its external stakeholders. Some of the lands crossed by the new highway had been occupied by families from neighboring communities, in violation of the legal rights granted to the company by the government. The company's initial reaction— sending their security staff to the conflict site—suggests low concern for those stakeholders' needs. Regardless of the company's formal organizational values, it seems fair to say that AUSOL was not deeply committed to community engagement.

However, as the relationship with Croce evolved, the company's real organizational values changed, as it built a new relationship with its external stakeholders. The company's collaboration with Croce went through three stages. In the initial stage (1994), Alberto Croce contacted the company as a leader of the Malaver cooperative, a grassroots organization he had been working with. As we mentioned when we discussed communication barriers, during those contacts the company perceived Croce to be a valid counterpart in negotiations and realized there was more to win through matching and aligning interests than through confrontation. Once the relationship proved to be beneficial for both parties,[22] it moved to a higher level. As of 1996, Croce became an external company consultant on social issues, acting as a liaison between AUSOL and other communities affected by the new highway layout. In this capacity, Croce continued to align the company's and stakeholders' interests. Finally, in 1999, the company substantially increased its commitment to Croce and his work by providing extensive funding in the creation of the SES Foundation (Sustainability, Education and Solidarity).

Each of these stages marked a change in relationship dynamics. In the first transition, both parties moved from a *negotiation* to a *collaboration*. They left the "one-time deal" paradigm behind to focus on developing a relationship; they ceased being counterparts and became partners. In the transition from the second to the third stage, AUSOL went from *crisis-management* (reactive) to *social investment* (proactive), with initiatives that gained in both depth and breadth. At the same time, it should be noted that, in each change, organizational boundaries became more pliable, and cross fertilization intensified. At the end of that process, social responsibility was deeply embedded in AUSOL's organizational DNA. Through this cross-sector collaboration, the company developed a new way to relate to internal and external stakeholders. According to Federico Giambastiani, in charge of institutional relations, "Internally, the relationship with SES has enabled AUSOL to develop the notion of social solidarity in its core."

La Nación's case also shows how collaborations may become instrumental to redefine partners' identities. Its relationship with the Solidarity Network (RS) drove the company to place social responsibility at the core of its organizational identity, raising it to a higher level. When the collaboration between both organizations started in 1996, the newspaper had recently gone through changes in management. The new board chairman, Julio Saguier, was determined to systematize the company's social policy to make it more high-profile. However, the relationship with the RS significantly marked the specific shape and underlying values of that policy. In 1998, when the company decided to create the *La Nación* Foundation, the priority set for the new organization was "to promote volunteer work and turn it into a cultural phenomenon" in Argentine society—a mission virtually describing RS's model. As collaboration actors acknowledged, the newspaper's interaction with RS had a lot to do with this development. According to Javier Comesaña, *La Nación*'s organizational development manager, the partnership with RS enabled the newspaper to become aware of the power the media has to drive cultural changes in society and, especially, to promote the values underlying the company's social policy. Through cross fertilization, the company and its foundation managed to instill the solidarity and anti-paternalistic values upheld by the RS in their activities. This value match led to a strong strategic consistency in the collaboration, which had not been present at its inception. The process leading to the creation of the Foundation resulted from both an internal company transformation and its relationship with the RS.

The collaboration between Itaú Bank and the Center for the Study and Research of Education, Culture and Community Action (*Centro de Estudos e Pesquisas em Educação, Cultura e Ação Comunitária*, hence CENPEC), also illustrates how companies may change their self-image and their strategy on the basis of interactions with third-sector partners. The CENPEC was founded in 1988 by Maria Alice Setúbal, who had become nationally renowned for her leadership and intellectual contributions in the field of public education. Maria Alice Setúbal was the daughter of Itaú Bank's chairman of the board and one of its major shareholders. Until that time, the bank's social policy had been limited to sporadic and unsystematic donations. After its creation, CENPEC became just one more beneficiary of the bank's philanthropy, in a relation that consisted mostly of check-writing and lacked any strategic dimension. Between 1988 and 1992, the relationship between Itaú and CENPEC remained low intensity and low profile on the surface, but underneath, a transformation process unfolded during those years which would emerge later. The collaboration fueled an intense dialogue between Maria Alice (M.A Setúbal) and her brother Roberto (R. Setúbal), who was a member of top management at the bank and had developed an interest in its social activities. Through these interactions, Roberto envisioned a new role for the bank as a change agent in Brazil's society.

When Roberto took over the bank's leadership (1993), the discussion and re-definition process gathered speed. The board of directors plunged into a deep soul-searching process featuring frequent arguments on the need to systematize the bank's social commitment. The three board members—Olavo and Roberto Setúbal, and Carlos da Câmara Pestana—believed they had to contribute to solving basic Brazilian social problems. Maria Alice Setúbal frequently attended these brainstorming sessions, to supply ideas and alternatives to help materialize those intentions. This process led to the decision of consolidating the bank's social policies into a strategically addressed and clearly defined plan called the Community Support Program (*Programa de Apoio Comunitário,* hence PROAC). Created in 1993, PROAC was the institutional channel chosen to launch the bank's strategic alliance with CENPEC—a collaboration which turned the bank into a first-tier actor in the Brazilian social responsibility field. In the following years, the bank increased its institutional commitment to social issues. In 1998, as part of this process, PROAC became the Itaú Social Program, and, two years later, the Itaú Social Foundation was created to provide continuity to the bank's social programs.

Between 1988 and 1993, until the creation of PROAC, the bank "rediscovered" its social calling and repositioned it in its organizational structure. In this process, the role of CENPEC and its director, Maria Alice, were instrumental. On the basis of the deep trust bred by family ties and her professional reputation, Maria Alice contributed "from the inside" to the development of the bank's new vision and its redefinition of corporate interests and responsibilities. Figure 7 below attempts to conceptualize that dynamic.

Figure 7: Changes in Strategic Alignment as a Result of Cross Fertilization

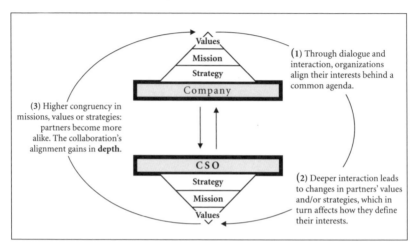

Shifts in Strategy

In some cases, alignment increased as a result of adjustments made in one of the partner's strategy. Such was the case of Tenaris, a company belonging to the Techint Group. In the early 1990s, this business holding was a diversified conglomerate including five areas of business devoted to steel, infrastructure, industrial plants and processes, energy and services, and operated in several countries, including Argentina, Mexico, Italy, Brazil, Venezuela, Peru, Ecuador, and Japan. In spite of its size and diversification, the Group was still under the control of the Rocca family. Engineer Agostino Rocca (1895–1978) had founded Techint. In 1995, when the Group celebrated 50 years, company owners felt the need to "give back to society" by means of a project that reflected its family values and had an impact on a needy section of the city of Buenos Aires. In addition, it was thought that a museum could have a multiplier economic effect, triggering new investments in the area by other institutional agents.

Adriana Rosenberg, who would later become *Fundación Proa*'s (Proa) president, strongly believed that there was an unmet demand in Buenos Aires for avant-garde art, but materializing this vision would require a patron's decisive support. Techint Group became receptive to Rosenberg's proposal, and helped her create Proa through solid financial backing and supporting services. Even if the center always remained autonomous to implement its mission, Techint realized that its original patronage project also had a great public relations potential. In 1996, Proa organized its first international exhibition, featuring the works by Mexican artist Rufino Tamayo. The event turned out to be highly relevant for the Group, since Mexico was one of its major areas of operations. However, the qualitative change in the collaboration took place a few years later. In 2002, as a result of the Group's international expansion in its steel tube area, a new global company called Tenaris was founded. This new organization came to replace the DST alliance—its name standing for the initials of their initial members: Dalmine, Siderca, and Tamsa. Tenaris represented a group of manufacturers from seven countries and had a marketing network covering over twenty nations.

Company executives decided that they needed to develop a new organizational identity for the emerging company. In the words of a senior manager "This re-branding was necessary because the group had ceased to be local and was now global, gathering new companies which felt that the DST initials no longer represented them, and were seeking a new position in the market." The new organization needed to acquire a strong corporate identity, in spite of its internal stakeholders' cultural diversity. To give an answer to this issue, the communications department's strategy was to build an identity that would turn diversity into a competitive advantage. Instead of the traditional "top-down culture" of U.S. corporations, in which headquarters defined a uniform and common identity, Tenaris wanted to be seen "as true locals and not as foreigners" in each of the countries where it operated. They called this the "multi-local approach." In order to build a common identity from multicultural and multi-local attributes, the relationship with Proa became a support for the Group because, in the words of a senior manager, "that partnership was a means to communicate Tenaris commitment to local cultures through art; valuing ties among countries, valuing one nation's art to make it known to others, is rooted in Tenaris as well as Techint corporate identity."

Through its collaboration with Proa, Tenaris managed to transmit a two-fold message: the company can handle the kind of business only a large company can manage, and it does so by appreciating local cultures in all the countries where the company operates. This identity turned into a competitive advantage. Due to a shift in overall strategy that called for a new organizational identity, the company increased its alignment to the collaboration, tightly linking it to its emerging needs. This connection affected all three previously mentioned dimensions: internal stakeholders (human resources), external stakeholders (clients), and positioning of the company's brand or its products/services. In regards to the first dimension, art turned out to be a tool, linking different cultures and showing employees—regardless of their country location—that the company was interested in local cultural expressions. In the opinion of a senior manager, "Proa basically helps us to strengthen our identity and our core values." The role played by the collaboration with Proa in providing internal coherence for Tenaris shows how these programs may become excellent "internal marketing" tools.[23]

This collaboration was also aligned to Tenaris' need to relate to various external stakeholders. The appreciation of local art implied in Proa's exhibitions allowed the company to show its interest in its markets' national identity. In the third dimension, the collaboration was aligned to Tenaris' product/services and corporate image needs, thus serving a vital purpose in its re-branding and repositioning process. The company intended to play a significant role in markets where the world's largest corporations competed. Although Tenaris was relatively small as compared to those groups, it needed to have the intangible attributes required to transmit a notion of leadership. Art became an extraordinary tool to communicate prestige and to consolidate the image of the company.

Dynamic realignment resulting from strategic shifts by one of the partners is also present in the collaboration between Coca-Cola de Argentina (CCA) and Junior Achievement Argentina (JAA). In contrast to the previous case, here the shift in strategy took place in the third-sector partner. The JAA Foundation was created in 1990, when its founder and executive director Eduardo Marty, decided to replicate the Junior Achievement program in Argentina. Its mission was initially defined as "educating and inspiring youths to value and defend the free enterprise system," adopting the mission of its parent organization, Junior Achievement International (JAI). The foundation would focus on entrepreneurship and individual responsibility—necessary values to the free market economy the country was striving to build. Early on it was decided the foundation would not accept public funding, since it was the organization's philosophy that the business sector should invest in the individuals who would join the labor market in the future. Funds would be strictly raised in the private sector, either from companies or individuals. JAA also started operating mainly in private schools, but only because it did not have enough funding to translate the materials "imported" from JAI. Thus, it was forced to focus on private bilingual schools.

Among the companies that rapidly agreed to collaborate with the new CSO was CCA. This relationship was traditionally philanthropic, consisting of a single, low annual donation to cover the cost of some courses. The collaboration only aligned the organizational values of both partners, and held no strategic relevance for either one: it was just one more donation for CCA and one more donor for JAA. That began to change in 1999, when JAA launched "Learning Entrepreneurship." This program differed from what the organization had done so far: it was funded by the Inter-American Development Bank and was delivered at public schools. This new program implied breaking away from several basic JAA values, and signaled the beginning of a shift in strategy. At that point JAA leaders decided that in order to scale up and gain impact, they would need to work with public schools and, therefore, to accept funding from public sources. In addition, they decided to broaden their definition of entrepreneurship, expanding it beyond the mere economic field to engulf the social and environmental dimensions. What the JAA heads realized was that they would need to adjust their vision in order to remain relevant to the needs of Argentine society. In turn, the new vision called for adjustments in JAA mission definition and the strategies needed to accomplish it.

This change in the organization had a direct impact on its collaboration with CCA, since social responsibility involving environmental issues was a core value for the company and its strategy, as we have seen in the previous chapter. The partnership increased its strategic relevance for both parties and became more intense. In 1998, JAA and CCA launched a jointly designed program, "Learning Environmental Entrepreneurship," closely aligned to both organizations' values and strategies. As explained by CCA's external relations director, María Marta Llosa, "This program, as opposed to the project undertaken with the *Fundación Compromiso* [devoted to strengthening CSO management], has *a lot to do with the company's beliefs,* policies and interest in environmental issues concerning waste management, and in consequence, it is *closer to our core business.*"

Competitive Pressures

In other cases, alignment increase was not the result of internal company dynamics, but the consequence of changes in context. When the company's environment becomes more competitive, it will tend to become more receptive to market requirements. In our sample, this change brought about new incentives for companies to align their cross-sector collaborations to their competitive strategy.

Such was the case of the Mexican food industry Bimbo Group and the Brazilian Itaú Bank. Both are top-tier companies that, in spite of their size and sophistication, are still run by the founders' family descendants. These two companies were committed to active social policies reflecting their owners' personal values. When we reviewed organizational motivations, we found that family businesses were reluctant to align their cross-sector collaborations to their commercial strategies, and Bimbo and Itaú were no exceptions. However, as we will see next, the increase in market competitiveness fueled by a strong multinational presence drove these companies to review some of their assumptions.

In 1993, Bimbo, entered into a collaboration with the newly created Papalote Children's Museum (*Papalote Museo del Niño,* hence Papalote), located in Mexico City. At that time, the company was still controlled by its founder, Don Lorenzo Servitje, a philanthropist who, as mentioned in the previous chapter, was already renowned for his social commitment. Don Lorenzo had a clear vision of the role his company should play in society and had instilled this vision in Bimbo's organizational values. As he himself put it, "Since the company was created, we have shared this vision. We knew where we were headed, and we knew we wanted to be active members of society, developing our people first and our environment later."

The company was especially interested in supporting early education for children. Thus, in building the collaboration with the Papalote, the value dimension was all-important since both organizations shared these core values. However, the relationship was not fully deprived of a utilitarian dimension. As the Group's marketing director, José Manuel González Guzmán, admitted, 60 percent of Bimbo's interest lay in the philanthropic aspect of this assistance, while 40 percent had to do with brand positioning. "Don Lorenzo has always told us to display our brands, to have people see them and remember them, always bearing in mind our social responsibility and ethical values." "However," he pointed out, "at the time, our core purpose was to help children;

we weren't looking for a direct economic value for the company." To describe the values fueling company's social investments, Martha Eugenia Hernández, institutional relations director, referred to the biblical metaphor "do not let your left hand know what your right hand is doing."

Until 2001, the collaboration with the Papalote was a low-priority relationship for Bimbo, involving a reduced resource allocation. However, some changes developed that year. The marketing head, González Guzmán, had to launch the new "Bimbo Kids" line targeted to children, consisting of top-quality, highly nutritional products that would yield a good margin for the company. "Why not use the alliance with Papalote?" González Guzmán thought, "If we are going to launch a children's product, we should try it at a place where children usually go. I think we'll be very successful. Now that we have this special line for kids, I think we could get a lot more from this alliance."

The change in alignment in this cross-sector collaboration coincided with a more aggressive institutional marketing approach developed by Bimbo, which included sponsoring a major league soccer team from Monterrey and several football teams. What drove the company to this new approach? It was certainly a combination of factors, both internal and external. Among them, we have already mentioned the generational change produced at the top management level. That year Don Lorenzo had been succeeded by his son, Daniel, at the helm of the group. In addition, as González Guzmán explained, this new line launch had been postponed because the company felt the conditions were not right. Only in 2001, according to AC Nielsen, the "children-targeted products" concept had become strong enough as to merit its own market segment.

However, the group also experienced a significant change in its competitive environment. Already in the early 1990s, Bimbo had withstood some competitive challenges, which were not severe enough to challenge its position of leadership.[24] When the collaboration started, the company was still leading most of the markets it operated in. However, in 1997, Gruma S.A. entered into a strategic alliance with the American food industry group Archer Daniels Midland Co. to compete in the packaged bread market, the industry that had fueled Bimbo's growth and diversification, and one of its strongest areas. Bimbo held a 95 percent share in that market,[25] and had not faced any real competition since 1986, when it acquired its competition, Wonder Mexico.[26] Coincidentally, in 2001, Bimbo decided to add a strongly strategic dimension to its collaboration with the Papalote. By definition, that institution was a perfect environment to reach its target segment and sample its new products. In addition, associating its new brand to the museum—which in its short life had become highly popular throughout Mexico—would surely help its positioning. This new dimension increased the collaboration's importance for Bimbo; accordingly, the company increased its commitment to the partnership.

The Brazilian Itaú Bank also had to face similar pressures. In an earlier section[27] we discussed how, between 1988 and 1993, the bank had rationalized and systematized its social policies through its collaboration with the Center for the Study and Research of Education, Culture and Community Action (CENPEC). The bank was also a family business, and its social policy was deeply related to the values held by its owners, the Setúbal family. For them, the bank's social assistance should not be aligned to its business strategy. This was the domain of the company's marketing efforts, based on a benefit-oriented rationale, as opposed to its social investments, exclusively aimed at creating social—not private—benefits. This clear-cut division based on the perceived incompatibility between social and economic value creation was reflected in the bank's organizational design. On the one hand, the bank handled its social investments through the Community Support Program (PROAC), later to become the Itaú Social Program (in 1998), and finally, the Itaú Social Foundation in 2000. On the other hand, its institutional marketing policy was channeled through the Cultural Itaú Institute. This institute had made significant investments in the development of national culture, promoting the work of Brazilian artists.

In 1995, the alliance between Itaú and CENPEC launched its first product: the Education and Participation Award, also involving UNICEF. This award intended to encourage the work of community organizations in charge of educational programs to supplement public schools' basic teaching. The contest, carried out every two years on a nationwide basis, required CSOs to submit their projects. The winner obtained technical and financial support for implementing and monitoring its project. The contest was so successful that organizers decided to carry it out again in 1997, 1999, and 2001. Also, a series of complementary activities were designed to expand its focus.

However, as the collaboration evolved positively, the bank's operating environment changed substantially. Here too, as in Bimbo's case, the 1990s were intensively competitive years. In 1992–93, the Brazilian financial sector underwent a severe adjustment process, which gathered momentum in 1994 with the implementation of the stabilization *Plan Real*. This process featured the sector's consolidation through a series of mergers and acquisitions that drastically reduced the number of relevant players, as well as the privatization of public banks and the arrival of foreign banks in the local financial market. These changes resulted in an increasingly competitive environment, where service quality ceased to be a differentiating factor. To face the new competition, the main players sought to develop symbolic aspects related to their brand image as competitive advantages.

In August 2002, Antonio Jacinto Matias, Itaú's vice-president in charge of the Social Itaú Program and the bank's marketing area, was shocked when he read a report on the competition's social activities. The publication, entitled "Keeping an Eye on the Competition" (*De Olho na Concorrência*), described the social programs developed by major banks operating in Brazil—Bradesco, Unibanco, Amro Bank, Banco do Brasil, Santander/Banespa and BankBoston—between 1999 and 2002. Matias was impressed by the intensity of these social programs, as well as the fact that all those institutions had not hesitated to use their social investments as competitive instruments, publicizing them in their external communications. He wondered if the time had come for Itaú to cash in on the company's sponsorship of the Education and Participation Award to support the bank's strategy. The success attained by the award and the developments that had taken place in the bank's competitive environment drove the principle set by owners—namely, that social investments should not be used for institutional marketing—to the heart of the debate. Matias pondered, "What if the bank's social responsibility efforts also involved publicizing our initiatives in order to encourage other social agents into action?"

The year before, the British consulting firm Interbrand had carried out a survey to test the bank's brand, and it had concluded that it was among the most valuable in the Brazilian economy. The survey revealed that the bank's brand was one of its main assets, thus leading top management to consciously manage it as a highly valuable intangible. Moved by this data, some of the bank's managers carried out an informal survey among the firm's human resources asking about their opinions on the bank's social activities. The results surprised several top executives, since the data collected conflicted with some of the basic premises set by the bank for its social investments.

The survey showed: (1) bank officials only had a very basic knowledge of the bank's educational and cultural programs, which had drawn substantial bank investments in recent years; (2) the bank's social initiatives had extremely low exposure; (3) the bank's social activities were poorly and ineffectively communicated outside interpersonal relationships, and, more importantly, (4) employees did not object to communicating these actions extensively to external stakeholders. On the contrary, they *wished* these actions became public because they were actually proud of the bank for engaging in these activities.

The bank's marketing area concluded that raising the profile of the alliance with CENPEC would strengthen the bank's brand and become a competitive advantage to face its tough competitors. In their view, even with the existing low-profile policy, almost 15 percent of the brand's value resulted from the bank's successful social aid projects, the alliance with CENPEC being the most significant. As the relational marketing superintendent, Oriovaldo Tumoli, put it, "A requisite for success in this area is for the bank to show, at all times during contacts with consumers, the same image, the same message, the same DNA, regardless of the business segment or location. A solid and consistent message should be offered to all current and prospective customers."

At the time of the writing of this book, Itaú Bank had yet to make any radical changes. The question remains: if the competition is doing it, if the market approves of it, if internal stakeholders wish for it, *why not?* The answer is that, in addition to going against the Setúbal family's values, part of the bank's top management fears that such a shift would jeopardize the credibility the organization worked so hard to build and damage its brand. Also, that decision could alienate its partner, CENPEC, which objects to the bank's using the collaboration as a competitive tool. The policy pursued by the bank has been to gradually align its social investments to its institutional marketing efforts, thus blurring the line between both areas.

Key Points to Consider

On account of the reasons explained in this chapter, those considering cross-sector collaborations should devote significant time to thinking about partnership alignment, both before initiating relationships and during the life of a partnership. The questions that follow can guide the process of alignment analysis.

Ideally, before seeking any contact, each potential partner should carry out an introspective analysis, since self-knowledge will facilitate alignment building. However, as we have said, this analysis should be a continuous and iterative process that covers the entire life span of the collaboration. It is useful to review periodically these questions, both individually and jointly, to explore possibilities for expanding alignment both in terms of breadth and depth.

Since most of the collaborations in our sample were initially built around partners' values, these could constitute a good starting point. What are the values that are fundamental to the organization? As a preventive mechanism, it will always be useful to explore possible inconsistencies between declared values and real values. Are those the values guiding everyday decision-making processes? Are they shared by people throughout the organization?

Once organizational values have been identified, the next step consists of looking around for the links between the social environment and these values. For private companies, the questions will be: What social issues are directly related to them? Which third-sector organizations have been working on these issues? In turn, CSOs should find companies having similar values. Which companies have publicly committed themselves to values matching the organization's core goal? Which ones have recently been working for that cause? Who are the individuals truly committed to those values and who may hold key positions in companies upholding compatible values?

The second dimension most organizations in our sample managed to align in their collaborations was strategy. The key questions on this topic are: What are the performance bottlenecks and main success factors in this organization? How could a cross-sector collaboration contribute to overcoming bottlenecks or to reinforcing strengths? It is especially useful to take a look at three dimensions that emerged as important connectors of collaborations to strategy: links to human resources, to customers or followers, or to brand or product positioning needs. Also, it is important to check the connection between values and strategy. If in fact collaborations solve strategic problems, how do those solutions fit in with organizational values? A scheme that creates practical solutions but runs contrary to the organizational values may backfire.

Finally, it will be necessary to explore the mission alignment between partners. Which organizations in the "other" sector have a matching mission? Even if missions do not match exactly, complementarity should be explored: can our missions strengthen each other?

In addition to exploring the breadth of the potential alignment, managers should also investigate depth. How tightly aligned is the connection for any single variable—values, strategy, or mission? While there are no objective parameters to measure the range of possible intensities of these connections, one can draw up a list of ways in which each of the key dimensions are misaligned. The length of the list will reveal, inversely, the collaboration's alignment depth. While a short list will indicate a deep and coherent connection, a long list will signal a superficial or absent connection.

Notes

1   James E. Austin, *The Collaboration Challenge: How Nonprofits and Businesses Succeed through Strategic Alliances*, 1st ed. (San Francisco: Jossey-Bass Publishers, 2000) 61.

2   Peggy H. Cunningham Minette E. Drumwright, Ida E. Berger, *Social Alliances: Company/Nonprofit Collaboration* (Cambridge, Mass.: Marketing Science Institute, 2000) 15.

3   Lynn Sharp Paine, *Value Shift: Why Companies Must Merge Social and Financial Imperatives to Achieve Superior Performance* (New York: McGraw-Hill, 2003).

4   See the discussion following the heading "Individuals" (p. 58.)

5   As we shall see later, eventually the collaboration also developed a strong connection to both partners' values triggered by a review of AUSOL's organizational values.

6   Honold and Silverman coined the expression *organizational DNA* to refer to organizations' basic identity, which should be consistent with daily practices in order to reach its effectiveness potential. In our work, we have used the expression in its conceptual dimension: "belief systems... and frameworks that often provide justification and guidance to our life and work." Linda Honold and Robert J. Silverman, *Organizational DNA: Diagnosing Your Organization for Increased Effectiveness* (Palo Alto, CA: Davies-Black Pub., 2002) xii.

7   "Lo social paga," presentation by Rubén Darío Lizarralde, Indupalma president. Bogotá, March 11, 2003.

8   Michael E. Porter and Mark R. Kramer, "The Competitive Advantage of Corporate Philanthropy," *Harvard Business Review* 80, no. 12 (2002).

8   Jeffrey Abrahams, *The Mission Statement Book: 301 Corporate Mission Statements from America's Top Companies* (Berkeley, Calif.: Ten Speed Press, 1995) 40.

10 The collaborations between H-E-B and the BAM, and between *La Nación* and the *Red Solidaria*, though featuring medium alignment, share some

of this group's characteristics. We will discuss these specific cases when we analyze the relationship between alignment and value creation, in the next chapter.

11 James E. Austin and Ezequiel A. Reficco, "Forest Stewardship Council," HBS Case No. 9-303-047 (Boston: Harvard Business School Publishing, 2002); James E. Austin and Cate Reavis, "Starbucks and Conservation International," HBS Case No. 9-303-055 (Boston: Harvard Business School Publishing, 2002).

12 Refer to p. 82.

13 In 2002, the raw materials for the Ekos product line came from the Brazilian states of Amazonas, Amapá, Pará, Rondônia, Piauí, Minas Gerais, Bahia, São Paulo, Paraná and Rio Grande do Sul. To illustrate the isolation these groups usually experience, it should be noted that a new indigenous group was discovered in 2002. It had never had any contact with the outer world, and no one had ever heard of it before. Leonêncio Nossa, "Os últimos povos desconhecidos da Amazônia brasileira," *O Estado de São Paulo*, 24 de noviembre 2002.

14 James E. Austin and Ezequiel A. Reficco, "Forest Stewardship Council," HBS Case No. 9-303-047 (Boston: Harvard Business School Publishing, 2002).

15 This alliance is discussed in James E. Austin and Cate Reavis, "Starbucks and Conservation International."

16 "Companies with strong brands (sometimes called "brand equity") can sell the same products as their competitors for more money. Starbucks is a case in point: they can sell a $5 cup of coffee because their customers are also buying the Starbucks experience, the Starbucks brand." Dan Saffer, *Building Brand into Structure* ([cited March 23, 2003]); available from http://www.boxesandarrows.com/archives/building_brand_into_structure.php.

17 *Social Responsibility and Environment*, Groupe Danone, [cited June 23, 2003]. Available from http://www.danonegroup.com/Social_Responsibility/.

18 See "CSOs Supporting Danone's Brands and Social Strategy" (p. 321.)

19 The connection between individuals is also relevant in another aspect: if there is no "personal chemistry," communications are more difficult, and collaborations hardly manage to get feedback. We will deal with this issue when we review alliance management.

20 Report submitted at the *Primer encuentro universidad–colegios: un espacio de reflexión sobre la educación*, Universidad de Rosario, [cited November 1, 2002]. Available from www.urosario.edu.co/lau/planeacion/encuentro01.htm.

21 See the discussion following the heading "Individuals" (p. 58.)

22 A detailed description of this alliance, evolution and impact may be found on Mario Roitter, "Developing Allies and Alliances: *Autopistas del Sol* and SES Foundation," SEKN Case No. SKE001, (Boston: Harvard Business School Publishing, 2003).

23 "Cross-sector collaboration can also be focused on strengthening the company's internal organization." James E. Austin, "Marketing's Role in Cross-Sector Collaboration," *Journal of Nonprofit and Public Sector Marketing* 11, no. 1 (Spring 2003): 35.

24 At the beginning of the decade, Unilever acquired Gamesa, a leader in the cracker market, which, combined with its subsidiary Sabritas, became a strong actor in the industry. However, competition was not up-front, since both led different market sectors. Bimbo's leadership focused on the cookie market, with a 90 percent share. Sabritas, instead, was a market leader in crackers, holding an 80 percent share. Bimbo was a smaller player at the crackers' industry (only 15 percent market share). Cecilia Bouleau, "Unilever, Pepsi invest in Mexico," *Advertising Age* (1990): 26.

25 "Gruma to Compete with Bimbo in Mexico's Bread Market," *Milling & Baking News* 76, no. 31 (1997): 14.

26 "Magic Pan," *Snack Food & Wholesale Bakery* 88, no. 5: 28.

27 Refer to p. 96.

4

Value Generation

James Austin, Ezequiel Reficco, and SEKN Research Team

We maintain and intensify interpersonal relationships when they gratify us in different ways. Likewise, value generation is what fuels an organization's active and committed involvement in collaborations. If a cross-sector partnership stops benefiting partners, it will soon fall into benign oblivion, the prologue to doom. Since the final goal of any collaboration is to create value for all parties, our analysis should start by reviewing the factors involved in their creation. Which collaborations manage to create the most value for partners?

As we mentioned in our opening chapter, previous research revealed that collaborations between businesses and CSOs may be conceptually plotted, according to their features, along the Collaboration Continuum that was presented in the first chapter, in any of its three stages: philanthropic, transactional or integrative.[1] Among the characteristics of these stages, is that each has more value creation potential than the preceding one; organizations only move ahead on this path as they discover that doing so will bring increased benefits.

The stages in the Collaboration Continuum can be helpful in structuring this chapter's discussion. Due to the subjective nature of value, it is impossible for external observers to measure its magnitude, which is solely determined by the partners' preferences, expectations, and context. Since we cannot measure value itself, we may use the developmental stage in the Continuum reached by collaborations as a proxy variable to estimate it. We may assume that collaborations will have a greater potential for value generation the further they have managed to advance along the Continuum.

At this point it may be useful to keep in mind that the stages in the Collaboration Continuum are not self contained, hermetic categories, nor meant to represent incompatible or self-exclusive models of partnership. What these categories depict are stages along a fluid and dynamic spectrum, meant to bring conceptual clarity to scholars and practitioners. While the three phases of the Continuum can be a useful device to think about the different requirements and distinct qualities of particular partnerships, it is important to recognize that in the real world very often collaborations will be best categorized as hybrids, which will not fall neatly into one single category.

The rest of this section explores the two sets of factors that condition this value creation process: the level of alignment and the sources of value creation.

Alignment as a Value Generator

In this analysis, we suggest a positive relationship between collaborations' level of alignment and their potential to create value: the higher the alignment between partners' missions, values, and strategies, the more value a collaboration will tend to generate. As we will explain, highly aligned collaborations are capable of creating *customized* value for partners' needs. In addition, the value generated by these collaborations will be harder to imitate, as it results from the unique and distinctive features of the organizations involved.

Philanthropic Collaborations

Philanthropy, mainly motivated by altruism, has been the prevailing pattern for collaborations between businesses and CSOs. Even in this kind of collaboration that creates predominantly social value, the benefits gained by partners will be closely related to their level of alignment. As Michael Porter and Mark Kramer point out in a recent article, "The more tightly philanthropy is aligned with a company's unique strategy—increasing skills, technology or infrastructure on which the firm is especially reliant, say, or increasing demand within a specialized segment where the company is strongest—the more disproportionately the company will benefit through enhancing the context."[2]

As Table 5 will show later, in our sample cases these philanthropic collaborations tended to feature a narrow alignment, involving a connection at only one dimension. Thus, in these partnerships the potential to generate value was in principle limited to that single dimension. In the previous chapter, we explained how this might change as partners get to know each other and realize they may be able to align more organizational dimensions to the collaboration. As alignment broadens, its value generation potential increases. An example of a traditional philanthropic collaboration was the School Sponsorship Program launched in Nicaragua in 1999 as a result of an agreement between the education committee of the American Chamber of Commerce (*Cámara de Comercio Americana de Nicaragua,* hence AMCHAM) and Nicaragua's Ministry of Education, Culture and Sports (*Ministerio de Educación, Cultura y Deportes,* hence MECD). AMCHAM's members agreed to work with primary school principals, under the supervision of the MECD, to identify their most urgent needs in order to provide for them through cash or in-kind donations.

Our sample also included some cases of what is sometimes referred to as high-impact philanthropy or strategic philanthropy, which tends to be built around a deeper connection than traditional philanthropy. An example of this kind of partnerships is the Pro-Council (*Pró-Conselho*) program, undertaken jointly in 2001 by the Telemig Celular Institute and the so-called Volunteer Support Groups, made up of several CSOs of the state of Minas Gerais in Southeast Brazil. The purpose of this alliance was to create and strengthen two municipal institutions— the Tutoring Councils and the Municipal Councils for Children's and Youths' Rights—whose functions were, respectively, to guarantee the enforcement of children's rights legislation, and to design public policies to that end. The Telemig Celular Institute was the social arm of Telemig Celular, a cellular telephone company operating in Minas Gerais. This company had adopted the concept of "capillarity" as its guiding principle: building a sound and long-lasting connection with its customers, wherever they might be located throughout the state. Its social policy strengthens its strategy by contributing to that objective.

In the previous chapter, we stated that narrow connections among organizations might be compensated by depth, which is illustrated by the collaboration between the Chilean *Empresas Ariztía* company and the Melipilla Municipal Corporation (*Corporación Municipal de Melipilla,* hence CMM). Philanthropist Manuel Ariztía, company president and owner, had been actively committed to the CMM since its creation in 1981. His leadership and managerial skills were instrumental in the process that led Melipilla's educational system to rank among the best in the country. At the time of our study, the collaboration had lasted over 20 years and was still vigorous and dynamic. As we have said before, both partners remained closely linked on account of Ariztía's values and strong commitment to public education in Melipilla.

However, although commitment may be deep, a narrow alignment conditions the collaboration's potential to generate value for organizations. For two decades, Ariztía struggled to *broaden* the partnership with CMM, trying to integrate company managers by clearly communicating the shared mission of both organizations aimed at improving Melipilla's education. Still, his efforts seem to have had little effect. *Empresas Ariztía* executives tend to be somewhat skeptical about the collaboration with CMM, which is viewed as the company owner's personal initiative. Even though the company mission was defined in such a way as to include educational promotion, the lack of an objective convergence between education and food manufacturing constrains the evolution of a collaboration, limiting strategic alignment.

Transactional Collaborations

Collaborations in this stage feature a focus on specific activities, in which each partner generates value for the other. As shown by Table 5, alignment in this group is mostly medium[3]; that is, connecting two organizational dimensions—usually partners' values and strategies. When a collaboration acquires strategic relevance, participants have strong incentives to deepen their involvement, allocating more resources to it.

This situation was quite clear in the cases reviewed when we discussed dynamic alignment,[4] for example, the collaboration between the Mexican food industry Bimbo Group and the Papalote Children's Museum (*Papalote Museo del Niño*). The partnership started out as a philanthropic effort providing emotional reward (the so-called feel-good effect), goodwill, and brand exposure for the company, but lacking a strategic dimension. However, eventually, competitive pressures led the company to align explicitly this collaboration to its competitive strategy. Since then, the value drawn by the company increased considerably, along with its commitment and resource allocation.[5]

Integrative Collaborations

Only highly-aligned collaborations (those featuring medium-deep and broad-deep alignment) managed to reach this stage. In these collaborations the incentives to capture efficiencies and create more value were strong enough to blur organizational boundaries in the partners' joint activities. While partnering organizations maintained their separate identities, the level of commitment and intimacy attained from these experiences were so deep that they tended to leave indelible marks in participants. The companies involved were impassioned and motivated by the collaboration. Far from being a burden on their budgets, social ventures strengthened these companies' core businesses, while they generated value for their partners and communities. At the same time, CSOs participating in these collaborations gained institutional capacity and sustainability.

Here, too, the level of alignment had an impact on the collaborations' potential for value creation, as one might conclude by comparing the case of *Meals de Colombia* (Meals) to the experiences undertaken by *La Nación* and H-E-B International Supermarkets (HEB). In 1994, the Presidents Forum of Bogotá's Chamber of Commerce launched its Twenty-First Century Leaders initiative (*Líderes Siglo XXI*, hence *Líderes*). Participating companies would work with schools to adapt the techniques of total quality to the challenges of managing educational institutions. From the outset, Meals, a frozen-food marketing company, became one of the most enthusiastic supporters of the initiative. As we have seen in the previous chapter, the company joined this collaboration strictly on philanthropic grounds, disregarding any strategic utilitarian calculation. However, shortly afterwards, Meals began to receive unexpected benefits in terms of exposure, goodwill, and human resource management.[6] This flow of value led the company to increase substantially its commitment to the initiative. For example, it hired a specialist on both educational and total quality issues to work for *Líderes*.[7] The company's discovery of this strategic dimension was soon reflected in changes in its organizational chart, where *Líderes* was incorporated as an area of the human resources department, with its own allocated budget.

Although protagonists do not hesitate to describe the experience as successful, by the time of conclusion of our study, the value the company was obtaining from its participation in *Líderes* seemed to have reached its peak. Why not further the commitment and drive the collaboration to the heart of its commercial strategy, so as to further advance along the Collaboration Continuum and generate more value? The answer has to do with the fit between partners' missions: they are compatible but not convergent; that is, both missions can co-exist comfortably within a collaboration as long as they remain at a certain distance. Since children are included in Meals' target population, one could think that a partnership with schools could facilitate a connection to its market. However, access to schools constitutes a delicate area, which needs to be handled carefully. It is not hard to imagine that if Meals should attempt to align the collaboration directly to its marketing strategy and its core business (which the company never did), it could raise ethical issues for some stakeholders and cause a negative backlash, hurting the company's interests.

As opposed to Ariztía's case, Meals was successful in instilling a strong strategic dimension into a collaboration that had been born by means of a deep value connection, as a philanthropic initiative. However, here too, the objective characteristics of partners' missions conditioned the collaboration's level of alignment, thus, its potential for value generation. The collaborations developed by *La Nación* and H-E-B supermarkets (HEB) with their respective CSO partners display an opposing picture: both companies *chose* to avoid full alignment, in spite of an objective convergence that would have facilitated their matching.

As we have mentioned, the Argentine newspaper *La Nación* entered into a partnership with the Solidarity Network (*Red Solidaria*, hence RS) to connect individuals or groups with specific needs to those who could provide the necessary help. One of the products developed by the collaboration was the "solidarity classified ads," a regular section in the newspaper that listed unsatisfied social needs. Although the company tried to keep the collaboration out of its core business, the objective matching between both organizations' missions drove the collaboration towards integration. As one of the newspaper reporters said, "The RS is the best possible partner for us because our missions are similar." The collaboration involved core business staff at both organizations: RS staff and writers from several of *La Nación*'s sections (general information, classifieds, and Sunday magazine). It would have been hard for casual observers to tell the difference between operations involving news related to *La Nación*'s core business and those associated with the solidarity section. Newspaper editors admitted that the working dynamics involved in solidarity classified ads turned this collaboration into something rather special: "Our relationship with the RS is more intense because it is an everyday deal."

Similarly, the collaboration between HEB and the Monterrey Food Bank (*Banco de Alimentos de Monterrey*, hence BAM) involved a strong strategic dimension for both partners, while their missions are clearly matching. Both organizations' personnel interacted on a daily basis in collaboration activities. For example, BAM staff monitored and reported on HEB store operations regularly—thus undertaking tasks that belong to the company's internal functions. In this case, too, external observers would have had a difficult time separating operations related to products used for HEB core business and those destined for food banks. The partners are part of each other's operating chain.

Both companies decided to separate collaborations from their core business area on account of a value judgment, but there was no objective boundary demanding that separation. If *La Nación* decided to do so, it could consider solidarity classified ads as another one of its products, an addition to its core business. It could view these ads as a source of both economic and social value. It is also possible to imagine HEB incorporating its damaged goods' management through food banks as part of its business, as do many of its competitors. In both instances, however, the company owners' altruistic motivations led them to consciously not pursue a full integration with their commercial strategies.

Mobilizing Resources to Create Value

The second factor that determines the magnitude of value that a collaboration can create, is its source. The value created in collaborations may come from transferring *generic* or *key resources,* or from jointly creating value through the *combined use of key resources.* Within a given level of alignment, the use of one or the other kind of resources will bear a significant impact on a collaboration's potential to create value.

Generic resources are fungible, generally consisting of undifferentiated goods or services—commodities. These are assets that any business company or CSO will have. Usually, they are mobilized in cross-sector partnerships through donations, of cash, in-kind, or of professional services that are not directly associated to the company's core business—such as manufacturing companies' accountants or lawyers. Key resources are core capabilities, specific organizational skills or assets that are relevant to an institution's main line of business. They may be tangible, such as high-technology equipment, or intangible such as highly specialized services and skills, knowledge, access to formal and informal networks, contacts with governments, media exposure, credibility on any given subject, and others.

In general terms, generic resources act as enablers: they remove hurdles and clear the path. Instead, key resources hold the potential leverage to generate exponential growth or impact for partners. Therefore, other things being equal, collaborations involving the transfer of key resources will generate more value, both for partners and the community. Generic resources are unquestionably important. Schools need erasers and desks; low-income neighborhoods need sewers. And all organizations—social or private—need financial resources to operate. However, creating value from generic goods is limited on two accounts. First, these goods are more vulnerable to the economic environment: donations may be among the first to go during hard times. (We will discuss this topic in depth when we deal with value renewal.) Second, donations have a rigid ceiling: they are strictly limited to donors' budgets. When the last cent is gone, there are no more chances to collaborate.

When cross-sector collaborations create value from key resources beyond money, boundaries are far more flexible: economic downturns are easier to handle, and value can be replicated and scaled up. Even though cash may be scarce, partner's competencies still exist. Manuel Ariztía led the transformation of Melipilla through good and rough times. When he was invited to participate in the Melipilla Municipal Corporation (CMM), his company was in dire financial straits and he recalled, "I didn't have a dime in my pockets." He knew he could not donate any money, but he also knew his managerial experience could have a great impact on local public education. In the Twenty-First Century Leaders' program (*Líderes*), *Meals de Colombia* documented the experiences and learning generated by participants in their efforts to adopt the total quality models to school management. That intellectual capital was distilled and later published in a series of booklets, which are distributed to new entrants to the program, speeding up their learning curve. The primary contribution of the companies in *Líderes* is not money but their time and expertise.

A skeptical reader could think that money is a generic resource, and that, with enough of it, you could generate all the impact you want. In a way, this is true: the difference between both categories is not absolute.[8] However, paying attention to the source of value creation is useful, because it helps us understand an important fact: not everything can be bought with money. In general, core organizational competencies are not for sale. In addition, donors will seldom be willing to provide enough money for enough time to generate a strategic impact. In practice, donations of generic resources tend to remain purely tactical, helping merely to fill organizational gaps. Instead, key resources usually have a strategic and transforming impact. They are more productive and can generate greater value, thus, their deployment is usually more cost-effective for the organizations that command them. Finally, as key resources are often points of differentiation, the value they generate is harder to imitate.

A quick glance at a recently cited example shows these points. In its alliance with *La Nación*, the Solidarity Network (RS) secured newspaper space to regularly publish its solidarity ads nationwide, in exchange for providing *La Nación* with a stable flow of life experiences, which were journalistically interesting and socially valuable, among other things. How much money should *La Nación* have donated in order to generate the same value in terms of public visibility for RS? How much money would RS have needed to generate a similar cultural change in Argentine society, had not *La Nación* been its partner? In all likelihood, a lot more than any donation budget could have afforded. While anyone can write a check, only an organization having *La Nación*'s exposure, credibility, and distribution channels may contribute to a cultural change favoring solidarity.

Additionally, the impact of key resources tends to be more lasting and sustainable. Windows may break again, and eventually desks will need repainting, but the exposure obtained by RS and the cultural change both partners worked for will certainly last a lot longer. Let us consider the Amazon Lodge (*Posada Amazonas*), the result of the already mentioned alliance between the Peruvian Ese'eja native community and the eco-tourism firm Rainforest Expeditions. When the collaboration concludes in 2015, community members will be equipped with the necessary knowledge and experience to manage a proven business yielding sound profit margins and significant social and environmental benefits. At that moment, they will be *able to choose* whether they seek another private partner or not, and they will not need to depend on the presence of another organization to provide employment for the community.

The collaboration between the Brazilian company Natura and the Matilde María Cremm (Matilde) public school shows the difference in sustainability and impact derived from generic and key resources. By 1992, Natura had a typically philanthropic collaboration with the school near its *Itapecerica da Serra* plant. However, as we mentioned in Chapter 2,[9] Natura's management was not satisfied with the situation and was seeking "a different kind of relationship," in the words of company president, Guilherme Leal. Together, both parties developed a common vision: Matilde would seek to become a transformational agent in its community. To meet this challenge, these organizations resorted to the Center for the Study and Research of Education, Culture and Community Action (*Centro de Estudos e Pesquisas em Educação, Cultura e Ação Comunitária*, hence CENPEC), a CSO devoted to public education strengthening. The school was used to following rigid and bureaucratic models favoring form over content. The other two partners helped Matilde in its soul-searching process, involving all its stakeholders. After a lot of hard work, the results became visible: Matilde, a public school located on the outskirts of a county near the São Paulo state capital, ranked fifth among the best schools in that region. Most interestingly, the change that this partnership brought about was permanent and sustainable. The management skills and self-evaluation techniques acquired by Matilde were imprinted in its institutional memory and will be reproduced. According to Leal, "We were instrumental in opening up a path for them to give the school an identity of its own. We facilitated a movement that contributed to its autonomy." For Irineu de Oliveira Cintra, Matilde's teaching coordinator and head of the collaboration between 1992 and 2001, "In many ways, our partnership with Natura taught us to stand on our own two feet."

Finally, the third source of value creation involves the combined use of each organization's key resources. When this happens, both parties create a new asset, which could not exist if the collaboration had not been in place. In 1982, Esso Chile entered into an alliance with the Assistance Corporation for Burned Children (*Corporación de Ayuda al Niño Quemado*, hence COANIQUEM), a CSO providing free medical treatment for children who have suffered burns. In 2001, both organizations launched the "Help Us Help" campaign for Esso to donate approximately US$ 0.001 for every dollar sold in fuel throughout Chile. The goodwill associated with the CSO was leveraged for fund-raising purposes, while increasing company sales. Esso covered the campaign's promotional costs, but at the same time COANIQUEM negotiated preferential advertising fees for both organizations with the media. That same year, COANIQUEM started to sell mandatory car insurance policies at Esso gas stations. Several companies provided the insurance coverage, COANIQUEM charged a broker's commission, while Esso benefited from the addition of another customer service and the additional exposure and the high profile granted by its association with COANIQUEM. It should be noted that funds for these activities did not come from Esso's budget; rather, they were generated by the joint use of partners' key resources.

The experience of *Farmacias Ahumada S.A.* (FASA) and *Fundación Las Rosas* (FLR) is especially interesting because their collaboration was never purely philanthropic: the resources received by the CSO came exclusively from joint value creation. The first collaboration product was the "Your Change Heals" campaign launched in 1999. During the campaign, all cashiers at FASA drugstores throughout Chile asked customers if they wanted to donate their change to FLR. Both partners agreed that 10 percent of the funds raised would be used to cover the campaign's marketing expenses, to build brand awareness for FLR, and to strengthen the association of both brands in the eyes of the public. The next year, FASA decided to provide incentives to its personnel, in order to stimulate value creation. The company would grant monetary rewards (vouchers for US$ 40) to those salespeople who raised more funds for FLR. To fund these bonuses, FASA would deduct US$ 2,000 a month from the donations received from customers. Since the rewards increased the net amount received by FLR, it turned out to be a win-win initiative.

In 2001, FASA's new human resources manager, Enrique Mendoza, discovered that the best fund-raisers for FLR were also the salespeople with the best selling performance at the drugstores. Spotting the opportunity to enhance the help provided to FLR while promoting personnel productivity, he decided to incorporate fund raising in the supervisor performance evaluation criteria. "They were astonished," recalls Mendoza, "because they were used to evaluations measuring number of clients served, average sales tickets, cost reduction, and service quality, but not their involvement in the company's social activities."

Generating incentives for FASA human resources to work harder and better for the collaboration not only turned employees into better fund-raisers, but it *also turned them into better salespeople.* By creating value from joint key resources, as the collaboration deepened, both the funds raised for the CSO and company sales increased. Mendoza himself was very clear in this regard. At one point, supervisors told him that there were salespeople who did not feel comfortable about asking for donations for FLR. Mendoza's reply was adamant: "Contributions for FLR are solicited not because our salespeople 'feel like' doing it, but because *it's important for our company.*"

Although the combined use of key resources turned out to be common in our case sample, the FASA-FLR experience is outstanding, because it relied exclusively on this value source. From the beginning, it was understood that FASA would not donate any funds. Thus, FLR never expected its partner to engage in "one-to-one" campaigns, in which companies match the amount donated by the public with their own funds. This lack of philanthropic spirit drove some observers to claim that "It's not FASA that helps the foundation, but its customers."

However, what this view is missing is the dynamics at play in this case's value creation: neither partner "helps" the other one; rather, they combine their core assets to generate resources benefiting both of them. As Felipe Morán, who has been in charge of the alliance at FLR since the beginning, puts it, "FASA is the channel; without that channel, we get nothing."

We close this section with a table (see next page) summarizing the results of our sample, according to the concepts developed in the previous pages. Cases were ranked according to their potential to generate value following the stages in the Collaboration Continuum—philanthropic, transactional, and integrative. The next column indicates each collaboration's level of alignment and its value source. As we discussed in Chapter 3, alignment in collaborations often changes over time; this table ignores this dynamic dimension and shows the maximum development attained by each alliance. We only include references to alignment depth when the qualitative analysis of collected materials proved there was a particularly intense connection. Value sources shown in each case do not exclude any others. When we specify key resource transference, it does not mean that there was not sporadic use of a generic resource. On the contrary, higher categories (key resources) usually include inferior ones (generic resources).

The Virtuous Circle of Value Generation

Several partnerships in our sample originated from philanthropic collaborations, involving disinterested and sporadic donations by companies, where value flows tended to remain one-way, with CSOs at the receiving end of the relation. However, in some cases, CSOs realized the key to receiving more laid in balancing those flows, thus generating value for companies. At the beginning of the chapter, we said that when Danone approached the Friendship Home (*Casa de la Amistad,* hence CdA) the company was looking for a sales promotion campaign, not an alliance. "At first, they gave and we received," remembered CdA founder, Amalia García Moreno. However, this CSO realized such a collaboration would not be sustainable and worked hard to balance the relationship. "Later, when we got to know Danone, we became more active," added García Moreno. As we will discuss subsequently, CdA's efforts to generate value for its partner were especially effective.

From the beginning, the *Fundación Proa* (Proa) helped to generate value for the Techint Group. Among other initiatives, it created a design area to sell services. This activity started as a peripheral dimension

Table 5: Value Determinants in Our Case Sample

Value magnitude	Alignment	Resources	Cases
Philanthropic Prevalence of narrow alignment. Traditional philanthropy cases involved only generic resources. The rest were high-impact philanthropy cases involving deeper connections and key resources.	Narrow	Generic	AMCHAM
	Narrow	Generic	Texaco – EJN
	Narrow	Key own	LSXXI – Multidinamics
	Narrow	Key own	LSXXI – Manrique
	Narrow-deep	Key own	CMM – PA
	Narrow-deep	Key own	Banco Itaú – CENPEC
	Medium	Key own	Telemig Celular – Support groups
	Medium-deep	Key own	BCI – CCM
	Medium-deep	Key own	Natura – Matilde
Transactional Prevalence of medium alignment. Some cases featured narrow-deep alignment, and others broad alignment, but not particularly deep. This category was marked by the use of key resources, and in some cases, partners used key combined resources.	Narrow-deep	Key own	Tetra Pak – JLCM
	Narrow-deep	Key own	Fuprovi – Repretel
	Medium	Key own	Bimbo – Papalote
	Medium	Combined key	DANONE – CDA
	Medium	Combined key	JAA – CCA
	Medium	Combined key	FASA – FLR
	Medium-deep	Key own	Manuelita
	Medium-deep	Key own	Indupalma
	Medium-deep	Combined key	AUSOL – SES
	Broad	Key own	CGH – Gen Méd
	Broad	Key own	CGH – J&J
Integrative Only collaborations built around a high level of alignment (medium-deep and broad-deep alignment) reached this stage. The most common value source was the use of key resources, either by each partner individually or combined.	Medium-deep	Key own	LSXXI – Meals
	Medium-deep	Key own	Techint – Proa
	Medium-deep	Combined key	ESSO – COANIQUEM
	Medium-deep	Combined key	HEB – BAM
	Medium-deep	Combined key	LN – RS
	Broad-deep	Combined key	Ese'eja – RFE
	Broad-deep	Combined key	GGH – FC
	Broad-deep	Combined key	Natura – Cognis – communities
	Broad-deep	Combined key	Starbucks – CI

in the collaboration, but eventually Proa also added corporate image consulting to its service portfolio and offered its advice to the Group as well as to other clients. In neighboring Chile, Felipe Morán, who has been in charge of *Fundación Las Rosas* (FLR) alliance with *Farmacias Ahumada S.A.* (FASA) drugstores, recognizes that generating value for its partner is precisely the challenge his organization is currently facing to bring about a stronger commitment from the company. "If we show FASA that, through our collaboration, they can stand out from the competition, maybe we will be able to open new collaboration channels, tighten our relationship and, perhaps, even get the company to commit as a partner, more than it is today."

Invariably, this awareness about the need to generate value for partners was the prologue to a new stage in the relationship, in which value flow became more bilateral and intense. In other words, it was the onset of what we call the virtuous circle of value exchange. Let us consider the collaboration between Esso Chile and the Assistance Corporation for Burned Children (COANIQUEM), a Chilean CSO providing free medical treatment for burned children. When the collaboration started in 1982, Esso was not COANIQUEM's partner, but its *donor*. However, Jorge Rojas, the CSO's executive director, realized that situation could change if his organization generated value for the company. "Early in our partnership, it dawned on me that Esso could also benefit from its relationship with us: goodwill in the media and increasing public awareness of its generous support," he explained.

COANIQUEM's success in generating value for the company triggered a new dynamic in the collaboration, which eventually translated into a paradigm change: Esso stopped contributing to specific *projects*, and became a more stable partner of an *organization*. The next step takes place when the partner responds in kind to that initial drive, thus completing the virtuous circle—Figure 8 below captures this dynamic.

The collaboration between H-E-B supermarkets (HEB) and the Monterrey Food Bank (BAM) is a good example of this process, in which:

- **Both partners try to find new opportunities to generate value**. Norma Treviño, HEB Mexico public relations manager, says, "The relationship is both ways: Blanca [Castillo, BAM's head] and her people let us know when they find opportunities for improvement in our operations."

- **Each partner thinks in terms of other's needs**: Treviño adds: "BAM people *know our warehouses better than many of our employees*… They usually come up with some very positive suggestions for HEB."

- **When partners receive value, they return it enriched, in a self-propelled circle of constant reciprocal feedback**. Initially, HEB trained its partner in food bank creation. However, when HEB expanded regionally and needed to develop new

Figure 8: The Virtuous Circle of Value Generation

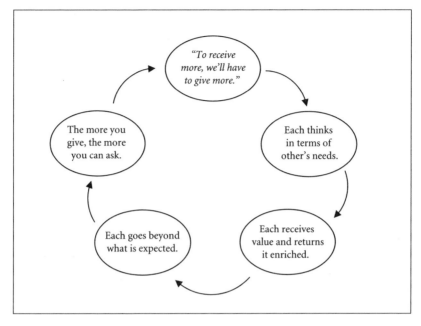

food banks, it relied on its partner to spread this knowledge. Treviño recalls that, "When we had to open three food banks in three months—insane!—Blanca brought her manual on how to open a food bank, step-by-step. This attitude helps processes flow."

- **Partners go beyond what is expected from them and proactively strive to generate value for the other partner.** Norma Treviño, HEB Mexico public relations manager, admits that, "Sometimes the bank overwhelms us with ideas and proposals, and that is very important, very good for us."

- **The more you give, the more you can ask for.** Castillo, BAM's head, shares her experience: "I've learned it's a process… You can ask for more if you are delivering results to your donor."

Once a strong bilateral flow is secured, the next challenge lies in working towards balance. Even if both parties strive to prevent alliance depreciation, collaborations may suffer if they are "too good" for one of the partners, generating far more value for only one of them. We have mentioned the Twenty-First Century Leaders (*Líderes*) program, gathering a number of companies working with Colombian schools to adjust management quality techniques to education. The specific value drawn by each participant was different, depending on its degree of commitment to the collaboration. However, at the aggregate level the initiative has been undoubtedly successful in transforming participating educational institutions. At first, schools were reluctant to join in, but, once the program proved it could create value for the sector, there was a wave of interest that engulfed more and more schools. The private sector's interest did not grow as rapidly, thus generating an imbalance. Sandra Velasco, program coordinator, explains,

> Our major problem lay in getting companies. Now, we have 189 educational institutions and 109 companies. It would be great to have the same number of companies, but it has been impossible so far. Selling the program to a school is a lot easier; in fact, I have almost 50 schools waiting to join. Desertion is also higher among companies than among schools, which spot the benefit immediately. Companies know there is a benefit for them, too, but it is very small, and it implies some contribution.

In light of this imbalance, the company leading the project, *Meals de Colombia* (Meals), filled the void by increasing its commitment and contributions. As we discussed at the beginning of the chapter, the company obtained several initially unexpected benefits in the process. However, the value drawn by the company seems to have reached its peak, while collaboration costs climb as the program grows. In order to meet the increasing demand, Meals implemented a new working system: instead of working one-on-one with a private-sector leader, schools join a group, and the company works with several schools at the same time. Still, despite Meals' efforts, the increasing imbalance between the number of schools and companies is starting to appear in project management indicators through a decrease in participants' satisfaction levels.

The problem lurking behind this is an imbalance in value flow. Companies find it harder than schools to identify the advantages of this collaboration. According to Velasco, "Companies know there is a benefit, but *it is very little.*" The value of collaborating with a school will depend on each company's values, strategy, and mission, but the evidence suggests that, in aggregate terms, schools are finding the collaboration more rewarding than the private sector. While educational institutions have a knowledge base that is not apparently crucial for most companies, the latter's know-how seems to be critical for all schools. At the time this study was undertaken, parties were still trying to figure out how to balance the value flow in this program.

A similar challenge arose in the already mentioned collaboration between AUSOL and social leader Alberto Croce. After five years of joint work, eventually the company decided to commit itself to supporting the creation of the SES Foundation (for Sustainability—Education—Solidarity), headed by Croce and his professional team. This organization's mission was defined as, "Promoting sustainable educational strategies to facilitate a true integration of these [needy] youngsters in society." The first joint product was the Community Study Groups (CSGs), which later gave rise to other complementary programs and activities. The CSGs intended to tackle the school desertion problem by means of tutoring support and financial incentives for the performance of needy students.

As we will discuss later,[10] the program created significant benefits for the company in various dimensions. However, by late 2001, the alliance seemed to have reached a plateau. From the beginning, AUSOL encouraged SES to seek other funding sources, but agreed to provide the necessary funds if no other partners were found. Of course, this was a risky bet; according to Luis Freixas, AUSOL's CEO, "From the start, the main risk was that the program would overwhelm us: if all the kids who can study enrolled, our numbers would triple. We run the risk of not getting other sponsors and having to afford a budget twice as large." That feared scenario was unfolding at the time of completion of this study. The CSGs started in 1998 with 88 participants and a US$61,000 budget. By 2001, the estimated budget for AUSOL's social program rose to over US$130,000, and there were more than 180 teenagers at the CSGs. Program heads expected more than 200 youths to register in 2002 and 220 for the next year. Since SES has grown so rapidly, it is starting to get out of the initiative more value than what AUSOL may obtain from it. If the process continues, it will probably outstrip the company's possibilities. Of course, a way out of this dilemma would be to balance costs and benefits by adding new partners, in order to distribute the financial burden among more companies. From the beginning, AUSOL was open to incorporating other companies, as was also the case with Colombia's Meals. However, in both instances, the invitation has not found an echo in the sector. Freixas elaborates, "We are finding it hard to get other partners. We need them because one of our premises is that all the youngsters from the neighborhoods surrounding the Tigre highway who want to study or are attending public schools have the right to take part in our program. There are no specially privileged."

Partners are discovering that it is not easy to turn a bilateral-born collaboration, which became more integrative over time, into a multilateral partnership involving several companies with different shares of responsibility. The collaborations' original high profile, the strong link between both brands in the eyes of the general public, the daily work entwining both organizations—all value sources in a bilateral association—seem to deter new potential partners. New companies are reluctant to join in because they see AUSOL's *fingerprints* all over the program, although the company does not have an exclusivity attitude. According to Alejandra Barczuk, AUSOL's communications and customer service head, "When we set out to get voluntary contributions from other companies, we found one of the program's characteristics stood in the way. The program is labeled: it is AUSOL's."

The tensions between bilateral and multilateral collaborations' requirements are not only perceived by potential new participants. Some insiders wonder if the incorporation of new organizations could undermine some of the basic principles on which the program's success has been built: the partners' enthusiasm and commitment, resulting from shared beliefs and a common goal. Some point out that this commitment is usually closely related to the program's *paternity* and doubt the former may exist without the latter. As Croce puts it, "If AUSOL had to give up its leading role in order to secure other partners, its enthusiasm and commitment might be jeopardized. *We should think about it.*"

Value Renewal

So far, we have reviewed how organizations in our sample have created value for themselves and their partners. However, the above examples also indicate that in order to ensure a collaboration's vitality, partners should not only strive to create value, but also renew it. In partnerships, value is a highly depreciating asset; if it is not renewed, it decays and vanishes. Among the several causes that may lead to value impairment in collaborations are changes in the contextual environment. What is important to partners today may not be so tomorrow, especially if organizations have to face a sudden slump in economic cycles.

At the beginning of the chapter, we mentioned the School Sponsorship program launched by Nicaragua's American Chamber of Commerce (AMCHAM) and the local Ministry of Education, Culture and Sports (MECD). Euronica, a local company engaged in marketing and post-sale service for Daimler-Chrysler vehicles, participated in the program. Its general manager, Werner Ahlers, was the program promoter in the company and, during 1999, invested a substantial amount of time and energy in it. However, Euronica's commitment dwindled considerably the next year on account of the hard times experienced by the company. The general manager focused his attention on company problems, and the collaboration stopped operating effectively.

Value may also decrease due to the emergence of more appealing alternatives. In general, leaders have no shortage of proposals competing for their attention and resources. Unless the connection with the collaboration is deep, there will always be other projects to explore. We have already mentioned the collaboration between the television network REPRETEL and the CSO Foundation for Housing Promotion (*Fundación para la Promoción de la Vivienda*, hence FUPROVI), which worked jointly in the "A Roof for the South" project to solve the housing shortage caused by Hurricane César in Costa Rica. After the partnership successfully accomplished its objectives, FUPROVI representatives approached their partner with a proposal for continued joint work in a similar project benefiting senior citizens. However, REPRETEL's top executives seemed to have lost their interest in working together. Why? FUPROVI's counterpart in the company, reporter René Barboza, says, "The network started to think about more feasible projects, and there were new goals." Federico Zamora, REPRETEL's corporate sales head, adds, "The problem is that life is *very hectic* at the network… In my opinion, we should do a lot of social work, but it's hard because, obviously, the television business is profit-oriented, and *social work sometimes becomes less of a priority*."

As in human relations, both organizations have to work hard for their proposal to remain relevant for one another, in spite of changing circumstances. COANIQUEM's director unhesitatingly uses a marriage metaphor to refer to his organization's collaboration with Esso Chile, which has already lasted over twenty years:

> Our accomplishment is the result of deep commitment, similar to marriage. Esso discovered COANIQUEM and fell madly in love. Undoubtedly, a good start, *but it wasn't enough*. Then, we moved on to the following stage: nurturing the relationship

to grow together, as a couple. We strengthened ourselves mutually and looked for opportunities to share each other's dreams.
*We are constantly seeking new ways to link and synchronize our
lives,* just like any married couple should do.

No organization is indifferent to economic downturns, but it
should be interesting to take a look at their impact when the value
an organization obtains from a collaboration is renewed dynamically,
evolving according to its changing needs. The partnership between the
Argentine road building company *Autopistas del Sol* (AUSOL) and social leader Alberto Croce underwent various stages, in which partners'
value propositions changed.[11] But despite those changes, both partners
constantly generated value for each other throughout the collaboration, building an intense and bilateral value flow. When in 2001, the
company struggled with adverse economic conditions, its management faced the need to make internal cost-cutting adjustments. According to its CEO, Luis Freixas,

> We are trying to cut back on expenses that do not bear a sig-
> nificant impact on our mission's four axes. In principle, we
> considered cutting back on salaries, our social program, divi-
> dends, or customer service. *But our social program is one of
> the key elements we are determined to spare from those cuts. It
> provides benefits that greatly offset its cost.*

What Freixas is telling us, is that a dynamic value flow consolidates
the partnership in a unique way. At the same time, as we have explained
at the beginning of the chapter, value generation depends on the level
of alignment in the collaboration. On the one hand, FUPROVI and
Euronica cases registered narrow alignment levels: in the former's case,
the connection was purely at the level of strategy; in the latter, it was
only aligned at the level of values, and not particularly deeply. On the
other hand, AUSOL developed a deep and broad alignment, which encompassed its values and strategy.

This process of shared growth and periodical renewal is also a dis-
tinctive feature in the evolution of the Hospital Management Center
(*Centro de Gestión Hospitalaria,* hence CGH). At first, companies com-
mitted to CGH in response to a proposal by the National Planning
Department that intended to transform the Colombian health sector.
Involvement in a national cause is certainly a mobilizing and invigo-

rating value proposition, but it is also highly perishable: it is depleted once stakeholders respond to the call. However, shortly after CGH started operating, it began to generate value for its participants in another dimension. According to Patricia Gómez, CGH executive director, by joining the center,

> Companies have come to understand the sector problems discussed at board meetings, and to know their peers in other sector organizations. Businessmen have their unions, while hospitals have their Hospitals Association, but the CGH has provided a new meeting ground for suppliers, insurers, customers and universities. The CGH promoted their interaction with players to which they were not related.

The access to other sector actors became a new magnet to encourage involvement. Yet, here, too, the "acquaintance" with others is also a depreciating asset: once they meet, its utility starts to decrease. Fortunately, when CGH consolidated, it started to generate value in a third dimension: as an engine for ideas and intellectual capital creation, catering to participating companies' needs, and even proactively getting ready to respond to their future demands, as shaped by the government's new regulations for health institutions. Gómez explains, "We have paved the way for a transformation that sector organizations were not even requesting. We are ready to serve a demand that doesn't exist yet."

Finally, value may decrease when one of the partners fully internalizes an asset that had originally been deployed by its partner. When, through the resource transfer from one partner to the other, organizations develop their own capability to produce those resources, alliance value will fall abruptly. In several cases, partners did incorporate skills acquired from their counterparts, but new collaboration assets were rapidly recreated, following the "virtuous circle" mechanics described in the previous section. Furthermore, our sample shows that continuous value renewal may turn into a virtual barrier to exit from a collaboration.

Let us take a look again at the collaboration between Danone's Mexican subsidiary and the Friendship Home (CdA), a CSO providing medical care for cancer-afflicted children. Initially, Danone approached CdA exclusively to launch a sales promotion campaign. The company cautiously prevented the creation of any exit barriers, preserving its right to discontinue the partnership at any point in time. Still, the success attained by the "Let's Build Their Dreams" campaign (which, by the time this book was released, had already reached its seventh edition) became a significant barrier in itself. Aminta Ocampo, Danone public relations manager, admits, "If we don't have a 'Let's Build Their Dreams' campaign this year, we'll have a lot of explaining to do." A similar situation unfolded in the collaboration between the Chilean Credit and Investment Bank (*Banco de Crédito e Inversiones,* hence BCI) and the Corporation for Children's Credit (*Corporación de Crédito al Menor,* hence CCM), a CSO created by one of the bank's executives to provide protection for abandoned girls. The bank's general manager, Juan Esteban Musalem, commented on the chance that a new president might discontinue the initiative:

> If, one of these days, Luis Enrique Yarur no longer chairs the bank, it will be very hard for the new president to hand the home over to Father Poblete. *He will have to continue because it would be very detrimental to the bank's image, both internally and externally.* At this point in time, *it would be unthinkable for players to get out* of the game.

As collaborations broaden, encompassing new groups of stakeholders and generating their enthusiasm and commitment, it is progressively harder to undo what has already been done. According to Patricia Martínez, Danone's public relations and corporate communications director, "At first, it was something completely new; no one had ever done anything like that in Mexico. Companies donated money or things, and that was it. Now, people are very motivated to help; they are practically involved in the project. Every time we launch the campaign, *it becomes more of a commitment for the company.*"

Value Created for Companies

All companies in our sample report they have benefited from their involvement in cross-sector collaborations, though the magnitude and kind of value generated in each case depended on the factors discussed at the beginning of this chapter—namely, the level of alignment and the type of resources committed to collaborations. Figure 9 summarizes the concepts discussed in the next pages. The forms of value at the base of the pyramid were generated in almost all sample collaborations. Companies involved in collaborations that registered a higher alignment degree and involved key resources reached other forms of value, located in the pyramid's narrower levels.

Figure 9: Value Created for Companies

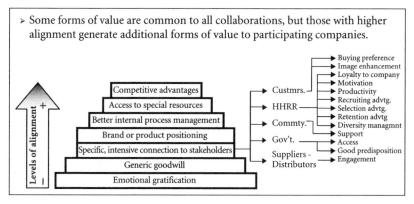

The most commonplace value form received by participating companies was *emotional gratification* and personal growth for those directly involved in the collaboration's management. Multidinamics was one of the companies committed to the Twenty-First Century Leaders (*Líderes*) program for Colombian schools. According to its CEO, Jorge González,

> Personally, participating in *Líderes* has been really rewarding. I was pleased to participate and help in the educational field. It helped us understand other sectors that are very different than those where we had worked and confirm that other small national institutions can also become successful. Now we understand—in principle—the way teachers view the world, which is a different vision to that of businessmen.

A second value dimension generated in most cases was community *goodwill* as a result of companies' involvement in social causes. In 1997, Texaco's subsidiary in Nicaragua entered into a partnership with The Resource Foundation through the "Adopt a School" program. As part of its involvement in the program, Texaco built a primary and secondary vocational school near one of its plants to provide education for low-income sectors, that otherwise would have been deprived of access to technical training. The school itself was a constant reminder of Texaco's social commitment, thus increasing community goodwill towards its brand. According to the company's brand, advertising and customer service coordinator, "Texaco has benefited from the positive media and public relations coverage that resulted from the association between the company and the project, both well respected on the local level."

In collaborations registering medium-level alignment, the emotional connection we mentioned at the beginning reached not only direct participants, but encompassed also other *stakeholders* of participating organizations, with significant implications. Let us consider the already mentioned case of Chile's Credit and Investment Bank (BCI), that, in 1990, launched a collaboration with the Corporation for Children's Credit (CCM). Because of this partnership, the company developed a stronger emotional connection with its *customers*. In turn, this led to two distinct benefits. On the one hand, *image enhancement*. As Pedro Balla, the bank's general controller points out, "People like to feel they keep their money in a bank that is not only concerned with making money but also with contributing to the common good. It removes the image of the 'cold and insensitive world of money.' It also matches our slogan, 'the people's bank.'" On the other hand, customer's stronger emotional connection led to their loyalty and *buying preference*. Rafael Pamias, Danone Mexico marketing director, commented on the campaign launched in partnership with Friendship Home (*Casa de la Amistad*): "During the campaigns, our prices remain the same. We don't raise them, but we don't lower them, either; we keep our regular prices. The competition lowered theirs in response, and, though we didn't, we still kept our share."

Emotional connections also reached companies' *human resource management*, generating value in several dimensions. As a generator of pride, social involvement increased employees' *loyalty*, through a more intense identification with the organizations to which they belong: they "wear the company colors," as Enrique Mendoza, human resources manager of *Farmacias Ahumada S.A.* (FASA), put it. Stemming from that identification, employees became *motivated*. For Luis Freixas, general manager of the Argentine road building company *Autopistas del Sol* (AUSOL),

> Employee motivation is essential to company success; it encourages people. AUSOL's 600 employees are aware of this program and feel truly proud. There are neighborhood kids

working in the company. I believe our service quality is a result of the incredible motivation of our employees. Everything done in the company motivates them, and this program is a part of that.

Because of the specific characteristics of this industry, when it comes to motivating its workforce AUSOL faces significant constraints: there are no opportunities to stir enthusiasm by the creation of new products, or the opening of new branch offices; there is no sales force to drive the entrepreneurial spirit. Thus, the motivation provided by the collaboration is especially valuable, since it could hardly be accomplished in other ways. As Freixas suggests, motivated employees amount to greater *productivity*. In this regard, at the beginning of the chapter, we have mentioned the experience reported by FASA's human resources manager, Enrique Mendoza, who discovered that the employees who raised more funds for its partner, FLR, also turned out to be the best-performing salespeople at company drugstores.

At the same time, the emotional connection also turned into *recruiting* advantages for companies. According to the recently alluded to Pamias, "Many people answer Danone's call when we are hiring. They say they want to work for Danone because they think it is really cool what we are doing. They are very specific about it, too; they mention the "Let's Build Their Dreams" campaign [implemented in collaboration with Friendship Home]."

Through cross-sector collaborations, some companies improved their personnel *selection* process. We have also referred to *Meals de Colombia* (Meals), the company that led the Twenty-First Century Leaders initiative for Colombian schools. The company president, Alberto Espinosa explains,

> The "Meals profile" was largely the product of a definition of a quality people profile elaborated with the schools. Many of the processes of personal growth and holistic development arise from the notion of what really constitutes a quality individual. Actually, what really happens is that motivational mechanisms for students and workers are very similar. Then, it all comes down to finding what really motivates people.

In addition, employees' emotional connection also produces *retention* advantages to companies. We have already talked about the collaboration between Starbucks with Conservation International and the cooperatives gathering small coffee growers from Chiapas, Mexico. This company has driven social responsibility to the heart of its organizational identity and its competitive strategy, and cross-sector collaborations are a core feature in its social work. This strong social dimension is an important source of pride and loyalty among its employees, thus contributing to company personnel retention. While the average industry turnover rate is 200 percent, at Starbucks it is 54 percent.[12] Since the company spends around US$ 500 to train each new employee, its higher retention rate accounts for yearly savings of approximately US$ 35 million.

Cross-sector collaborations also served as *diversity management* tools for companies featuring heterogeneous internal stakeholders. In Chapter 3, we analysed in detail the case of Tenaris, a company belonging to the Techint Group, developed as a result of a merger between several companies in seven countries, which until then, had been part of an alliance. The collaboration with the Fundación Proa, through its cultural initiatives, became a tool in developing a link to their various stakeholders, in spite of the diversity of perspectives and nationalities involved.

The case of the Colombian company Indupalma shows how cross-sector collaborations may generate value by helping build a connection with *communities* and *governments*. In the first case, that stronger connection turned into *support* for the company; in the second, companies accrued higher *access* and *good predisposition* from the authorities. It should be noted that the significance of that connection for Indupalma goes beyond the usual generic goodwill any company needs. As we have said, the polarization and radicalization of Colombian politics threatened the lives of company management and drove Indupalma to the verge of bankruptcy. Therefore, the support of external stakeholders was a vital dimension for this company. Indupalma carries out a community-bonding strategy it calls "construction of pacific coexistence," basically implemented through cross-sector collaborations. Claudia Calero, Indupalma's advisor, comments on the company's collaboration with the Rafael Pombo Foundation (*Fundación Rafael Pombo*, hence FRP), which hinges on the programs called "Good Manners Agreement" and "Hands for Peace."

> At first, obviously, we had to focus on internal strengthening, but, then, we have always understood we had to reach out to

the rest of the community. The "Good Manners Agreement" and "Hands for Peace" programs are not restricted to the Indupalma community; they are totally open. That's how we relate to the local community.

At the same time, through the connection to the community, Indupalma reached the local government, with whom relations had not been easy in the past. According to Calero, the collaboration provided "a different way to approach the local administration, not directly, but through the community, empowered for that purpose." A representative from the FRP adds,

> At the time, Indupalma did not have a good relationship with the mayor, Javier Zárate. But, since the collaboration started, the mayor greatly appreciated what a company such as Indupalma means for his county and recognized its merits, which we reported to Indupalma in writing.

CSOs proved to be an effective vehicle to connect with companies' external stakeholders. For this task, they leveraged a strong comparative advantage: their credibility. We mentioned earlier[13] the case of Tetra Pak, which needed to persuade both the general public and the government that waste recycling was not the sole responsibility of producers, but, instead, of a group of several actors. According to its environmental head, Sergio Escalera, the program objective was "for value chain actors (…) to gradually align to our message." For this purpose, the partnership with Mexico City Junior League proved to be a very effective tool. In Escalera's words,

> We believe the Junior League is the perfect counterpart for this, because its image enables it to communicate these messages adequately. The public sees it as a committed organization, fully altruistic, devoid of any partisan ideology. It doesn't have communication problems, and, therefore, there is no interference in the messages it conveys.

Collaborations also generated a new connection to other companies' stakeholders, such as *suppliers or distributors*. Esso Chile president, Alejandro Sanin, explains that the emotional link to its partner, COANIQUEM and its work began "at the top of both organizations,

but eventually it grew and it engulfed Esso employees, gas station owners all over the country, and even the stations' employees!"

The emotional connection and goodwill developed were very useful
for the company during hard times. In 1999, a series of earth tremors
in the northern region of the country damaged diesel depots in the
city of Antofagasta. There was a fuel spill that leaked into the city's
sewer system. At the same time, a strong odor invaded a section of the
city, though its cause was never accurately determined. Immediately,
community leaders publicly blamed Esso Chile for the incident. The
ensuing controversy had negative repercussions for the company, but
the damage was controlled and lessened due to the goodwill developed
through the collaboration with COANIQUEM. Guillermo García,
company public relations head, asserts, "We owe COANIQUEM for its
loyal support during the Antofagasta incident. [Its director, Dr. Jorge]
Rojas helped us recover the community's goodwill."

Collaborations were also instrumental in *repositioning* brands or
products. We have already discussed the case of Danone Mexico, whose
brand was perceived as detached and cold by consumers. According to
its marketing head, Rafael Pamias, "We detect a brand image evolution
in some key attributes related to proximity, as a company that cares
about children. We have turned from a cold top-quality brand into a
partnering and social citizen brand." These new attributes became a
powerful point of differentiation.

In collaborations involving the transfer of intellectual capital, knowledge tended to return, enriched, to its original owners. Often, this dynamic resulted in an *improvement of internal process management* for
companies. Early in their collaboration, the H-E-B supermarket chain
(HEB) trained the Monterrey Food Bank (BAM) on the creation and
management of world-class food banks. However, through the collaboration, the company improved its internal processes as well. BAM
used to submit detailed reports on the goods it received from HEB.
The supermarket used that information to work on enhancing its internal operations in order to reduce its damaged goods' volume. When
we discussed the value renewal circle, we explained how its partner's
keen observations on store internal processes were systematically used
by the company to seize efficiency-enhancing opportunities.

Colombian companies participating in the Twenty-First Century
Leaders program transmitted their management expertise to partnering schools, but in the process they also learned to be better managers. "Multidinamics and the Santa María School jointly developed a

strategic planning methodology we have been using for our own businesses," reports the company's CEO, Jorge González. Sandra Velasco, from Meals, adds,

> You learn a lot. You think you know about quality and processes, but you only know the theory because you studied it at the university or here. However, the real test is to apply it to an organization. This has been one of the greatest benefits for businessmen: applying something they know theoretically, checking whether it works or not, and finding ways to adjust it to each organization's needs.

In a few collaborations featuring significant levels of alignment, companies accessed third-sector partners' *special resources*—inputs deriving from their nature as NGOs that would have been difficult or impossible to imitate—which were successfully incorporated into their value chains. We have mentioned the alliance between the Argentine newspaper *La Nación* and the Solidarity Network (RS) several times already. The CSO's mission was to improve the quality of life of the needy by connecting them to those who could help them. Once this organization contacted *La Nación*, it rapidly turned into a reliable source of interesting and genuine stories, which nurtured several products: the "solidarity news," the "solidarity section," the "to lend a hand" column, the "solidarity classifieds," and a specific Sunday magazine section. This asset would have been very hard to replicate by another organization that lacked the enormous legitimacy and capillarity commanded by the RS.

In cases of broad and deep alignment, these idiosyncratic resources were used to generate unique *competitive advantages*. Chapter 8 discusses how the cross-sector partnership between Rainforest Expeditions and the Ese'eja native community turned into a source of strong advantages for the company. Here, we will only add that these advantages translated into solid profit margins. Locally, Amazon Lodge competed with six other similar facilities, and, internationally, with several eco-lodges in Ecuador and Bolivia—all of them offering, generally speaking, the same product. Despite the strong competition of these alternative destinations, the competitive advantages featured by Amazon Lodge enabled it to keep its prices between 5 percent and 40 percent above them.

The exact magnitude of the value generated by collaborations was more obvious for companies that systematically measured their costs and benefits. However, those companies tended to be the exception in our sample. The reluctance to measure costs and benefits was explicit in the case of the Argentine newspaper *La Nación* and its alliance with the Solidarity Network (RS). From the beginning, the newspaper refused to measure the value of its in-kind contributions as well as the economic impact of its social work. The internal perception was that assigning an economic value to the project would *deprive it of its solidarity nature* and would undermine the motivations that had led the company to launch the initiative. In that view, assigning a dollar value to the benefits accrued by the collaboration with the RS would have conveyed the impression that the partnership had been about institutional marketing, something the company tried to prevent at all costs. This was not an isolated case, either. In the previous chapter, we described the case of the Brazilian Itaú Bank, which strove to keep its social work decidedly apart from its institutional marketing, in spite of the strong competitive pressures at play that were leading in the opposite direction.

The companies that carefully measured costs and benefits tended to be those that had no reservations about aligning their social strategy to their competitive strategy—mostly multinational companies, such as Danone, Coca-Cola, Esso, and Starbucks. For example, Coca-Cola de Argentina outsourced the supervision and operations of its collaboration with Junior Achievement Argentina to a private consulting firm, which, among other things, was in charge of monitoring program results. Of course, underlying this disparity, there is a different attitude in regard to the relationship between individual profit and social benefit. It should be interesting to compare the vision described in the previous paragraph with the one voiced by Starbucks president, Orin Smith, who believed that "*aligning self-interest to social responsibility is the most powerful way to sustaining a company's success.*"

In Chapter 2 we mentioned that the search for profit does not appear to be fully legitimized in Latin American societies—a perception that somehow calls into question the role of businessmen in society, and their legitimacy. According to Jorge González, CEO of the Colombian company Multidinamics, "Businessmen are viewed as people exploiters, seeking profits and benefits at all costs." For the Chilean businessman Manuel Ariztía, most Chileans "are under the impression that business executives have no soul." Considering such a negative presumption, it is understandable that regional businessmen may be reluctant to look like they are profiting from their social ventures, which might reinforce those initial suspicions.

Thus, what appears to be behind companies' efforts to separate social work from core businesses is the intention to show the truly disinterested nature of their ventures. Yet, in this battle, the odds seem to be against companies. We have seen that even the most altruistic efforts end up generating undeniable benefits for the partners, even when they were not actively sought. This is obvious to everyone, and particularly to those who are skeptical and even scornful of the private sector's altruism. Proclaiming, once and again, the lack of advantages for organizations does not seem to be a good choice: it is neutral for converts and counterproductive for skeptics, who will always find "evidence" of allegedly hidden agendas.

Furthermore, winning that battle is not only highly improbable; but it may also be dangerous. Social enterprises are disinterested when they are not connected to any business objectives; in other words, when they *are not aligned to* utilitarian organizational needs. This rationale goes against the dynamics described in the preceding analysis of the value creation process, which states that a cross-sector collaboration's potential *increases* through higher alignment levels. Taken to the extreme, the sad conclusion of that rationale would be that only *social ventures with a low potential to benefit society are genuine.* Altruism has a core role in social initiatives, but, perhaps, the time has come to expand our vision, to try new paths to reach the same destination. One may wonder why social solutions that do not generate private value are better than those that do. Moreover, the outcome in both cases is not identical: it is worth recalling that, as our analysis has showed, the solutions resulting from highly integrated collaborations tend to be deeper and more lasting.

The social delegitimization of the search for profits in the region, compounded by the local business sector's "shame" and its struggle for credibility and legitimacy, could produce the paradoxical and undesired effect of restricting the quantity and quality of resources potentially allocated to the solution of social problems. The consolidation of the new vision that is emerging in Latin America's business sector and civil society will help reverse this dilemma. In this new vision, utilitarian drivers may coexist with and *reinforce* altruistic drivers in pursuing the creation of economic and social value.

Value Created for CSOs

In general, CSOs that participated in cross-sector collaborations benefited from the experience, though here, too, the magnitude of value accrued was conditioned by alignment and the kind of resources used for value generation. Figure 10 summarizes the concepts discussed in this section in a similar fashion to the chart presented at the beginning of the previous section. Once again, the base of the pyramid includes those value forms that were generated in all cases of cross-sector partnerships, while the top houses the benefits provided by highly aligned collaborations.

Figure 10: Value Created for CSOs

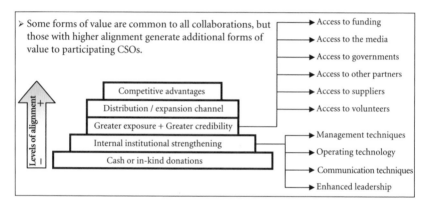

The most general form of benefit for the CSOs in our sample was the reception of cash or in-kind *donations* from the companies involved in collaborations. For example, through its involvement in the School Sponsorship program organized by Nicaragua's American Chamber of Commerce (AMCHAM), the Simón Bolívar Nicaraguan Professional Education Center (*Centro de Formación Profesional Nicaragüense Simón Bolívar*) managed to get the Shell company to donate US$ 7,500, which proved quite valuable to the school in refurbishing its infrastructure. When financial donations were made in the context of collaborations with broader or deeper alignment, their impact tended to be stronger and more enduring. For example, in the already mentioned collaboration between Natura and the Matilde School, cash donations were a significant component. However, they were part of a broader relationship, which also encompassed ongoing assistance and support for the school's process of soul-searching and transformation. Largely, these resources were used to finance this self-assessment process assisted by

CENPEC, the CSO specializing in public education. Consequently, as we have seen at the beginning of the chapter, donations had a deep and lasting impact on the school.

Those CSOs that managed to become partners of their private counterparts enhanced their *institutional capacity*. In the Twenty-First Century Leaders (*Líderes*) program, which brought together Colombian schools and businesses, companies did not transfer any money to schools,[14] only their management knowledge and experience, which generated a series of specific benefits to the schools. When Sofía Ramírez, Rafael Uribe Uribe public school principal, describes the results of her involvement in the program, she says, "One of the first results was *strategic planning*. We teachers understood we could not work in isolation; we had to set institutional goals and design a four-year plan and a shorter-term plan for a year. We had some academic and administrative objectives, and we started working on our mission, vision, values, and principles."

A second related benefit was the development of a habit to define *measurable indicators* to assess management quality, a basic notion in the private sector (*"what you measure is what you get"*) that the third sector and the government usually lack. Ana María de Samper, the Santa María School principal and a participant in the *Líderes* program, admits that "schools had and still have difficulties in evaluating ourselves. We are very keen on academic evaluation, but we find it very hard to use management indicators." The private sector contributed a new perspective. Remembering his interactions with Bogotá's Secretary of Education, Francisco Manrique, CEO and owner of Manrique Santamaría construction company, points out, "We used to insist time and again on measuring. We just had to measure stuff; we would ask them 'where are your management indicators?' Then, they started to gather the information. At first, it was a mess, and they were embarrassed every time we brought it up."

Through their joint work with companies, participating schools adjusted total quality techniques to education and designed new processes. Sofía Ramírez, Rafael Uribe Uribe school principal, recalls that "we used to work a lot, but we never sat down to review our work. Now, any activity—no matter how small—is evaluated. *Participating in Líderes means planning, doing, checking, and redoing things.*"

The schools' association with companies also allowed for the transfer of state-of-the-art *operating technology* to CSOs. By entering into a collaboration with the H-E-B supermarket chain, the Monterrey Food

Bank (BAM) accessed the most advanced food bank management and quality control technologies and practices. It would be safe to say that the collaboration completely reshaped the way in which BAM carried out its mission, strengthening it institutionally. Its operating head, Blanca Castillo, does not hesitate to state that "the history of our Food Bank is divided in two: before and after H-E-B."

CSOs involved in collaborations registering high or medium alignment also learned how to design and execute an effective *communication strategy*. Discussing the benefits drawn from his collaboration with *La Nación* newspaper, Juan Carr, leader of the Solidarity Network (RS), says, "I learned the rationale of communications and everything it implies. Our practical manual on solidarity now includes a last chapter on the topic of communications." Dr. Jorge Rojas, director of the Chilean CSO Assistance Corporation for Burned Children (COANIQUEM), reports that "Guillermo García [Esso Chile's public relations head] has been a key actor in our alliance. I have learned a lot about communication strategy from him."

In some collaborations, CSOs were able to rely on their business partners' leadership to gain *greater capacity to engage other social actors* in support of their mission. Building on the institutional strength accrued from private partners' ongoing support, organizations such as the SES Foundation or COANIQUEM became undisputed national leaders in their field of action, capable of engaging other public or private institutions as equal partners.

Partnerships that were highly exposed over time also provided CSOs with two additional associated benefits: *enhanced visibility* and *public credibility*. The collaboration between Esso Chile and COANIQUEM constitutes an especially rich example of these beneficial effects. As a result of strong and sustained support over a period of two decades, by 2002 COANIQUEM had increased its exposure to the point of ranking as the third most recognized CSO in the country. Dr. Jorge Rojas, COANIQUEM's director, explains, "After we received the first donation from Esso, people stopped seeing us as a bunch of dreamers, and came to regard us as a group of professionals sponsored by a corporation that shared and supported our dream."

In turn, that credibility opened the door to a series of other benefits derived from it. The first was access to other *funding sources*. "After receiving the first donation from Esso, we were in better shape to request a land donation from the city administration," reports Rojas. "When a mayor sees that a corporation such as Esso is willing to support a bold initiative, he dares to get involved as well." The partnership with Esso also enabled COANIQUEM to access the media. As Rojas explains, "Esso helped us build our public image when we were perfect strangers for Chilean society at large." With its new credibility and Esso's supporting influence, COANIQUEM became more influential before *government officials*. Through an intense lobbying campaign at the National Congress and media support, in 1998, COANIQUEM succeeded in getting fireworks banned for private use, which was the first cause of children's burns. Its new exposure also enabled COANIQUEM to reach out for *new partners*. For example, it built a collaboration with *Cristalerías Chile*, a glass industry leader, to recycle glass containers. With the resources generated from this collaboration, COANIQUEM was able to build and operate the "Open House" (*Casa Abierta*), a facility that offered free lodging to burned children and a relative during treatment.

Finally, the exposure warranted by partnerships with private companies enabled CSOs to rely on their partners' contact networks to seek *suppliers* or *volunteers*. For example, the *Fundación Proa*, a contemporary art center located in Buenos Aires that built a collaboration with the Techint Group, takes into consideration its partner's contacts and social networks to plan and organize events. The SES Foundation, led by Alberto Croce, tapped into the supplier network of his partner, *Autopistas del Sol* (AUSOL), as well as its employee list, to recruit volunteers.

Often, when collaborations had a high and sustained profile over time, CSOs could use their business partners' infrastructure as a *distribution* or *expansion channel* to increase their geographical coverage. We have already mentioned that COANIQUEM sold car insurance policies at the gas stations in Esso's network. In its collaboration with Coca-Cola de Argentina, Junior Achievement Argentina also took advantage of its partner's infrastructure to expand its coverage throughout the country. The "Learning Environmental Entrepreneurship" was launched in 1999 at four schools in Buenos Aires. After a few adjustments, the following year, it expanded nationwide to the locations where Coca-Cola had bottling plants. The program reached 15 schools and 900 students in 2000, and 30 schools and 2,520 students the next year.

In a few cases of collaborations featuring deep alignment, CSOs managed to gain *competitive advantages*. In Colombia, Law 100 of 1993 transformed the whole national health social security system, substituting a subsidy offered to hospitals for a demand subsidy to service providers (EPS). Since the new law granted EPS the freedom to determine where to send their patients, hospitals were forced to compete, improving their accounting, billing and stock systems, as well as their service quality standards. In a brief period of time, organizations that had been vertically integrated into a bureaucratic system, had to start acting like social companies. As they were not ready to undergo such a transformation on their own, there was a significant demand for counseling services to assist in the transformation of hospital management.

The Hospital Management Center (CGH), which had been created in 1991, spotted in this development an opportunity to carry out its mission—"to promote and lead health management transformation in order to contribute to overall industry development." However, CGH was not the only organization eager to respond to that demand. On the contrary, in doing so it competed with a series of public, semi-public, and private organizations, such as (a) the Quality Corporation, another mixed corporation, similar to CGH; (b) the San Vicente de Paul Hospital, a hospital in Medellín selling consulting services that also organized a sector congress in the city of Cartagena; and (c) an assortment of private consulting firms, both local and multinational. In this competition, a key asset for CGH was the involvement of all actors in the industry, including business companies, which provided it with a bulk of experience and knowledge hardly replicable by competitors.

Value Created for Communities

In a way, the collaborations in our sample cases would have failed had they only benefited the partners. In the end, all these ventures have a social purpose component, which, by definition, entails reaching out and bettering society. A quick glance at our data reveals that cross-sector collaborations did have a positive impact on their respective communities. By 2001, COANIQUEM had provided free medical treatment to more than 50,000 burned children in Chile. Between 2000 and 2001, the Monterrey Food Bank (BAM) distributed a total of 6,120 tons of food products, benefiting 493,241 people. Between 1997 and 2001, the Friendship Home (CdA) had provided free medical treatment for 419 cancer-afflicted children in Mexico. In all instances, their collaborations constributed significantly to the increased magnitude of these impacts.

Some of these collaborations managed to alter the terms of public debate in their societies. For example, the *Programa Pró-Conselho* (Pro-Council program) was extremely effective in raising the visibility of children's rights in the Brazilian state of Minas Gerais. As we have mentioned before, this program came about by an initiative developed by the Telemig Celular Institute and the many CSOs participating in the Volunteer Support Groups, supported by UNICEF. The number of Municipal Councils for Children's and Youths' Rights, one of the institutions promoted by the program, increased 50 percent. In just 18 months, the program managed to generate half the number of Councils that had been created in the 11 years preceding it.

Also in Brazil, the Itaú-UNICEF Award definitely incorporated the topic of educational quality into the nation's social agenda. In Chile, as we have said before, COANIQUEM's work made the public aware of the dangers associated with the private use of fireworks. Its efforts were rewarded in 1998, when an act of Congress banned its private use on the grounds that it was the first cause of children's burns. In Colombia, the Twenty-First Century Leaders program improved the climate of labor-management relations in the educational sector. In spite of belonging to one of the most combative unions in the country, teachers of participating schools decided to stay out of strikes that they perceived to be harmful to the students' interests. According to Sofía Ramírez, principal of the Rafael Uribe Uribe school,

> It's been three or four years since we last went on strike. It's hard to miss class and ensure quality teaching for students. We are fully autonomous in that; if a teacher here wants to go on strike, it's OK. But here, we respect children's rights. They are the ones strikes affect the most.

Other collaborations provided stability for needy and excluded communities. Through its alliance with the Rainforest Expeditions, the Ese'eja native community managed to change their living conditions substantially. Juan Pesha, a native from the community, says that "We're *being given a chance, an opportunity*, a new working system [tourism]… because these activities are largely new; we had never seen this kind of work before." Becoming part of international tourism circuits implied diversifying the community's sources of income, making it less exposed to the recurrent fluctuations in the price of agricultural commodities. Another community member, Hernán Arrospides, elaborates, "Here you have some security; if you work so many days, you

get so much money. To the contrary, in agriculture, there is no security… you take your products and prices are too low… Then, it means
you worked very hard for almost nothing." Income has become more
stable; it is also higher: salaries at the lodge are 38 percent higher than
the traditional family income generated by hunting and agriculture.
With higher and more stable income, the almost disintegrating community envisioned a new horizon. Arrospides adds, "With the Amazon
Lodge the whole community is fine. Now, kids don't leave after high
school to go to other places… They used to go to Puerto Maldonado
and now they don't anymore, because the contract says the company
has to provide jobs for everyone."

The collaboration between RFE and the Ese'eja native community
also brought about environmental benefits for the Tambopata-Candamo Reservation, in the Peruvian Amazon. The environment is the
classic example of a public good, where the absence of private property
generates a tension between the short-term interest of the individual of
maximizing profits and the long-term social interest in resource preservation. The collaboration did away with the problem of free-riding,
generating market incentives for the community to preserve the environment, since it is the source of the income provided by tourists. At
the same time, tourism and conservationism are positively associated.
As more individuals become employed in tourism-related ventures,
fewer engage in activities that may harm the environment—such as
unregulated hunting or fishing. The community is now aware of the
fact that the lodge's success depends on the reservation's biodiversity,
and, accordingly, it has created wildlife conservation mechanisms.

The already mentioned collaboration in Brazil built around the
Ekos product line[15] has also generated significant social and environmental value in needy areas. The communities involved in this alliance
improved their housing, health, and educational conditions. Additionally, according to its key actors, community members have developed
new habits to protect endangered local species, while their example
generated collaboration ventures at similar communities, outside the
project led by Natura.

Other collaborations made governments more receptive to citizens'
needs and opinions. The partnership between Indupalma and the Rafael Pombo Foundation (FRP) had a strong impact on the San Alberto
County. Partners organized a public hearing, and city officials listened
to local children's requests. After the hearing, the city administration
recognized the need to incorporate children and youth-related issues

into its local development plan. Thus, it created the Youth Municipal Council Committee and invited local youths to participate. According to a FRP official,

> When we called [city officials] to tell them "Indupalma is providing its support; we want to hold a public hearing at San Alberto," they shrunk back and thought "what are they going to do?" They realized the development plan was totally mute on issues relating to children and youths. Then, they confessed, "we are terrified of a public hearing, of children and youth coming and demanding things." We told them, "*No, it's just that we need to start...*"

Another effect from these successful experiences was the prominent display of a proven model to create economic and social value, facilitating the emergence of new collaborations between organizations in the sample with other parties. Several companies involved in the Hospital Management Center (CGH) launched other cross-sector alliances. For example, General Médica decided to get involved in two new collaborations: the "Hospitals and Clinics Association" and the "Health Chamber" at the Industrial National Association. As its president, Orlando Sánchez, explains,

> We have liked the idea [of belonging to the CGH] so much that, later, when the Hospitals and Clinics Association was created, we also joined in as sponsors. We want to learn everything and have them get to know us.

However, the demonstration effect of these successful ventures was not limited to their direct participants. On the contrary, these experiences showed a tested model of collaborative work that was replicated by others, which suggests the strengthening of solidarity as a shared value in these societies. In Argentina, as a result of the high profile attained by RS on account of its collaboration with *La Nación* newspaper, *fourteen* solidarity-based networks replicating its format were created all over the country: in Pilar, Azul, Rauch, Bariloche, Jujuy, Salta, Rosario, Córdoba, Alto Valle, Mar del Plata, Junín, González Chávez, Pergamino and Chascomús. Based on the leading case supplied by the collaboration between the H-E-B supermarket chain and the the Monterrey Food Bank, new food banks were created in the Mexican cities of Saltillo, Matamoros, Reynosa, and Nuevo Laredo. In both cases, emerging organizations were supported by their *alma mater,* though they remained fully independent. These examples suggest a positive externality created by cross-sector partnerships: the multiplier effect in the aggregate endowment of social value, which appears to lower the costs of replicating these ventures.

Key Points to Consider

This chapter explored the dynamics at play when alliances create value and the factors that condition those processes. The centrality of value creation in any cross-sector collaboration makes it imperative that partners should devote a substantial amount of time working on this. Below we offer some guidelines for that analysis.

Any organization—whether it is a business or CSO—should start by asking which of the value dimensions delineated in the final section of the chapter (Figures 9 and 10) are being generated by its collaboration. The key question here should be, *how much* value is this collaboration producing? Is it enough, suitable for my needs and proportional to its costs? If not, is it possible to identify the bottlenecks hindering value generation? Often, as we have seen in our sample cases, small adjustments may have a significant impact on a collaboration's potential to benefit actors.

A way to increase collaboration productivity consists in analyzing the resources being deployed in the venture. We have seen that there are major differences in productivity between partnerships using generic resources and those contributing their own key resources, or creating value through combining key resources. The task is to identify the kind of resources currently transferred in this collaboration and to explore the possibility of upgrading them. Does your organization have key resources that may be leveraged to generate more value to the alliance? Does the other partner have key resources that could be combined with your own in an original fashion to generate a new resource source?

The second question should be: which of the potential value dimensions specified in the figures *are not present* in this collaboration? This will lead to analyzing how to *broaden* the partnership. Are there any dimensions that were not obvious at the beginning of the collaboration that could generate new value dimensions, thus enriching it?

Partners should also focus their attention on the value flow, and especially to the notion of the *virtuous circle* of value creation. Is that dynamic present in this collaboration? If not, the key question will be, "How can my organization generate more value for my partner in order to trigger the process?" The next question should be, "Is my value proposition still fresh and relevant?" If an organization discovers that there is a mismatch between what it produces and what its partner needs, it should work on renewing its value proposition by taking a new, candid look at its partner's needs. What are your partner's needs and how could your organization cater to them? Finally, value renewal will require partners to think strategically about the future and work proactively. Has my past source of value depreciated? What will be your partner's *future needs* and how can your organization get ready to serve them?

Notes

1   James E. Austin, *The Collaboration Challenge: How Nonprofits and Businesses Succeed through Strategic Alliances*, 1st ed. (San Francisco: Jossey-Bass Publishers, 2000).

2   Michael E. Porter and Mark R. Kramer, "The Competitive Advantage of Corporate Philanthropy," *Harvard Business Review* 80, no. 12 (2002): 56.

3   In this group, there were also cases featuring narrow but very deep alignment, and others with a broad, though not very deep, connection on all three dimensions.

4   "The Dynamic Construction of Alignment," p. 93.

5   This case is discussed under the heading "Competitive Pressures" (p. 102), and analyzed in depth in Chapter 11: "Mexico: The Business Sense of Cross-Sector Alliances" (p. 311).

6   Reference to p. 94, where those are discussed in detail.

7   The expert was Sandra Velasco, who had worked at the Quality Corporation as an ISO internal auditor. At the same time, she had also served as juror and evaluator for the National Quality Award and the Educational Excellence Prize sponsored by the Colombian Education Secretary.

8   For example, services provided by a single professional may belong to either category, depending on the circumstances.

9   Refer to p. 47.

10 See "Value Created for Companies" (p. 132.)

11 A brief summary of that relationship was offered in Chapter 1 (p. 9). For a more in-depth description readers may consult the discussions under the headings "Individuals" (p. 58), and "Cross Fertilization" (p. 94).

12 James E. Austin and Cate Reavis, "Starbucks and Conservation International," HBS Case No. 9-303-055 (Boston: Harvard Business School Publishing, 1996).

13 Refer to p. 35.

14 The exception was *Meals de Colombia*, which paid for coordination and management costs since it led the program. However, those funds were not transferred to the schools either; they were program transaction and governance costs.

15 The alliance structured around the Ekos line was discussed in pp. 40 and 82. It is also the subject of an in-depth analysis in Chapter 7.

5

Alliance Management

James Austin, Ezequiel Reficco, and SEKN Research Team

Collaborations are built on a daily basis, through joint work. The way in which partners go about organizing their joint assignments has a direct impact on alliances' capability to yield results. Previous chapters have shown that cross-sector collaborations have the potential to generate benefits for participating organizations and society. Yet, the greater the potential for value creation, the more complex alliance management will prove. Therefore, the challenges involved in successfully managing a cross-sector partnership call for a thorough analysis. This chapter draws lessons on collaboration management from the experiences analyzed in our sample of Latin American alliances. We will start by considering the importance of focused attention on collaborations, and then move on to the advantages of institutionalizing them. Next, we will talk about the role of communications in collaborations and the different resources for building trust among partners. Our analysis will close with a discussion on the role of collaborations as learning tools.

Focused Attention

Collaborations will hardly become a growth driver for participating organizations if partners assume it can develop on *automatic pilot*. Focused attention on the part of leaders capable of making decisions, allocating resources, and committing their organizations to the partnership, is a vital input for its successful management. At the Colombian Hospital Management Center (*Centro de Gestión Hospitalaria,* hence CGH), for example, as explained by its managing director, Patricia Gómez, "everyone who sits on the board is CEO of his or her organization. Nobody sends a second or third-rank executive to the CGH. Businessmen commit to it as if this was their most important project, and they will devote all their time to discuss how to help the CGH face the challenges that lie ahead." This investment of time and energy guarantees that the partnership remains strategically relevant for all parties.

The management of the alliance is also facilitated when its daily operations are clearly defined and assigned to specific individuals in each organization. As cross-sector alliances deepen and grow more complex, it may be necessary to turn collaboration management into a core responsibility for some individuals, and in some cases, even a full-time job. A key success factor in the management of the partnership between *Farmacias Ahumada S.A.* (FASA), a Chilean drugstore chain, and the *Fundación Las Rosas* (FLR) was the fact that the latter had an executive especially assigned to the task: Felipe Morán. Assigning the collaboration management to specific individuals makes communications consistent and smooth, and promotes a constant search for improvement opportunities. "We have to devote some time to thinking and discussing how to improve the collaboration for both parties," explained Morán.

Until 1995, the collaboration between the Natura company and Matilde Maria Cremm public school was handled by the company's executive board, including Luiz Seabra, founding president, Guilherme Leal, executive president, and Pedro Passos, operations president. Although the board's support of the partnership had started to prove fruitful, Leal realized that the intensity of the collaboration demanded a time commitment that the board would not be able to sustain for long. "Who will ensure continuity for the quality improvements our partner has begun to experience?" he wondered. The answer came with the creation of the social enterprise area within the company, led by Angela Serino, exclusively in charge of the company's social endeavors. Serino's appointment and the excellent working relation she quickly developed with Maria da Graça Fernandes Branco, the school principal, galvanized the collaboration.

As collaborations move along the Collaboration Continuum stages, alliance management grows more complex. Eventually, partners may consider establishing joint management structures. For example, the partnership between the newspaper *La Nación* and the Solidarity Network (*La Red Solidaria*, hence RS) started out in a philanthropic stage, in which the newspaper donated sporadically advertising space to the network. Then, the collaboration moved on to a transactional phase, in which RS became a fluent provider of material for different publication sections. However, with the launching of the *solidarity classified ads*—a joint product—the alliance entered an integrative stage that required the creation of a common management structure.

The Amazon Lodge (*Posada Amazonas*) case provides perhaps the best example of a sophisticated integrative management structure, the result of the collaboration between the Ese'eja Native Community and the eco-tourism firm Rainforest Expeditions. Here the Management Committee (MC), made up of five representatives from each party, served as an efficient channel for community representation vis-à-vis the company, which was in charge of the lodge's daily management. At the MC, partners jointly defined the strategy for *Posada Amazonas* and made key decisions, such as capital investments, loan payments, and personnel management.

In principle, there are good reasons to put the day-to-day management of the collaboration in the hands of each organization's own human resources. In the previous chapter, we saw that parties may accrue substantial benefits when its internal stakeholders connect personally with the partnership. Still, some companies in our sample opted for outsourcing this task. We have already mentioned the case of Coca-Cola de Argentina (CCA) in its partnership with Junior Achievement Argentina (JAA), in which the company turned over its collaboration management to a private consultant firm experienced in public relations.

To a great extent, this option may be explained in terms of economies of scale and specialization. When the scale of an organization's social portfolio does not warrant having in-house specialized human resources, some companies hand over daily management of their social initiatives but retain control of their general strategy and critical decisions. At the same time, outsourcing might be more appealing for companies in which, on account of their industries, internal stakeholders do not hold a prominent weight. CCA's business is franchising: it only manages a brand and its image, since the real product is handled by bottling plants and distributors. Therefore, the company mainly focuses on connecting strongly with its external stakeholders. Service providers, on the contrary, as we have seen in the cases of FASA, the Chilean drugstore chain, or the Argentine road building firm AUSOL, will have powerful incentives to boost internal stakeholders' motivations and identification, since a good part of their productivity will stem from those factors.

Given that effective collaboration management requires significant investments of time and attention from top leaders, and considering these resources are scarce, there are also good reasons to restrict the number of collaborations in which an organization participates. Several of our sample alliances received a disproportionate amount of resources and attention from their participants. For example, *La Nación* newspaper developed several collaborations with other CSOs, but none of them matched the commitment, continuity, and intensity achieved by its alliance with RS. Developing a single, sound alliance that can manage ten projects, instead of managing ten projects through ten different partnerships, will generate internal economies of scale. Externally, concentrating efforts in a single area, where the organization has key resources that could make a difference, will tend to maximize impact.

At the same time, focusing the execution of all social initiatives in a single partner may entail risks. For example, H-E-B International Supermarkets (HEB) only channels its damaged goods systematically through the Monterrey Food Bank (*Banco de Alimentos de Monterrey*, hence BAM). If we bear in mind that HEB has also made substantial investments in training and equipping its partner, we might think that the collaboration creates a vulnerable spot for the company. However, BAM is also highly exposed to HEB, a fact that does not worry Blanca Castillo, BAM director. "What we have in mind is for HEB to continue being our main donor, not only through cash donations, but also through in-kind contributions to our food bank." When dependence is mutual, it becomes interdependence, and it is thus neutralized. Moreover, as we explained in Chapter 4, as long as a partnership creates value for its partners, there will be few incentives to withdraw from it.

Institutionalization

Cross-sector partnerships are born from leaders, but they grow and consolidate through institutions. Collaborations will be sound if they are deeply ingrained in institutionally solid and stable partners. Achieving that ideal state may demand efforts to institutionalize the partnership within organizations themselves and their stakeholders, to contribute to partners' institutionalization, or to reproduce or replicate collaborations.

Institutionalization within Organizations Themselves and Their Stakeholders

Although individual mentorship may prove beneficial for partnerships, it is also desirable that, at some point, collaborations exceed them. When collaborations are overly associated with specific individuals, the risk of discontinuity increases. The previous chapter broached the collaboration case between a Chilean company *Empresas Ariztía* and the Melipilla Municipal Corporation (*Corporación Municipal de Melipilla,* hence CMM), an autonomous organization. As a result of the deep commitment of the company president, Manuel Ariztía, the collaboration between *Empresas Ariztía* and CMM has lasted over two decades. However, management is uncertain as to what will happen with the collaboration upon Ariztía's retirement, since the leader's passion and enthusiasm do not seem to have stretched to other company executives, although Don Manuel's son has indicated willingness to follow in his father's footsteps.

Even if organization leaders are deeply committed to collaborations, partnerships will not reach their full potential if commitment does not permeate the whole organizational pyramid. The challenge will thus lie in incorporating collaboration to real organizational cultures, so that their members do not consider it as something temporary that happened to land on their leaders' desks. Yet, this will not always be easy: the following examples show how surveyed organizations set about achieving this purpose. For example, Enrique Mendoza, FASA operations director, considers it vital for management to send out *clear signals* to its staff about the importance they assign to collaborations:

> If management is deeply committed to the alliance, subordinates at the drugstores receive the signals, and they make it a priority. This happens at all levels. When the marketing assistant manager sees that the general manager asks him why there was no mention of the alliance with the FLR in the periodical bargain offer catalogue, he will realize that his boss is concerned with the issue and he will bear it in mind for the next catalogue. For an alliance to perform successfully, top management should convey clear messages.

Thus, when visiting the drugstores with the general manager, Mendoza not only asked "how are margins doing?" or "what products do you need?" but also *"how's the FLR doing?"*

> At first, drugstore managers would answer "I don't know," but soon word got around and suddenly all of them knew how

much the monthly collection of donations had been, how much they had raised the previous day, which salesperson collected more...

In this regard, perhaps the most powerful and clear signal a company may send out to its human resources is *integrating into its incentive structure* the consideration of individuals' performance in and commitment to the collaboration. In the previous chapter, we pointed out that Mendoza had decided to incorporate fund-raising to the criteria used for evaluating supervisors' performance, thus increasing results and highlighting the importance of the alliance among employees. Another good example is the *Meals de Colombia* case, that integrated Twenty-first Century Leaders (*Líderes Siglo XXI,* hence *Líderes*) project management to its organizational chart, as an area of its human resources and quality department. Adriana Hoyos, area manager, explained,

> Once we entered the Leaders' Program, my job description was reviewed, and I now have a key performance area called "community contribution." It is weighed into my work plan and rated every three months. My performance indicators are recruiting, personnel development, something we call "insight process," employee satisfaction, total quality, community contributions, and personnel production.

Efforts to institutionalize collaborations through incentives may also encompass external stakeholders. When Manuel Ariztía joined the above mentioned CMM, he realized that alliance efforts to improve education would not prosper without teachers' active commitment. Therefore, he insisted in creating a set of incentives targeted at them, which included annual bonuses related to improvements in key indicators, premiums for teachers who sent their children to schools managed by the CMM, for those whose sons or daughters graduated from schools in Melipilla and were accepted in higher education institutions, and for those who showed perfect attendance to work, among others. In time, those incentives yielded results. According to Ariztía, "*Teachers learned to trust the CMM.* They also developed a sense of belonging and ownership as regards the system, and they realized their efforts could produce an impact." Ariztía also tried to incorporate parents to the new operational culture under way at the Melipilla educational system. In his opinion, "Schools can't generate results without active parent involvement." To discourage school desertion, he convinced the CMM to reward parents whose children never missed a day at school and got the best grades.

Another effective step was to *walk your talk*. Initial efforts by the Argentine road building company AUSOL to institutionalize its relation with the SES Foundation did not work out as expected. Internal communication activities were unable to permeate the company culture or shake off the inertia of an organization unfamiliar with social involvement. "We held information meetings and invitations to participate and to learn how we were doing were not enough," recalls Alejandra Barczuk, communications and customer services manager,

> At that time [the company CEO, Luis] Freixas resorted to "asking"—or "forcing," to put it right—the 14 operation area managers in the company to get involved. We came up with the mentor idea. Freixas considered it a good starting point. At a given time, managers heading those groups started getting more personally involved, and that proved useful. We kept on channeling information as we had always done. *The difference was that now, instead of reading a report in a meeting, they described their own experiences.*

A first result of these efforts will be when collaborations manage to overcome what a Bayer executive once called the "oh, yes…I've heard something about it" category.[1] Still, a second stage in collaboration institutionalization should aim at getting *each company department to think how the alliance can contribute to its work*, and vice versa. In the case of Techint, several of the Group's areas became involved with the *Fundación Proa*. For example, the human resources area often engages in culture-related activities, and they usually resort to Proa for advice.

Institutional Development of Partners

Working to institutionalize collaborations within organizations themselves and their stakeholders may not be enough. In some of the sample alliances, a participating actor concluded that resources had to be invested to build institutionally its partner. When a cross-sector alliance becomes embedded in the company DNA, and all of its departments come to be connected with it, the collaboration can generate demands that the partner may not be ready to serve. For example, a company fueled by a successful collaboration may seek to expand its breadth to gain access to new stakeholders, only to discover that its partner lacks the necessary institutional capability to do so.

That was the case of the road building company AUSOL, which as we saw earlier, initially approached community leader Alberto Croce to handle a potentially explosive social situation.[2] However, once the objective was achieved, company commitment did not dwindle, but rather, it increased. After five years of joint work, AUSOL strongly committed to help Croce create the SES, devoted to fighting social exclusion through informal education.

The rich and dynamic evolution of the association between AUSOL and Croce, can be seen as a process in which AUSOL expanded the realm of its collaboration, in order to encompass new stakeholders as beneficiaries of the value being created. From a legalistic approach in 1994, which only served its *shareholders'* interests, AUSOL shifted to a negotiation approach that incorporated *neighboring communities'* interests in 1996. Finally, by institutionalizing its social involvement through the SES Foundation in 1999, it went on to include its *employees*, its *clients*—indirectly benefiting from a better service—and other sectors of the *community at large,* since its social activities expanded both in content and in geographical coverage. Thus, AUSOL's investment in institutionalizing its partner cleared a bottleneck brought about by the limitations implicit in a value creation process that to a large extent relied on a single individual.

We have already mentioned that during almost two decades, the H-E-B supermarket chain had entered alliances with food banks in the United States on the basis of its owners' deep convictions and links with its core strategy. In the mid 1990s, when the company decided to venture out of the United States and into the northern Mexico, it also took along its culture of strategic alliances with food banks. Upon its arrival in Monterrey, it encountered a professional and enthusiastic organization, which at the same time was somewhat lacking in technical standards and institutional capability. Far from being put off, the company committed to helping its partner overcome that capability gap. Eddie García, the executive in charge of collaborations with food banks at Texas headquarters, informed its future partners that the company would not restrict its assistance to quick fixes. HEB intended to collaborate in the creation of a food bank with a capacity to serve the whole northern Mexico region in 15 or 20 years' time. Living up to such an ambitious objective involved substantial transfers of technology, equipment, and management techniques, which were elaborated on in previous chapters.

Expanding the Collaboration?

Sometimes, the institutional development of partners and/or strengthening collaborations may imply taking in third parties, or else replicating similar associations between partners and other companies. Both alternatives may help scale up, reduce costs, or increase the impact of the program. Javier Comesaña, *La Nación* organizational development director, reports that "we have tried to connect the Solidarity Network (RS) to our competitors because, that way, they will have more chances to communicate what the organization is doing." Thus, in 2001, the RS carried out a nationwide high-profile campaign with the *Clarín* newspaper, a direct competitor of *La Nación*.

This course of action was considered by several of the organizations surveyed. The previous chapters mentioned the cases of *Meals de Colombia* and *Autopistas del Sol*, and how both of them went to great lengths to include other companies in their collaborations, so as to strengthen and institutionalize them. However, in both cases, those efforts did not prove wholly successful on account of the intimate association between the companies' brands and the collaboration in the public eye. A similar approach prevailed in the case of Bimbo Mexico; referring to its collaboration with the Papalote Children's Museum, Martha Eugenia Hernández, Bimbo institutional relations director, pointed out, "the more companies that partner with the museum and contribute, the better for them. Bimbo does not feel affected by that."

However, that open and candid attitude had its limits: in establishing its partnership with Papalote, Bimbo clearly stated that the Museum was not to enter an alliance with a direct competitor of Bimbo. The same happened in the collaboration between Coca-Cola de Argentina and Junior Achievement Argentina, developed through the Learning Environmental Entrepreneurship program (*Aprender a Emprender en el Medio Ambiente*, hence AEMA). María Marta Llosa, public relations director, explained: "I would love for Coca-Cola to implement the AEMA worldwide, but *I wouldn't like for a competitor to do it*." The difference in attitude between these two cases and *La Nación*'s can be understood if we bear in mind the different motivations that drove the companies to collaborations. While in Bimbo and Coca-Cola's cases cross-sector partnerships had a strong competitive dimension, the newspaper's motivation was more philanthropic than utilitarian.

Alliances may expand through the inclusion of a partner for a limited time, or on a limited role, if these command a key capability to contribute to alliance objectives. For example, in the collaboration between the Brazilian cosmetic company Natura and Matilde public school, the partners summoned the educational specialist CENPEC to join them for a couple of months in their efforts to change school culture and align it to collaboration objectives. In the partnership between the television company *Representaciones Televisivas* (REPRE-TEL) and the *Fundación Promotora para la Vivienda* (FUPROVI), a Costa Rican CSO, both partners called in Mutual Heredia. As mentioned in Chapter 3, the purpose of this collaboration was to provide homes for the victims of Hurricane César that had devastated Costa Rica in July 1996. Whereas REPRETEL and FUPROVI were the most visible alliance partners, Mutual Heredia played the more restricted but nonetheless important role of collecting cash donations.

In spite of its potential advantages, expanding the alliance may not be risk-free. Consider the collaboration between the Telemig Celular Institute, social arm of the Brazilian mobile telephone company Telemig Celular, and the Volunteer Support Groups. As explained earlier, the alliance aimed at the creation and strengthening of Councils, municipal institutions that guaranteed the enforcement of children's rights and designed public policies to protect them. In order to achieve that objective, in 2001, the company invested resources to reinforce the institutional capability of its partners by means of training programs. Although the collaboration succeeded in fulfilling its objectives, by year end, partners were considering the possibility of further strengthening it through the incorporation of the office of the Justice Attorney General.

The reasons for this incorporation were powerful, since the Justice Attorney General was the Minas Gerais state agency in charge of Councils' creation and development, the very same objective pursued by the alliance. At the same time, the decision entailed substantial risks. Telemig Celular's senior management, represented in the board of the Telemig Celular Institute, was very concerned with the potential consequences to its corporate image that such an association with a public sector agency could bring about. In their view, alliances with the public sector were perceived as being more complex and having less chance of success. In particular, the company feared that the new incorporation became a *Trojan horse*, introducing partisan or ideological dynamics into the collaboration, and slowing down decision-making. By the time this study was completed, the emerging consensus was that if the idea were to prosper, it should be implemented coupled with built-in guarantees, aimed at managing those risks. It is important to ensure that an expansion originally meant to strengthen a partnership, does not end up having the paradoxical effect of weakening it.

Another possible risk emerges from the comparison between Twenty-first Century Leaders (*Líderes*) initiative in Colombia and the school sponsorship program carried out by Nicaragua's American Chamber of Commerce (*Cámara de Comercio Americana de Nicaragua*, hence AMCHAM) with the support of Nicaragua's Ministry of Education, Culture and Sports (*Ministerio de Educación, Cultura y Deportes de Nicaragua*, hence MECD). Both initiatives were launched by chambers of commerce—Bogotá Chamber of Commerce Presidents' Forum (*Foro de Presidentes de la Cámara de Comercio de Bogotá*), and AMCHAM—to contribute to the betterment of education in their respective communities. The Presidents' Forum had worked on the creation of intellectual capital around the strengths of the Total Quality management approach, and sought to adapt those techniques to education. To that purpose, it partnered with CSOs that had devoted themselves to the same field, such as the U.S.-based Koalaty Kid, or the Brazilian organizations Pitágoras and Christiano Ottoni. Joint activities carried out with these CSOs broadened the leaders' vision and influenced its later work with schools.

The AMCHAM-led initiative, instead, did not engage the third sector. Early on, AMCHAM Education Committee had explored the possibility of working with a local CSO called the Nicaraguan Education Forum "Let's Educate" (*Foro Educativo Nicaragüense "Eduquemos,"* hence "Let's Educate"), whose mission was to "facilitate the involvement of the business community and civil society in the betterment of the quality, equity, efficiency and relevance of education in Nicaragua…" However, when the time came to launch the initiative, "Let's Educate" was left aside. Businessmen insisted on "getting down to work" immediately, with a minimal paperwork to reduce bureaucratic proceedings, since "children and education couldn't wait." Thus, the decision was to work directly with the Ministry, without "Let's Educate" participation. This exclusion generated an implicit diagnosis that was never subject to public discussion: "The main problem at schools is financial." Without disregarding the obvious importance of financial resources, the absence of the third sector's specialized knowledge, by default drove money to the heart of the collaboration between schools and companies. As a consequence, most sponsorships inadvertently left out other dimensions of schools' problems, which companies could have contributed to alleviate, maybe even with lower budgetary costs, such as through management assistance as was done through corporate *Líderes* alliance in Colombia.

Communication

The notion of collaboration assumes that of communication, since it is obvious that one cannot exist without the other. Our main interest lies in examining how communication operates as a vehicle to generate and capture several different value dimensions in a collaboration. Successful collaborations require effective communication at each segment of their value chain, during their whole life span. Communicating is at the heart of the institutionalization process recently discussed, and is also fundamental in the trust-building process that, as we will later see, is a *sine qua non* in any collaboration venture.

Those contemplating entering a cross-sector collaboration should strive to achieve an effective communication with their partners, within their organizations, and with their environment. Next, we will elaborate on each of those dimensions.

Communication between Partners

A stable and fluid flow of communications between organizations is central to any successful partnership, and its significance increases as organizations move along the Collaboration Continuum and their relationship grows in complexity. Communication requirements are relatively low in traditional philanthropic cases: for example, in the above mentioned AMCHAM-led experience, schools were the last to find out about their involvement in the program. Each company, together with the Nicaraguan MECD, unilaterally chose which institution to support. Educational centers had no say in the selection of their sponsors, and it usually came as a surprise when they learned that a company had selected them. Once the initial contact was established, the school role was restricted to "informing the company of its needs," so that the sponsor could evaluate how to contribute within its possibilities.

High-impact philanthropy, which entails a higher level of commitment, places higher communication demands on partners. For example, in the recently mentioned *Líderes* program, businessmen started by carrying out a meticulous and systematic campaign to elicit the support of school principals. One of its main actors described it as a real "preaching mission." Once the initial obstacles to communication—which were dealt with in Chapter 2—were overcome, each working group set a routine of frequent meetings.

When collaborations enter the transactional stage, communication becomes crucial. Collaborations grow stronger when parties clearly communicate what they expect to receive and what they are in a position to offer. In the collaboration between Esso Chile and the Assistance Corporation for Burned Children for instance, protagonists consider that one of the key success factors was clearly enunciated mutual expectations and the precise definition of the products to be generated by the alliance and the benefits to be generated and distributed. Fluent communication facilitates sorting out misunderstandings or misperceptions that may arise, especially when collaborations grow very rapidly, thus forcing parties to continually readjust.

The partnership between Coca-Cola de Argentina (CCA) and Junior Achievement Argentina (JAA) provides a good example of it. Both organizations had developed in the early 1990s a traditional philanthropic relationship. On the surface, CCA seemed to be satisfied with the partnership until, one day, its partner suddenly found out it was not so. Paula Bullrich, JAA director of primary school programs, reported:

> You have to listen candidly to your sponsor to learn that, despite what you might have thought, it is not being fully satisfied. At the first meeting where we found out that JAA was not living up to Coca-Cola's expectations and interests, we were shocked. That's why at the second meeting we focused on how to move on together.

As a result of this awareness, the collaboration grew to new heights and produced the already mentioned "Learning Environmental Entrepreneurship" (AEMA) program. To implement it, parties set down formal communication mechanisms that included periodical evaluation reports and regular monitoring meetings to discuss those reports. As the program expanded its geographical coverage, its day-to-day management grew in complexity and incorporated new layers of interaction, such as communication and public relations professionals in both organizations. But in spite of these preventive measures, fast program growth kept on imposing new challenges to communication, with contrasting interpretations on issues that had not been present in the initial agenda, all of which required constant communication to integrate criteria. Solange Coquet, AEMA coordinator for JAA, explained,

> With the expansion to the provinces, the alliance grew in all dimensions: it covered more courses, larger geographical areas, and rendered the close working relationship between the JAA and the CAA even more intense. The program was developed, but *nobody ever mentioned how it was to be communicated* or what part each organization should play in that communication process.

We come back to these challenges below, where we discuss the need to communicate effectively to audiences outside the alliance.

Internal Communication

Communicating effectively within the organization itself helps to consolidate the collaboration, as it permeates the company organizational culture and becomes institutionalized. At the same time, an internal communication policy sustained over time becomes the channel to capture several of the value dimensions discussed in the final part of the previous chapter. For example, Techint Group has used its Intranet to disseminate throughout the Group its collaboration with the *Fundación Proa* (Proa). Company managers report that through "Techint Today", a communication and information portal distributed through their intranet, the entire Group learns about the activities carried out by Proa. If all different departments of a company are not informed about the development of the collaboration on a regular basis, they will hardly come to see how it relates to their specific area, and how they can serve each other.

Ineffective communication can block value creation. The dilemma faced by the Brazilian Itaú Bank in 2002[3] supplies a clear example. Opinion surveys had revealed that the bank's social initiatives had an extremely low exposure and that bank officials only had a very basic knowledge of them, despite the substantial investments Itaú had made in previous years. It was clear that these activities were poorly and ineffectively communicated beyond that occuring through interpersonal relationships. To avoid jeopardizing its brand credibility—which the organization had worked so hard to build—and alienating its partner, CENPEC, the bank was reluctant to give more visibility to its social initiatives. However, at the same time, management learned that *not having a determined communication policy implied giving up a powerful motivation source for its human resources:* surveys had also shown that the few employees acquainted with the bank's social policy were actually proud of it and wished these actions would become public.

External Communication

Effective external communication is the vehicle to capitalize on the several value dimensions mentioned at the end of the previous chapter. Both companies and CSOs require exposure, reputation, and brand recognition. However, communication is even more important for the CSOs; since usually their funding is not provided by the direct recipients of their services, an effective communication of their activities to current and potential donors is vital for their survival.[4]

At the same time, public recognition constitutes a powerful tool for CSOs. Companies always value positive public exposure, and CSOs can provide them a *quality* of exposure that all of their money cannot buy: the one backed by civil society credibility. Properly used, external communication may become a key instrument in collaboration management, keeping it active and creating incentives for its renewal. The Friendship Home (*Casa de la Amistad*, hence CdA) experience illustrates this point.

In 1997, the CdA entered a collaboration with Danone Mexico that was implemented through annual cause related marketing campaigns. At the end of the 2001 edition, the CSO procured—without the company knowing—an advertising space donation in one of Mexico City most important avenues (the *Periférico*), where millions of people pass by every day. In that space, the CdA placed a huge ad publicly thanking Danone for having collaborated with its cause. The gesture strongly impacted its partner. In this respect, Aminta Ocampo, Danone public relations manager, commented, "I think there has never been anything like that on the Periférico before. People remember the campaign every time they see it. No other institution advertises like that!"

COANIQUEM's experience also shows how public recognition may produce a deep impact on the partner. The collaboration between COANIQUEM and Esso Chile had started out with a specific donation for the building of a burn treatment unit at the Roberto del Río Hospital. But COANIQUEM director, Dr. Jorge Rojas, harbored more ambitious plans. "When hospital refurbishing was over, we invited Ralph Gassman, Esso president, to the inauguration," recalled Rojas.

> We wanted to impress him, because we needed Esso's support to our cause. After all, it was the only donor in sight! We organized a cocktail party and we invited public health officials and the media. And then we seized the opportunity to present our dream project: the plans for the building of a new assistance center for burned children. Ralph Gassman welcomed the idea and said that Esso would maintain its support. And so it did, very loyally, for the next twenty years...

To Communicate or Not to Communicate?

Companies viewed external communication through two different prisms. On the one hand, some companies attached great importance to the external communication of collaboration results; for the most part, these were multinational corporations and/or companies that aligned collaborations to their marketing needs, as was the case of Coca-Cola de Argentina (CCA). In fact, external communications were so important in those collaborations that they became a source of tension between partners. For example, the first AEMA brochure printed by Junior Achievement Argentina (JAA) was never used. Its text defined it as "a program *supported* by CCA, and *developed* by JAA." "After a long debate," recalled Solange Coquet, AEMA coordinator for JAA, "we settled on 'a program *jointly developed by* CCA and JAA.'"

Interestingly enough, the first radio spot prepared by CCA did not mention JAA either,[5] and could not be used. The latter's complaints forced CCA to rewrite the spot script to include its partner. Geraldine Campbell, CCA public affairs manager, remembered:

> There was a lot of internal discussion at CCA. The issue raised opposing positions. Some said it was our advertising; we were paying for it. It was a long argument. Several of us thought that JAA often did not mention CCA. Actually, it mentioned us as *sponsors*, and we didn't feel like *sponsors*. It was not just that we had given them money and forgot about the whole thing. That would have been *sponsorship*. AEMA had been the result of joint work, of joint concern.

On the other hand, a second group of companies in our sample, mainly made up of family-owned businesses, was reluctant to publicize their collaborations. Underlying that decision was the intention to clearly signal that their social involvement was not linked to their marketing needs. In explaining his position in this regard, Manuel Ariztía, owner and CEO of *Empresas Ariztía*, resorted to a gospel passage stating that charitable deeds should not be made public: "So when you give to the needy, do not announce it with trumpets, ... do not let your left hand know what your right hand is doing, so that your giving may be in secret." (Matthew 6:1–4). The same verse was used as metaphor by managers of other important family companies, such as Bimbo and the Investment and Credit Bank (*Banco de Crédito e Inversiones*, hence BCI), to illustrate owners' reluctance to communicate their social activities to the general public. However, in these last two cases, that policy was reviewed. Carmen Achondo, director of the Corporation for Children's Credit (*Corporación de Crédito al Menor*, hence CCM), BCI's third sector partner, declared,

> It's been hard work convincing Luis Enrique [Yarur, BCI owner] of the importance of exposing the collaboration, because if we hide it, how will we motivate others to replicate the experience? He firmly believes that the right hand should not know what the left hand is doing, but we are bringing him around... This may be a first step leading to many other events to raise funds and create awareness in the public and other companies as to the possibility of responsibly assuming from the business sector the challenge of overcoming social problems.

Chapter 3 mentioned the cases of Bimbo and Itaú,[6] both family-owned companies which were forced to review this position as a result of competitive pressures exerted by multinational corporations. In the first case, a significant shift in communication policy conveyed a higher profile to the collaboration; in the second, the bank opted for a gradual and cautious change in its external communication policy.

External Communication Risks

Philanthropic collaborations feature low communication needs because the association between the partners' brands in the public eye is superficial and brief. Therefore, it is not surprising that businessmen participating in the school sponsorship program sponsored by

Nicaragua's AMCHAM systematically pointed out that the initiative entailed no risks to their companies' image. However, as collaboration intensifies and the association of both brands becomes more intimate, ensuing risks will be higher. A recent case study shows how the lack of transparency in external communication in a cross-sector collaboration backfired, damaging the participating company's brand image.[7]

In our sample case that extreme did not materialize, although the case of *Representaciones Televisivas* (REPRETEL) and the *Fundación Promotora para la Vivienda* (FUPROVI) provides a good example of the difficulties that may arise in handling the partnership's external communication. As we have mentioned, in 1996, the television company REPRETEL engaged in an alliance with FUPROVI to provide housing to Hurricane César victims in Costa Rica. After weeks of hard work, the campaign came to an end, having successfully achieved its objectives. "In my opinion as well as the board's, it was a successful campaign," stated Federico Zamora, REPRETEL corporate sales representative.

With the campaign's work completed, all that remained was to stage a grand closing event, to celebrate and generate the image impact both partners had sought. What could be better to accomplish that goal than inviting to the closing event the nation's president, José María Figueres Olsen? Such a presence, it was thought, would undoubtedly enhance the event's visibility and impact. At first sight, it seemed that risks had been left behind, and all there was left to do was the reaping of benefits. But things did not turn out that way. The presence of the president eclipsed the work of both the OSC and the private companies, and "families ended up thanking the government instead of the campaign promoters," according to Carmen González, FUPROVI development manager and project director. In spite of the campaign's success *in itself*, an external communication difficulty deprived one participant of the expected benefits it had set out to obtain, and the campaign was not repeated. Other factors seem to have intervened in that decision, too; however, in the view of González, the impact of the closing event fiasco was not trivial. "I think REPRETEL saw that and didn't like it at all," she speculated in retrospect.

Therefore, it does not come as a surprise that, as a general rule, companies took steps to control collaborations' external communications, and particularly, brand use. "To protect and increase brand value," Jaime Augusto Chaves, Brazilian Itaú Bank's strategic manager, pointed out, "we need to have a permanent and strong control on our partners and the bank's social projects. It's the only way we can guarantee that our brand will live up to its promises."

The collaboration between Bimbo Group and the Papalote Children's in Mexico City exhibits an interesting example of how surveyed organizations attempted to keep control of external communications. The company allowed the museum to use its brand in Papalote's public relations, but had its marketing personnel closely monitor that use by means of an internal media center that allowed them to check how the brand was presented in television, radio, or the printed media. Also, brand managers kept in close contact with the museum during all exhibits or events in which the Group's brands were displayed to the public.

Finally, both potential benefits and risks for participants' brands increase even more in the integrative stage, in which organizations develop an almost symbiotic relationship, with whole segments of the value chain controlled by partners. For example, the eco-tourism firm Rainforest Expeditions, associated with the Peruvian Amazon Ese'eja community and responsible for running the Amazonas eco-lodge, has had to deal with problems in its partner that could potentially undermine the joint venture's reputation, such as community employees' absenteeism or alcoholism.

The collaboration between the Brazilian company Natura and traditional communities, aimed at manufacturing the Ekos product line,[8] constitutes another excellent example. Company commitment to this alliance is almost at a point of no return, on account of the considerable investment made in educational and technical training for the associated communities. Despite the high stakes, external stakeholders command vital parts of Ekos' production chain, over whom the company does not exercise any direct control. If one of the partnering communities producing a key and hardly replicable ingredient decided to defect from the collaboration and sell the product to a competitor, the Ekos brand would lose a good portion of its value. Even the work of the OSC Imaflora, whose participation in the scheme was limited to certification activities, is critical to the company's image. If that ONG failed to comply with its oversight responsibilities, the Ekos brand and, by extension, Natura's, could be seriously damaged.

Trust Building

Trust is an intangible asset essential in cross-sector collaborations; without trust, parties would be unable to effectively explore, discover, and seize value creation opportunities, and the relationship would become stagnant. As we have seen, effective communication contributes to trust building, but the process may involve additional factors. Next, we will distill some lessons from the experience accumulated in our sample cases, meant to offer some guidance on how to develop and multiply this indispensable input.

Refrain from Making Promises You Cannot Keep

"Deals should be honored," reads a classical Roman aphorism.[9] The significance of building credibility on the basis of a strict observance of the given word emerges as a common element in all cases surveyed. The seed capital, in the form of trust, that partners invest in one another, will only be reciprocated if each member lives up to expectations. In the words of Luis Freixas, CEO of *Autopistas del Sol* (AUSOL), "When both parties keep their promises, trust is born, and the partnership is galvanized."

This initial observance prompts a moral commitment from the other party to reciprocate in kind and display a similar performance. When H-E-B Supermarkets public relations manager, Norma Treviño, analyzed trust consolidation with its partner, she remarked, "Eddie [García, executive in charge of the food bank's program at Texas headquarters] set conditions, and, as the [Monterrey] Food Bank met them, HEB kept its promise and delivered."

Showing Results

Sometimes, keeping promises is not enough if efforts do not go beyond mere futile good intentions. Instead, verifying *tangible results* from the collaboration is almost an infallible tool for trust development. The case of the Hospital Management Center (CGH) provides a pertinent example. During the board's first strategic planning meeting in May, 1992, members stipulated six work areas to be addressed in the following months,[10] and defined specific projects for the organization's first operational year. At the second strategic planning meeting, carried out 16 months later, CGH's executive director, Patricia Gómez, reviewed the guidelines set in the first meeting one by one. Once the presentation was over, partners reported "a very positive advance in almost all areas."[11] Gómez's professionalism and her capability to show results facilitated the emergence and consolidation of a trust-based working relationship and the commitment of sponsoring companies.

Similar dynamics developed between Bimbo Mexico and the Papalote Children's Museum. According to company marketing director, José Manuel González Guzmán, "at Bimbo, we are really satisfied with these types of programs. *When you see that programs meet their objectives, trust naturally grows.*"

Transparency and Accountability

Another element present in all sample cases was the importance of transparency in fund management. Highly transparent cross-sector collaborations serve the interests of both parties: mere suspicions to the contrary on programs aimed at the common good could have a devastating effect on the reputation of participating organizations. This explains why most of the organizations surveyed went to great lengths to establish procedures that left no doubt on that account.

A good example is the accountability structure set up in the collaboration between the Chilean Investment and Credit Bank (BCI) and the Corporation for Children's Credit (CCM), a CSO devoted to providing care to abandoned girls. As already mentioned, the CCM was the result of an initiative launched by a group of bank executives, and it received sizable monthly contributions from the bank. In return, Carmen Achondo, CCM director, reported on a monthly basis on funds allocation to that OSC board, where several BCI executives sit. In addition, Achondo also made two annual presentations to the BCI board, where she gave account of the OSC management and received recommendations from the directors. Another useful example is that of *Fundación Las Rosas*, also from Chile, which long ago has unilaterally adopted the customary practice of subjecting itself to regular external financial accounting audits, thus guaranteeing transparency to its current partners and other potential donors.

When in doubt, it is better to err on the side of being *too transparent* than the opposite, as the partnership between Danone Mexico and the Friendhip Home (CdA) shows. From the very beginning, the CdA systematically outdid its partner's expectations in its accountability procedures, so much so that Danone ended up asking for *less detailed* and *less frequent* reports. At the company's request, CdA's weekly reports became first biweekly, and then monthly, and came to contain broader statements and fewer minutiae. Aminta Ocampo, Danone public relations manager, commented, "When I read some of the CdA reports, I feel like screaming, 'enough already!' They report every time one of the kids sneezes, how he's doing with the treatment... it's unbelievable." What this attitude inspires in the other party, for obvious reasons, is unfettered trust.

The Rainforest Expeditions and the Ese'eja community alliance, displays an interesting feature: over time, transparency in decision-making and resource allocation helped build trust between the partners, although at the beginning, the community *was not prepared* to assume the partner role it had been assigned, since it lacked trained leaders who could fully understand the challenges entailed by the venture. However, both partners' involvement in the Management Committee generated reciprocal trust. In time, the community bred a new generation of leaders, highly committed to project success.

A Routine of Joint Work

Trust cannot be built in the abstract, without creating a work relation that contains it. The Pro-Council program, developed by the Telemig Celular Institute with several CSOs participating in the Volunteer Support Groups constitutes an enlightening example of this point. An initial challenge faced by this program was to build trust and turn a large and varied group of civil society representatives, coming from the 12 regions of the Minas Gerais state, into a cohesive team. To confront the challenge, the Institute designed and implemented a series of regular meetings, where its social project managers met systematically with social leaders from each of the 12 Support Groups, in order to listen to their perspectives and promote their interaction.

These meetings pursued two objectives: on the one hand, they aimed at training participants through the transfer of project management techniques. Yet, at the same time, the meetings were meant to strengthen a common organizational identity among support groups, and to develop trust, both among its members and between the groups and the Institute. Without that trust, the Program could not achieve its goals. Fernando Silveira Elias, project manager at the Telemig Celular Institute, elaborated on the topic. "We needed to secure a deeper involvement of the community in the creation of councils. And that cannot happen overnight; *it had to be constructed.*" Regular meetings between Institute managers and Support Groups established a joint work routine that contributed substantially to trust building in the collaboration.

Putting Yourself in Your Partner's Shoes

Earning partners' trust requires getting to know how their minds work and understanding their needs. Consider how companies participating in the Colombian Twenty-first Century Leaders (*Líderes*) program managed to gain their partners' trust. Jorge González, Multidinamics CEO, initially faced serious resistance from the priest who led one of the participating educational institutions. The clergyman was not interested in incorporating quality systems because, in his view, "it was all a Japanese fabrication," as González recalled. To overcome this opposition, González toiled patiently to develop empathy.

> To understand him better, we started studying the Catholic social doctrine. In doing so, we realized there were no major differences between what total quality proclaimed and Jesus Christ's preachings. *From then on, the father opened up to us,* and though he hasn't become our "friend," at least he no longer shows opposition.

Respecting Partners' Expertise

Just like in human relationships, institutional collaborations are based on respect, and that includes valuing and respecting partners' specialized knowledge. In the *Líderes* initiative, early mistrust between parties was overcome because both sides recognized the complex and valid knowledge the other held: businessmen admitted they did not know about education, and educators recognized that they knew nothing about management. As a result of this attitude, each member focused on learning from the other and on checking whether Total Quality techniques could contribute solutions to the unique challenges posed by educational management. Equally important, businessmen willingly accepted the limitations of such techniques, a knowledge they later applied to their own organizations.

Respecting Autonomy

Another relevant dimension of mutual respect is the acceptance of the areas that fall outside the collaboration, pertaining to the exclusive domain of partner organizations. On the relation with the Solidarity Network (RS), Javier Comesaña, *La Nación* organizational development manager, explained, "The fact that there is no symbiosis contributes to prevent conflicts. Each partner has its own activities aside from the collaboration." Social leader and SES Foundation director, Alberto Croce, confirms this idea: "Working with companies, I have learned to keep out of their businesses, and I have done just that with AUSOL. They just want me to tell them what I want to do and let them do the numbers."

Joint Challenges

Occasionally, interpersonal relationships consolidate when people involved undergo risk situations together. Our sample cases display a similar effect in cross-sector collaborations. Thus started the partnership between H-E-B supermarkets (HEB) and the Monterrey Food Bank (BAM), with a challenge both organizations came together to face. In October, 1996, HEB put forward a proposal to jointly organize with BAM the first *Fiesta de Compartir* (Feast of Sharing) in Monterrey at the end of the year. Through this initiative, the company was exporting a long-time tradition of the parent company, which held a similar event every Thanksgiving Day in Texas. The prospects were not the best, since partners only had three months to organize the event, in what would amount to be HEB's first public appearance as a local player; a major failure would certainly impair the brand. To make it happen, HEB contributed supervisors, know-how and training, while Cáritas supplied volunteers and most of the organizational work. The event was a success, and it strengthened the fledgling association.

Something similar happened in the partnership between Danone Mexico and the Friendship Home (CdA), in the initial stages of the collaboration. To build on the basis of success is always easy, but it is a very different story altogether to make a fresh start from a setback. In 1997, both organizations launched a cause related marketing campaign called "Let's Build their Dreams." However, the campaign did not reach the fund raising goals that the parties had publicly announced. There were two options: to withdraw or to double the bet, acknowledging the gap and increasing commitment and public exposure. Danone decided on the second alternative: it contributed the resources to fill the gap in the funds raised for the CdA and decided to work to educate the public about the initiative and enhance public responsiveness to the cause. This decision reinforced CdA's trust in Danone's firm commitment.

Giving Before Asking and Putting Your Money Where Your Mouth Is

The best guarantee for an organization entering a collaboration is to see that the other party takes the initiative in offering its resources to the collaboration with a view to achieve the promised objectives. We have already pointed out that the Colombian Hospital Management Center (CGH) was created to gather institutions that until then had been strangers, or even competitors. When one of them, *General Médica*, offered its premises to house the Center, it sent out a strong signal that reflected its deep commitment.

A similar occurrence cropped up in the dynamics of the Melipilla Municipal Corporation (CMM), a decentralized organ in charge of managing public health and education in that Chilean district. We have made several references to *Empresas Ariztía*'s commitment, and that of its owner, Manuel Ariztía, to this entity. According to participants' reports, Ariztía was a source of ideas and work proposals during meetings and was usually willing to fund them with his own means, for lack of alternative sources. Ariztía's readiness to back up his ideas with his own resources, revealed to the other participants his earnest commitment to the social cause he supported.

Long-Term Commitment

When an organization articulates long-term expectations, it is also conveying a powerful signal about the magnitude of its commitment. At the beginning of the chapter, we mentioned that H-E-B supermarkets informed its partner at the very start of the collaboration that it would set out to create a food bank with a capacity to serve the whole Northern Mexican region in 15 or 20 years' time. The partnership between Rainforest Expeditions and the Ese'eja community aimed at a 20-year period collaboration, at the end of which parties would decide whether to continue or terminate the association. Such a long-term perspective spells out clearly that the partner is here to stay and that its commitment is forceful enough to overcome possible temporary setbacks in the accomplishment of common objectives.

Trust is also strengthened when long-term commitment is not only proclaimed but validated with facts. The previous chapter addressed the collaboration between Esso Chile and the Burned Children Assistance Corporation (COANIQUEM), including a detailed description of the 1999 Antofagasta crisis. In that incident, several sectors blamed the company for a pervasive odor that affected various city areas. The *deep trust developed in 17 years of joint and productive work* between both organizations, helped them endure this difficult time and prevail. Furthermore, as we have already indicated, the partnership with COANIQUEM helped the company in its damage control efforts to restore its public image.

Cross-Membership in Governance Bodies

Another way to show commitment to partners and to build trust is cross-involvement in organizations' governance bodies. For example, it is a common practice for the Monterrey Food Bank (BAM) to invite its main donors to participate in its board. When BAM became aware of HEB's deep commitment, it invited its manager of food bank program at Texas headquarters, Eddie García, to join BAM's board. García, who was based in the U.S., declined the offer, but the position was taken over by HEB Mexico public relations managers instead.

Cases in which companies contributed to create their third-sector partners may constitute an extreme example of this point. For example, the *Fundación Proa* (Proa) was created with the substantial support of the Techint Group, which also provides it with an ongoing sponsorship. Accordingly, four out of the five members in the Proa's board are company executives. Another illustrative example is the recently mentioned collaboration between BCI and the CCM. This CSO had been created by initiative of a group of bank executives, and was basically funded by employees and clients' donations, all of which accounts for a peculiar partnership. Its president and owner, Luis Enrique Yarur, explained: "In time, the CCM and the bank have developed a *symbiotic* relationship. The CCM is already incorporated into the bank. We have two thousand people contributing." As from 2001, CCM's internal statutes established that its board of nine members should include at least six BCI officers, with a minimum of 5-years seniority; the remaining three may be former officials. In the words of Juan Esteban Musalem, the bank's CEO: "knowing who sits on the board is a *trust guarantee* for partners. Former executives do not serve this aim, because new company people will not know them."

Small First Steps Lead to Big Accomplishments

Starting off with a low-risk, low-cost pilot project may facilitate trust building. In 1995, when *La Nación* newspaper and the Solidarity Network (RS) engaged in initial contacts, they were far from imagining the magnitude their joint ventures would reach in time, or the deep bond they would later build. An initial project contemplating these objectives would have been futile; instead, it all began with a telephone call and a small advertising space donation in the newspaper. "I took his call the first time he phoned," recalled Marta García Terans, general information reporter at *La Nación*. After several unsuccessful attempts, RS leader, Juan Carr, managed to have an article published about a deaf family that lived in a tent and needed help to get a suitable home. This first article produced a great impact, on account of the numerous help offers received by the newspaper and the immediate solution provided to the needy family. "Two days later, I was informed that the deaf family had a place to live in," continued García Terans. "For all of us at the paper, this article became an eye-opener that showed what could be done. We all realized that people do read this news." The discovery encouraged the newspaper to explore further the possibility of an association with RS.

Building Interpersonal Relationships in Collaborations

Collaborations are built on human relations. Though these may crop up spontaneously, intense experiences may help initiate or speed up the process. In 1998, Starbucks entered a collaboration with the CSO Conservation International (CI) to work for sustainable development in Chiapas, Mexico. The aim was to encourage local coffee growers to go back to traditional shade coffee production.[12] Soon after the memorandum of understanding was signed, members of both organizations traveled together to Chiapas. During four days of busy activities, the group met with farmers and hiked the 13 craggy miles to the top of the El Triunfo Biosphere Reservation. As reported by Ben Packard, Starbucks environment manager, "The trip enabled us to see each other's dirty laundry. We were able to build trust by sharing that intense experience." The CI team discovered that Starbucks people not only had a business interest in procuring the supply of a high-quality product, but were also really concerned with environmental preservation. "We realized during the time we spent together that we were not that different from one another," commented Amy Skoczlas, CI representative.

This trust building experience was not planned as such. However, the experience of these organizations suggests that it may prove useful for other partners to actively seek opportunities to build interpersonal relations among personnel at both organizations. This could be accomplished through the implementation of intense and focused bonding activities, aimed at generating similar results.

Big Brands

The presence of big brands may also represent a significant trust driver for partners, both current and potential. Chapter 2 analyzed in detail the Mexico City Junior League (*Junior League de la Ciudad de México*, hence JLCM) case and its collaboration with Tetra Pak (TP), a container manufacturer.[13] When in 1993, JLCM submitted an association proposal to TP, it encountered a cold reception. After a year and a half of patient efforts, JLCM managed to persuade Kimberly-Clark (KC) to join in the project. The company's direct contribution to the project did not produce a significant impact, but the fact that its name was associated with the initiative turned out to be a powerful asset. Martha Rangel, JLCM president, elaborated on the topic, "When [TP] found out that Kimberley had joined in, it suddenly became very eager to participate." KC participation in the project provided TP with the guarantees it needed to put its brand at stake.

Something similar came up in the already mentioned collaboration between Bimbo and the Papalote Children's Museum. José Manuel González Guzmán, Bimbo marketing director, stated, "We are reliable, traditional, and very Mexican." Thus, continued González Guzmán, Bimbo's presence drove other companies such as Nestlé, Telmex, and Bancomer to associate with the Museum; in short, "it encouraged trust" in the project.

Collaborations as Learning Tools

The strongest collaborations are those that participants view as learning opportunities. A share of that learning revolves around the collaboration process itself, which some companies have cashed in on as part of their own organizational growth. The experience of Natura, the Brazilian cosmetic company, provides a good example. As we saw in Chapter 2,[14] the company has driven its social involvement to the core of its organizational identity and competitive strategy. However, this was not an overnight occurrence, but, rather, the result of a process initiated in 1992 with its first cross-sector collaboration with Matilde public school.[15] This high-impact philanthropic relationship enabled Natura to explore its own potential in the social field, thus developing the skill to establish and deepen its relations with other stakeholders.

Company leaders believe that this learning process allowed Natura, almost 10 years later, to engage in another more ambitious and riskier alliance, one in which it would strengthen its competitive edge while reinforcing its role as a catalyst for social change. This was the collaboration shaped around the Ekos line, which involved Natura, Cognis, and several traditional communities.

In addition, collaborations offered its participants opportunities to acquire new capabilities, which went beyond the realm of the collaboration per se, spilling over to enrich other operating areas of the organization.[16] This organizational enhancement tended to result from collaborations with an intense and two-way value flow that reproduced itself in a virtuous circle of innovation and value creation. One of such collaborations was the alliance between H-E-B supermarkets (HEB) and the Monterrey Food Bank (BAM). The company, with a large experience in working with food banks, made a sizable investment in technology and management techniques transfer to its third sector partner. But, at the same time, through the alliance, HEB increased its food bank management knowledge, thus adding value to its services. For example, as a result of the collaboration with BAM, HEB's food packages started to be prepared catering to the specific nutritional requirements of the target regions.

When the knowledge required to strengthen the collaboration was not available in the partnership, it had to be sought out elsewhere. For example, we saw that the Chilean drugstore chain *Farmacias Ahumada S.A.* (FASA), discovered that employees more motivated by the collaboration with the *Fundación Las Rosas* (FLR) were also the most productive. The experience of its partnership with FLR prompted the company to focus more attention in its sales-force communication with clients. To beef up those skills, the parties resorted to the services of a labor psychologist, paid by FASA, who helped develop employees' communicational capabilities in order to turn them into better *sellers-collectors*. Moreover, together with an advertising agency that usually collaborated with the FLR, the partners designed training, instructional, and motivational videos for drugstore personnel. Thus, drugstores ceased to be mere points of sales, to become true *communication outlets* towards society.

Key Points to Consider

This chapter has examined the ways in which alliance management shapes collaboration effectiveness to create value for the parties, and has contemplated the use of different resources to optimize it. The next paragraphs recapitulate the key points an organization must bear in mind when analyzing its performance in a cross-sector collaboration.

The first point to consider is whether the collaboration is receiving enough attention. It is important that the entire organizational pyramid is clear on the breadth and depth of top leadership commitment. One way in which that commitment is signaled is through the process and structure with which the collaboration is managed. Is there a clearly defined channel to maintain regular and fluent communications with the partner, or to systematically explore new possibilities? Are there specific individuals in my own organization formally in charge of the collaboration? How many are they, and what position do they hold in the organization? It is worth recalling that those in charge of the collaboration should be in a position to make decisions, allocate resources and commit their organizations. Likewise, it is also important that leaders' commitment to the collaboration is clearly signaled to the partner. Can leaders of my own organization be readily reached by their counterparts, when the situation calls for it?

A way of ensuring that a cross-sector alliance receives adequate attention would be to review the number of collaborations in which the organization is engaged. Would it be wise to consolidate the organization's portfolio of cross-sector alliances into a smaller, more manageable size? In that case, which alliance or alliances should be strengthened? Answering this question should involve determining the areas in which my key capabilities may make a difference, and those in which a strategic alliance may generate a greater impact. At the same time, potential risks that may eventually derive from concentrating social activities in a reduced number of relations should also be taken into account.

For a collaboration to reach its full potential, it is essential that it becomes part of the organizational culture of its members. Are all departments and functional areas *imbued* with it? Does senior management send out clear enough signals to the rest of the organization? Should one of these answers be negative, it will be worthwhile to review the resources suggested in this chapter. These include managers' participation in follow-up meetings, their personal involvement in collaboration activities, or the integration of the collaboration's indicators into the company's reward system, among others. Do all relevant stakeholders perceive these signals as clear? If not, what incentives could the organization offer them to galvanize its commitment and earn their trust?

We have mentioned that collaboration productivity may increase when organizations contribute resources to building their partners' organizational capability. Would my partner create more value to me if my organization contributed to its institutional strengthening? On the other hand, collaborations may be strengthened through expansion. If a new partner entered the alliance—whether on a temporary or a permanent basis—would that lead to cost reduction, scale increase, or impact enhancement? Another way of strengthening a partner would be to encourage replication of the collaboration model with other companies. Is that compatible with the value my organization is accruing from the collaboration? Finally, potential risks involved in expanding collaborations and different ways to eventually neutralize them should also be considered.

We have also analyzed how a collaboration's productivity is shaped by the quality of its communications. Is the partnership adequately leveraging its potential to create value through appropriate external communications? Of course, all communication efforts should include a deep analysis of the benefits and risks that joint exposure may bring to the organization's brands. Is the organization extracting from the collaboration its full value vis-à-vis its human resources through an adequate internal communication policy? If not, how can it be reinforced?

As we have seen, no collaboration will be able to move forward if partners fail to generate and reproduce trust. A close examination of the resources analyzed in the chapter may suggest several working lines. What can I do to better understand my partner and its needs? How can I clearly convey to my partner the magnitude of my commitment to the collaboration? It will always be useful to plan joint, focused, and intense bonding activities to enable the emergence and consolidation of interpersonal relations between both organizations' staff. Would considering cross-member participation in governing bodies be a viable alternative?

Finally, participating organizations will draw greater value from collaborations if they consider them as an experimentation and learning arena. Is the organization capitalizing on the joint work experience, thus learning to collaborate better? Furthermore, the impact of lessons drawn should not be restricted to the specific domain of the collaboration. How can this learning strengthen other functional areas of the organization? Does the other partner have any critical skill to enhance the organization that has not been tapped into yet? If not, can the collaboration become an opportunity to acquire new capabilities from third sources?

Notes

1   James E. Austin, *The Collaboration Challenge: How Nonprofits and Businesses Succeed through Strategic Alliances,* 1st ed. (San Francisco: Jossey-Bass Publishers, 2000) 125.

2   A brief summary of that relationship was offered in Chapter 1 (p. 9). For a more in-depth description readers may consult the discussions under the headings "Individuals" (p. 58), and "Cross Fertilization" (p. 94).

3   For a more detailed description refer to Chapter 3, "Competitive Pressures," p. 102.

4   James E. Austin, "Marketing's role in cross-sector collaboration," *Journal of Nonprofit and Public Sector Marketing* 11, no. 1 (Spring 2003): 28.

5   "No matter what you like, what you think, what you feel or what you are, we all share a common concern: the environment. Thus, we created Learning Environmental Entrepreneurship, a program for primary schools starting from the beginning: children's education. The idea is to encourage their natural creativity to find small solutions to improve the environs in which we live, so that our shared environment does not come to an end." (Source: company documents).

6   Refer to "Competitive Pressures" (p. 102), under Chapter 3.

7   "Another factor to be taken into account when explaining these very critical attitudes is the lack of informative transparency shown by Pepsi so as to explain the quantity and destination of the funds obtained in their CRM [cause-related marketing] campaigns (…) In this light, firms implementing these programs ought to consider the convenience of devising parallel communication campaigns so as to provide stakeholders with accurate and thorough information of objectives, procedure, results and thus avoid suspicion, and consequently a negative effect upon the brand." Iñaki García, Juan J. Gibaja, and Alazne Mujika, "A Study of the Effect of Cause-Related Marketing on the Attitude towards the Brand: The Case of Pepsi in Spain," *Journal of Nonprofit and Public Sector Marketing* 11, no. 1 (Spring 2003): 35.

8   To recall basic characteristics of this partnership, refer to p. 83.

9   *Pacta sunt servanda.*

10   These areas included (1) defining the CGH operational range, (2) defining

its clients, (3) outlining how to respond to customers' needs, (4) analyzing how to retain CGH partners' commitment, (5) working out how to make the public and private sectors view the CGH as a stable organization and a transformation agent, and (6) providing a management model and to gain financial soundness.

11 Centro de Gestión Hospitalaria Board of Directors, Minutes No. 20, 15 September, 1993, p. 3.

12 James E. Austin and Cate Reavis, "Starbucks and Conservation International," HBS Case No. 9-303-055 (Boston: Harvard Business School Publishing, 1996).

13 Refer to p. 68.

14 Refer to p. 40.

15 To recall basic characteristics of this collaboration, refer to Chapter 4, p. 119.

16 "Today several leading companies (...) have learned that applying their energies to solving the chronic problems of the social sector powerfully stimulates their own business development." Rosabeth Moss Kanter, "From Spare Change to Real Change: The Social Sector as Beta Site for Business Innovation," *Harvard Business Review* (1999): 124.

PART

II

Country Topics

6

Argentina: The Role of Social Entrepreneurs in Alliance Building

Gabriel Berger and Mario Roitter

Introduction

The role of social entrepreneurs in building and maintaining cross-sector collaboration processes demands special attention. Probing their role is highly useful in understanding some of the factors that contribute to the successful development of joint work by Non Governmental Organizations (NGOs) and business companies. In this regard, the collaboration cases studied in Argentina illustrate well how social entrepreneurs deploy valuable attributes to build these initiatives, which encompass actors with significantly different objectives, norms, cultures, and working styles. However, they still manage to create value, provide solutions, or improve general living conditions for communities, thus helping to achieve fairer, more sustainable societies.

The chapter begins with an outline of the overall conditions in Argentina during the second half of the 1990s, which set the stage for the emergence of a new type of social entrepreneur. Then, it moves on to describe briefly the so-called third sector in that country, and the development processes undergone by NGOs in recent decades, enabling readers to gain a better understanding of the new social entrepreneurs. The cases of alliances between companies and nonprofits studied by the SEKN team in Argentina offer examples of this new social entrepreneurship profile, displaying the common attributes and characteristics that serve as enablers in alliance building. Finally, the chapter concludes by drawing lessons from this analysis to enlighten both social entrepreneurs and private companies.

Argentine Entrepreneurship in the 1990s

In the past few years, Argentina has experienced a renewed interest in entrepreneurship, or better stated, a renewed interest in the role played by certain individuals as energizers of the productive fabric,[1] as drivers of process innovation and employment creation opportunities, both in the business and the nonprofit sectors. This new approach focuses on entrepreneurship and "business demographics,"[2] drawing attention to the role played by entrepreneurs as economic and social development promoters. Entrepreneurship development should be viewed as a systemic phenomenon, both causing and resulting from deep social building processes, featuring macro/microeconomic and idiosyncratic issues in both a cultural and institutional sense.

The social context in which this phenomenon emerges constitutes an essential factor. Though the first half of the 1990s brought Argentina remarkable growth in GDP and social indicators improved temporarily, the growth model adopted by the government also led to increasing social fragmentation, inequity, and exclusion. In the mid 1980s, the greater Buenos Aires area reported 9 percent of households with incomes below the poverty line. By the end of the 1990s, that figure had doubled, as unemployment and under-employment were on the rise beginning in the mid 1990s, reaching 18 percent by 2001. The acute economic recession that started in 1998 worsened the social situation, affecting a large number of households that up to this point had always been part of an extended middle class. By the end of 2002, the unemployment rate had reached a startling 25 percent.

In this contradictory yet fertile environment, the early 1990s brought on the emergence of numerous business initiatives, especially in the service industry. Regionally speaking, Argentina registered outstanding entrepreneurship behavior. According to the 2002 Global Entrepreneurship Monitor (GEM)[3] indicators, Argentina's 14.2 percent entrepreneurial activity rate was fifth in the world, second in Latin America. In the most recent survey, Thailand leads this ranking, followed by India, Chile, South Korea, and then Argentina.

The resources available to entrepreneurs allow for a distinction inside this universe. As Silvia Carbonell[4] points out, entrepreneurship is a multi-layer phenomenon, and *need-based entrepreneurs* should be distinguished from *opportunity-based entrepreneurs*. The first group includes individuals who have no choice in the face of poverty, low salaries, and worse yet, a weak labor market. Conversely, the second group is comprised of those who take advantage of specific market conditions to develop new businesses, and are therefore prepared to make a decision regarding the launching of a particular business endeavor following the premises of economic theories regarding agent rationality, guided mostly by profitability expectations.[5]

Then, we should wonder about the specific nature of Argentine entrepreneurship. The data provided by the GEM become more relevant when analyzed in terms of the kinds of entrepreneurs found. Indeed, this report explains that, contrary to what happens in developed countries, where opportunity-based entrepreneurs prevail, developing countries like Argentina tend to breed entrepreneurs born out of "need." Thus, there seems to be a link between unemployment rates and entrepreneurship levels. Although the evidence is not conclusive as to the effect produced by a rise in this indicator, it would apparently foster the emergence of small firms in less capital and knowledge-intensive industries, where the so-called need-based entrepreneurs may find feasible niches.[6]

Argentina also showed a significant development in opportunity-based entrepreneurship. A clear example was provided by the "dot.com" business phenomenon. In the early 1990s, the combination of technological breakthroughs and the Internet boom produced a remarkably high number of entrepreneurs. Argentina had a high schooling rate and educational institutions that had trained several generations in the use of new technologies. These factors provided the adequate environment for these new ventures, but they were not enough to ensure sustainability for businesses that required increased capital resources and growing markets. Initially, financing facilities and the existence of expanding markets created favorable conditions for the emergence of a large number of business initiatives. These conditions were present during the early 1990s, and the ensuing opportunities were seized by innovators who were willing to enter the fledgling industry. Financing was readily available, and good educational standards supplied the necessary knowledge base to enter this new market. The "dot.com" experience clearly illustrates the influence of macro and micro-economic factors in entrepreneurship. However, these factors do not explain the whole phenomenon, because though environmental variables were relatively similar throughout Latin America, Argentina registered additional enablers (educational background, entrepreneurial attitude) that turned its website creation and content production into the largest in the region. Years later, when international (especially the NASDAQ fall) and local conditions changed, there were a significant number of bankruptcies in the sector. Nevertheless, some entrepreneurs managed to develop highly attractive and successful products that have survived the crisis either by selling out or merging with other companies.

In regard to the recent recessionary period that began in 1998 and deepened in the years that followed, the GEM report indicates that those who started their own businesses in Argentina faced pros and cons in their decision. Among the positive changes brought about by the economic crisis, there was the opening of new markets resulting from reduced external competition, but among the hurdles existed the lack of marketing, professional, financial, and public policy infrastructure.

The results of the 2002 GEM survey show that, in spite of the overall entrepreneurship decline registered by all countries, Argentina boasted a 40 percent increase in comparison to 2001, which the authors attribute to social impairment and the subsequent emergence of need-based entrepreneurs, as well as the existence of new business opportunities resulting from economic changes associated with the devaluation of Argentina's currency.

These developments seem to confirm the notion that crises are opportunities in disguise. In this line of thought, these recent macroeconomic changes have yielded new alternatives for exports or import-substitution that are being exploited daily by an assortment of firms and entrepreneurs.

Recent Dynamics of Argentine NGOs

The existence of NGOs is not a new phenomenon in Argentina or the rest of Latin America. Even before Argentina consolidated as a nation-state in the late nineteenth century, there existed welfare institutions devoted to education, culture and most importantly, social aid.

However, the growth experienced in size and public exposure of this sector is a rather recent occurrence. The rapid creation rate of NGOs represents an expression of a new kind of social entrepreneurship.

Since the mid-1980s in Argentina and throughout most of Latin America, NGOs have captured renewed relevance. This phenomenon was fostered by democratic processes, state decentralization policies, and service transferences to provincial and city administrations that had started to rely on NGOs to "outsource" social programs. In addition, multilateral credit agencies began assigning tasks associated with social public policy implementation to nonprofits; this action coupled with the worsening living conditions afflicting a significant portion of the population triggered the emergence of numerous initiatives. These institutions are grouped in what is almost indistinctly known as the "nonprofit sector," "non-governmental organizations," "Civil Society Organizations," or the "third sector."

The lack of updated information available for this sector in Argentina makes it difficult to describe accurately the current situation. According to 1995 data, there were 57,321 of the so-called "open" NGOs, which provided services to third parties, beyond their membership.[7] These institutions spent slightly over 3.3 billion Argentine pesos (Arg$)[8] and employed 118,720 people.[9] These figures do reveal how relevant these organizations were to the country when the social entrepreneurs featured in the cases studied by the SEKN-Argentina program began planning their initiatives.

Volunteer involvement is also an indicator used to determine the dimension of the third sector. In this regard, the Gallup-Argentina survey on Donations and Volunteer Work carried out in March, 1999 shows that 20 percent of the adult population reported having been engaged in volunteer work during 1998. Later estimates published by the same consulting firm raised this percentage to 33 percent,[10] proving that significant growth had taken place in public involvement experienced by Civil Society Organizations during the second half of the 1990s. It should be noted that this growth includes many social entrepreneurs who, out of their own needs or solidarity, launched new ventures or contributed to already existing organizations.

In addition to quantitative indicators measuring the increase in individual involvement in social organizations, the Argentine third sector has registered significant growth in recent years, both in its level of institutionalization (with the emergence of second-tier institutions) and exposure in the most influential media, as well as through academic recognition in undergraduate and graduate university program offerings, participation in international advisory organs, and public policy-making involvement in almost all state areas. The role of alliances among social organizations and the public or private sector in this growth, calls for deeper analysis.

Concerning the new trend towards alliances between the state and nonprofits in social policies, this is a phenomenon that should be the object of further research to check whether it has resulted in a stronger nonprofit sector having a greater social impact, or whether it has been a response to the need for filling the void left by the state in its neglected welfare obligations[11] Similarly, the impact of the greater business involvement in social and community programs on the growth of the third sector registered in Argentina during the second half of the 1990s has yet to be determined.[12]

In short, during the expansionary period experienced by the Argentine economy up until 1997, the social sector underwent a dynamic creation and growth process. In particular, groups of professionals launched technical assistance, research, training, and consulting programs to strengthen NGOs. The latter, in turn, took advantage of these new opportunities to become service providers for public-sector projects. New undergraduate and graduate programs were also created to train professionals. There was a significant flow of new proposals coming from the private business sector and several foundations to develop joint programs with third-sector organizations.

During the second half of the 1990s, the third sector continued to grow at a rapid rate, and though no systematic studies have measured this growth with precision, it is reasonable to assume that the greatest expansion has been experienced by the NGOs providing services to poverty-stricken population groups. This phenomenon had already sprouted as a response to the two hyperinflation episodes that Argentina had undergone in 1989 and 1990. In the late 1990s it gathered renewed momentum on account of the increase in poverty and social exclusion afflicting large sectors of the population, in spite of the improvement shown by macroeconomic indicators. In general, these were small-sized organizations in terms of number of employees, but they assembled substantial numbers of volunteers, many of whom lived in poverty and joined these organizations to find solutions for food and family care problems. Their funding sources were private donations, modest fund-raising activities, and mostly state subsidies. Though these organizations may collaborate with the public sector or manage state-funded social programs, for the most part they lack the institutional capacity to work with business companies.

The emergence of new social ventures and organizations grew remarkably since 2001 as a result of the social crisis that was already reaching emergency proportions. The political turmoil that erupted at the end of that year when President De La Rua resigned, significantly changed the conditions upon which the Argentine economy had been functioning. A compulsory blockage of all bank deposits was followed by the collapse of the fixed currency exchange system, upsetting all productive and financial activities and unleashing a deep stagnation process comparable to that experienced during the 1930 crisis. Living conditions were severely impaired, while poverty and unemployment rates rose to unprecedented heights. This negative scenario for business entrepreneurs paradoxically triggered numerous entrepreneurial social initiatives among affected sectors. In the middle income population layers, there were neighborhood movements to seek collective solutions and demand government action. Also, new efforts were geared to promote and support productive micro-companies, oriented mainly to self-sufficiency, and solidarity-based initiatives to serve the most affected sectors. This rapid rate of social enterprise emergence posed new challenges for organizations' medium-term sustainability on account of their improvised and unstable nature.

Social Entrepreneurs in Argentina

In what unfolded as a truly paradoxical social climate, Argentine entrepreneurship bloomed in the social sector. Several companies launched new expansion and diversification projects, and many organizations and individuals felt compelled to channel their energies towards the common good, which propelled the creation of various business foundations and corporate social responsibility programs. Others came to see NGOs as a means for responding to the contraction in the labor market that had affected a large portion of the population, and the increasingly unsatisfied social needs that were produced by rising unemployment and income loss. Those were the two primary power sources that fueled the vigorous expansion in entrepreneurship registered throughout the decade. As a response to the deterioration of living conditions and labor shortage, many entrepreneurs set up food shelters, children day-care centers, productive microenterprises, and other social-oriented projects. This situation also encouraged several other individuals from higher social layers to collaborate actively in these initiatives or to develop new organizations to support the needy.

The appearance of need-based social entrepreneurs, to use Carbonell's definition, has been significantly acknowledged by Argentine media in recent years. Two emblematic examples of this media exposure have been the efforts of Mónica Carranza and Margarita Barrientos in founding and directing their own community organizations, *Los Carasucias* and *Los Piletones*, respectively, to provide basic food services in extremely poor neighborhoods in the greater Buenos Aires City area. Both entrepreneurs come from the same low-income communities that they serve, and they have managed to create precarious food shelters and social service centers for hundreds of people. These community leaders have been able to organize fellow community members to help provide staple services (starting with food) and obtain resources from other social sectors through contacts with newspapers and television networks. Thus, they have managed to broaden their offerings through agreements with other institutions and professionals who volunteer their expertise. These two women constitute true examples of individuals who overcome their own needy status and apply their communication and leadership capabilities to solve (or serve) community problems.

Social entrepreneurs with similar characteristics have surfaced throughout the country, providing other clear examples of individual responses to the state's deterioration as the basic social service supplier, in addition to the general difficulties usually experienced by communities in organizing themselves and collectively seeking solutions for their problems. Numerous entrepreneurs with strong personal leadership have emerged in this environment, and in some cases, have even become more visible than the projects themselves. This characteristic often hinders the development of sustainable social organizations and their continuity, a phenomenon clearly associated with Argentine institutional weaknesses. Despite these limitations, the rapid emergence of these need-based social entrepreneurs has been a fast and spontaneous response mechanism to the social crisis that has besieged Argentina in recent years.

Our work has focused primarily on social ventures featuring successful alliances with business companies. These entrepreneurs have managed to secure a broader social impact and greater sustainability from their ability to build effective collaborations with companies. In these cases, we have found social entrepreneurs who share some of the same characteristics as need-based entrepreneurs, but who also display differentiating attributes.

It is convenient to start off by establishing a more "idealized" definition of social entrepreneurship that has been used by several authors and organizations. For example, one of the pioneering organizations in social entrepreneurship promotion and support defines this kind of entrepreneurs as follows: "Social entrepreneurs have two salient features: an innovative idea for producing significant social change and an entrepreneurial vision for executing their projects. Social entrepreneurs are committed to generating systematic social changes instead of being motivated by a profit-oriented spirit."[13] Another similar definition is offered by Dees, who points out that social entrepreneurs are transformation agents that behave according to the following patterns: (a) "adopting a mission to create and sustain social value," (b) "recognizing and relentlessly pursuing new opportunities to serve the mission," (c) "engaging in a process of continuous innovation, adaptation, and learning," (d) "acting boldly without being limited to resources currently in hand," and (e) "exhibiting a heightened sense of accountability to the constituencies served and for the outcomes created."[14] In Argentina, we should probably add to this ideal model two additional attributes:[15] a strong capability to achieve public exposure for their actions and a disorganized (even "chaotic") working style as compared to more traditional labor models. The social entrepreneurs studied in our sample show some of these behavioral patterns in varying ways and degrees, thus approaching the ideal model.

The cases studied for the SEKN-Argentina project illustrate the trends described above and allow for the identification of some characteristics shared by recently emerged social entrepreneurs. Therefore, we will focus on the four leaders involved in the cases analyzed for this project, as well as other cases still in progress.

Creativity and Innovating Capability

The cases examined in this project describe NGOs that, for the most part, were created by entrepreneurs who have built alliances with companies. This entrepreneurial generation has created organizations that are both new and innovative in Argentina. The first example is Juan Carr, who created the Solidarity Network (*Red Solidaria*, hence RS) on the basis of a simple idea and a simple operating process: linking those who have extreme needs to those who have the resources to satisfy them, and appealing to volunteers who handle the requests over the telephone and to the media in order to communicate those requests. The second example is Alberto Croce, who created the SES Foundation to promote continued schooling for youths through the construction of peer groups that study together, under the supervision of adult community members acting as tutors. Third is Adriana Rosenberg, who created *Fundación Proa* (Proa) to provide a forum to foster avant-garde art in a traditional environment. The final example is Paula Bullrich, who did not found her organization (Junior Achievement Argentina Foundation), but who served as the main change agent in a strategic shift towards the development of local programs as an alternative to the use of materials developed in the United States and translated into Spanish. The behavior exhibited by these four examples is comparable to that seen by other entrepreneurs involved in other study cases: Carolina Biquard, who created the Commitment Foundation (*Fundación Compromiso*) to offer up-to-date management technical counseling and training for social organizations, and Victoria Shocrón, founder of the Dialing Foundation (*Fundación Discar*) for the social integration of mentally handicapped individuals through art and work opportunities. It should also be noted that our case selection criterion was based on the existence of successful alliances between companies and NGOs. Therefore, the creation of innovative nonprofits is a common trait among the leaders in the sample, which may be identified ex post facto.

Another significant aspect is that the innovation supporting these ventures (RS, *Fundación SES, Fundación Proa,* and *Fundación Discar*) was locally conceived on the basis of these entrepreneurs' own ideas. One of the cases analyzed did, however, involve innovation that resulted from the local application of a model designed abroad (Junior Achievement). The same goes for the *Fundación Compromiso,* which was inspired by the U.S.-based Drucker Foundation for Nonprofit Management. As these two cases demonstrate, innovation may also result from successful adaptation of foreign models. In certain cases, this form of innovation appeals to companies with a strong international background, such as Coca-Cola and McKinsey. Nevertheless, these are not cases of mere replication, but examples of clever adjustment of the external model to local conditions, thus creating a new version that differs significantly from the original. Such is the case of the Junior Achievement-Coca-Cola alliance, which focused on the development of a new program that would later receive a Junior Achievement International award. Similarly, the *Fundación Compromiso* developed a variation based on a Drucker Foundation publication. This NGO changed the target population (originally schools) and created an innovative program that provided technical assistance to social organizations. Again, this program later received recognition from the Drucker Foundation.

The innovative nature of these organizations constituted a valuable attribute for the companies involved in the partnerships: a) the business culture tends to relate more easily to new ideas that break away from the traditional image associated with welfare organizations (associated with charity), and b) it provides an additional differentiating factor for the company because of its association with a novel venture.

Credibility and Sector Leadership

These entrepreneurs have also held positions of leadership in their respective fields, and gained a level of experience that commanded respect. They were widely recognized, not only by the followers and volunteers directly working with their organizations, but by every individual working on similar issues, for whom they were role models. For example, Juan Carr has become a national figure in the solidarity field, while Alberto Croce is renowned in education and youth-related issues; the same goes for Adriana Rosenberg in the area of avant-garde art, for Carolina Biquard in NGO support, and Victoria Shocrón in social integration of the mentally-handicapped. In the case of Paula Bullrich and Junior Achievement, the organization itself is nationally recognized for its school work in developing entrepreneurial skills. The social recognition of these entrepreneurs as specialists in their fields has been instrumental in obtaining the support of companies. Their sector leadership role is something that is valued by companies because it establishes the legitimacy and credibility of the entrepreneurs involved. Also, the alliances built with companies contributed to the strengthening of their sector leadership, because the companies' endorsement enhances credibility and subsequent dissemination of their work to new environments.

Ties with the Media

The entrepreneurs in our sample have been able to build ties with the media, especially newspapers, thus providing public exposure to publicize their ventures, obtain funds for their initiatives, and strengthen their leadership in the sector. Juan Carr has been particularly proficient in this matter, experiencing tremendous success in contacting reporters, newspapers, and television heads. Adriana Rosenberg has also demonstrated capabilities in contacting specialized reporters, though the quality of the exhibitions organized by Proa ensures a certain level of art and culture media coverage. This high profile is useful for fundraising and mobilization to respond to social needs, but also plays an instrumental role in positioning the protagonists as potential partners with companies.

The ties that these entrepreneurs built with the media allowed them to show their results. Public exposure then becomes a source of credibility. Using the media to communicate results and achievements entails the risk of taking the information provided by the entrepreneurs themselves to prove their impact. Though the cases we have studied display a significant concern for showing results as a measure of performance, it is not always possible to check the authenticity of the data provided because these organizations lack formal and systematic mechanisms and procedures to record, monitor, and evaluate performance. Regardless, media exposure allows social entrepreneurs to commit themselves publicly to their goals and results.

In some cases, companies obtain additional visibility from media exposure of the social entrepreneurs; in others, the entrepreneurs' visibility only serves to strengthen their prestige in the eyes of the business community. At times, external recognition and exposure are achieved through awards and subsidies granted by organizations, such as Ashoka or AVINA. Ashoka has developed a communication strategy that supports media exposure for its fellows like Juan Carr, Carolina Biquard, and Victoria Shocrón. AVINA's support for social entrepreneurs went to Alberto Croce and Carolina Biquard, enabling both to access new social and professional networks. In the case of Paula Bullrich, this ability to use external recognition as a means to boost reputation was developed after the Learning Environmental Entrepreneurship program received the Junior Achievement International award and the Corporate Citizenship prize, granted by the American Chamber of Commerce in Argentina. Ultimately, this kind of recognition is very valuable in the business world, and can factor in quite largely in the overall success of certain programs.

Capability to Attract Volunteers and Other Collaborators

In three of the cases analyzed, social entrepreneurs exhibited a remarkable ability to attract volunteers and collaborators to their initiatives. This ability to motivate, inspire, and gain commitment from others to pursue their mission provides further evidence of their leadership capabilities. Undoubtedly, Juan Carr is the most accomplished entrepreneur in this field, but Croce and Rosenberg have also proven quite successful in recruiting volunteers (the number of people is less than Carr on account of their initiatives' smaller requirements). The fact that both entrepreneurs have managed to secure assistance from companies in building of their organizations clearly illustrates their ability to attract other collaborators. In addition to the support provided by AVINA to create the SES Foundation, Croce secured the cooperation of *Autopistas del Sol* (AUSOL), (it contributed the funds required by law in addition to initial legal counseling). Adriana Rosenberg created Proa with the support of the Techint Group, and of the Foundation run by the family controlling that company, which contributed the building in which that NGO operates. In Patricia Bullrich's case, this capability is the core feature of the Junior Achievement organization, which actively recruits volunteers to deliver courses. Also, since the organization already existed before she joined, this attribute soon became a requisite for her work.

Resource Mobilization

Regardless of the strategic relevance that alliances with companies had for these social entrepreneurs, they have all shown an impressive ability to mobilize additional economic and material resources from other sources. Juan Carr has secured printed media attention, in addition to a section developed by *La Nación* newspaper. Alberto Croce managed to get the support of other companies. Adriana Rosenberg brought renowned art exhibits to the country through her contacts with the visual art world. Paula Bullrich (from Junior Achievement) worked on the basis of several corporate sponsorships. Companies value this resource generation capability for several reasons. First, it implies that social entrepreneurs do not entirely and exclusively depend on one single donor or company to carry out their activities. Companies tend to avoid exclusive economic dependence, and this ability to mobilize additional resources guarantees that organizations will not become a burden for them. Second, companies value entrepreneurs' ability to multiply or leverage available resources as a sign of efficiency. Finally, obtaining additional resources may provide external recognition and exposure, which strengthens the commitment of companies to these entrepreneurs.

This capability was tested in the alliances studied. These social entrepreneurs were able to gradually mobilize additional resources from the very same companies, broadening the contributions by adding new types of assets (e.g., in AUSOL's case, managers started to volunteer their time) and increasing the economic value of those contributions (as in the case of *La Nación* and its solidarity classifieds, or at Techint/Tenaris, where other group companies funded Proa exhibitions).

Unbiased Attitude towards Companies and Valuing Their Distinctive Resources

Another important attribute shared by these 1990s social entrepreneurs is their lack of ideological biases against the business world. In the past, social entrepreneurs, founders of NGOs or grass-roots organizations, and human rights advocates, used to view companies as one of the agents responsible for many of the social problems that they were seeking to combat, and so they were reluctant to work with them. As part of their strategies to live up to their respective missions, the cases analyzed show that social entrepreneurs acknowledged work with companies as an absolute necessity, for their role in providing both monetary and non-monetary resources (know-how, management skills, networks, etc.) would be crucial.

This unbiased and rather pragmatic attitude towards bisiness firms stems from the fact that these social entrepreneurs understood the critical nature of building cooperation ties with companies in order to ensure sustainability. As discussed in Chapter 4, working with the private sector is not about seeking donations. It is about building collaborations with corporations so that they may contribute their key resources, which oftentimes are not "for sale." Accessing specific markets or customers (*La Nación* newspaper readers), developing logistics and administrative capabilities and international relations (*Fundación Proa* with Techint), securing legal assistance or corporate volunteer work (Alberto Croce and AUSOL), or achieving exposure and recognition as a prestigious brand (Paula Bullrich and Coca-Cola) were all considered by social entrepreneurs as resources that only companies could provide.

Flexibility and Complementarity

These social entrepreneurs displayed great flexibility in adjusting to company requirements and needs. In pursuit of their mission, they were willing to seek opportunities to develop products or programs that would ultimately enable companies to obtain benefits for themselves. This was clearly seen in the Junior Achievement case, when Coca-Cola was allowed to choose the cities where the environmental education program would be implemented, thus reaching places it would not have accessed on its own. Alberto Croce contemplated the needs of AUSOL in his initial work in neighborhoods that the company held as a priority or target area. Juan Carr adjusted to reporters' requirements in terms of news style and schedule, thus reaching more readers and enhancing campaign impact. Adriana Rosenberg took into account Tenaris' international expansion needs when she prepared exhibits, thus promoting expositions that featured the countries targeted by the company.

Throughout these collaborations, social entrepreneurs were aware of their potential to provide specific resources to the companies. They knew that the key to building successful alliances lay in creating value for companies while enhancing their impact as social entrepreneurs, and it appears that they did so without compromising too much of themselves or their programs.

Lessons for Social Entrepreneurs and Companies Interested in Collaborating

The attributes identified reveal four significant lessons that may be of use to social entrepreneurs as enablers for the development and management of alliances.

1. Think about companies' needs and explore ways of complementing them; it is not enough to have an innovative idea and management capabilities. It is paramount to take into account companies' needs and to consider the potential value that a social enterprise can create for the private partner.

2. Identify those elements in companies' needs that can be aligned with the mission, values, or strategies of the social venture. Oftentimes, working with companies to serve their needs proves to be the path to social mission attainment, value promotion, or strategy implementation.

3. Understand that nonfinancial resources provided by a company during collaboration may be just as or even more valuable than monetary contributions. This ability to take advantage of key capacities or assets of companies, to channel them towards social goals, may multiply the impact sought by the entrepreneurs. Also, companies may provide additional economic resources as a result of their gradual and increasing involvement.

4. Keep a flexible and pragmatic attitude in the search for collaborations. The willingness to change the means (the "How?" and "Where?") of ventures, without compromising core values and ultimate aims (the "What?" and "For what?"), provides for the generation, maintenance, and enhancement of company collaboration opportunities.

These cases also suggest three lessons relevant to companies in terms of their work with social entrepreneurs in jointly developed initiatives:

1. Understand the needs of social entrepreneurs and offer the necessary support. Social entrepreneurs usually have great visionary and motivating capability, but they often lack organizational management skills or tend to be somewhat reluctant to institutionalize their endeavors. Companies should be aware of the tremendous impact that their contributions may have in those areas, and focus on the substance of the demands of the entrepreneur, avoiding a critical view of their organizational style.

2. Value the significance of standing by the entrepreneur as the initiative develops and becomes institutionalized. For this purpose, companies need to learn about the organizational rationale used by social enterprises, while thinking how to apply private sector know-how to make them better and stronger. This implies "educating" social entrepreneurs, respecting their timing in understanding the need to build solid, efficient, and sustainable organizations.

3. Understand and accept cultural differences existing between companies and social entrepreneurs. Be ready to initiate and maintain a mutually beneficial communication. Social entrepreneurs' backgrounds, education, values, ideologies, and working styles often differ from those prevailing at the companies. Respectful and candid exchanges with social entrepreneurs may turn out to be enlightening for business executives and their own organizations.

The cases analyzed in Argentina show that social entrepreneurs are invigorating agents in the social fabric, who have the potential to build bridges between businesses and society. A better understanding of their traits and attributes becomes instrumental for the study of cross-sector alliances.

Notes

1 Hugo Kantis, Pablo Angelelli, and Francisco Gatto, "Nuevos emprendimientos y emprendedores: ¿de qué depende su creación y supervivencia? Explorando el caso argentino," (San Miguel: Universidad de General Sarmiento, Instituto de Industria, mimeo, 2000).

2 Gustavo Burachik, "Supervivencia de nuevas empresas industriales: una reseña de la literatura," *Revista Desarrollo Económico* 42, no. 165 (2002).

3   The 2002 Global Entrepreneurship Monitor (GEM) is an entrepreneurship survey including 37 countries—accounting for 62 percent of the world's population. See Paul D. Reynolds et al., "Global Entrepreneurship Monitor (GEM) 2002," (Boston, MA; London, UK: London Business School and Babson College, 2003).

4   Silvia S. de Torres Carbonell, "Global Entrepreneurship Monitor. Reporte ejecutivo Argentina 2002," (Buenos Aires, Argentina: Centro de Entrepreneurship, IAE, Escuela de Dirección y Negocios, 2003).

5   Burachik, "Supervivencia de nuevas empresas industriales: una reseña de la literatura."

6   There is relatively important evidence on this topic; see Kantis, Angelelli, and Gatto, "Nuevos emprendimientos y emprendedores: ¿de qué depende su creación y supervivencia? Explorando el caso argentino."

7   In other words, these figures do not include organizations serving their own members or providing services subject to fees. If these kinds of organizations are added, the number of jobs in 1995 climbs to almost 400,000, and operating expenses rise to almost 12 billion Argentine pesos.

8   At the moment these data were collected, the exchange rate was Arg$ 1 = US$ 1.

9   Mario Roitter, Regina Rippetoe, and Lester M. Salamon, "Descubriendo el sector sin fines de lucro en Argentina," in *Estudios sobre sector sin fines de lucro en la Argentina*, ed. Mario M. Roitter and Inés González Bombal (Buenos Aires: Centro de Estudios de Estado y Sociedad / Johns Hopkins University, 1999).

10 Survey carried out in 2001 through a sample of 1,323 people over 17 years of age, living in urban centers with a population of more than 5,000. See *Perfil de los trabajadores voluntarios* (Gallup Argentina, February 2002 [cited June 29, 2003]); available from http://www.gallup.com.ar/publi/pub025.pdf.

11 Eduardo Bustelo Graffigna, "El abrazo. Nuevas relaciones entre el estado y los organismos no gubernamentales en la Argentina," *L'Ordinaire Latino Americain*, no. 165–166 (1996); Andrea Campetella and Inés González Bombal, "Historia del sector sin fines de lucro en la Argentina," in *Estudios sobre sector sin fines de lucro en la Argentina*, ed. Mario M. Roitter and Inés González Bombal (Buenos Aires: Centro de Estudios de Estado y Sociedad / Johns Hopkins University, 2000).

12 Instituto Gallup de la Argentina and Universidad de San Andrés, "Estudio de filantropía empresaria," (Instituto Gallup de la Argentina and Universidad de San Andrés, mimeo, n.d.).

13 Ashoka, *¿Qué es un emprendedor social?* (Ashoka, 2003 [cited April 24, 2003]); available from http://www.espanol.ashoka.org/Public/FDA_QueEsUnEmprendedorSocial.asp.

14 J. Gregory Dees, Peter Economy, and Jed Emerson, *Enterprising Nonprofits: A Toolkit for Social Entrepreneurs, Wiley Nonprofit Law, Finance, And Management Series* (New York: Wiley, 2001) 5.

15 Romina Waldman, "Los entrepreneurs sociales argentinos" (Universidad de San Andrés, 2000).

7

Brazil: Understanding the Influence of Organizational Culture on Alliance Development[1]

Rosa Maria Fischer

Introduction

What is the influence of an organization's culture on the creation and management of cross-sector alliances? Cases reviewed under the SEKN project in Brazil indicate that cultural patterns and power relationships prevalent in the corporations are strong conditioning factors in the characteristics of cross-sector partnerships with Civil Society Organizations (CSOs).

There are two possible ways in which a cross-sector alliance may be established. On the one hand, the corporation may define a certain strategy for its social involvement, based on its own conception of corporate social responsibility, and then seek a partner in the third sector that adds specific knowledge and experience to manage the project. On the other hand, the corporation may be approached by an organization that needs financial and material resources and end up adhering to its proposals, deepening the initial relationship. In any movement that leads to the strengthening of collaboration, taking it from a philanthropic relationship to a deeper form of alliance, there is the need for a process, no matter how small, to establish the cultural identities of the organizations involved.

The purpose of this chapter is to analyze, on the basis of research performed with Brazilian cases, how the cultural and political aspects of the members of an alliance are critical for understanding the barriers and opportunities that influence cross-sector collaborations.

Though they may be found in specific aspects of the collaboration between the organizations, the contradictions and difficulties of partnerships are originated in the subjective sphere of expectations, perceptions, and representations. Hence, the analysis should take into account the objective factors that relate to the way in which actors deal with the issues, and, at the same time, with the more subjective characteristics associated with values and assumptions underlying their actions and decisions.

The theoretical framework that serves as a basis for analyzing our empirical research on cross-sector collaborations follows two dimensions. One is a macro approach that attempts to identify the cultural and political configuration of the environment surrounding the organizations that integrate a cross-sector alliance. The other focuses on the specific characteristics of the partners to understand if and how they influence the alliance composition, development, and management.

The contextual dimension is relevant insofar as the political and cultural aspects of the environment determine the strategic dimension of corporations and the way in which they relate to different markets, stakeholders, and civil society as a whole.[2] Government and CSOs, though perhaps more resilient than corporations, are also affected by contextual characteristics in the environment.

In the organizational dimension, we find the convergence between the personal characteristics of the actors directly involved in the alliance and the cultural patterns that define the identity of the partner organizations. The background of social entrepreneurs and business leaders explains many of the choices made when establishing a social action partnership. The clash between the "result-oriented culture" of businesses and the "process-oriented culture" of CSOs may impede the creation of alliances or, if formed, ultimately result in their painful break-up, or provide valuable lessons for partners. Alliance success may be interpreted differently by the parties, leading to a power conflict in the quest for process control.

This chapter attempts to generate insights for improvements in the management of alliances, opening a debate that highlights the cultural complexities involved in partnering across sectors and the importance of overcoming cultural barriers in order to make cross-sector alliances a powerful tool for sustainable social development.

Business Corporations and the Third Sector: The Brazilian Context

The cultural and political patterns found in any organization are strongly affected by the prevailing features of the surrounding culture.

A brief description of the evolution of businesses and CSOs in Brazil can be helpful in identifying the roles that these social forces have played in the emergence of cross-sector alliances. It can also show how the cultural and political characteristics of each organization influence the composition and development of partnerships.

From the colonial times and throughout the process of industrialization, Brazil's economic development was shaped by a strong presence of government in the country's social life. In the second half of the twentieth century, the Brazilian government carried out infrastructure investments and adopted fiscal policies to attract industrial foreign investment. Family businesses focused primarily on the domestic market under the protection of public economic regulations.

Though industrial corporations experienced the benefits of modernization, such as urban development, the formation of a consumer market, and the broadening of the so-called middle classes, this was not enough to build a solid economy that would lead to the distribution of wealth.

Furthermore, there was no fostering of an independent national business community that would assume a leadership role in the search for solutions to social problems. Brazil's history is filled with individuals that exercised personal initiative in the development of business philanthropy, yet social entrepreneurship was restricted to the individual level, and did not become a common trait of the business community as a whole.

Cyclical crises shattered the country's economy, the trust of foreign investors, and the confidence and self-esteem of Brazilian business leaders. During the 1990s, globalization forced Brazil to adopt liberal policies and to face up to the challenges of modernization. Local industry was overwhelmed by fierce competition that followed the lowering of trade barriers. Fiscal crises, the opening up of imports, privatizations, and the rise in foreign capital flows radically transformed the Brazilian economic landscape at the end of the century, a situation that was not conducive to the eradication of economic and social imbalances.

It was in this context that the third sector emerged as a strong actor in Brazil's society, defined as a group made up of private, nonprofit organizations, whose actions address public needs or issues involving social needs.

The third sector represents an "organizational patchwork" made up of a mixture of non-governmental organizations, private foundations, social aid and charity entities, religious organizations, and cultural and educational associations. These organizations play roles that do not differ significantly from the pattern established by analogous organizations in industrialized countries. They vary in size, degree of formalization, amount of resources, institutional objectives, and modus operandi. Such diversity stems from the richness and plurality of Brazilian society and the different historical backgrounds that frame the relationship between government, the market, and civil society.

The main components of the American nonprofit sector, frequently adopted as a standard for understanding the same sector in other countries, may be found in Brazil's third sector. According to Salamon/Anheier's "structural-operational" definition used by Landim,[3] those organizations are private, not for profit, formal, independent, and relying on some kind of volunteer work. Meanwhile, the notion that, in view of these common characteristics, such organizations constitute a specific "sector" of the social fabric is not sufficiently understood in academia or in the world of civic, associative, and solidarity practices. Even the name assigned to this field is in itself a bone of contention, in which different visions, values, identities, and ideologies—more than academic concepts—compete with each other.

A comprehensive categorization of third sector organizations, emphasizing their origin and historical development, allows us to classify them as traditional, religious, and lay entities; non-governmental organizations; para-governmental entities; associative organizations, and business-related entities.

Lay and religious associations date back to the Brazilian colonial period and gained relevance towards the end of the nineteenth century with the country's urbanization and industrialization. Mutual aid societies and unions were organizational forms brought by European immigrants. Solidarity, social aid, and the formation of political conscience were elements introduced by these entities in their quest for inclusion in the elitist and closed political system that prevailed in Brazil at that time.

The emergence of non-governmental organizations in Brazil is a more recent phenomenon. Throughout the past thirty years, a variety of movements, more or less formalized, emerged throughout the country, organized in response to social needs or as an expression of resistance to the military dictatorship. The efficacy of those movements was made evident by the achievements obtained in various fields, such as the defense of human rights, the recovery of the state of law, the enhancement of social policies involving health and education, and the 1988 Constitution itself, called the "Citizen Constitution."

Though growing rapidly, business initiatives in the third sector are relatively new, executed through foundations, institutes, and the individual philanthropy of business leaders. To this day, "philanthropy" is a term that has pejorative connotations. Meanwhile, in less than a decade, this perspective has been changing: corporations and business foundations lead discussions regarding the third sector, and their social initiatives are portrayed in the media as positive and concrete examples of a new alternative for national development, based on social responsibility, entrepreneurial spirit, and partnerships among sectors that did not previously interact with each other.

The elements that compose the third sector arena are intertwined in some rather complex ways, blurring the boundaries between the three sectors and making them less static. The activities, programs, and discourses within the third-sector field are also diverse: terms such as "the construction of civil society," "the scope of democratic participation," and "the promotion of sustainable development in the country" are used, although relationships between those expressions and the objective content of actions and projects are not always clearly understood.

The greatest challenge faced by the diverse group of organizations that make up the third sector is the increased demand for services and effective results at a time when there has been a reduction of financial aid in the midst of economic crisis. It is precisely the paradox of the need for self-sustainability and the generation of resources within a context in which beneficiaries rarely find themselves in a position to pay for services that leads to a path of cross-sector collaboration.

In order to overcome that vulnerability, CSOs need to develop certain basic competencies: those required to build institutional capabilities to conduct negotiations, to elaborate joint plans, and to operate within partnerships; those needed to report their operations with transparency; and those that enable them to produce services with a high standard of quality, generating effective results that can be perceived by society at large.

The Emergence of Cross-Sector Alliances

Until 1998, the involvement of businesses with social issues and in collaborations with CSOs was hardly seen in Brazil. Firms that carried out social projects did not publicize their actions or collaboration with third sector organizations. These actions were considered to pertain only to the internal life of organizations and to the realm of personal decisions of business leaders.

Since then, this outlook has been changing. There has been research, academic studies, dissemination pieces, and mainly, broad media coverage describing social endeavors performed by organizations acting in partnerships.

Initial studies of partnerships[4] show that the operation of cross-sector collaborations is not the simple process sometimes expected by the partners. The more common challenges found in our study are:

- Difficulty in sharing the power and control of decisions involving the partners. Each organization has a specific vision of the importance of its role in the alliance and tends to minimize the roles of the other partners, creating a conflict of perceptions that may obstruct joint actions.

- The time and energy required to match different organizational cultures, which generate divergent expectations on how the alliance should operate, on which success indicators it should be evaluated, and on its working style and rhythm.

- The lack of adequate management tools for cross-sector partnering. Corporations often tend to impose their procedures, considering them to be more apt given their proven efficiency in the business world. On the other hand, NGOs, zealous of their expertise, are often reluctant to share the organizational competencies they have developed, and restrict the exchange of knowledge amongst the partners.

Despite such difficulties, cross-sector partnering has boomed over the past five years, bringing together market organizations with CSOs to solve or reduce social exclusion problems.[5]

The political context of the 1990s favored the development of a positive climate for interaction among organizations belonging to different sectors. The return to democracy was consolidated, providing room for the exercise of civil citizenship and for organized forms of participation. The 1988 Constitution secured civil rights for all citizens and strengthened democratic principles of social tolerance. The proposal to decentralize government, though slowed by difficulties encountered in fiscal reform, stimulated the emancipation of local communities.

Following the redemocratization process, non-governmental organizations and grass-root organizations had to face up to the challenges of redefining themselves, finding new innovative ways to pursue their missions, and developing new organizational competencies. Due to the reduction of available financial resources,[6] CSOs had to learn fundraising techniques, financial engineering to optimize their use, and competitive positioning to guarantee their differentiation. A new discourse emerged in the third sector arena; one that introduced concepts such as efficiency, efficacy, and results, all ideas that used to be more common in the business world.

At the other end, that of the market, there is also a new trend that converges with the one that characterizes the third sector environment: proposals of business involvement in social causes. Some initiatives are of a predominantly political nature, such as the National Thinking of Business Foundations (*Pensamento Nacional das Bases Empresariais*) movement, that attempted to influence public debate over social problems without the intent of becoming a political party.[7] Other movements, often led by the same protagonists, assume from their inception the explicit mission of acting on a certain perverse feature of the Brazilian social reality. An example is the ABRINQ Foundation for Children's Rights (*Fundação ABRINQ pelos Direitos da Criança*), created at the beginning of the 1990s by business leaders that wished to influence legislation and public opinion to protect children's civil rights.

This trend gave rise to a proliferation of business-related foundations and institutes, meant to become a "social arm" of private enterprise. Other pioneering corporations involved in these initiatives started to implement their own social responsibility undertakings, approaching CSOs, or simply becoming more amenable to their requests and campaigns.

One instance that accelerated this process of social responsibility awareness was the Citizenship Action against Misery and for Life (*Ação da Cidadania contra a Miséria e pela Vida*), a campaign organized by sociologist Herbert José de Souza ("Betinho") in 1993. Upon describing the problem of hunger in simple terms and proposing that each citizen engage in its solution, this community leader touched a profound sentiment in Brazilian society at large. New initiatives were launched, old projects and programs were re-energized, and the magic of a key word was rediscovered: partnership.

Despite its newly found visibility, the notion of partnership was still difficult to implement in practice. Organizations in the third sector were more accustomed to promoting fund-raising campaigns and soliciting donations than elaborating joint projects with other institutions. Some NGOs felt uncomfortable in the new paradigm, with a feeling of invasion and loss, as if their identity could become fragmented upon allying with another organization.

Nevertheless, in spite of certain restrictions, these movements altered the conception of the roles played by government, the market, and the third sector. The business community warmed up to the idea of social action as a practice through which companies might voluntarily transcend their economic interests, starting a movement towards a more humane and social engagement at local, national, and world levels. As a measure of internal efficiency, corporate social responsibility was not opposed to financial gains, but rather, according to this view, a necessary condition for optimizing the utilization of resources and the mobilization of individuals.

This new vision, currently present in business executives and shareholders' discourse, is the result of a long and complex process of approximation between corporations and civil society. Before, companies used to focus exclusively on seeking profits for their shareholders, and their social role was viewed as limited to the generation of jobs, payment of taxes, and law abidance. In this context, donations were made by business owners as individuals and reflected a personal attitude of charity, disassociated from the company.

This attitude began to change over the last decade, marked by slower economic growth and widespread unemployment at the global level. The impact caused by industries in the ecosystem turned the threats of environmental destruction, by and large ignored until then, into a verifiable reality. Compounding this emerging scenario was strong social tension arising from the growing mobilization of segments of civil society, coupled with a clear perception of the impact of high levels of social exclusion on the consumer market. In different circles, civil society started to succeed in changing ethical business attitudes in their various areas of involvement and press for effective changes in the relationship of businesses with their socio-environmental surroundings.

Gradually, corporations began responding to these calls, reviewing their roles and opening up to the possibility of discussing novel approaches that previously were seen as incompatible with the primary objective of obtaining and maximizing profits. The strategy of businesses started to contemplate the need to revise their relationship with employees and suppliers; ethical principles were redefined vis-à-vis customers; the environmental consequences of companies' activities became a legal liability.

In time, neighboring communities and society as a whole came to be encompassed in this growing set of concerns, and began to be included in companies' strategic planning as relevant stakeholders.

Current Profile of Alliances

In an intentional sample of 2,085 surveyed firms conducted in 2001–2002, 385 reported being involved in social actions, with 85 percent of them relying on alliances with other organizations as a means of carrying out their social plans.[8] This finding highlights the plurality of the various forms of collaboration, since, for many firms, the concept of partnership ranges from a one-time donation to support a specific entity to the development of joint projects with various organizations. The analysis of the data in Figure 11 shows the following types of cross-sector collaborations:

- 15 percent resort to partnerships for all of their social practices.
- 37 percent are involved in partnerships, but not on a permanent basis.
- 33 percent carry out their social projects through occasional partnership practices.
- 15 percent of responding firms are not engaged in any sort of alliance.

Figure 11: Tri-Sectoral Model: Distribution of Alliances among Surveyed Companies

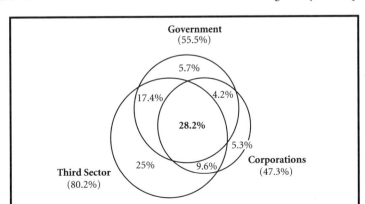

The above graph depicts the replies of all firms that resort to collaborations as a means of implementing their social action practices. Each circle represents a sector with the numbers within them relating to the percentage of existing alliances between the responding firms and organizations in each sector—corporations, third sector, and government. The numbers in the intersections represent the number of partnerships of firms with more than one sector. The first finding is that most firms maintain alliances with third sector organizations (80 percent), whereas 56 percent have partnerships with government agencies, and 47 percent with other business enterprises.

Yet, as the percentages indicate, these alliances are not established exclusively with organizations of a single sector:

- 17.4 percent of companies simultaneously establish alliances with third sector and government organizations.

- 4.2 percent establish alliances with government organizations and other business entities.

- 9.6 percent establish alliances with third sector organizations and other business entities.

- 28.2 percent of firms establish alliances with organizations in all three sectors, configuring the nucleus of the graph in which the more complex relationships are encountered. Yet, these are also the ones that observe the highest potential to attain their objectives.

These percentages indicate the intensity in relationships among sectors as a means of enabling firms to engage in social action practices. This movement that brings business organizations and CSOs closer together may be indicative of a cultural change. Corporate leaders who are responsible for strategic decisions in their firms can no longer ignore the "social function" of businesses. On the one hand, we find entities, such as GIFE, Instituto Ethos, the Institute for Business Citizenship, and others, that promote the concepts and practices of corporate responsibility and organizational citizenship with the purpose of informing and mobilizing decision-makers. On the other hand, the media, through various vehicles, disseminates the best practice examples that demonstrate and encourage positive behavior on the part of businesses and executives.

Only 47 percent of surveyed firms establish alliances with organizations in their own private sector. This is probably the result of a search for specific competencies in their field. In other words, when businesses decide to initiate social activities, they try to ally with governmental and non-governmental organizations that already muster social management know-how. This reduces implementation and operating costs for business projects in social activities, and may imply recognition of the competence of CSOs.

In some instances, businesses have dealt with their social involvement as a differentiating factor in competitive environments, leading them to consider exclusivity in the alliance established and express an unwillingness to accept other companies into the partnership. This factor has frequently been identified as a barrier in the formation and sustainability of cross-sector collaborations.

By carrying over certain typical business patterns into social practices, some private companies constrain the potential for growth and consolidation of partnership networks. Demand for exclusivity often discourages organizations in the third sector from engaging in an alliance with a corporation, or if they do engage, it generates a conflictive relationship in which the entity feels restricted in its autonomy. An interesting example among the cases studied was Itaú Bank, which went from being the sole business partner in the alliance that created the Education and Participation Program (*Programa Educação & Participação*), to encouraging the creation of the 2001 Partners Program, which sought to launch a multi-sector network that would include other firms.

Another aspect revealed by our data has been the trend to use collaborations as a means of enhancing the existing synergy among companies in the same supply chain. In this case, the established acquaintance provided by the business relationship facilitates the creation of a partnership for the social practice, neutralizing competition issues. It is observed that suppliers and service providers do partner with their clients to pursue a joint social project.

This configuration may be very efficient when allied companies come together for a specific cause. The ABRINQ Foundation, a non-governmental organization focusing on children's rights, promoted an initiative in 2000 called the Bandeirantes Pact. Its objective was to gather agribusiness producers of sugar and alcohol located alongside the Bandeirantes Highway in the state of São Paulo and bring them together with their suppliers and outsourcers to gain a commitment to refrain from employing child labor in sugar cane harvesting tasks.

It should be noted that the percentage of alliances of firms encompassing organizations in the three sectors is higher than the percentage of alliances involving only two sectors. It may be inferred that the engagement of the corporation in cross-sector alliances makes for broader awareness of social problems and adds to their drive to act in search of solutions. The quest for various partners may indicate a change in perception by firms in the sense that they become more proactive in their social enterprise initiatives and more selective in their choice of partners.

Enhancement in the quality of their social actions is the main driver identified by surveyed firms in the use of alliances: 74 percent believe that this form of social action yields efficiency gains. Recognition of the fact that partnering organizations may improve their know-how to deal with social issues represents the second motive reported by participating companies, accounting for 64 percent of the sample.

These results seem to indicate a trend towards a change in behavior on the part of business leaders responsible for decisions shaping social action strategies within the firms. This search for efficiency, know-how, and specific competencies to generate social projects in partnership with the third sector is indicative of the fact that:

- Businesses' social activity starts to be viewed as a core component of the strategic direction of the corporation and thus, begins to be treated with the business rationality that demands efficiency, efficacy, and effectiveness.
- NGOs and social entities come to be valued as holders of expertise in dealing with social issues. They are invited into partnerships following the same rationale used for outsourcing and contracting with suppliers.

In the cases of two of the Brazilian firms studied, Itaú Bank and the cosmetics company Natura, alliances were established with the same nonprofit organization, the Center for the Study and Research of Education, Culture and Community Action (*Centro de Estudos e Pesquisas em Educação, Cultura e Ação Comunitária*, hence CENPEC), an entity renowned for its technical competence in educational issues, especially those affecting the performance of public schools and the education of children and adolescents from low-income segments.

Though they are firms with different cultural organizations, Itaú and Natura are both renowned for their selectiveness in hiring human resources and subcontracting services. Technical competence, solid skills in their area of specialization, good qualifications, and outstanding performance are requisites demanded by both firms from their executives, staff, and suppliers. Thus, it seemed natural that they should use the same criteria for selecting their social action partners.

Nevertheless, this observation that shows the influence of business culture over the composition of the partnership, also brings to the fore the question of the balance of power in the relationship among partners. If a company maintains a dominant role in this selection process, we may wonder whether it wishes to lead the partnership to a transactional or an integrative pattern. We could also think that, instead of investing in the creation of an alliance, these firms might be simply replicating the practices developed in dealing with other suppliers for specialized services.

CENPEC's statements regarding the many projects developed with Itaú Bank highlight the characteristics of their alliance as integrative, using the Continuum described in Chapter 1 (p. 4):[9] "We can no longer tell where the bank's involvement ends and where our technical activity begins;" or "Itaú cannot do away with the quality and the efficiency that CENPEC adds to the projects," are examples of opinions that reinforce the idea of an egalitarian, balanced, and synchronized relationship between two organizations. Meanwhile, the bank itself wonders about the opportunity gains that could result from the decentralization of the Education and Participation Program. By resorting to regional entities that would scale the work nationwide, the bank would broaden the scope of its social action, adapt it to local specificities, and ensure more visibility for the program.

Natura's alliance with CENPEC, focusing on the improvement of the quality of education at the Matilde school, did not last. School teachers did not accept that outside professionals dare propose changes in their programs, and pressured the company to dismiss the consulting team. The way in which the discontinuation of CENPEC's involvement took place, suggests that it was not considered a full partner from the perspectives of both Natura and the public school that benefited from its consulting support. Instead, that CSO was viewed as a consulting service provider, which could be retained or dismissed as needed.

In our research, the need to assure "better control of resources" was the main argument invoked by those firms that chose not to engage in cross-sector collaborations to carry out their social initiatives. These firms believe that they can manage their social actions more efficiently on their own; they show resistance to share resources, and tend to express mistrust regarding the technical and managerial skills of partners coming from other sectors. Interestingly enough, the same argument that calls for higher technical, managerial, and operating efficiency, is used both by firms that do not resort to cross-sector partnerships and by those that do.

Though these research findings may seem contradictory, it is not so, and reflects the variety of experiences in organizational collaboration. It provides evidence that the perceptions of those who did not engage in partnerships and those who underwent troubled experiences in other alliances were affected by mistrust and the lack of aptitude for cooperative endeavors.

The most common arguments expressed by firms resisting alliances emphasize the lack of professionalism, poor management training, and low administrative competence of third sector organizations. The latter, in turn, highlight the "bullishness" and "technocracy" of some private companies. They refuse to adopt a "result-oriented logic" that, from their perspective, would downgrade the quality of their work and the sensitivity to deal with social issues. These two conflicting rationales regarding the nature and value of social work are the two most frequent phenomena that may be found in cultural conflicts of cross-sector alliances.

These conflicts are greater when a multilateral alliance involves agents coming from the first, second, and third sectors. Governmental organizations are usually viewed as non-cooperative, bureaucratic, slow, and inefficient. Thus, it is common for business leaders to avoid partnerships with government agencies.

However, this challenge may lead to an effective process of organizational transformation. One of the spin-offs of the alliance between Natura and the Itapecerica da Serra public school resulted in the *Barracões da Cidadania* (Citizenship Barns) program. Managed by the Municipal Secretary of Culture, this program was able to serve needy children and youths with social and cultural activities and equipment.

In the multiple alliance of the Ekos project, one of Natura's private-sector partners, Cognis, preferred to stay out of the partnership with the indigenous communities in the Amazon region. Fearful of the potential hurdles that could be raised by the National Indian Foundation (*Fundação Nacional do Índio*, hence FUNAI), the federal agency in charge of relations with natives and their employment in forestry, Cognis chose to restrict its field of action to the process of collection and extraction of natural resources. Despite that decision, Natura decided to engage the indigenous tribes, established cordial relations with their leaders, and offered them the opportunity to work in the Ekos line production process.

These examples illustrate the novelty of experiences in cross-sector collaboration and the diversity of results and interpretations. It can also be noted that they incorporate the contradictions that are inherent in the class structure of a capitalist system that is characterized by economic inequality and social injustice. Yet, they reflect a trend toward social mobilization on the part of various agents, leading to specific cultural mutations on account of actions and decisions by those individuals and by the organizations that they command.

These analyses validate the importance of the cross-sector collaboration phenomenon in Brazil. Next, we will deepen our attempt to understand the role of organizational cultures in the composition and development of partnerships.

Sectoral Cultures, Organizational Cultures

Theories on the construction and consolidation of culture, whether within small social groups or in the broader dimension of society as a whole, highlight the decisive importance of certain factors: sharing a vision of the world and of basic assumptions; the process of identity creation in the field of ideas, ideals, values, and beliefs; and the process of aggregation of political legitimacy, which is essential for the recognition of power, authority, rights, and norms. These same factors, with different compositions and expressions, come together to cause the breakup of political and cultural patterns, configuring the phenomenon of cultural change.[10]

The prevalent culture in a particular social context permeates all forms of relationship and influences the cultural composition of specific organizations. In that sense, the corporations, the social entities, and the public agencies that interact in the cases of cross-sector collaboration that we have studied here are repositories of the more vigorous characteristics of the model of culture and power that prevails in Brazilian society.

In the cases studied, we found that the patterns present in the culture and in the relationships of power that make up the identity of corporations, have a decisive influence on the social actions that they pursue in their alliances. Itaú is a "bank of engineers" that not only maintains precise hierarchical relationships, but also works with an exclusive focus on actions and decisions. It prioritizes technical competencies, placing value on the field of knowledge, and investing heavily in state-of-the-art technology. Upon establishing the partnership with CENPEC, it made use of those parameters of competency and efficiency, maintaining control over the quality of its social action and keeping the Education and Participation Program within the realm of strategic decisions at the bank.

Itaú's partnership with CENPEC also reflects a mutual recognition of their respective identities: they both consider education to be a driving force for social development, and they both attribute that responsibility to the Government, seeking to influence the drafting of social policy and to invest in the betterment of public education. When summoning Ministry of Education and Culture and UNICEF[11] to join the alliance, they also showed consensus over the perception that the program had to reach a national scope, and that the legitimacy of the program had to be validated by the country's maximum authority on education, as well as an internationally renowned entity. Hence, the organizational-cultural trait of respect for institutionalized power hierarchies is made explicit.[12]

Itaú Bank is an organization known for its image of solidity, trust, and transparency. It operates as a full bank, with marketing structures that are able to serve different client segments that include small and medium-sized enterprises, large corporations, and high net worth individuals. It quickly absorbs technological breakthroughs, and defines its social action policy as a community investment that produces a return not to be measured by bank indicators, but rather by the benefits obtained by society. CENPEC designs and executes projects in partnership with the private sector, multilateral and national public agencies, focused on improving the quality of public education and of public policies that target formal education. Both organizations managed to align their social action missions along the same objectives, focusing primarily on the effective implementation of improvements in educational policies.

Furthermore, they agreed that the best strategy is to forge alliances, as a means to leverage their respective essential competencies to pursue their social objectives. CENPEC took responsibility for the relationship with schools, community groups, and other social entities engaged in the program. On the other hand, the bank focused on promoting events that targeted the business community, and sought the support of other corporations and professional organizations in disseminating the program.

When looking at the choices both organizations made upon defining their social action strategy, the influence of industry characteristics cannot be overlooked. Itaú is concerned with its institutional image, since it operates in a sector that is considered to be unpopular. This stems from Brazil's development model, overly dependent on the attraction of sizable quantities of foreign capital, which translates into significant pressure on fiscal adjustment and a restrictive monetary policy; this process led to high interest rates, favoring the financial sector, in detriment to other segments of the economy.

The bank vigorously seeks competitive advantages, since it is inserted in a sector that has undergone significant restructuring and consolidation, where attributes such as business reliability and their clients' identification with the brand have become key differentiators. Upon joining the group of companies that make up the Dow Jones Sustainability Group Index (DJSGI), the bank tries to leverage these differences through the acknowledgement of its social and financial performance, measured by external standards. The DJSGI monitors policies associated with the company's relationship with its stakeholders, such as those targeting environmental protection or contributing to social welfare. Upon being recognized as a member of this select group of institutions, the value of Itaú's brand was greatly enhanced in domestic and international financial markets.

CENPEC also benefited from the alliance. The Education and Participation Program allowed that CSO to accrue some competitive gains, such as gaining access to an enlarged pool of potential customers, incorporating performance indicators that allow them to better monitor their own efficiency, and obtaining nationwide recognition for their social action.

Like the financial sector, the telecom industry, in which Telemig Celular is inserted, also presents characteristics of high competitiveness and unpopularity. This unpopularity comes from the intense process of privatization of services that started in 1998. The private companies that entered the market at that time faced the need to enlarge and consolidate their market position. Satisfying unmet demand and overcoming the dissatisfaction of consumers caused by low quality of services, made for a very challenging transition for these companies.

Telemig Celular bears the burden of being a company which is currently under the process of creating its own culture and in which the internal political relations are not yet clearly defined. An outcome of a recent privatization, the company is a "patchwork" of inherited public cultural standards and those of the new controlling shareholders. The decision to create the Telemig Celular Institute (*Instituto Telemig Celular*) and the definition of its focus and scope, indicate the prevalence of a rational logic, which seeks synergies with the company's business while strengthening the company's image and brand equity in the eyes of the community.

In its search for partners for the creation of the Municipal Councils for Children's and Teenagers' Rights (*Conselhos Municipais de Direito da Criança e do Adolescente*), the Telemig Celular Institute chose to launch an alliance with an informal organization, which included members of civil society, volunteers, and government employees, prioritizing initiatives focused in the participation of various social agents.

The Telemig Celular Institute tries to create participation mechanisms with high community penetration, which lends legitimacy to its social action. The Municipal Councils for Children's and Teenagers' Rights and the Care Councils (*Conselhos Tutelares*) are authentic forums for popular participation in the formulation and assurance of national public policies dealing with children's and teenagers' rights. We see here a pattern of risk management, which is specific to the culture of the post-privatization sector. The company seeks competitive advantages by associating its social initiative with the construction and consolidation of effective popular participation tools leading to policy improvements.

Currently, Telemig Celular Institute is trying to enhance its social action strategy by establishing an alliance with the Attorney General's Office (*Procuradoria Geral da Justiça*)—related to the Ministry of Justice—which plays the most important role in the assurance of children's and teenager's rights. Considering the profound cultural differences between a judiciary organization and a telecom company, there are likely to be substantial difficulties in establishing and managing this new alliance. Taking into account the complexity involved in assuring that legislation that is essential to the future of the nation does not end up as a set of mute rules, it is understandable that Telemig Celular Institute would be monitoring this process with purposeful clarity of thought. Mobilizing volunteers does not suffice; the program would amount only to having capable municipal advisers, if the Judiciary were not committed to enforcing the law in all spheres of every day life.

Natura is a company that transforms and recreates itself through the experiences it accumulates, driving itself to create new product lines, to use innovative marketing and advertising approaches, and to associate its brand with concepts of responsibility. Company founder Luiz Seabra emphasizes that the main sustainability principle in Natura's culture is the "value of relations." He even goes as far as saying that cosmetics production and marketing are only activities that provide opportunities and offer support for the development and expansion of interpersonal relationships. The slogan "Well Being Well" was coined to convey just how important it was to the company for people to feel good about themselves, building pleasant relationships with one another.

These cultural patterns, which sometimes seem excessively abstract for a business environment, took shape in features like the architectural design of company facilities, the product packaging styles, and the workstation layout at the manufacturing plant and office buildings.[13] Less explicit, though even more obvious, these traits emerge in the company's management policies: employees are referred to as associates (*colaboradores*), promotions and career developments are explained candidly, and management practices and relationships aim to reduce interpersonal distance and encourage egalitarian perceptions. Some outstanding initiatives confirm the internal coherence of this culture, such as the environmental protection policies in place at company plants, the concern for occupational health and safety conditions in working environments, and the hiring of handicapped individuals and subsequent efforts to integrate these new employees into company life.

Also in its social action practices, Natura has progressively accumulated experiences with a variety of partners in different modalities, building up an organizational learning process that reflects the growth and consolidation of the company and its brand. In its partnerships, Natura stresses the significance of direct quality relationships, as it has always valued the direct sales format as an ideal vehicle for positioning its products in the market.

The questionings and issues involving the development of the new Ekos line emerge precisely because, according to company culture, it is very important to determine the degree of commitment in the multiple alliances included in their proposal. Previous alliances have increased Natura's collaboration competencies. With the bulk and richness of that learning process, it was possible for the company to replicate its social actions successfully, consolidating some positive practices that included the clear definition of partners' roles, the continuous clarification of mutual expectations, and the creation of a dynamic and constant interaction process ensuring social action efficiency.

The Natura-Ekos project involves the incorporation of multiple stakeholders, with different profiles and motivations, in a supply chain whose core value added lies in Brazilian biodiversity, exploited through management and work processes that respect the culture of the social groups involved. This chain includes Cognis—a multinational chemical company in charge of processing oils extracted from natural resources. Both companies share the same sustainability values. However, as mentioned before, Cognis decided not to deal with the indigenous communities in raw material collection processes in order to avoid the complicated and bureaucratic contacts with FUNAI. Cognis' decision did not prevent Natura from initiating and maintaining relations with the indigenous communities. This initial clarification was important because it portrayed the differences and similarities in each company's definition of the value of the relationship with the communities in the Amazon region.

For the partnering companies, the success of the Ekos line is a sine qua non condition. The cosmetics manufacturing and marketing industry is highly competitive and is currently undergoing a cartelling process in the world market. The differentiation of Natura products not only needs to ensure their local market position, it must also offer international leverage. To face this challenge, the concepts of "natural/native/Brazilian" should be associated with the proper environmental sustainability procedures: conditions for natural recovery of collected resources, preservation of original sources, and environmental balance maintenance. The product to be offered in the international market should be attractive on account of its extravagant content, but should also assure consumers that they are not accomplices to an aggression against nature or to exploitative labor practices.

To ensure that all these abstract concepts are incorporated in the specific product it manufactures and markets, Natura has to trust Cognis's procedures. The latter, in turn, must strive to keep that coherence, not only to guarantee its client's loyalty, but also to attract other companies that are interested in "being and seeming politically correct." Both companies need the Forest and Agriculture Management and Certification Institute (*Instituto de Manejo e Certificação Florestal e Agrícola,* hence IMAFLORA) to audit efficiently the processes employed, since only IMAFLORA may assure the legitimacy of its certification to both the market and society.

Though each of these organizations has its own culture, they were forced to become compatible through numerous meetings, agreements, and negotiations to make the partnership more viable. Natura's value-based culture is carried over to the product it manufactures and shows that relationships among people are capable of transforming society. Social involvement through alliances is conceived as a means for promoting such transformation.

Social Actors in the Collaboration Culture

The study of strategic alliances formed between sectors allows us to foresee the materialization of what can be called a "collaboration culture" among organizations that had previously been held separate as a result of their different natures, their different "forms of existence." Basically, it is the people involved in establishing these new partnerships who are responsible for forming these new cultural standards.

There are at least three determinant factors involved in the configuration of behavior and a culture in a collaboration process between sectors: the existence of personal relations between partners preceding the formation of the alliances; the disposition of allies to set an environment of trust and mutual respect; and the care taken in the establishment of communication channels, which strengthen and ease the management of such alliances.

Relations between Actors

The dynamics of the initial contacts between the elements of private corporations and CSOs are a key determinant in the building process of an alliance. These early interactions constitute the basic pillar for the collaboration effort, as it is from this initial dynamic that roles, mutual expectations, and expected results are defined.

Companies and organizations of the third sector generally do not establish partnerships on a random basis. Rather, these connections are established by active members of both partners who already know each other from diverse social and professional contacts, or who are introduced and brought together by a third actor who has trust in both. Maria Alice Setúbal, founder of CENPEC and educator with a consolidated academic career and renowned competence, is the sister of the president of Itaú, Roberto Setúbal. In 1992, Itaú managers expressed their dissatisfaction with the dispersive form in which social action was being implemented. It was necessary to carry out those initiatives focusing on well-defined objectives and establishing structured procedures. Maria Alice's experience in the field of education, added to the confidence level from the family relationship, enhanced the initial contacts that preceded the Itaú-CENPEC partnership.

Guilherme Leal—one of the presidents of Natura—knew Maria Alice quite well, serving on several boards of various CSOs like ABRINQ Foundation with her. In planning an alliance for the enhancement of education in the state-owned primary and secondary school Matilde Maria Cremm, Natura agreed upon hiring an entity that possessed both experience and a strong reputation in improving public education. In this context the reference to CENPEC naturally emerged, on one hand, as an entity renowned for its competence, and on the other, by its accessibility as acknowledged in the personal relationship between the executives and the educator.

Luiz Gonzaga Leal, former president of Telemig Celular, had worked with the Minas Gerais Children and Teenagers State Council before the creation of Telemig Celular Institute. This experience allowed him to meet social actors involved with issues centered on children's rights, and later led him to envisage a partnership between Telemig Celular Institute and Volunteer Support Groups (*Grupo de Apoio de Voluntários*).

When invited to structure Telemig Celular Institute, Francisco Azevedo was an executive of *Fundação ACESITA* (Acesita Foundation), already recognized as one of the corporate foundations most active in the strengthening of community organizations like the Council of Children and Teenagers' Rights. The personal and mutual understanding between Francisco and Luiz Gonzaga Leal was decisive in gaining Francisco's acceptance of the invitation presented by Telemig Celular Institute. He not only brought to the post the asset of his prior experience with ACESITA, but also the network of relationships established with the Industries Federation of the Rio de Janeiro State (*Federação das Indústrias do Estado do Rio de Janeiro*, or FIERJ), the Industries Federation of the Minas Gerais State (*Federação das Indústrias do Estado de Minas Gerais*, or FIEMG), the Group of Institutes, Foundations and Corporations (*Grupo de Institutos, Fundações e Empresas*, or GIFE), and many other institutions that were all recognized in the business community for social entrepreneurship initiatives and corporate responsibility.

Thus, pre-existing relationships played a decisive role in the constitution of alliances between sectors. Organizations warmed up greatly to the notion of collaboration upon identifying that they shared similar principles and ideas with other individuals. This was crucial in reducing uncertainty and allowing groups to deal with the novel challenge of managing strategic alliances among sectors in safer fashion. From their perspective, a shared "world vision" reduced the risk of involving their companies and organizations in potentially dangerous or incompatible partnerships, which could ultimately do damage to the institution's reputation.

The Construction of Trust

The establishment of cultural identity among organizations is eased by the build-up of trust between allies. This build-up is the cornerstone of any model of cooperative social action, and manifests itself in interpersonal relationships between decision makers that guide the partnership.

Rubens Becker, president of the chemical enterprise Cognis, a partner organization of Natura's project Ekos, moved to Amazônia to make the initial contacts with IBAMA, the governmental organization responsible for the environment, an effort that would ultimately provide the company with the tools required for implementing its project. In this manner, the relationship was initiated with mutual recognition of governmental authority and the company's intentions, allowing the establishment of trust.

Natura directors personally visited the homes of indigenous people to explain how important the relationship with the natives was to the company. When the indigenous leaders expressed their interest in visiting the plant in São Paulo in exchange for this visit, they made an unprecedented gesture that demonstrated how important this gentle exchange had been in consolidating the beginning of a collaborative relationship.

The cases researched by SEKN in Brazil show that trust among partners developed in the following manner:

Prioritizing Trust in the Planning of the Alliance

The cases of Itaú-CENPEC and Natura-Ekos provide us with the best examples of this approach. The pre-existing relationships between the president of Itaú and the director of CENPEC, deeply grounded in trust, permeated the entire lifespan of this collaboration. The quality of the ensuing dialogue, as well as the complementarity of both organizations' core competencies and the level of alignment of both partners' organizational values, later reinforced on an ongoing basis this initial trust. In the case of Natura-Ekos, their experience with previous alliances led them to prioritize the establishment of trust relationships as the cornerstone for the creation of partnership networks.

Building Trust through Empathy, Transparency, and Frankness in the Relationships

The Natura-Matilde case illustrates the strengthening of trust along the lifespan of the partnership, mainly through frankness, transparency, and an intense exchange of perceptions and feedback. Telemig Celular Institute, during the creation and development of the Volunteer Support Groups, demonstrated an attitude of empathy by being a candid and attentive listener, eager to learn about the nature and needs of its partners. The simple act of listening pro-actively sets the foundation for building a firm and lasting relationship of trust. At the same time, the company also leveraged its competence in articulating interests, trying to instill in the ensuing dialogue a pattern of transparency and frankness.

Respecting the Wisdom of Each Partner

In this area, it is possible to trace a common line between the analyzed cases. In all of them, partnering organizations respected the core competencies of each other, and constantly sought for complementarity and synergies, in a process of continuous organizational learning. Itaú and Natura approached CENPEC for its competence in education. In the Ekos case, Natura tried to select its partners by summoning the most appropriate actors, even if doing so increased the complexity of managing the alliance. The Telemig Celular Institute sought the broadest possible participation in the Volunteer Support Groups, and perceived that the Attorney General's Office of the State of Minas Gerais also had a great deal to contribute to the alliance given its unique expertise and prerogatives established by law.

Creating Combined Work Procedures

In the majority of the cases analyzed, the frequent and systematic interaction between the allied organizations was a decisive factor for trust building and adjusting on a continuous basis. The physical proximity between the Matilde School and Natura facilitated a close contact between the organizations, creating a richer and more intimate relationship between the two groups. The constant presence of social project managers from Telemig Celular Institute in the Volunteer Support Groups leveraged the company's capacity for constructing enduring relations of trust among individuals. This experience suggests that partners need to go beyond sporadic personal encounters, and establish a routine of systematic meetings, which should encompass a substantial number of members from both organizations, in order to build effectively inter-organizational trust.

Establishing Communication

The analysis presented in Chapter 5 demonstrates the importance of communication in consolidating cultural standards, whether inside or between organizations. An effective communication may be even more vital across organizations, as it can serve to attenuate differences, removing resistances and reducing conflicts. The content of communication and the system and means employed by the organizations to communicate reflect the prevailing cultural standards.[14]

The analysis of Brazilian alliances researched as part of the SEKN project show that three dimensions merit attention: the internal communication of the alliance; the communication of the alliance towards the internal stakeholders of partnering organizations; and the communication of the alliance towards external stakeholders.

The Partners Communicate among Themselves

It was observed that the initiative and the tone of the communication process between the partners tends to be set by the private sector partner, at least initially, while the CSO tends to remain in a position of passive follower. However, as individuals from both organizations become progressively involved in the day-to-day management of the partnership, this initial imbalance is partially corrected.

In the case of Natura Matilde, dialogue between the company and the public school improved over time. The company's decision to create a technical and administrative department dedicated to the social action was made during its involvement in this alliance, and signaled the importance that the company placed upon the need to reach out and connect with its partners. In the Natura-Ekos case, which took place years after the Natura-Matilde alliance, from the initial planning stage the alliance contemplated the need for creating time and space to exchange information, seek agreements and make decisions.

Over time, the Education and Participation Program started to drift away from the restricted domain of Itaú Bank's strategic council, to the inter-organizational realm also occupied by CENPEC, MEC, and UNICEF. With the success of the prize and consolidation of the experience, the bank started to invite all participating entities to meetings where the program is systematically monitored and evaluated. The enlargement of these partnerships brings on new collaborations and reinforces the energy of the program, while at the same time maintaining Itaú's communications style, which the company commands from its center-stage position as host and articulator of the program.

In the case of Telemig Celular, the goal of strengthening the Volunteer Support Groups and opening a dialog channel with the attorney general, by itself makes evident the need to enhance the internal communication of the group in order to effectively carry out social work. For a telecom company, the value proposition of an alliance that offers the prospects of sharpening its social communication skills is extremely appealing.

The Alliance in the Internal Communication of Participating Organizations

In this area, our research revealed an ongoing process of change, that continues at the time of completion of our study. It is known that companies often have recurrent difficulties with internal communication: different operating departments tend to isolate themselves like "fiefdoms," plagued with groups and people that receive and do not disseminate information, obstructed channels and inefficient vehicles. The picture is not any better among the organizations of the third sector, characterized by the centralization of decision and information, as well as a lack of agility, precision, and a substandard flow of communication. It should come as no surprise that an alliance between sectors, when it comes to internal communication among partners, will suffer all these problems.

Adding to this, up until recently, the companies tended to be very reticent in the communication of their social actions, both to internal and external audiences. Oftentimes, institutions were more forthcoming in addressing their external audiences than engaging their internal stakeholders, as the Itaú case. Here, internal surveys revealed a complete lack of knowledge on the part of employees about the bank's social initiatives, and particularly about their major Education and Participation Program. This fact clearly indicated a managerial style that does not stimulate intensity of internal communication, generating employee dissatisfaction and, oftentimes, unfair criticism and scorn about the corporate responsibility actions of the company. This finding led the bank to consider investing in the improvement of its internal communication and to involve its human resources in its social initiatives.

Even in Natura, with a more open management style which continuously seeks to involve its associates in their social projects, our research identified deficiencies in the amount and intensity of internal communication about its alliances and partnerships.

This has been a dilemma for the companies: on the one hand, it can be an effective tool to increase the visibility of certain initiatives toward its employees; on the other hand, it may create backlash and generate criticism or cascading demands. Moreover, it can expose inconsistencies or contradictions between its management of human resources and its proclaimed corporate social responsibility.

The third sector did not fare any better in dealing with its internal communication, andthe fact that the private sector partner tended to hold a leading role did not help. This led the CSO to assume a subordinate role, in which the company was seen as the only holder of resources, and not as an equal partner. From this role, they tended to neglect the internal dissemination of the partnership, and when they did communicate it, it was portrayed as "our project" executed with the resources of company X. This dynamic clearly emerged in the collaboration maintained between Coca-Cola de Argentina and *Junior Achievement* of Argentina, a case analyzed in Chapter 5 *(To Communicate or Not to Communicate?" p. 168).*

The level, intensity, and depth in which alliances are disseminated in the internal communication of partners bring up a fundamental point for discussion: to what extent do these organizations really intend the partnership to become part of their own culture?

The Alliance in the External Communication

The companies surveyed were beginning to perceive and use their social actions as an element that adds value to their brand or image with the general public. In the cases researched, some alliances were established to assure this positive visibility, identifying the social action being undertaken with the company's product or service. The case that illustrates this aspect well is Telemig Celular, although the company is very discrete about publicizing its social actions.

Some alliances were established exclusively as a function of the nature of the social action of the company and, in practice, were only marginally used to promote its brand. Itaú Bank was always very reluctant to publicize the Education and Participation Program beyond the community of educators, CSOs, and other audiences targeted by the program. More recently, after it became listed in the Dow Jones Sustainability Group Index, the management of the bank became aware of the value that its corporate responsibility actions were adding to the Itaú brand. However, despite this finding, the company is still grappling with the dilemma of whether or not to widely publicize these actions, closely aligning its social action and cross-sector partnerships to its institutional marketing.

In turn, CSOs also have trouble in communicating with mainstream audiences. Due to their lack of experience, and even for ideological reasons, they are reluctant to be excessively visible. At the same time, they do seek a certain level of exposure that assures them enough visibility to access donors and sponsors. However, they fear that overly publicizing their alliances with companies can be ineffective or even backfire, harming them for being associated with a corporate image over which they cannot have any control.

The ample coverage that Brazilian media has been giving in the last years to social entrepreneurship and corporate responsibility, has added yet another complexity to the issue of communication of the alliances among sectors. This is a paradoxical and problematic issue, since it is at the core of these reflections: is there, effectively, a cultural change? Is this change leading towards the constitution of "a solidarity culture of cooperation and social responsibility"? If the answer to these questions is affirmative, the communication of the partnerships plays an important role in the validation of these forms of organizational articulation.

Final Considerations

The experience of our research on cross-sector strategic alliances, and the cases developed within the SEKN project, lead to a few considerations. Although strategic alliances' creation and management are undoubtedly a complex task, they have in general stood up as an interesting model for promoting the social action of organizations.

The last five years have seen an increase in the numbers of corporate-led social action initiatives, boosted by the new visibility of this field, and the action of entities that disseminate social responsibility values. Those companies that were already carrying such actions expanded their scope and started marketing them or showing a better appreciation of the value that those programs brought. On the other hand, companies that had not adopted social practices in a systematic way have started to gather information and technical support in order to make them part of their management practices and business culture. Taking into account that this movement seems to be expanding, it is fair to state that there is a "responsibility culture" trend, which aims at disseminating the concepts of the rights and obligations of a democratic citizenship.

Alliances are not the only way in which companies may go about fulfilling their social responsibility, although it is becoming the prevalent strategy of choice. Companies are resorting to such alliances in order to be more effective and efficient and reduce the costs of their social action. However, a significant portion of the private sector still prefers to maintain autonomy and full control in carrying out their social initiatives. Barriers such as lack of confidence, lack of information, and previous frustrating experiences have prevented them from taking the collaboration route. In this sense, the cases analyzed are not representative of the behavior of the vast majority of companies, although they could signal a qualitative shift towards the emergence of a "collaboration culture."

CSOs have proven to be ambivalent with respect to the interest of corporations to deploy efforts towards the solution of social problems. Some emphasize the benefits of partnerships: the development and improvement of their management skills, enhancement of their network, strengthening of their image, and access to more and better resources. Others who are reluctant to engage in cross-sector alliances, or which had frustrating experiences, prefer to touch on the weaknesses of the alliances: the incompatibility of mindset and working styles, the lack of knowledge and sensitivity of corporations regarding social problems, their arrogant and imposing behavior, the patron-like and lenient way in which corporations relate to social entities; the lack of transparency of the corporations' intentions, and the values that support their actions; and finally, uncertainty about the companies' commitment in the long run.

It is fair to say that, along the lifespan of the alliances, CSOs have tended to oscillate between these two positions, which would suggest that they are indeed being merely reactive to corporations' initiatives and decisions. Therefore, an important step in the development of cross-sector strategic alliances would be to encourage a more proactive outlook in civil society, as well as working to sensitize corporations, so as to bring about a more balanced relationship with regards to the vital decisions for the future of alliances.

The establishment of mutual trust among partners is highlighted as one of the most important drivers for forging and strengthening these alliances. This fact is directly related to the personal characteristics of the partners, with the patterns of interpersonal relationship established among them, and the predominant traits of the organizational cultures in which they are inserted.

Therefore, the kind of relationship that the players establish before and during the alliance building process is a key driver in its evolution. Brazil being a society still characterized for being patriarchal and conservative, it is only natural that the protagonists will tend to establish affinities on the basis of their social class, educational level, and professional status. This quest reflects the need for finding partners with similar values, as these shared reference points suggest that both parties might share a common "world view," structured upon compatible core principles.

The business leaders and executives of the companies surveyed stand up for their engagement capacity with corporate responsibility and social development propositions. Their approaching CSOs and governmental entities has fostered collaborative undertakings. This determines a relationship of power in which the balance between the company and the partners is subtle and requires constant maintenance. Part of that process of assuring equilibrium in the relation's balance of power consists of constructing communication processes that are both efficient and effective.

Notes

1   Prof. Tania Casado and researcher João Teixeira Pires, members of the SEKN team at CEATS, FIA/FEA/USP, collaborated in the development of this chapter.

2   Andrew M. Pettigrew, "Contextualist Research: A Natural Way to Link Theory and Practice," in *Doing Research That Is Useful for Theory and Practice*, ed. Edward E. Lawler (San Francisco: Jossey-Bass, 1985).

3   Leilah Landim, "The Nonprofit Sector in Brazil," in *The Nonprofit Sector in the Developing World: A Comparative Analysis*, ed. Helmut K. Anheier and Lester M. Salamon (Manchester, UK; New York: Manchester University Press: Distributed exclusively in the U.S. by St. Martin's Press, 1998).

4   *"Non-Governmental Organizations and the Marketization of Development"* was a research study carried out by IDR—Institute for Development Research with support from the Ford Foundation, under the coordination of Prof. L. David Brown of the Hauser Center for Nonprofit Organizations, of Harvard University. The mapping of Brazilian cases was done by CEATS—Centro de Empreendedorismo Social e Administração em Terceiro Setor of FIA/FEA/USP

5   Though Brazil is ranked among the ten largest world economies, it occupies one of the last four places in income distribution, with a GINI Index of 0.6, which puts it in the 73rd place in the ranking of Human Development Index. There are close to 50 million people who live with a monthly income of less than 30 dollars in Brazil.

6   During the time of the military dictatorship, independent centers of social research, CSOs, NGOs, and all other associative movements were supported by donations and funding from international organizations. With the re-establishment of the state of law in Brazil, these investments were directed to other regions of the world that were still struggling for democratization. Available resources were insufficient to serve the need for social activities and the expansion of the third sector. Competition caused the fragmentation, on the one hand, but, on the other hand, it led to profound changes in organizations and in their operating models.

7   Eduardo Rodrigues Gomes, "Um capítulo especial da responsabilidade social empresarial no Brasil: O papel do PNBE–Pensamento nacional das bases empresariais" (paper presented at the Responsabilidade social empresarial no Brasil hoje: Um balanço, Rio de Janeiro, Brasil, 2003).

8   *Alianças estratégicas intersetoriais* research project, part of the *Programa de pesquisa e capacitação-Cidadania organizacional e terceiro setor,* carried out by CEATS—Centro de Empreendedorismo Social e Administração em Terceiro Setor da FIA/FEA/USP, with financial and institutional support from the Ford Foundation.

9   A more in-depth discussion of the Continuum may be found in James E. Austin, *The Collaboration Challenge: How Nonprofits and Businesses Succeed through Strategic Alliances,* 1st ed. (San Francisco: Jossey-Bass Publishers, 2000); also available in Portuguese: *Parcerias—Fundamentos e benefícios para o Terceiro Setor* (São Paulo: Editora Futura, 2001).

10 Rosa Maria Fischer, "O círculo do poder—As práticas invisíveis de sujeição nas organizações complexas," in *Poder e cultura nas organizações,* ed. Maria Tereza Fleury and Rosa Maria Fischer (São Paulo, Brasil: Editora Atlas, 1989).

11 Ministry of Education and Culture of Brazil (*Ministério da Educação e Cultura da Presidência da República*; hence MEC); United Nations Children's Fund (UNICEF)

12 Max Weber, *Ética protestante e o espírito do capitalismo* (São Paulo, Brasil: Editora Pioneira, 1994).

13 Edgar H. Schein, *Organizational Culture and Leadership*, 2nd ed. (San Francisco, CA: Jossey-Bass, 1992).

14 Rosa M. Fischer, "Mudança e transformação organizacional," in *As pessoas na organização*, ed. Maria Tereza Leme Fleury (São Paulo: Editora Gente, 2002).

8

Central America and Peru: Dealing with Barriers to Inter-Sector Collaboration

Andrea Prado, Arturo Condo, Enrique Ogliastri, Felipe Pérez Pineda, Forrest Colburn, Francisco Leguizamón, Guillermo S. Edelberg, Jesús Revilla, John Ickis, Julio Ayca, Julio Sergio Ramírez, Luis Noel Alfaro, Luz Marina García, Mónica Azofeifa, and Wendy Rodríguez

Introduction

Poor countries have many needs. In Latin America it was the state that was long held to be responsible for promoting broad-based economic development. The embracing of political and economic liberalism—democracy and market economies—in the 1980s, though, left the "private sector" as the motor of economic development. The task is enormous. The World Bank gauges Latin America to have the most inequitable distribution of wealth and income in the world, with a significant proportion of the population mired in poverty. The social landscape is treacherous, all the more so because of the ideological clashes that were fanned by the Cuban Revolution in 1959 and only ebbed in 1989, with the withering of socialism as an ideal. Successful entrepreneurs and firms have long been distrusted by many. This distrust, and the faith entrusted to the state, has long resulted in an absence of private initiatives to meet social needs. Those with resources who did step forward to offer help frequently preferred to do so anonymously. Thus, the countries of Latin America do not have a tradition—a history—of private initiatives to meet social needs. And as a consequence, there is a paucity of knowledge about just how to pursue private initiatives and a scarcity of institutions for assisting such efforts.

The scaling back of expectations for what the state can—or should—do, however, has led to a growing sense among entrepreneurs and managers that they must step forward to help meet pressing social needs. The task is not easy, but it is important. In a bid to contribute to efforts to learn more about how the private sector in Latin America can contribute to social welfare, the faculty of INCAE explored 11 cases of what can be called "social enterprise" in the five countries of Central America and in Peru.

The six countries vary in size, from Costa Rica with a population of 4 million, to Guatemala with a population of 12 million, to Peru with a population of 26 million.[1] Surely more important, though, is the spread among the gross national income per capita of the countries: from a low of $400 in Nicaragua and $900 in Honduras, to $1,680 in Guatemala and $1,980 in Peru, to a high of $4,060 in Costa Rica.[2] With the notable exception of Costa Rica, though, these are all poor countries, with pronounced class disparities and gaping holes in social services. Moreover, four of the countries were traumatized by political violence in recent decades: Guatemala, El Salvador, Nicaragua, and Peru. Today, all six countries are committed to a model of economic development that highlights private initiative in unfettered markets.

The private sector in each of the six countries is heterogeneous and frequently at odds—still—with the state. For example, in Peru, an estimated 60 percent of the gross national product is in the "informal sector."[3] The Peruvian state may have scaled back its economic responsibilities, but it remains elephantine, resulting in high taxes for those in the "formal sector." Indeed, it is estimated that each state employee is supported by only two tax-paying employees of the private sector.[4] The opening of economies in Latin America to international competition has resulted, too, in many "losers." Still, in every economy—even in impoverished Nicaragua and Honduras—there are "winners," economic actors with resources to contribute to social needs. Anecdotal but persuasive evidence suggests, too, that there is a growing consciousness that the private sector—at least those with some resources—must contribute to the well-being of the countries in which they are situated. Likewise, though, competition in business has prompted many managers to find innovative ways "to market" their firm—and specific products. Social enterprise activities in Latin America are commonly driven by a murky combination of altruism and self-interest.

In searching for examples of social enterprise, the INCAE faculty was impressed with the diversity of ways in which entrepreneurs and managers are seeking to contribute to meeting social needs. In one case, for example, a prominent entrepreneur in El Salvador is seeking to revive cultivation of a crop important in the colonial era with the conviction that the endeavor will generate employment in impoverished rural areas formerly in the hands of guerrillas seeking radical change.[5] In this and other cases, barriers to communication and the paucity of institutions are the two key challenges. When there is a willingness to help, to contribute, it is often difficult to reach out to the less fortunate and to find—or build—institutions that can facilitate the transfer of skills or resources. Success demands commitment and creativity.

Although the diversity of efforts at social enterprise in Latin America needs to be highlighted, the discussion here focuses on four cases where institutions were present on both sides of the equation: firms at one end, and Civil Society Organizations (CSOs) at the other end. This kind—and level—of institutionalization is not the norm in the six countries studied, but it is probably the kind of social enterprise that is most favored by promient entrepreneurs and managers, and so likely to be more common in the future. Exploring cases of how firms work with CSOs in different settings illuminates the most telling challenges of social entreprise in Latin America: communication and institutional development.

The four cases reviewed involve projects in: education, housing, youths-at-risk, and environmental and cultural preservation in indigenous communities. The analysis presents a "longitudinal" discussion of the four cases that permits an insightful examination of all phases of the alliance.

The first case discussed is the *Fundación Promotora para la Vivienda* (FUPROVI) in Costa Rica, a "second generation" CSO that was looking for potential partners to finance housing projects for low-income families. Studied is its relationship with a Mexican-owned television network in Costa Rica, *Representaciones Televisivas* (REPRETEL), and with a financing institution, *Mutual Heredia*. Although all participating organizations benefited from the social project, suggesting that the alliance had overcome a mere philanthropic phase to reach a transactional stage, the relationship did not further evolve to an integrative or strategic commitment. Moreover, there are no plans for future joint projects.

The second case explored is Nicaragua's American Chamber of

Commerce (AMCHAM), which promoted the involvement of private companies in a school sponsorship program. The case allows for a comparison between the respective relations built by two companies, Shell and Euronica, with public schools. One of these relationships seemed to dwindle over time, thus restricting the alliance to a philanthropic gesture, while the other relationship showed signs of continuing mutual benefits, characteristic of an alliance that had moved on to a transactional stage.

The third case recounts the efforts of the Young Entrepreneurs Program (*Emprendedores Juveniles de Nicaragua,* hence EJN) and Nicaragua's Institute for Development (*Instituto Nicaragüense de Desarrollo,* hence INDE) to support youths-at-risk of prematurely ending their education. The case allows for an analysis of the two CSOs complex relations with both UNICEF (a possible strategic alliance) and with three firms having varied interests. Here the institutional and organizational challenges are truly complex.

The final case discussed is the Amazon Lodge (*Posada Amazonas,* hence PA), where a Peruvian ecotourism company seeks to assist an indigenous community in an isolated jungle. The partnership becomes a true "joint-venture." Moreover, resource exchanges are significant, and joint activities amount to much more than a merely philanthropic or transactional relationship. This case is special because it is a civil society alliance that reaches the integrative and strategic level.

The chapter ends with a discussion of the most salient conclusions of the analysis, and an effort to suggest how barriers in inter-sector alliances might be overcome in the difficult setting of Latin America.

A Roof for the South—Building with Love

"A Roof for the South" was a collaboration relationship between FUPROVI, REPRETEL and Mutual Heredia. FUPROVI was a non-profit private organization aimed at developing public housing and community strengthening programs. REPRETEL was the second leading television corporation in Costa Rica, which managed three of the six local channels existing at the time. Mutual Heredia is a financial institution.

The alliance arose from a shared interest in aiding low-income families who had lost their homes to Hurricane Ceasar in July 1996. However, in the case of REPRETEL, the corporation had an additional motivation: the company had been recently acquired by a Mexican group and did not enjoy a good image within Costa Rica. Thus, it sought to enhance its corporate image through collaboration with FUPROVI.

Participating organizations carried out a campaign to raise funds among private companies. Each institution contributed its expertise in its respective areas: REPRETEL in communication, FUPROVI in construction and working with low-income people, and *Mutual Heredia* in finance. Private companies could donate resources to finance one whole house, or half a house, to a family in exchange for free advertising on REPRETEL channels. All donations were tax deductible.

As a result of the campaign, 37 houses were built. This accomplishment was made possible in part through government support, which provided housing bonds, and in part by 16 private companies that donated cash and construction supplies. The project was deemed a success by all involved. Federico Zamora, REPRETEL corporate sales representative, reports, "In my opinion and the board's opinion, it was a successful campaign. The objective was accomplished."

Reflecting on the factors that ensured the project's success, Carmen González, FUPROVI development manager, explained:

> In the case of FUPROVI, one of the factors that led to project success was the Foundation's committed involvement since the very beginning. Also, both the director and her management team were keenly aware of the organization's nature and mission. The personal characteristics of the individuals involved in the campaign, especially at FUPROVI and REPRETEL, were also instrumental. We were very active and committed. We talked by cellular phone every day to handle everything: 'Has so-and-so's donations been picked up yet?' For months, we all did something for the campaign every single day. Then, one day, we said, 'That's it; this is as far as we go.'

After the *A Roof for the South* project was over, representatives of REPRETEL and FUPROVI discussed the possibility of undertaking future joint projects.

Although FUPROVI submitted a formal proposal for a housing project for older people, it was never started. FUPROVI was willing to take on the new project, but REPRETEL's management decided against it. Reporter René Barboza, REPRETEL's promoter in the first project, commented: "The 'Houses for the Elder' project was not approved. I don't know why, but perhaps it was because *A Roof for the*

South had been very taxing for us. It wasn't that easy, and the company decided to carry out more feasible marathons, with new goals." Federico Zamora also expressed his opinion:

> I personally looked for some land to build small houses, like mini-condos for homeless older people, but, then, we sort of lost contact with FUPROVI. The problem is that life is very hectic at the network; we have priorities. We were airing a lot of new shows, and this project just slipped. Unfortunately, we lost contact. In my opinion, we should do a lot of social work, but it's hard because, obviously, the television business is profit-oriented, and social work sometimes becomes less of a priority.

It is true, social enterprise projects can be time-consuming.

However, if the campaign was deemed a success by both parties, why did REPRETEL decide to put an end to its work with FUPROVI? What reasons—other than fatigue—could have influenced the decision to end the relationship, and what steps could have been taken for the relationship to evolve from the transactional to the integrative stage?

A negative impact on alliance development was the fact that each company had its own working style and they were not compatible. Due to the nature of journalism, where time is of essence for reporting, REPRETEL's employees were always pressed for time. But FUPROVI employees were accustomed to a more relaxed schedule. González elaborated:

> Some things were hard for us, not impossible, but hard. For example, our working styles were very different. Reporters' work focuses on time; they are more impulsive. They want things now! They are used to doing everything fast; otherwise, the news is old. It was very hard for me to fit in that role. Sometimes, they called me for a last minute meeting or to get someone to go with a reporter. It was difficult, because Foundation officials who were involved in the campaign had previous appointments. However, we felt committed, and we knew we had to deliver.

Differences among actors, even just of "style," exacerbate difficulties.

When the working styles of alliance partners differ extensively, it is advisable, insofar as possible, to define a working agenda. Taking this step should help to minimize "improvisations" and last-minute changes. Planning is especially important when top officials are in charge of the project, since their time is limited and they have other pressing tasks. A possible alternative would be to assign someone exclusively to follow up on the project and report on its progress. Nevertheless, for an alliance to evolve to an integrative stage, senior managers should be involved.

A second factor that influenced the development of the relationship was an unfortunate misunderstanding. When the journalist Barboza visited the project site and found that families were discouraged on account of the slow progress in construction, she complained to her colleagues. REPRETEL's representative sent a letter to FUPROVI, complaining about its lack of project supervision: "I sent a letter to warn FUPROVI, to let them know we had a problem. But I didn't have the whole picture; I mean, I made it out to be more than it was. I never intended it as a reprimand or a complaint from REPRETEL." FUPROVI's director replied to the letter, refuting all accusations and stating that, "FUPROVI cannot allow these kinds of situations to impair our image as a serious, responsible and technically efficient institution." A simple complaint led to a strained relationship.

For an alliance to develop successfully, partners should strengthen their ties and mutual trust. The furor over the letter exerted a negative impact on the relationship. Parties should refrain from making accusations and value judgments that may "hurt" their partner. However, trust is built—or reinforced—when misunderstandings are addressed directly and honestly.

The bulk of REPRETEL's contribution to the campaign consisted of free advertising offered to donating companies, as well as the time contributed by the company's staff assigned to the project. According to data provided by the companies, this investment amounted to approximately $350,000. In addition, private companies' donations totaled $70,000, while government bonds added another $222,000. Overall investment thus was about $642,000. The total cost of the 37 houses built was estimated at $480.000. From the economic point of view, the campaign was perhaps unsuccessful, since the imputed value of the inputs exceeded the value of houses by $162,000. Perhaps tangible benefits for each party were not cost-effective, especially for REPRETEL, whose donations may have greatly exceeded the material benefits obtained. However, since image enhancement was an additional motivation, value creation to corporate image should also be evaluated and estimated in addition to economic results. Benefits of improved company visibility and image are difficult to quantify. However, for an alliance to reach the integrative stage, intangible benefits drawn from contributing to this type of campaign should be considered. Otherwise, involvement in the project may be difficult to justify before shareholders or the board, thus jeopardizing continuity of social enterprise activity.

Another aspect that could have influenced REPRETEL's decision not to engage in the new project with FUPROVI was the immediate beneficiaries'—the families'—lack of recognition of the company's assistance. González shared her views: "I should say that, in my opinion, we were a little disappointed when, at the inauguration ceremony, upon the president's arrival with his entourage, the effort undertaken by FUPROVI, REPRETEL, *Mutual Heredia* and all other donating companies was undermined, and families ended up thanking the government instead of the campaign promoters. I think representatives of REPRETEL saw that and didn't like it at all." The future of a collaboration relationship, especially when one of its participants aims at image enhancement, is highly linked to the recognition shown by the beneficiaries. If the recognition is low, advertising campaigns may be carried out to expressly indicate each partner's contribution to the project. Also, one of the partners may publicly thank the other one for the support provided, or it may encourage the media to provide desired coverage.

Finally, participating companies failed to choose an adequate type of project that would have proved profitable and sustainable. REPRETEL had no specific interests in public housing construction, as would have been the case of a building company or a manufacturer of building materials. If alliance members aim to build a long-term relationship, they should seek partners with common interests or, at least, with the potential to develop them. There is no substitute for a "good fit" between firms and Civil Society Organizations.

AMCHAM of Nicaragua

This case describes the school sponsorship program promoted by Nicaragua's AMCHAM, through its education committee. The program arose from a philanthropic initiative shared by some AMCHAM members to respond to the reality of poverty-stricken Managua. Since poverty was associated with street children and deficient education, efforts were focused in this direction. The program intended to promote private companies' support for the neediest educational centers in Nicaragua. Public schools and technical schools in urban and rural areas lacked appropriate infrastructure, equipment and teaching materials. Furthermore, teachers' wages were very low. These shortages were reflected in the low education level of youths entering the labor market. Nicaragua's Ministry of Education, Culture and Sports (*Ministerio de Educación, Cultura y Deportes,* hence MECD) participated in the program, selecting the most deprived institutions and submitting them to the education committee for companies to choose support targets. A direct relationship was developed between the company and the selected school.

The sponsorship program began in 2000, with 45 participating companies, and by 2002, more than 50 schools were involved in the project. Sponsors' aims were fairly similar: improving educational conditions at sponsored schools and providing a better education for Nicaraguan children. However, in addition to philanthropic desires, some companies pursued additional and more self-serving agendas. The objectives of the schools were in improving facilities, providing a better education, delivering the necessary materials, and finding support for additional needs, such as breakfast for needy children. The match of objectives encouraged participants to build the alliance.

The INCAE study analyzes the associations of two companies, Shell of Nicaragua with the Simón Bolívar Training Center, and Euronica with the Josefa Toledo 2 public school. The desire to support their communities triggered Shell and Euronica's participation in the program.

Shell Nicaragua mainly contributed materials and equipment to be used in technical labs. The company also granted scholarships, and its staff delivered seminars to school students. Corporate support during 2001 exceeded $7,500, and a similar amount was forecasted for 2002. Two years into the project, the initial expectations remained unaltered. Both Shell and the school were satisfied. The company considered that it had accomplished its purpose of contributing to education enhancement, and the school knew it could count on the company's cooperation.

For its part, Euronica offered materials and funding for facility renovation works at the Josefa Toledo 2 school. The relationship started in February 2000, and, during the first year, the company's donations were used to finance the building of a pedestrian bridge, bathrooms, and two classrooms, and to support roofs repairs and school ceremonies, among other things. Total contributions in 2001 amounted to approximately $30,000. Some of the funds were obtained through the sale of trucks coming from foreign donations. The trucks had been repaired by company mechanics and later sold to get cash. Although the company intended to contribute a similar amount in 2001, the actual figure decreased significantly. The company continued delivering materials and supplies, however construction works were interrupted.

Why did Euronica reduce its support to its sponsored school? And why did Shell continue to support its own? Did the program's structure impose barriers that curbed the progress of collaboration relationships between companies and schools towards the integrative stage? If this was the case, how could these barriers have been overcome?

Chapter 3 shows that the prospects of continuity of an alliance are influenced by the degree of alignment between partners' objectives, missions, values and strategies. And Chapter 4 argues that the higher the alignment, the higher the value created by the relationship, and its level of commitment. Shell chose an educational center with a mission and objectives aligned with the company's technical orientation. Therefore, the support provided was highly related to its core competencies, favoring the assistance and also allowing for ongoing support, and not only the constant allocation of new resources.

Both Shell of Nicaragua and the Simón Bolívar Center were devoted to maintain or improve the operation of internal combustion engines; the former through the production of lubricants to lengthen engines' useful life, and the latter through training human resources to repair and maintain the engines. Thus, the objective driving Shell's involvement in the project was not merely philanthropic. For instance, the company sought to make use of the program in order to develop brand "loyalty" among students. The idea was that upon entering the labor market, they would prefer their products.

Euronica, on the other hand, selected the Josefa Toledo 2 school as requested by its general manager, who lived near the school. The motivation was personal, and it responded to a desire to support a school in his community. Also, the contribution offered by the company was not directly related to its core competencies, and thus implied direct resource allocation. When the depressed local economy affected the firm's revenues, Euronica decided to reduce its support.

In the face of economic crises, many companies trim their budgets allotted to social projects, especially if they are judged to represent only a resource expenditure and not an enhancement of the firm's core business. It is important to choose a partner with the capabilities, or potential, to develop mutually beneficial activities. These activities should be somehow aligned with the company's mission, values and strategies, so that the alliance may evolve beyond the philanthropic stage.

Another important factor that helped strengthen the relationship between Shell and the Simón Bolívar Center, which was not present in the relationship between Euronica and the Josefa Toledo 2 school, was the attitude displayed by the Center's principal. At the Simón Bolívar Center the administrative staff was very active. The principal prepared a list of needs and, with the aid of his staff, outlined new projects to submit to Shell. Initiatives came from both parties, and this participation contributed to a healthy, active relationship. The purchase of gas emission equipment provided an example of this commitment. The principal requested financing for this purchase in August 2001, and the company responded it would supply 50 percent of the funds as long as the school managed to find the balance elsewhere. The school finally secured the remaining 50 percent in 2002, and Shell delivered the promised funds. Euronica did not encounter, in contrast, an active school board. Consequently, there was no pressure to regain initial collaboration levels. The principal, with the modesty that characterized her, chose not to press the company through telephone calls to maintain support. She did not wish to appear demanding before the sponsor.

A successful alliance requires the active participation of both partners. In a philanthropic relationship, the benefactor may have no incentives to invest resources in improving the alliance. However, if the recipient is not encouraging, there may be a lost opportunity to receive larger benefits, or to contribute to the building of a sustainable relationship. Moreover, many CSOs display weaknesses in their administrative capabilities, hindering the development of sophisticated alliances with private companies. Personnel training in this area may help overcome this obstacle, a process to which the partner may also contribute its own expertise.

Chapter 5 shows that the development of communication channels and the strengthening of trust-based relations between project coordinators in both organizations are vital for alliance development. Also, it is helpful if both senior management and mid-level employees are involved in projects. Shell had scheduled meetings every two or three months to submit projects and to monitor continuing projects. This commitment allowed for an organized monitoring of working plans. The company's employees also delivered seminars to school students on topics related to their own knowledge and skills, such as lubricants and industrial safety.

Euronica adopted an unusual and highly elaborated organizational response. The creation of three committees and their monthly meetings accounted for a fluent and rich relationship during the first year of work. However, after an active first year, communication decreased, since meetings were no longer held at regular intervals. The involvement of the company's general manager, Werner Ahlers, who had been the initial promoter of the alliance, proved to be fundamental in the beginning. However, in spite of his effort to encourage senior executives and mid-level employees to participate in the project, enthusiasm dwindled during the last year, and many lacked the necessary time to devote to the project. Commenting on this decline in participation, Ahlers said: "It was difficult to motivate people; I tried with managers. Although, at the beginning, they went to the school, then they stopped going. Maybe they weren't really motivated. I wanted mid-level employees to be motivated as well, to feel the school was like a 'godchild,' so they would come up with support ideas or go there on Saturdays or any other day. I wanted this to be a project for all of us, not just for senior management." This decline in participation was detrimental to the relationship.

Lack of time on the part of the managers involved in the program was noted by all. It was one of the usual topics of discussion at the meetings between the education committee and the sponsors, since it affected several participating companies. Given the philanthropic nature of the initiative, managers had to "steal" part of the time they devoted to their work at the firm to see to the needs of the school. At committee meetings it was proposed to hire someone exclusively to work with the schools, a proposal—that if it had been accepted— probably would have helped maintain the vitality of the alliances.

Incentives to maintain participation is a pressing need in collaboration relationships, especially for firms, where personnel are under pressure to contribute to the profitiablity of the company. In most instances it is probably advisable for firms to hire someone to be responsible for the success of the relationship and to report directly to senior management. If, for budgetary reasons, this tack is not possible,

then responsibility for coordinating work with the CSO should be assigned to an individual with a position tied to the project's objectives.
Likewise, firms can devise incentives to motivate employees to volunteer their time and expertise. Such incentives might include free
transportation, a T-shirt, and/or a participation certificate.

The *Nicaraguan School Sponsorship Program* organization model
was framed within a philanthropic initiative without strategic alignment, and sponsors offered their help according to their possibilities.
The companies participating in the program chose the schools they
wished to sponsor from a list supplied by the MECD. There was no
predetermined selection criterion: each company could choose according to its own motives. The schools did not participate in the selection process, and, in fact, they were usually taken by surprise on
learning that a company had selected them. Schools had to submit
reports on their needs and educational projects to the sponsoring
companies, which, in turn, tried to meet those needs depending on
their resources.

Choosing a partner in a unilateral way may hinder alignment of
objectives, exert a negative influence in future alliance development,
or limit the possible value created by the relationship. Selecting the
correct partner is essential for alliance success. Merely requesting potential beneficiaries to submit a list of their needs to companies willing
to make donations is likely to restrict collaboration to a philanthropic
stage. Matching firms with CSOs deserves more care and attention.
Representatives of both parties should exchange opinions on what is
expected from the relationship, and on possible value creation strategies, before choosing their partner.

AMCHAM's education committee did not set minimum support
requirements, compulsory regulations, or create supervision or control
procedures. On the contrary, companies and schools were responsible
for deciding future courses of action, alliance organization models,
and their priorities. In these kinds of programs, the coordinating organization—if one exists—may play a more active intermediary role,
setting minimum commitments and exercising quality control. However, this role should not curtail the creative nature of the sponsorship, or the active participation of all actors. At a minimum, everyone
involved in the relationship should have well-specified goals and the
opportunity to communicate with partners.

An important lesson from this case is that business organizations,
commonly called "chambers" (*cámaras*), have significant opportu-

nites in the development and implementation of social program development. These organizations, common throughout Latin America, may employ several strategies to encourage members' involvement. For example, awards can be granted to companies with the best social programs or offering the most creative or sophisticated support to organizations helping the needy. The coordinating entity may also measure the accomplishments of collaboration with CSOs and publicize them. Participating firms would benefit from greater value creation, new companies would be encouraged to participate in the program, and commitment to social welfare would be enhanced.

The creation of an advisory committee on social issues may prove instrumental for business organizations to stimulate initiatives. Prominent business leaders could be asked to chair meetings, inviting their colleagues to participate, too. Those with successful experiences in collaborative relationships could be asked to speak at public gatherings. Even examples of unsuccessful alliances may merit public discussion. There surely are many ways entreprepreneurs and managers can be enticed into entering into collaborative relationships for the purpose of meeting social needs.

Finally, it may be important to engage the endorsement and support of political parties and their leaders. Private initiatives can usually benefit from political support, including from the governing party or the institutions of government. Of course, as was seen in the Repretel and FUPROVI case, engaging the government runs the risk of having the credit for doing the good work be given the politicians rather than to the business and CSO. Reworking legislation can also stimulate private initiatives by providing various types of incentives for the private sector to contribute to eradicating poverty and other social ills. For example, AMCHAM of Nicaragua had submitted a project to the National Assembly titled, "Corporate Involvement in Education Act." The bill was intended to: (1) promote initiatives to complement government performance in public education; (2) make managers and society at large aware of the significance of investing in education as a way to foster competitiveness; and (3) encourage tangible support actions for schools. More legislatuion of this kind is needed.

Nicaragua's Institute for Development and the Young Entrepreneurs Program

By mid-2002, the *Emprendedores Juveniles de Nicaragua* (EJN) program was undergoing difficult times. An important company had withdrawn its support, and the project faced the challenge of overcoming barriers for its social mission. The program, implemented by Nicaragua's Institute for Development (INDE), had started in 1991 as an affiliate of Junior Achievement International (JAI), with support from the United States Agency for International Development (AID). The aspiration was to develop managerial capabilities in youth and to enhance their self-esteem, empowering them to improve their living conditions. These goals were pursued through educational activities and selected school events.

After creating its board of directors, composed of renowned local businessmen, and designing a work plan, EJN sought the support of the private sector. In 1991, the first EJN program was launched. Named, "The Company," this first effort included 300 youths from five public schools. The program consisted of a series of brief courses, following a "learning by doing" methodology, delivered by the executives of companies associated with the program. Participants exhibited their work at fairs well attended by entrepreneurs and managers from the private sector.

In 1992, EJN courses targeted primary, secondary and university students. Programs for primary schools consisted of a series of seven topics for children from kindergarten to the sixth grade, sequentially covering basic economic and business concepts suitable for their ages.

In 1993, AID, which had supplied the necessary funds for the program's fixed costs, cancelled its support. EJN sought assistance from various sources to continue its operations. The Austrian government agreed to provide funding, and the private sector offered contributions to meet EJN's operating expenses.

In 1997, the program was refocused to youths at risk, a very serious problem in Nicaragua where school drop-out rates reached 50 percent. The process to identify youths at risk started at the shelters housing these youngsters when they were rescued from the streets. The program provided lodging, clothing, food and education for abandoned and unemployed youngsters, and so helping them to adjust socially. It also assisted them in creating a small company, so that they could earn their living while strengthening themselves as individuals.

UNICEF financed the development and execution of the project, which in 1998, received JAI's international innovation award for adjusting the traditional program to meet local needs. Basically, both organizations shared a common goal: children's welfare. Also, UNI-

CEF had resources to allocate to cooperation projects, and the EJN was committed to sustainable and participative development; it conformed to local regulations; it was apolitical, nonprofit and had so far shown executive capabilities, thus meeting several significant requirements set by UNICEF. As of 2003, UNICEF was considering expanding its support, incorporating seed capital to turn the business proposals created by participating young entrepreneurs into "real-world" ventures. The alliance was becoming increasingly integrative for both parties—and continually successful.

According to EJN executives, there were several factors hindering the support of private companies, including the country's political unrest and the shortage of funds for social assistance in corporate budgets. EJN's 2003 objectives focused on strengthening the relationship with UNICEF, and procuring more extensive and sustainable support from the private sector. The relationships that EJN developed with three companies—Texaco, Coca-Cola, and Pizza Hut—are illuminating, and so described.

The Relationship with Texaco

For years, Texaco headquarters allocated a social contribution budget to each subsidiary. This budget varied among countries and was based on several criteria, the most important ones being forecasted yearly earnings, program contribution to corporate image enhancement, and aid in solving pressing needs. Texaco's brand, advertising and customer service coordinator was in charge of managing the contribution budget. Texaco Nicaragua had supported the EJN since 1999, but in 2002 the company canceled its support. According to a representative of the company, this decision was made because EJN had not turned into a sustainable initiative, and did not provide any follow-up for youngsters once their involvement in the program ended. In addition, Texaco's 2002 budget had been reduced considerably.

EJN surely could have overcome these obstacles and profited from its alliance with Texaco Nicaragua. The company was building an educational center aimed at providing education to low-income students; therefore, it had the necessary facilities and equipment to provide permanent room and support for youths-at-risk. It was a potential opportunity for the EJN. Moreover, if UNICEF provided the seed capital needed to create new companies, Texaco would have had a project that met its support requirements.

Other factors that supported the possibility of a long-term alliance were: (1)Texaco Nicaragua had benefited from positive media coverage resulting from its relation with the EJN, and had received direct recognition from program participants; (2)Texaco had supported the program during three consecutive years (1999–2001), thus promoting working relations between both institutions; (3) the active participation of Texaco officials in social-oriented activities; (4) the EJN could have leveraged its agreement with UNICEF to improve different aspects of its programs, such as strengthening the support to "graduates" of the program or the quality of the business training offered; (5)Texaco's brand, advertising and customer service coordinator was willing to participate in a team that would have explored ideas to render the EJN program self-sufficient.

The Relationship with Coca-Cola

In 2000, Coca-Cola supported an EJN program aimed at primary-school children, between seven and ten years of age, as it aimed at the same segment targeted in the company's marketing efforts. The resources came from the company's marketing budget, which had an "educational channel" program aimed at improving brand recognition since early childhood. For Coca-Cola, the experience with the EJN was highly positive, since participants in the program identified with the brand and with the firm's representatives. In their final exam, the majority of children said they wanted to work for Coca-Cola, or to have their own business to sell their products and Coca-Cola. Once the program was over, the company received around 500 letters from the children, thanking Coca-Cola for its involvement in the program and expressing their admiration for the firm.

Coca-Cola and the EJN were able to align their objectives and strategies in segments that proved appealing to the firm. However, Coca-Cola did not participate in the EJN program in 2001 and 2002, years in which it focused its efforts on raising its sales volume. The educational channel program coordinator believed that the company would accomplish that goal by the end of 2002, allowing the firm to support social initiatives the following year. He anticipated Coca-Cola's willingness to support EJN's program "The Company" with an annual contribution of $10,000 during the following four years, coupled with volunteers from among the company's managers speaking in workshops.

The Relationship with Pizza Hut

The company started supporting the EJN in 2000, helping low-income fourth-grade children with the "Our Community" program. This program required the presence of Pizza Hut personnel at least during seven sessions for ten-minute lectures, either at the beginning or the end of the class. Eight–year-olds were the company's target market in Nicaragua, so its marketing efforts and budget were focused on families with children that age. However, youths-at-risk had no purchasing power, and, therefore, were not a target segment for Pizza Hut.

The company supported the EJN program because its executive director—a former chairman of the CSO—had somehow managed to instill his personal interest in social work in Pizza Hut. "The Young Entrepreneurs' Program" was not included in the social program budget—which depended entirely on children's program earnings—because it was very costly, so contributions to the EJN came directly from Pizza Hut's general budget. Social program activities were not publicized; rather, the company kept a low profile since the board did not want the program to be public or to be used for marketing purposes. The children's program, in contrast, was strongly promoted as a marketing tool. Pizza Hut and the EJN did not achieve a total alignment of objectives and strategies. Pizza Hut did not support the EJN's core objective—the development of "The Company" program for youths-at-risk—however some benefits accrued to all involved.

This case illuminates the three common types of alliances between private companies and CSO. The relationship between EJN and UNICEF represented an integrative alliance, whereas with Texaco, the partnership was still at a transactional level. The relationships with Coca-Cola and Pizza Hut remained at a philanthropic stage. What measures could the EJN take to enable these alliances to move on to an integrative phase, or to secure additional corporate support for its youths-at-risk program?

In the case of Texaco, creating a seed capital fund with UNICEF to launch the business ventures created by young entrepreneurs could help renew the company's enthusiasm. Also, Texaco and the EJN director could together define the social responsibility and corporate image objectives that the company wishes to achieve through the partnership. The EJN might also benefit from Texaco's proposal to create a "work team" to generate initiatives that could make the program self-sufficient. The EJN could view Texaco's reasons to cancel its support as a valuable evaluation of its operation, recognizing that improvements are necessary to secure financial support from other firms.

With Coca-Cola, the EJN could clearly define the financial and human resources support the company might provide to the program. Also, to foster the company's involvement with a program that targets youths-at-risk, it should create incentives for the company, making sure it obtains benefits from the engagement. For example, the EJN could resort to an advertising campaign thanking Coca-Cola's collaboration in this social enterprise. Initiative and creativity are likely to bear fruit.

The relationship with Pizza Hut illustrates the traditional Latin American practice of businesses maintaing a low social profile, even when contributing to social welfare. This attitude, expressed in the saying "do good without saying from whom," is perhaps linked to a strong Catholic tradition in Latin America of piety. Many entrepreneurs who contribute to social projects consider it "inappropriate" or even "immoral" to use chairty as marketing tools. Still others worry that social contribution could hinder rather than serve their personal or corporate objectives, attracting undue and risky attention (including from criminals and cash-starved politicians). More progressive, and less fearful, entrepreneurs and managers, with a social conscious, pragmatic attitude, and a "cost-benefit" calculation ever-present in their analysis are more likely to consider an evolution from the philanthropic stage to the transactional stage as a legitimate and desirable step in alliance development.

However, if the EJN expects to take its partnership with Pizza Hut to an integrative level and to keep its support for the youths-at-risk program after the executive director retires, it should focus its efforts on ensuring value-creation for the company. The EJN could seek government support to create a tax incentive act for participating companies, or it could also plan activities in collaboration with the company to obtain an enhanced value from its employees' volunteer involvement in the program.

An agreement between UNICEF and the EJN to carry out the Young Entrepreneurs' program for a period of five years in several locations, and the inclusion of a seed capital fund to finance start-ups would constitute a qualitative and quantitative leap for the CSO's activities. Its capability as a strategic partner for private companies' social programs would be enhanced, and, as a result, there would be a greater inclination to move from mere philanthropic relationships to long-term strategic alliances.

Posada Amazonas

This case describes the strategic alliance between a private company and a native community in the Peruvian Amazonia. The Amazon Lodge (PA) was a jungle lodge with 24 double rooms that combined native building techniques and materials with contemporary architectural concepts and designs used in eco-lodges around the world. PA was the result of a joint venture between the Ese'eja de Infierno Native Community (EINC) and Rainforest Expeditions (RFE), a small eco-tourism firm whose objective was to promote the preservation of the natural locations through a combination of tourism, research, and education.

Built by RFE to lodge tourists and researchers working on macaw preservation projects, the Tambopata Research Center (TRC) had 13 double rooms. During the TRC's early years, RFE used to hire half a dozen members of the Ese'eja community. But EINC representatives approached RFE to express their concern about the lack of other employment opportunities. They desired RFE to hire more workers to benefit more members of their community. RFE, for its part, had identified the need to build another lodge in the area, not only because the ride to TRC was too long (eight hours), but also because of the number of tourists visiting the lodge. The land owned by the Ese'eja community was suitably located for another lodge.

Given the alignment of needs between both parties, in May 1996, RFE submitted a formal partnership proposal to the community. In 1997, a joint venture was signed to build and operate a lodge in the EINC territory. RFE assumed lodge management responsibility, agreed to hire community members to work in the lodge, and received 50 percent voting shares in business decisions. Profits were split between the community and the firm. The contract covered a period of 20 years, at the end of which the community had the option to continue or terminate it.

RFE partners recalled that they went door-to-door, explaining the terms of the agreement to all members of the Ese'eja community, who had no previous understanding of such things as tourism, foreigners, dollars, and investments. Members of the community got a basic picture of the project and signed the agreement almost unanimously. This accomplishment highlights the role that a firm may play in fostering a project, despite its partner's initial lack of understanding of what might be possible.

In seeking financing for the project, RFE found some difficulties. Kurt Holle, RFE marketing manager and founding partner, explained: "It would have been insane to go to banks or financial institutions; they would have thought us mad. Our clients were not interested, basically because of the size of the investment. Development cooperation agencies left their doors open." After searching for nine months, the Peru-Canada Fund (PCF) was persuaded to support the initiative through a low interest rate loan. Moreover, to provide further financial support, the PCF purchased from the EINC everything that was produced for exchange or sale by the community. Although social projects may not always qualify for bank financing, this example suggests it is useful to explore how other kinds of institutions might provide some kind of support to enable desired projects to be implemented. Once again, commitment and creativity are likely to be rewarded.

The scarce knowledge of administration among members of the Ese'eja community could have stalled alliance progress to the integrative phase. However, although the contract established that RFE would be responsible for the joint venture's management, the community had 50 percent voting shares and exercised a supervisory role through the Management Committee (MC), composed of ten members of the community. The MC was responsible for overseeing, evaluating and monitoring contract provisions and results. Through this committee, members of the community reviewed business information and defined business strategies jointly with RFE. The MC was an effective representation and decision-making institution. RFE's ability to build institutions where none existed was key to its success.

Institution-building was complemented by the training of personnel. The aspiration of RFE was to increase service quality and ensure the continuity of the project, since in 20 years the Ese'eja community was expected to run the lodge on its own. Successful training programs created benefits for community members, while RFE also benefited from PA's success.

As this case illustrates, it is sometimes necessary for one of the partners to invest sizable resources, not just to get the project started, but also to build sustainability. However, as long as this partner obtains a return on the "investment," the relation may evolve to the integrative stage, and not just be "stuck" in the philanthropic stage. Success at PA was welcome by all. The Ese'eja community provided their intimate knowledge of the region, and RFE contributed its institutional, operational and marketing knowledge.

RFE had been mainly responsible for the initial success. However, the association with the Ese'eja community contributed a unique source of assistance and a "market positioning" without which the lodge would not have stood out in a sector in which competition was rapidly increasing. PA prices were between 5 and 40 percent higher than those of other private lodges; it was the market leader in the region and was financially sound. Moreover, the relationship with the indigenous community had given it an additional competitive advantage in advertising. For example, the tourist guide Lonely Planet included a ten-sentence reference of PA, while other lodges were described mentioned in one or two sentences. Holle recalled:

> They are not saying we are better, but we get more press; they talk more about us. So, we become more interesting for the same price. Why? Because they talk about our relationship with the community, about the community owning the place, and so on. The same happens with travel agencies. Many agencies mention that the lodge belongs to the community, and tourists view the fact that part of their money goes to community development as an additional benefit.

Although the relationship between both parties was predetermined by an agreement, the fact that both RFE and the community benefited from the project contributed to an enduring relationship.

The joint venture granted benefits to RFE: corporate image, publicity, and enhanced revenues. Also, the preservation of natural resources in the area, one of the company's main objectives, was achieved. In general, members of the Ese'eja community were clearing less jungle for agriculture and hunting fewer animals. The more community members worked at PA, the less time they spent in collection and agricultural activities.

For its part, the Ese'ja community obtained numerous benefits, too: "secure" employment, training, a decrease in the need to emigrate to cities in search of employment (with all of its risk to family unity and cultural cohesion), and a rise in household income.

The project is truly a testament to the rich possibilities of collaboration between the private sector—the entrepreneurs and managers that are its foundation—and the leaders and partners of CSOs.

Conclusions

The analysis of the cases studied by the faculty of INCAE illuminate the obstacles that frequently hinder the evolution of collaboration relationships to an integrative stage. Cross-sector partnerships develop more successfully and for longer periods of time when parties formally set forth their objectives in an agreement, specifying prospective results, respective contributions and responsibilities, and fixing criteria and approaches to determine the achievement level of established objectives. Thus, each participant can focus its efforts and draw the value expected from the relationship. Otherwise, the alliance may not create value for any of the partners, and thus may not endure.

The process of choosing the correct partner is a key factor to alliance evolution and value creation. The more the objectives between both partners match, the longer and more profitable the relationship. The less the objectives of the partnership matched, the more precarious and short-termed the collaboration is likely to be. It is advisable that both partners jointly analyze their mission, strategies, and value alignment, investing the necessary time and resources to ensure an appropriate choice, before engaging in the partnership.

CSOs should be aware of the objectives driving companies' involvement in the project, and vice versa. There should be a definition of the joint goals to be attained throughout the project, and a careful effort to delineate how each partner can contribute to project success. Adding guidelines for supervision and periodic evaluations should also contribute to project success—as well as a more fluid relationship between partners.

Value creation is essential for an alliance to overcome the philanthropic stage, and also crucial for relationship sustainability. Institutions that pursue image enhancement or seek to use their support to the project as a marketing tool should get recognition from beneficiaries and/or consumers. Otherwise, project involvement and contributions may be hard to explain or justify before the shareholders or the board, jeopardizing partnership continuity. CSOs may publicly thank companies for their help, or a joint advertising campaign may be carried out to disclose project results. Developing mechanisms to quantify the benefits obtained in terms of corporate image, or to measure the project's impact on specific variables, such as sales or brand positioning, may also be helpful.

Differences in working styles between parties may produce a negative effect on partnership development. Potential differences should be acknowledged from the beginning and measures taken to avoid misunderstandings or unnecessary friction in the partnership. Communication is essential. Strong organizations are helpful, too. Chaos is everyone's enemy. And in Latin America, communication is frequently complicated by social cleavages—prominently of class—and by the paucity of institutions. CSOs are frequently organizationally weak, as well as financially limited. These obstacles—and barriers—are best addressed with commitment and creativity.

Social problems are too large for CSOs and private companies to tackle alone, though they surely can contribute to alleviate them. Latin America's social ills demand the combined efforts of productive sectors, local organizations, governments, international institutions—and society itself. The challenge is so immense that all must contribute. Governments, in particular, should assist private efforts, if only by providing incentives.

However desirable it may be for strategic alliances to move from the philanthropic stage to transactional or integrative phases, it is equally important that alliances be reworked over time in order to fulfill changing needs and objectives. Alliances need to be dynamic. Both parties should consider the alliance as a self-discovery and learning opportunity, supporting, in turn, a constant exhange of information useful for building stronger and more useful institutions. Agreements should be modified—or reworked—if necessary to attain project sustainability. Commitment, communication, creativity, innovation, and institutional development are all key factors in successful collaborative relationships to meet social needs.

INCAE's Social Enterprise Cases

Ayca, J, Alfaro, L. N., "ACODEP," INCAE case #10963, 2003.

Ayca, J, Edelberg, G. S., Ickis, J., "Amcham de Nicaragua," INCAE case #10959, 2003.

Azofeifa, M, Leguizamón, F, "IFDC Emprendedores Juveniles de Nicaragua," INCAE case #26334, 2003.

Azofeifa, M., Condo, A., Prado, A., "Banco Solidario del Ecuador," INCAE case #26708, 2003.

Colburn, F., "Indigo," INCAE case #25984, 2001.

García, L. M., Pérez, F., "Construambiente," INCAE case #10997, 2003.

Ogliastri, E., "La Equidad," INCAE case #26586, 2003.

Ogliastri, E., Alfaro, L., et alli, "Alianzas intersectoriales para el desarrollo social. Seis casos latinoamericanos", INCAE, 2004.

Ogliastri, E., Alfaro, L., et alli, "Estrategia y sostenibilidad de empresas sociales. Cinco casos latinoamericanos", INCAE, 2004.

Pérez, F, Revilla, J, "Posada Amazonas," INCAE case #25440, 2003.

Ramírez, J, Revilla, J, "Techo para el Sur-Construyendo con Amor," INCAE case #26116, 2003.

Rodríguez, W., Alfaro, LN, "La Estancia," INCAE case #25528, 2002

Rodríguez, W. Ogliastri, E., "RDS Honduras," INCAE case #26646, 2003.

Notes

1   Population data are from The World Bank, *The Little Data Book 2003* (Washington, DC: The World Bank Group, 2003).

2   Ibid. and (for Nicaragua) The World Bank, *The Little Data Book 2002* (Washington, DC: The World Bank Group, 2002).

3   Data on Peru are from Fritz Du Bois, lecture at the Universidad de Lima, Lima, Peru, August 22, 2003.

4   Ibid.

5   Forrest Colburn, "Indigo," INCAE case #25984, 2001.

9

Chile: Building Trust in Alliances[1]

Mladen Koljatic and Mónica Silva

Introduction

"Better a known devil than an unknown saint," is a popular Chilean saying that reveals the tendency of nationals to mistrust strangers. Chile's geographical isolation may account for this phenomenon, which favors restricted personal interactions between individuals belonging to a small group of close-knit relations, where "everybody knows everybody."[2] However, whatever the origins of this preference for the familiar, there is no doubt that it exerts both positive and negative influences on a community. A clear and almost extreme example of the latter would be the inclination to offer job positions to relatives and friends rather than to strangers, thus creating a kind of nepotism or favoritism that would be frowned upon in other cultures. In Chile, however, this "job-for-one-of-the-guys" practice enjoys widespread tacit approval and is only condemned when the individual in question proves to be inefficient or performs illegal or immoral acts.[3]

This preference for the familiar underlies many successful cross-sector partnerships in the region, and, particularly, in those discussed in this chapter. Many of the partnerships in Chile originated as the result of trust-based relations between acquaintances, friends or family members. As shown in Chapters 2 and 3, and especially Chapter 5, trust contributes to the emergence of collaboration processes, spurs their development over time, and becomes one of their key assets.[4]

In this chapter we explore the role played by trust in alliance initiation and strengthening through the example of four successful cross-sector collaborations in Chile: *Empresas Ariztía* and Melipilla Municipal Corporation (*Corporación Municipal de Melipilla,* hence CMM); *Farmacias Ahumada S.A.* (FASA) and the *Fundación Las Rosas* (FLR); the Credit and Investment Bank (*Banco de Crédito e Inversiones,* hence BCI) and the Corporation for Children's Credit (*Corpo-*

ración de Crédito al Menor, hence CCM); ESSO-Chile and the Burned Children Assistance Corporation (*Corporación de Ayuda al Niño Quemado,* hence COANIQUEM).[5] The discussion is based on a qualitative analysis and constitutes an exploratory approach to the study of trust as a key factor to cross-sector alliance success. Two important questions were explored: what factors promoted trust development at the initial stages of a collaborative effort? and what factors have contributed to the sustainability and growth of trust over time?

Different Standpoints on Trust

Trust is a key concept to understand people's willingness to volunteer their involvement in groups, organizations, and society at large. Moreover, some authors claim that trust is essential to the creation and survival of civil society.[6] The actual scope and significance of trust in social life is often downplayed, and it usually crops up in situations of social disintegration where trust has been undermined, jeopardizing the stability of social relations.[7]

Trust is a core element in the development of current, complex and interdependent societies. Thus, various disciplines have studied it.[8] The willingness to take the risk of investing in something or someone can be explained by the existence of trust. Both concepts, risk and trust, are closely related and interdependent: risk creates an opportunity for trust, which in turns leads to a willingness to take risks. Thus, from an economic standpoint, trust constitutes a paramount feature, since democratic and free market societies could not do without it.[9]

Likewise, trust also plays an important role in regulating interpersonal relations and collaboration processes among institutions in society.[10] The significance of trust in the initial stages of cross-sector alliances seems to be of crucial importance, since trust mechanisms basically rely on individuals rather than on external sources of control, such as formal contracts that serve to regulate exchanges in strategic alliances between businesses.[11]

In this section, we opted for a broad concept of trust, making a distinction between trust built among individuals and among organizations. Trust among individuals is understood as the degree of willingness to believe in others' good intentions, accepting the risks and the vulnerability entailed.[12] Trust in organizations or institutions appears to rest not in individuals, but in institutionalized practices or procedures, based on the belief that if followed they will produce a positive outcome.[13]

Trust among individuals has played a significant part in the creation of some cross-sector collaborations in Chile between an already established company and a nascent NGO. In these cases, trust is placed in the social organization's leader, for he/she has nothing tangible to show to its partner in terms of organizational outcomes. Since the organization does not exist in operational terms, its leader can only offer his/her vision of future results derived from the collaboration process.

For long-standing NGOs that have a history in the community and that are in a position to show positive outcomes, trust operates differently than in the case of a budding institution. For the former, trust rests on a collective belief that the group or institution will be true to its commitments.[14] Trust is not placed on an individual, but transcends to the organization as a whole.

It should be noted that the distinction between trust in individuals and institutional or organizational trust is not absolute. Both seem to be different but related forms of the same phenomenon, and both are important when analyzing cross-sector alliances over time. Trust is not a static occurrence; on the contrary, it is dynamic and changes as the relationship evolves in time. As a result, the processes involved in trust building at initial stages may not necessarily be the ones operating in subsequent phases.[15]

Additionally, cultural nuances in societies must be taken into account as key determinants to understand the role of trust in alliance building. International research studies have demonstrated that the levels of social trust vary over time among countries and within a country itself.[16] An understanding of how societal norms and values influence trust appears to be very important in the context of cross-national strategic alliances. Along the same vein, the understanding of the emergence and evolution of cross-sector collaborations could be enhanced by considering societal norms and value influences in trust processes. For example, the predominant role played by certain cultural variables, such as the predominance of familiarity in trust building and the reluctance to engage in interaction with strangers, serves as a crucial factor to understand the emergence of collaborative relationships in Chile.

To sum up, trust building, and the processes through which it evolves and strengthens in time, takes place at individual, organizational and societal levels (or in a micro-, media- or macro-system).[17] Therefore, an adequate understanding of trust and its role in a successful cross-sector alliance should engulf all three levels. Although most research on organizational trust has been conducted about relationships between for-profit organizations, many of the findings appear to be applicable to the framework of cross-sector alliances.

Trust in Alliance Emergence

Friendship or direct family ties among NGO founders and company representatives seemed to facilitate the emergence of a collaborative relationship, and later, continued alliance development. Initial contacts in three of the four local cases analyzed started in this familiarity context. Such was the case of Dr. Rojas, the founder of COANIQUEM—the center for treating burned children—who during a family gathering came across an in-law who worked at ESSO-Chile. Thus, he found out that the company supported social community projects. According to Rojas, should this contact have not existed, he would have never dared to knock at ESSO-Chile's door, since he knew no one at the company. His attitude reflects the prevalent culture of distrust, which narrows down the pool of potential partners for interaction and discourages the initiation of interactions with strangers.[18]

Trust based on friendship and camaraderie also played an essential role in the alliance between BCI bank and CCM.[19] Its founder, a bank manager, started out by seeking support for his endeavor among his co-workers. He first approached the comptroller, who, in addition to being his friend, enjoyed great trust within the company. The comptroller's endorsement of the initiative proved crucial for BCI executives agreeing to donate money to the emerging organization.

In the alliance between the agribusiness *Empresas Ariztía* and CMM, the mutual trust between its CEO and the mayor who invited him to join in the collaboration was reinforced by their ideological affinity and the respect and affection that the company president enjoyed in his close-knit community.

The emergence of these alliances can be explained as a function of affect and emotional ties between individuals. It is interesting to note that affect also appears to play a role in the selection of alliance partners in business organizations in the U.S. Alliances appear to be facilitated by pre-existing and ongoing social relations and networks of personal rapport.[20]

In the literature in organizational trust, some authors draw a distinction between trust based on emotional bonds and positive feelings towards individuals (labeled affect-based trust) and trust based on evidence of trustworthiness on the part of individuals (cognition-based trust).[21] Emotional trust is founded on the historical interactions with a certain individual, and is marked by positive feelings for the person, whereas cognition-based trust or calculative trust is based on the expected behavior of the person in his/her role, independent of friendship considerations.[22] In the initial stages of the cross-sector alliances studied, affect-based trust appears to be the predominant type of trust that operates. Thus, a common family or friendship background drives one of the parties to approach the other and request a collaborative effort.

However, as already noted, an approach to understanding the link between friendship ties and collaboration development should go beyond the individual or interpersonal standpoint to encompass a macro context, regulations, and cultural standards. Although trust may form in a variety of ways, whether and how trust is established appears to depend upon societal norms and values that guide people's behaviors and beliefs regarding whom to trust.[23]

Researchers studying the realm of trust and human relations have identified distinctive features shaping friendship patterns in different countries.[24] In Chile, as opposed to other countries, trust is highly restricted to family and friends; whatever may lie beyond that close context is construed as a potential menace. Thus, family and friendship ties are highly treasured in Chile, accounting for a tacit cultural norm that considers almost inadmissible refusing to do a favor for a friend. This idiosyncratic trait, coupled with the fact that Chileans tend to distrust strangers, substantiate the notion that family and friendship ties constitute a powerful factor in the development of collaborative relations.

Contemporary and historic evidence shows that, while some societies develop solid trust cultures, others feature an endemic mistrust. These tendencies are not static: they vary over time, depending on a complex interaction of factors. According to some authors, during the past decades, the North American culture has evolved towards a diffuse and generalized mistrust, while post-communist societies have moved towards a greater comprehensive trust.[25]

The Chilean society displays a low level of social trust that undermines potential relationships with strangers. This lack of social trust is counteracted, as already explained, by a strong and intense trust towards family members, acquaintances and friends.[26] Moreover, Chileans appear to be more mistrustful than other Latin American nationals. Thus the influence of family and friendship ties in the emergence of alliances may not be a mere coincidence, but an expression of the Chilean cultural idiosyncrasy and predominant model of association between individuals.

It is noteworthy that in the three collaborations previously mentioned (that is to say, COANIQUEM with Esso Chile; CCM with BCI; and CMM with *Empresas Ariztía*), the role of affect-based bonds in the emergence of the collaboration is self-evident, since the NGOs did not exist, or had only legal status. Consequently, trust at this stage, was fully placed in project leaders, since NGOs were not operational. The support of these social ventures on the part of the companies, entailed a greater leap of faith than contributing to philanthropic or social welfare initiatives promoted by NGOs that were already established in the community.

So far, no mention has been made of the fourth cross-sector collaboration case, the partnership between the largest Chilean drugstore chain, FASA and the FLR, an organization devoted to assisting older people in need. FASA, as part of its business strategy, was looking for a partner to enhance its corporate image and to develop a closer relationship with the community.

At first sight, this alliance seems to be an exception to the rule, in that it lacked the bond of friendship or family-ties component in its initial stages. However, this alliance illustrates the intervention of the so-called "third party mechanism" or trust intermediary.[27] In this kind of collaboration process, the relationship develops between groups that do not know each other, but that come together through a common link, usually an individual that belongs to both groups. In this instance, the liaison was Alex Fernández, FASA board member and executive president of the insurance enterprise Compañía Interamericana de Seguros. Fernández was well acquainted with the work of the foundation in the support of the elderly, since the insurance company he presided over had been contributing to this social institution for several years. When FASA's board decided to seek an alliance with an NGO that could contribute to enhance its corporate image within the community, Fernández—acting as a trust intermediary—facilitated the company's decision to choose FLR over other welfare institutions that had also been identified as potential partners.

In a culture characterized by low levels of trust, the tendency to mistrust others goes beyond individuals to include institutions of the civil society. However, an exception to this pattern of generalized distrust towards institutions is the Catholic Church, which has traditionally inspired confidence in Chileans.[28] Our cases showed a positive impact of religious affiliation of both business and social leaders, facilitating trust-building among parties. Many of the leaders who were involved in the early stages of the partnerships were described by other protagonists interviewed as religiously inclined individuals, with strong connections to the Church.[29] The leaders' affiliation with the Catholic Church may have contributed to legitimize their embryonic institutions.[30] In other words, in a country featuring a low level of interpersonal trust, added to a relatively low trust in secular organizations and a deep trust in religious institutions,[31] the participation of the leaders as conspicuous members in the Church may well have favored the emergence of credibility in their initiatives.

The bond of the leader of FLR with the Church was very evident. The Foundation was managed by a charismatic priest who was widely respected for his social initiatives aimed at protecting destitute senior citizens. In CCM the leader was an individual with an intense social and religious zeal according to his associates. On account of his acquaintance with a Jesuit priest, and director of a renowned Jesuit institution devoted to helping the needy, the nascent organization was loaned a building site. In COANIQUEM, its president was a devout Catholic who decided to build a sanctuary to the Flagellated Christ at the patient care center in the city of Santiago,[32] and invited a Catholic bishop to participate in the board of the institution. Finally, the president of *Empresas Ariztía* was an active member in local Church movements, making contributions to its philanthropic activities. He also had incorporated explicit references in his company's Mission Statement to Christian ethical values and the need to foster community development.

In brief, from the beginning of the alliances, the element of trust was present between the leaders of both organizations. This trust originated either from family, friendship or acquaintance ties among the leaders and company executives. In some instances, trust was enhanced and encouraged by the leaders' close connections with the Church. Affect-based trust placed in the project leader explains the surge of confidence in social venture, even when the social institutions were not operational, as is the case with the alliance between BCI and CCM, and between COANIQUEM and Esso Chile.

As previously stated, some authors believe that trust is not only a necessary prerequisite for cooperative relationships, but that it also undergoes changes during the collaboration process.[33] Following this notion, the next section will tackle the role of trust in alliance strengthening.

The Role of Trust in Cross-Sector Alliance Strengthening

The previous sections have analyzed the role played by family and friendship ties in trust building during the early stages of alliance development in Chile. Trust, in these terms, implies an initial bet about the future contingent actions of others, based on kinship and friendship networks. However, as collaboration relationships progress over time, the line between interpersonal relations and relationships with larger social organizations becomes blurry, resulting in a form of trust that transcends individuals to encompass the institutions.

Some authors have described the relation between interpersonal trust and trust placed in more abstract social objects—among them, organizations—as concentric circles in gradual expansion.[34] In describing institutional trust, this model illustrates the significance of an individual tie even when trust expands to the organizations. After all, alliances are created, nurtured and strengthened by individuals.[35]

For an alliance to develop and become institutionalized, parties must consistently engage in activities conducive to that end. Chapter 5 showed that, in all collaboration cases studied, frequent interactions between the parties, an open and candid communication, institutional involvement at all levels, and the performance of joint activities, such as personnel training or technical assistance sessions, proved to be facilitating factors.[36] Many of these factors were operating in collaborative relationships developed in Chile and contributed to promote trust and positive feelings among members in the two institutions.

The alliances hereby analyzed included frequent interactions and contacts that went beyond top executives of both organizations to involve a larger number of members. Although key individuals may manage the alliances and act as liaisons between the organizations,[37] they also promote the collaborative participation of other members.[38]

Integrity and transparency are crucial in promoting trust across the organizational boundaries. Trust appears to be enhanced by actions such as periodic management audits of the NGOs, or by making income and expenditure reports available to the companies. Such transparency procedures imply a willingness to display achievements and to assume responsibility for them, and they strengthen mutual trust. Among the cases studied, FLR, for example, audited its statements and made them public, while CCM submitted a semester income report to the board made up of members of BCI management. Likewise, COANIQUEM had sought to achieve transparent management and to improve its administrative processes over time, and CMM was particularly careful in reporting its financial statements, since it received public funding from the government.

All alliances featured frequent interactions between partners, even beyond their working environments. COANIQUEM's president, who is also a concert guitarist, for example, offered lectures on prevention of burn accidents and performed at musical events for ESSO employees. Companies' employees were encouraged to visit the institutions during working hours, like in the case of FASA, or in off-hours, as was the case of ESSO-Chile and BCI employees. These direct contacts promoted close relationships among organization members and built interaction networks that strengthened the alliance through enhancing the development of affective bonds between individuals.

For alliances, it is of key importance that the NGOs show accomplishments to support the confidence placed in them by businesses. Alliances gain in strength when expectations of performance are met, and there is evidence that the time and resources invested in the organization has translated into measurable outcomes. The examples that follow reflect this pattern. In the alliance between CCM and BCI, the bank's president pointed out that it was possible to see the results associated to the efforts when he stated: "in this kind of project, results are plain to see." Results are also clearly evident in the case of FLR, which managed to grow from 18 to 39 homes for the elderly in less than a decade. Likewise, the CEO of *Empresas Ariztía* explained that he had withdrawn from another corporation's board because he felt that his participation in it "would bear no fruit," as opposed to CMM that had yielded tangible results. The display of positive results was also important for ESSO-Chile. An executive noted, "COANIQUEM is a rare case. It shows short-term results and is very transparent as regards to resource allocation. ESSO-Chile will continue supporting COANIQUEM as long as it submits adequate projects."

Eventually, gradual strengthening of the relationship may lead to a kind of trust where companies identify themselves with the mission of the NGO and vice versa. The advance or progress attained in mission fulfillment, the feelings of ownership and participation in those achievements, and the existence of transparent management practices reinforce the mutual trust between organizations, giving way to a solid relationship. Or put another way, the partners eventually adopt the other organization's identity as their own, thus generating trust based on identification.[39] How could this type of identification-based trust be developed in cross-sector alliances? What factors would support it? A common and long history of collaboration, interwoven with shared values and expectations, and rooted in the close-knit relationship between the parties are likely factors that facilitate the construction of a shared identity. This shared identity and mission is a distinctive feature of collaborative alliances that have reached the integrative phase.[40]

Alliance Trust and Risks

All personal relationships entail some level of risk, namely that one individual might fail to live up to the other's expectations. Obviously, alliances of any kind between institutions also imply risks. In the case of cross-sector alliances, if social organizations fail to comply with their mission, business companies may experience a negative reaction from their stakeholders for sponsoring unreliable organizations. Along the same lines, if NGOs enter into alliances with companies whose ethical practices are questioned, their standing in the community will be undermined, and they run the risk of getting bad press for their poor judgment in choosing partners. If alliances have become public, the success or failure of one of the parties will affect the other's image in the public eye. To a certain extent, partners will have to account for the other's performance, much in the same way as a husband and wife who are bound together "for better and for worse."

The levels of commitment in relationships are clearly appreciated in the face of crises or external threats to one of the partners. Such was the case in the alliance between COANIQUEM and ESSO-Chile: when the company was drawn into a controversy due to an unfortunate incident, COANIQUEM stepped in to provide its public support contributing to the strengthening of ESSO-Chile's image in the community.

Part of the alliance trust-building process lies in the expectation as to whether the other party will meet or fail to meet expectations, and how supportive the partner will be in the future. Whether trusting someone was or was not a wise decision will depend on the odds that the other party will live up to his/her commitments in meeting objectives, and the potential effects of failure.[41] Thus, the question "Do you trust them?" must be qualified: "trust them to do what?" [42] The latter implies having clear expectations of what are the objectives that are being sought. Trust is enhanced when the impact of the social endeavor undertaken is clear to all parties. Clear objectives combined with efforts conducive to higher levels of accountability, transparency, and performance measurement can only lead to higher levels of trust among parties.

Nowadays companies and NGOs attach great importance to the exposure derived from entering an alliance, and oftentimes one of the benefits that accrue to a collaborative effort is media coverage. However, advertising the alliance may entail a risk if the trusted partner fails to achieve its objectives. If trust is lost or damaged, the odds of a continuing and successful collaborative effort are at risk.

Final Thoughts

Previous sections have discussed several facets of trust in alliances. Trust is a variable that adds value to a relationship from the moment of its very inception and tends to grow and develop as the partnership itself evolves and consolidates.

The Chilean cases served to explore in retrospect the role played by trust at two different moments in time: when NGOs had not yet been created and were a mere project in the minds of their leaders, and when they already enjoyed a sound reputation and standing in the community. In all the cases analyzed, initial trust appeared to be facilitated in these successful alliances through family, friendship or third party ties.

However, regardless of how the collaborative effort is launched, trust between the parties must be nurtured. The attainment of explicit goals and objectives, the display of tangible outcomes associated to the collaboration, frequent interactions between participants and relational transparency are instrumental to maintaining confidence. Sound trust in a relationship is a powerful ingredient associated to successful alliances.

A future and more thorough study of the influence and value enhancement potential of trust in collaboration relationships seems appropriate, especially along the different stages in the alliance-building process. Some authors in the context of business alliances have claimed that alliances originating from friendship ties may experience a different developmental path from those arising without personal ties between participants.[43] This matter has not yet been explored in cross-sector alliances, but due to its potential relevance for successful collaboration it appears to merit further study.

Likewise, the role of trust in the emergence of cross-sector alliances in other countries, with their own idiosyncratic features and cultural standards, calls for further investigation. Knowledge obtained through the study of local collaboration relationships may not necessarily apply to other countries. Chile, for example, does not display the more open American attitude of engaging in social relations with strangers, which reflects a stronger sense of community, and the characteristic pattern of establishing friendship and partnership bonds that is typical of contemporary U.S. culture. A possible strategy to create alliances in societies featuring a low level of social trust and unwillingness to relate to strangers is to start the search for potential partners among the close family and friendship circles. Should this fail, it appears that a sound strategy might consist of identifying a third party to serve as liaison between the organization leader and the company. This strategy may help overcome distrust towards strangers and profit from the spontaneous trust stemming from common roots.

The adequate strategies to facilitate the emergence of bonds between businessmen and NGO leaders may vary among countries. The liaison role between institutions may be achieved or at least facilitated by institutions enjoying trust within the community.

Finally, as indicated at the outset, all the previous discussion is founded on qualitative data. As in any exploratory study, the major value of the findings consists in raising questions to be explored by future practice and research. For instance, at present, it is not possible to state whether trust is to be considered a cause or an effect of a sustainable collaboration, nor if it is an exclusive feature of successful alliances. Still, the analysis of the cross-sector alliances discussed here, offers reasonably credible—albeit not conclusive—evidence that trust played a key role in the genesis and evolution of these successful collaborative efforts.

Notes

1   We are grateful to Eduardo Valenzuela, Director of the Institute of Sociology at the *Pontificia Universidad Católica de Chile*, for his valuable contributions to this work.

2   Hernán Godoy, *El carácter chileno: Estudio preliminar y selección de ensayos* (Santiago, Chile: Editorial Universitaria, 1981).

3   Eugenio González, *La importancia de ser pariente* (August 5) (Ercilla,

2002 [cited April 3, 2003]); available from http://www.ercilla.cl/nanterior/n3195/edito.html.

4   The role of trust in cross-sector collaborations is also discussed in James E. Austin, *The Collaboration Challenge: How Nonprofits and Businesses Succeed through Strategic Alliances*, 1st ed. (San Francisco: Jossey-Bass Publishers, 2000).

5   A summary of each of those cases can be found in Chapter 1.

6   Russell Hardin, *Trust and Trustworthiness* (New York: Russell Sage Foundation, 2002).

7   Karen S. Cook, *Trust in Society* (New York: Russell Sage Foundation, 2001).

8   Denise M. Rousseau et al., "Not so different after all: A Cross-Discipline View of Trust," *Academy of Management Review* 23, no. 3 (1998); Megan Tschannen-Moran and Wayne K. Hoy, "A multidisciplinary Analysis of the Nature, Meaning and Measurement of Trust," *Review of Educational Research* 70, no. 4 (2000).

9   "Confianza social para el desarrollo," (Santiago, Chile: Fundación Chile Unido, 2002).

10   Antonio Argandoña, "Sharing out in Alliances: Trust and Ethics," *Journal of Business Ethics* 21 (1999).

11   Deepak Malhotra and Keith Murnighan, J, "The Effects of Contracts on Interpersonal Trust," *Administrative Science Quarterly* 47 (2002).

12   Taggart Frost, David Simpson, and Micol R. C. Maughham, "Some Correlates of Trust," *Journal of Psychology* 99 (1978); Julian B. Rotter, "A New Scale for the Measurement of Interpersonal Trust," *Journal of Personality and Social Psychology* 35 (1967); Rousseau et al., "Not So Different After All: A Cross-Discipline View of Trust."

13   Piotr Sztompka, *Trust: a Sociological Theory* (Cambridge, UK: Cambridge University Press, 1999).

14   Larry L. Cummings and Philip Bromiley, "The Organizational Trust Inventory," in *Trust in Organizations: Frontiers of Theory and Research*, ed. Roderick M. Tyler and Tom R. Tyler (Thousand Oaks, CA: Sage Publications, 1996).

15   D. Harrison McKnight, Larry L. Cummins, and Norman L. Chervany, "Initial Trust Formation in New Organizational Relationships," *Academy of Management Review* 23, no. 3 (1998).

16   Wendy M. Rahn and John E. Transue, "Social Trust and Value Change: The Decline of Social Capital in American Youth," *Political Psychology* 19, no. 3 (1998); Jan W. Van Deth, ed., *Private Groups and Public Life: Social Participation, Voluntary Associations and Political Involvement in Repre-*

sentative Democracies, European Political Science Series (London; New York: Routledge, 1997).

17 Tom R. Tyler and Roderick M. Kramer, "Whither Trust?," in *Trust in Organizations: Frontiers of Theory and Research*, ed. Roderick M. Tyler and Tom R. Tyler (Thousand Oaks, CA: Sage Publications, 1996).

18 Sztompka, *Trust: A Sociological Theory*.

19 According to Chilean law there are two types of nonprofit organizations: *corporaciones* and *fundaciones*. The statutes of a *corporación* require that it be created through the association of a group of individuals who pursue a nonprofit social purpose, but it exacts no assets or equity for its creation. On the other hand, *fundaciones* do require the existence of an endowment since their purpose is to finance social endeavors.

20 Hitoshi Mitsuhashi, "Uncertainty in Selecting Alliance Partners: The Three Reduction Mechanisms and Alliance Formation Processes," *The International Journal of Organizational Analysis* 10, no. 2 (2002).

21 Daniel J. McAllister, "Affect and Cognition-Based Trust as Foundations for Interpersonal Cooperation in Organizations," *Academy of Management Journal* 38, no. 1 (1995).

22 Paul Olk and Marta Elvira, "Friends and Srategic Agents," *Group and Organization Management* 26, no. 2 (June 2001).

23 Patricia M. Doney, P. Cannon Joseph, and Michael R. Mullen, "Understanding the influence of National Culture on the Development of Trust," *Academy of Management Review* 23, no. 3 (1999).

24 Barbara A. Misztal, *Trust in Modern Societies: The Search for the Bases of Social Order* (Cambridge, U.K.: Polity Press, 1996).

25 Sztompka, *Trust: A Sociological Theory*.

26 Eduardo Valenzuela and Carlos Cousiño, "Sociabilidad y asociatividad: Un ensayo de sociología comparada," *Estudios Públicos* 77 (Summer 2000).

27 Hardin, *Trust and Trustworthiness*.

28 Numerous studies uphold the trust generated by the Catholic Church as an institution in Chile. See *Pulso de la política* (Fundación Futuro, April 2000 [cited June 25, 2003]); available from http://www.fundacionfuturo. cl/estudios_pub.php?id=24&valor=1; Paola Sais, *El 80 percent de los chilenos no confía en los políticos* (La Tercera, April 2000 [cited December 13, 2002]); available from http://www.tercera.ia.cl/diario/2000/04/23/ t-23.06.3a.CRO.PNUD.html. In another comparative study among seven Latin American countries, Chile ranks as the second country in terms of the Catholic Church's institutional trust. *Golpe de opinión* (August 19) (Qué pasa, 1997 [cited March 15, 2003]); available from http://www. quepasa.cl/revista/1375/11.html.

29 This is consistent with the view developed in Blair Sheppard and Dana Sherman, "The Grammars of Trust: A Model and General Implications," *Academy of Management Review* 23, no. 3 (1998). These authors mention the role of the church as a mechanism to facilitate the emergence of trust among relative strangers.

30 McKnight, Cummins, and Chervany, "Initial Trust Formation in New Organizational Relationships."

31 Carla Lehmann, "¿Cuán religiosos somos los chilenos? Mapa de la religiosidad de 31 países," *Estudios Públicos* 85 (Summer 2002).

32 *El ser profundo, del dolor a la plenitud* (Coaniquem, [cited June 18, 2003]); available from http://coaniquem.cl/ponencias.htm.

33 Sztompka, *Trust: a Sociological Theory.*

34 Ibid.

35 See "The Power of Pre-Existing Relations" (p. 48), "Alignment's Personal Dimension" (p. 90) and "Trust Building" (p. 171). The subject is also discussed in Austin, *The Collaboration Challenge: How Nonprofits and Businesses Succeed through Strategic Alliances.*

36 Ibid.

37 Steven C. Currall and Timothy A. Judge, "Measuring Trust between Organizational Boundary Role Persons," *Organizational Behavior and Human Decision Processes* 64, no. 2 (1995).

38 In dealing with the search for an adequate spokesman, Chapter 2 discussed the role of alliance "sponsors" within each organization.

39 Blair H. Sheppard and Marla Tuchinsky, "Micro O-B and the Network Organization," in *Trust in Organizations: Frontiers of Theory and Research,* ed. Roderick M. Tyler and Tom R. Tyler (Thousand Oaks, CA: Sage Publications, 1996).

40 Austin, *The Collaboration Challenge: How Nonprofits and Businesses Succeed through Strategic Alliances.*

42 Sztompka, *Trust: A Sociological Theory.*

42 Roger C. Mayer, James H. Davis, and F. David Schoorman, "An Integrative Model of Organizational Trust," *Academy of Management Review* 20, no. 3 (1995).

43 Olk and Elvira, "Friends and Strategic Agents."

10

Colombia: Multi-Party Alliance Development

Roberto Gutiérrez, Diana Trujillo and Iván Darío Lobo

Introduction

Collaborations are phenomena that, under the right circumstances, have the potential for great value. Since they are not a trivial practice and certainly imply some risks, they are not always successful and a general aversion to risk means their potential value is at times untapped.[1] If it is hard for collaborations to fulfill their potential, why then would organizations want to multiply that effort and embark on collaborations involving multiple parties? The cases studied in Colombia are characterized by multi-party alliances. As opposed to bilateral alliances, where a single member of the private sector interacts with a single member of the social sector, multilateral or multi-party alliances involve the interaction of many agents from both sectors; one private company involved with several social organizations or one social organization involved with several companies or multiple companies interacting with multiple social organizations. This chapter intends to shed some light on the ability of organizations to create and maintain multi-party partnerships.

Developing the potential of alliances involves building trust, as was emphasized in the previous chapter, and deploying considerable coordination. Thus, it is important to explore how organizations overcome the challenges posed by multi-party alliances. This chapter introduces some of the characteristics that differentiate multilateral alliances from bilateral partnerships in terms of initial contacts, strategic alignment, value creation methods, and institutionalization formats.

This research is not intended to draw definitive generalizations, which is impossible because of the few cases surveyed. However, we do intend to sketch out hypotheses that will help guide the approach of other observers to similar situations.

Colombia in the Nineties

In Colombia, as well as in other Latin American countries, the State underwent a process of downsizing, modernization and decentralization during the nineties. As mentioned in chapter one, these drives brought along several phenomena uncommon in the region: partial or total privatization of State agencies, a move towards provision of public goods and services by private organizations, and the adoption of development models with a stronger role for civil society, among others. In Colombia, government promoted free trade and enacted legislation to decentralize its operations. Within these elements, some structural characteristics of Colombia—such as the weakness of the State and the pressing needs of a large portion of its population—have had an effect on the development of the multiple alliances reported in this chapter.

Governmental Policies and New Legislation

Trade liberalization, a central policy during the presidency of César Gaviria (1990–1994), was promoted with the argument that foreign competition would stimulate the internal development of the economy. The State's decentralization gave fiscal autonomy to the regions and made it possible for them to take education, health, and regional development policies in their hands. In such a context, two laws were key for the alliances studied within the Colombian sample:

- Law 100 of 1993, which created the Health and Social Security General System. This decentralized health model, with its participatory and solidarity characteristics, aims at promotion, prevention, treatment and rehabilitation coverage for all Colombians. In essence, it replaced a subsidy for the suppliers, paid to the hospitals, with a subsidy to the demand paid to insurers who send those insured to hospitals that compete through a better service.

- Law 115 of 1994, the Education General Law, which defined the Institutional Education Projects as a required activity for every educational institution in the country. These projects attempt to articulate the interests of the different actors within an educational community and they respond to a strategic exercise carried out within educational institutions.

Pressing Needs

In the last decade, social problems in Colombia have become more acute. The armed conflict has escalated and the social fabric has suffered as a consequence. Poverty levels remain high and increasing numbers of Colombians are excluded from the benefits of economic development. However, as needs become more pressing, many citizens take on a more active role. Behind their activism there are two different motivations: one, a survival instinct for those who cannot satisfy their basic needs and, two, the energy originated by a service drive within some of the privileged ones who have the opportunity to help others.

State Weakness

The weakness of the Colombian State is manifest in different ways. In many regions of the country, the State is absent and its place is occupied by private interests. Corruption has increased in the past years, its costs have gone up, and the solutions posed by governments have not been very effective. Public services, for example, have been affected by the derailing of public funds or by the lack of transparency in biddings that result in the lowering of the quality of the services. Within this panorama, other actors have begun to play an important role in changing such situations. Multiple alliances have been an answer by the private and social sectors to pull needed resources together that fill in the void with social control as one main characteristic.

Four Colombian Experiences

The four experiences studied were selected because agents from various sectors were involved, they lasted several years as strategic alliances, and they focused on different social issues. The sample includes collaborations devoted to housing projects, enhancement of education, management improvements within health-sector organizations, and promotion of regional development. Two of the experiences were led by social organizations, while the other two were undertaken by private companies.

The first case describes the *Corporación Minuto de Dios* (MD, One Minute for God), a nonprofit founded in 1958 to "organize a Christian community to try to provide comprehensive solutions for the social problems of their affiliates."[2] This nonprofit and seven others form the One Minute for God Organization (*Organización Minuto de Dios*), an institution committed to the overall development of needy communities and their inhabitants, both urban and rural, on the basis of the Christian Gospel. MD has built approximately 60,000 different solutions, with social housing projects being their principal line of work. They also offer disaster assistance services, micro enterprise support, care for the elderly, spiritual aid, and youth development programs. Since its inception, the MD has built alliances with high-powered companies like Manuelita S.A. (Manuelita), one of the largest sugar producers in Colombia. In the 1990s, MD developed partnerships with *Servibanca*, a Colombian nonprofit organization engaged in the promotion of Colombian banking automation, with the electronic banking division of the *Banco Davivienda*[3] and with the Carulla-Vivero Supermarket chain. In these three alliances, the companies provided their own infrastructure in order to raise funds for MD services. The MD case shows social problems with such a complexity that concerted efforts are required. For example, demand for affordable housing projects has not been fulfilled by the State nor by the market. When an organization like MD seeks to satisfy this demand, the resources needed (financial ones in particular) are proportional to the magnitude of the problem, and it is not possible to gather them without the concourse of financial or commercial businesses.

The second case is a program called The Twenty-First Century Leaders (*Líderes Siglo XXI,* hence *Líderes*) created by businessmen of the Forum of Presidents of Bogotá's Chamber of Commerce, with the purpose of contributing to the improvement of educational quality through a program that paired companies and schools. Each company accompanied a school in the design, implementation, and evaluation of management models. The program was launched in 1994 with ten company and school pairs. By 2002, the program had expanded to include 189 schools and 109 companies. The involvement of *Meals de Colombia S.A.* (Meals) has differed from that of other companies. This private company, manufacturer and marketer of frozen foods, assumed the coordination of this multi-party collaboration in 1997, and has since built alliances with over 20 educational institutions. In the development of the *Líderes* Program two elements of the socio-economic context came together. First, highly trained young professionals, sharing a learning and service approach, decided to participate in social initiatives after some contact with similar international experiences. Second, the recession has pushed several companies that participate in the program—and others interested in joining it—to rationalize their resources. This has affected their participation and generated an imbalance in the number of companies and schools. As one result, Meals has had to increase its efforts and resources to face the unmet demands of participating educational institutions.

The Hospital Management Center (*Centro de Gestión Hospitalaria,* hence CGH) was founded in 1992 as a mixed public-private partnership that allowed private sector executives to lend their skills for the improvement of management in Colombian hospitals. The CGH has built and maintained alliances throughout its history with business foundations and several health-sector organizations that have included both private companies (Johnson & Johnson and *General Médica*) and social institutions. These alliances enabled the CGH to provide better advisory and training services for hospitals. They worked with 125 hospitals (25 percent of the total hospital beds in Colombia at the time), ten health care providers (35 percent of all health and social security systems affiliates), five Health Secretaries (that covered 34 percent of the total Colombian population), and 35 walk-in clinics. The creation of the CGH would not have been possible had there not been a strong interest from the National Planning Department top directors in promoting alliances between public health institutions and companies within the sector. Ideas of State's downsizing and modernization have become alive as the private and social sectors take over some of the activities that the State had performed in the past.

Finally, Indupalma S.A. is an agribusiness company founded in 1961 in the town of San Alberto. In 1993, internal factors (costly union policy and tense labor management relations) and external conditions (local political unrest and the opening of the economy in Colombia) pushed the company to the verge of bankruptcy. In an attempt to rescue the company, top management decided to redesign its organizational strategy. They focused on four community development axes: the generation of income opportunities, the strengthening of education, the construction of a culture based on peace and tolerance, and the development of citizenship and solidarity. This management model links together multiple alliances that the company built with social and state organizations for the promotion of regional development. The alliances included an effort with the Rafael Pombo Foundation to train communities in the area of peaceful conflict resolution, collaboration with an NGO called Urban Context for the development of the "Soccer for Peace" program, a partnership with *Fundalectura* to create San Alberto's public library, and an association with the Children's Day Organization to build playgrounds. Both the escalation of the Colombian armed conflict and foreign competition played a role in Indupalma's crisis. Armed actors took part in the polarization between workers and management, and had great weight in the labor agreements negotiated from the last part of the seventies to the first part of the nineties. Later, foreign competition forced management and workers to restructure the operation and costs of the company.

Moving from One to Several Alliances

Given the complexity of most alliances, organizations usually begin with a single alliance before embarking on several others. The CGH may be viewed as an exception to this usual progression. Created as a meeting ground for numerous health-sector agents, CGH was aware of the need to count on different contributions and complementary alliances, and so its founders invited several agents to join. The group launched what they called a "national project" to improve hospital management, and each organization has contributed resources and knowledge. In this experience several simultaneous alliances emerged, while all three remaining cases involved the creation of an initial alliance and the subsequent progression of others.

Alternative Structures

The organizations in our sample have increased their number of alliances in three different ways: by (a) replicating the same project several times with different partners, (b) by summoning various organizations to join in successive projects and (c) by incorporating independent alliances to their collaboration portfolio (see Figure 12 below).

The first of these formats is illustrated by *Meals de Colombia* when it took over the *Líderes* program. One of the first tasks undertaken by the company was the elaboration of textbook guidelines on the processes followed by schools. Thus, they managed to work alone with groups of ten schools each, replicating the process over and over in order to improve school management. According to Sandra Velasco, program coordinator at *Meals de Colombia* since 1997, program textbooks were instrumental in achieving a systematic methodology. "The *Líderes* Program started to become a policy. Meals sees that the program has a structure, and the board decided to continue its support to strengthen and expand the initiative." Expansion in this type of structure means adding associated organizations to an existing project.

The second type of structure was pursued by Indupalma when it sought partners for specific projects. For example, to carry out their "Soccer for Peace" program, Indupalma, Urban Context, the National Routes Program of the President's Office, and the San Alberto administration all worked together to promote the creative use of leisure time for children and adolescents, promote the prevention of drug addiction, and create peace-learning spaces for the community. For this project, the National Routes Program contributed funds to pay for the work of Urban Context, this NGO contributed to the design and implementation of the program, the town administration agreed to adjust fields and public areas to make them more suitable for community involvement, and Indupalma provided transportation and lodging for program coordinators, along with materials such as balls and nets. Expansion in this type of structure means adding a new project between a coordinating and several associated organizations.

MD illustrates the third kind of structure that involves organizations adding alliances to their portfolio on the basis of their own specific needs. All along its relationship with Manuelita, a partnership that involved interactions ranging from economic contributions to company participation in MD's board, MD built alliances with Davivienda, Servibanca, and Carulla-Vivero in order to raise additional funds.

Figure 12: Three Possible Structures for Multiple Alliances

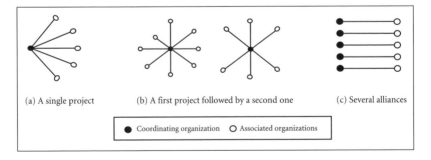

(a) A single project   (b) A first project followed by a second one   (c) Several alliances

● Coordinating organization   ○ Associated organizations

These three structures may develop simultaneously or independently. A common characteristic in the first two alternatives is the existence of a project. The alliance is based on the project and exists while the specific project is being developed, but partners withdraw once it has concluded. On the other hand, alliances of the third kind, those that are independent from previous ones, are maintained even if there are no specific projects at hand. These alliances may exist with or without projects, and their collaboration intensity varies over time.

Why Move from One Alliance to Several?

We identify three reasons for organizations to move from one alliance to several. Not only does such expansion increase the number of project beneficiaries, it also takes advantage of organizational learning in order to produce greater benefits, and it responds to offers of building new alliances. The decision involves consideration of not just the advantages, but also the potential risks and operational hurdles associated with taking on additional alliances. Thus, more than one reason has been behind these decisions in the four experiences studied.

Increasing the Number of Beneficiaries (Scaling up):

When a social organization tries to carry out a particular mission, it looks to resolve problems of great magnitude, usually associated with basic needs of the general population that require urgent attention, as is illustrated in the following testimony by Father Diego Jaramillo, president of the Minuto de Dios Organization:

> Father García Herreros once asked the National University for help in building houses. Dr. Alfonso Cleves, University dean at the time, responded to the request arriving for a meeting with the Father, who told him, "I want you to build a house here." Alfonso replied, "Very well, Father. We'll have the lot plotted and measured, and we'll draw the plans for the house." The Father quickly interjected, "No, no, no. The poor can't wait. We have to start building the house right now." Alfonso tells that they took their shoelaces off and tied them together to make a rope to measure the lot and sketch it.

Awareness of the magnitude of a problem indicates a recognition of the inability to solve it alone. First of all, the size of a problem poses difficulties for organizations, as there are limitations to resources. When MD tried to provide housing solutions for Colombians, it was aware of the amount of resources needed and looked for alliances to obtain them. Some alliances channel different kinds of resources provided by organizations such as Manuelita, or they channel donations from individuals through technology supplied by Servibanca and Davivienda. In addition to needing large amounts of a single resource like money in the case of the social housing projects, there is also the need to complement resources with technical institutions like a bank of materials to lower construction costs, legal firms to handle administrative procedures, financial institutions, etc.

Likewise, when private companies want to enhance their social contributions and reach more people, they also find it hard to do so on their own. Given the nature of certain targeted issues, financial resources are not the only need, as specialized competency is also relevant. In other words, the problems to be addressed are not the exclusive responsibility of a couple of organizations. According to Trist, social problems belong to inter-organizational domains and should not be approached by organizations acting on their own.[4] For example, Indupalma has realized that in order to work for San Alberto's development it must help to strengthen both regional civil society and state organizations. Otherwise, the company could end up assuming roles that do not belong to it.

Capturing Organizational Learning and Multiplying Value Creation:
Learning is another reason for broadening organizational alliances. The main aspect of learning related to alliances involves value creation. It is through alliances that organizations create benefits for their partners and ultimately receive benefits as a result of their joint effort. Alliance benefits also drive organizations to seek other alliances in order to increase those benefits.

MD executives have confirmed that, through collaborations, the organization has obtained benefits that would have otherwise been impossible to achieve. Also, they have tried to identify the needs of potential partners in order to find ways to create value for them as well. MD is aware of the need to give in order to receive. That is why they make sure to use the majority of their media exposure to thank their collaborators.

Indupalma views alliances as a means to leverage its resources. Thus, the company makes a contribution and demands matching funds from its partners in order to enhance resources devoted to its end beneficiary, the population of San Alberto. Clara Teresa Arbeláez, Rafael Pombo Foundation director, explained, "When you are dealing with Indupalma, to put it some way, first you need to tell them if you have matching funds. They are very careful with their resource distribution; they always ask if we have financing alternatives with other institutions."

In addition, Indupalma understands that it must create value for its partners, and it takes advantage of its strengths to do so. For example, the company knows its workers are an interesting target for *Corpoeducación* because that organization designs educational methodologies, and so by developing a program for a rural area adult population, they can provide themselves with a new useful competency in other regions of the country. At the same time, this methodology development provides an opportunity for better training of Indupalma workers. Thus, the company receives and adds value in the process. Claudia Calero, a consultant for Indupalma, elaborates:

> There is a great responsibility in adult training programs. We need to develop skills and competencies, especially in regard to symbolism in mathematics and communication, both oral and written. With *Corpoeducación*, we have thought about developing a program to strengthen symbolic skills in adults. They are interested because they would have a captive community to design this program.

There are two types of learning related to alliances; one associated with value creation and the other involving collaboration processes. The former makes organizations seek new alliances, while the latter helps facilitate and enhance these new partnerships. These two types bring us back to the categories of drivers and enablers proposed by Austin in his analysis of bilateral alliances.[5]

At the CGH, systematic and visible management results allow the Center to use a language that businessmen understand, thus facilitating communications and accountability. The meeting minutes of the strategic planning workshops of the CGh board of directors often include specific exhibits listing accomplishments versus guidelines set at previous meetings. Also, a systematic approach to school management processes was summarized in six textbooks by the *Líderes* Program, serving as a guide for any professional who worked with a school and was interested in replicating the process. In other experiences, process learning has been much less systematic and formal. The MD, which has intuitively built alliances since its inception, was invited by the

World Bank to participate in the National Alliance Program in 1997. One of MD's top executives then set out to understand the way in which they had developed its collaborations with various partners. This knowledge has yet to be systematically documented for others to use; it is instead part of the expertise embedded in the organization's culture.

In these cases, process learning allows for a reduction in transaction costs during the process of building an alliance. There is a virtuous cycle: alliance partners create value, learn from their interaction, and repeat the process at a lesser cost, thus getting a wider margin between costs and benefits and enhancing replication appeal. In addition, a higher degree of formal documentation of learning allows for an easier and wider acquisition of knowledge for organizations in regards to alliance work.

Responding to Offers:

One last reason to broaden alliance portfolios lies in the reception of proposals by other organizations that want to work together. When the MD started to name its sponsor during its television show in 1955, many companies became interested in this kind of relationship. The first sponsor was Beneficencia de Cundinamarca, and nine months later, Manuelita offered to cover show production expenses and donate sugar to be distributed among needy families. When they saw how Manuelita's image grew on account of its daily appearance on television, many other companies offered to contribute cash and in-kind donations in exchange for MD's announcements. Though some companies still wanted to contribute to MD and receive television recognition, the National Television Commission implemented a 1990 ban on all advertising announcements in institutional time slots. Manuelita's mention was the only one preserved as a result of Father Diego Jaramillo's negotiation with the commission.

Alliance propositions may also come from the public sector. In all four cases studied, results have caught the attention of state officials. Subsequent proposals to businessmen and civil society organization leaders have been varied, including invitations to undertake joint projects and create public-private partnerships. For example, three years after the *Líderes* Program was launched, the secretary of education of Bogotá challenged involved businessmen to develop the program at public schools. In the words of Adriana Hoyos, manager of human resources at Meals,

There was a group at the Presidents' Forum already working with the secretary of district education. They started telling us: "You have an interesting program, but you are only implementing it at expensive private schools in Bogotá. Why don't you consider this project for the public sector?" We then built a small second group that included only public schools located at Ciudad Bolívar, and we started working there.

Since there were not enough companies to pair each school, Meals decided instead to work with groups of schools. Through these new groups, Meals went from having a single alliance to coordinating over twenty. Thus, Meals was the prime coordinator of the overall multi-party collaboration involving other companies and their partner schools, but also it was managing multiple alliances with its assigned schools.

Multilateral Alliance Complexity

In multi-party alliances, there are additional variables and interactions that are not present in bilateral partnerships. Two possible paths exist for partner organizations to deal with this complexity: a decrease in environmental variety or an increase in their own variety.[6] Since there are some alliance factors that organizations do not control (those related to the operations, structures, processes, or cultures of their partners), it is more feasible to think that an adequate mechanism to regulate alliance complexity would be an increase in the organizations' own variety. Thus, the management of multiple alliances requires more organizational variety, understood as the ability of organizations to respond to the multiple states that the environment may adopt. In short, increased variety is a mechanism that helps adjust the capabilities of management to the demands of multiple alliances. Some of the characteristics present in multi-party alliances are described next. Our hypothesis states that the different mechanisms that organizations use to respond to these characteristics contribute to the increase of organizational capabilities to control the multiple states adopted by alliances. Therein lies its importance.

Initial Contacts

The critical role of initial contacts in bilateral alliances is preserved, though slightly varied, in multilateral alliances. Two factors determine variations: alliance portfolio structure and how organizations apply the knowledge acquired in previous alliances.

Two of the three structures previously described for multilateral alliances render top management's involvement in initial contacts even more crucial. The first structure described in which a single project is replicated with several organizations, is the only one that does not require constant participation by the heads of coordinating organizations, since that participation may be replaced by accomplished results and systematic processes. The growth in *Meals de Colombia*'s alliance portfolio, based on a defined process repeated several times, features great clarity in proposals for new partners and the kind of partners to seek, thus allowing for systematic searches in data bases and effective identification of numerous prospective partners. Initial contacts are distant, but once new partners have been chosen, relationships benefit from regular and direct contact between organizations. Contacts are useful in strengthening partnerships and detecting the failure of partners to deliver. According to Sandra Velasco,

> We have left several institutions out of the process because their expectations were very different. Some of them wanted to have a company that provided jobs for their last-year students or to have a place for them to practice. Others wanted to get money to improve their facilities. When we find these kinds of expectations, we work very hard from the beginning to let them know the process is not like that. But if institutions insist on playing that role, we just stop working with them (...) We evaluate attendance at meetings and response to the commitments made. I monitor that very closely; institutions missing meetings are called and questioned, and commitments are once again renewed.

For prospective schools, Meals' history within the program and the results obtained by other participating schools constitute a quality guarantee. The company invests very little in locating new schools, as the experiences of participating schools serve as incentive enough for others to apply to the program. The systematic process has allowed the program to face the difficulties arising from organizations' cultural differences, lack of a common language, stereotypes, and different rationales and operational rhythms.

Learning from past alliances is the second factor shaping initial contacts in multiple alliances. Although there were no formal mechanisms in place to record knowledge acquired from other alliances, the cases of Indupalma and MD illustrate how previous relationships affect initial contacts in new partnerships. In both cases, prior alliances and their results, exposure, and knowledge accounted for specific advantages in finding new partners. However, these cases differed in the approaches chosen by each institution, for while Indupalma uses what we call strategic opportunism, MD starts off with direct contacts with the needy individuals that will become the main beneficiaries in a future alliance.

If the project is new, there is a need to have initial direct contacts with end beneficiaries. Some MD officials have understood that alliances require trust building and constant presence at the target site to consolidate the joint-effort. Trust and presence turn some of these officials into joint work "preachers." Their alliances respond to the needs of some sectors in the population and feature close and fluent relationships between stakeholders. For example, to consolidate the Sewing Future (*Cosiendo Futuro*) alliance, the president of the MD University spent some time in the coffee production region to define the area best suited for a contribution to assist victims of the 1999 earthquake. He identified stakeholders in unemployment issues and contacted them directly. Father Camilo Bernal, the University's president, remembers:

> At the time of the Armenia incident [...] I made up a series of educational, energy, and communication missions, and I went there myself. We ended up working on unemployment issues because there were no satisfactory solutions. We had a meeting with representatives from the government reconstruction agency (FOREC), a clothing manufacturer in Pereira, the Labor Minister, and the Chambers of Commerce, and we began thinking about a project to create jobs. We sought FOREC's resources and signed an agreement in July, 1999.

Incorporating new organizations into an ongoing project constitutes a strategic decision to be made by top management. In Indupalma's case, management was fully aware of the difficulties involved in independently carrying out a development program for San Alberto. Thus, every time there was an opportunity to work with others in pursuit of that goal, company management did not hesitate to seize it. These contacts were eased by the exposure that the Indupalma case acquired, transforming the company into an appealing contact for many.

Alignment

In a collaboration portfolio, there are two strategic factors that should be taken into account: alliance mix and portfolio size.[7] According to Austin, focus and balance are to be held as priorities in deciding upon an adequate mix for a collaboration portfolio. Focus helps select collaborations to match core organizational interests and competencies. Balance implies a combination of different kinds of alliances (philanthropic, transactional or integrative) based on their relevance and contribution to the organizational mission and values.

In regard to the element of focus, the more aligned the alliance objective is to the organization's mission, the more relevant and valuable the collaboration will be. Another aspect to be considered is the mission alignment between involved organizations. Both aspects have been discussed at length in Chapter 3.

In bilateral alliances, when the missions of partner organizations are compatible, alliances can create similar value for both organizations. In multiple alliances, however, there is greater potential for complications. When coordinating organizations seek various other organizations with compatible missions, there is the tendency for competition. This difficulty may be overcome if a general goal becomes more important than individual agendas. The CGH provides an example of this situation. It has built alliances with several health-sector organizations, including some private companies. The CGH's mission, "to promote and lead health management transformation in order to contribute to overall industrial development," only contributes to company business if benefits are collective. No company is allowed to obtain individual benefits from its relationship with the CGH. According to Patricia Gómez, former executive director of the CGH, two things have been instrumental in keeping motivation high among partners through the years: they "feel part of a national project" and the CGH provides "a forum where suppliers, insurers, customers, and universities can interact." She also adds,

I remember an instance in which a board member tried to

influence a decision for his own benefit, and the whole crowd stepped in to tell him, very quickly and very softly, that that was not the idea here. If the question is whether they may influence things to benefit themselves, I don't think so, but there are other general benefits: their image benefits to some degree in every forum, in the things that we do for the whole sector where the board of directors shows up, and it is important for the members as supporting organizations who are interested in sector quality and improvements. That's a specific benefit.

One way to deal with the search for private benefits is to find a higher motivation that gathers all stakeholders above and beyond their private interests.[8] For competing companies that participate in the CGH, a joint effort to improve the health sector becomes more important than individual profits. In the long run, companies may benefit from having a stronger sector. Chapter 2 has already introduced the notion of "co-opetition," a dynamic that simultaneously combines aspects of cooperation and competition.[9] CGH also exemplifies the benefits of strategic philanthropy accruing to companies from what Porter and Kramer refer to as collective enhancement of the industry context.[10]

Due to alignment restrictions, organizations with a collaboration portfolio search for a mix of different kinds of partnerships. This is when a balance is necessary in portfolio mixes. Not all alliances should be integrative because, among other reasons, the degree of commitment required reduces organizational resources. Thus, integrative alliances can be combined with transactional and philanthropic alliances. MD's alliance portfolio provides an example of balanced relationships. Although the objective of each alliance is different, all of MD's alliances find a way to match its interests with those of partner organizations. In cases such as Manuelita's, both organizations share not only their objectives but their values as well. The three kinds of collaborations (philanthropic, transactional, and integrative) are included in MD's alliance portfolio: philanthropic collaborations with individuals, transactional collaborations with most business companies, and integrative collaborations, at some points in time, with Manuelita. Also, MD's partnerships are not static. For instance, its 48-year-old relationship with Manuelita has been, at times, a philanthropic alliance, while at other times it has reached an integrative phase.

In addition to being mutually complementary, multiple alliances have the potential to facilitate alignment processes on account of the formal status that they eventually reach. For example, when organizations are clear about the kind of partners that they are seeking through initial contacts, there are more chances for adequate alignment. Meals demands that schools applying for the program have educational quality as a value. Once these schools actually join the program, it is probable that they already have or eventually must adopt a highly aligned strategy. MD also looks for companies that view social responsibility as a priority, where there is coherence between mission, strategy, corporate values, and everyday operations. Clarity and formality in new partner selection are associated with future alliance alignment.

Value Generation

Value generation and its magnitude, along with exposure and the possibility of influencing public policy, are significant attractions for multiple alliance partners. The effect of multilateral alliances may be appreciated on three levels, and has the potential for a broader impact when compared to that of bilateral alliances.

Effects of Multilateral Alliances

The most obvious effect is for *alliances* themselves and it shows in the experience accumulated during the process of consolidating collaborations with multiple partners. That experience is demonstrated in various ways: the acquisition of a deeper knowledge regarding sectors served by alliances, greater access to assorted resources, and a strengthened ability to build new alliances. An example of enhanced sector knowledge is provided by the Meals' case. According to Adriana Hoyos,

> When the program was extended to public schools, several adjustments had to be made to the model. We had to learn more about educational laws because there are very clear regulations for public school management; resources were different, and many other things that we had handled with the first group were no longer applicable. For example, I have been involved in human resources and recruiting during my whole life, and I used to talk about the importance of the selection of a teaching staff as a crucial educational issue. Then, I came to realize that it wasn't like that there.

The overall effect of accumulated experience is that of a positive feedback spiral: each cycle provides results that would not be possible without the knowledge acquired in the previous cycle.

The second effect of multilateral alliances is for *partners*. In multi-party alliances, there is a limit to the value generated for the partners of coordinating organizations because the existence of several alliances jeopardizes the ability of the latter to serve all of the partners' inter-ests. In MD's case, for instance, mentioning more than one sponsor in the media would lower the image impact obtained by these sponsors. However, one effect that could appeal to partners in a multilateral alli-ance is the achievement of complementariness. Meals offers to schools the opportunity for colleague interaction that they would otherwise lack, and so the alliance is perceived as producing a valuable result. The same happens at the CGH. Health-sector companies appreciate the ability to have a forum to interact with other value chain mem-bers (hospitals, labs, equipment marketing companies, physicians, etc.). According to Orlando Sánchez, General Médica's president, "We wanted to get to know and understand the sector better, to know more about health. I was not interested in selling more; we didn't think we would. We are interested in learning, and we have learned a lot from this organization because they are very good at what they do." He also added,

> I communicate many of the things I learn. We have learned how and when to invest or not invest our scarce resources in first-tier organizations. We have begun to understand the dif-ficulties faced by health institutions and the constant struggle of directors to get resources for their institutions. We have learned about the current conflicts with doctors and about the importance, for example, of nurses by shift, which I never even imagined. [In the board of directors] there were so many people who knew so much about the sector that it was like attending free lectures or a graduate program on Hospital Management.

The third effect of multilateral alliances is for *beneficiaries*. Direct beneficiaries, to whom collaboration projects are directed, are the most important judges of any alliance. The following testimony by a member of the Rafael Pombo Foundation illustrates this fact: "Indu-palma understood the importance of interaction in its community, in its school, and in its own company... There is something very interesting there, which I had never seen in a private company, and it is their interest in improving via education. They believe education is the vehicle for improving the lives of those who work with them."

Although our research has focused on observing alliance building processes and not the impacts of alliances on the living conditions of end beneficiaries, it is still relevant to explore a few questions pertaining to this subject. As in the case of restrictions affecting value creation for shareholders, it is possible to question value creation for end beneficiaries in multiple alliances. Although coverage expansion becomes feasible through multi-party alliances, there is the possibility that coverage and quality may not always be adequately balanced. In the case of Meals, for example, a company associated with over 20 schools is a model of overwhelming coverage; however, the impact on each educational institution may not be the same when the company is working with so many partners. Is depth being compromised by coverage? What is the effect of this decision on the end beneficiaries, school students? The type of multi-party alliance can lessen this trade-off. If instead of a single company having relations with multiple Civil Society Organizations CSOs, which can dilute the company's resources, you have multiple companies collaborating with counterpart CSOs, as is the structure of the overall *Líderes* multilateral alliance with schools, the dilution risk is reduced.

As mentioned in Chapter 4, value generation in bilateral alliances is highly dependent on the degree of strategic alignment. The same applies to multilateral alliances. Equally important for both kinds of alliances is the balance in value creation for every partner and the mechanisms used to renew value creation over time. Balance becomes acutely significant in the second type of structure for multiple alliances, when many organizations are involved in a single project. If value creation for all participating organizations is not balanced, the collaboration may fail. In regard to value renewal, multiple alliances afford the possibility for value sources to last longer than in bilateral alliances. For instance, in the case of the CGH, the knowledge of management models and their application to hospitals constitutes a source of value for these institutions. Once hospitals have depleted this source of value, the CGH may use it with other partners that have yet to benefit from it. Apart from these common traits shared with bilateral partnerships, multiple alliances have their own value creation mechanisms, such as higher exposure or greater influence on public policies.

Exposure

Multilateral alliances have greater breadth because they operate in larger networks than bilateral alliances, thus increasing their exposure. Though there are exceptions, such as MD, whose exposure results from a mass media communication strategy that has been in place for half a century, exposure usually increases in time through organizational involvement in multiple alliances. By participating in the communication networks, institutional messages, or social balance sheets of its partners, MD's exposure is enhanced. In an editorial published by the *Asocolflores* Magazine, the description of the "Asocolflor-es Hogar" Program points out: "MD, a non-governmental organization that has been our partner since the beginning of the program, shares in its Community Building proposal our sector's approach, which is focused on human development and social welfare around families and communities as the main objective in housing programs."[11]

Another possibility for greater exposure through multilateral alliances is presented by the state when it requests the advice of allied organizations for policy making or when it invites them to bid on specific projects. Local or national organizations broaden their experience and exposure when they participate in public policy making. Our cases provide two examples that illustrate this point: the CGH won the contract to design the quality guarantee system that was later adopted and regulated by the Health Ministry. According to the CGH director,

> If we didn't win the bid, one of two things could happen: either another company won with a lousy project, which would mean trouble because that would be the quality evaluation system implemented here and people would be measured with the wrong yardstick. Everybody would work according to the wrong yardstick because it would be mandatory, and even if you came up with great ideas about doing some very nice things, you wouldn't be able to withstand pressure from the government's wrong yardstick. The other possible scenario was that if another company won with a good project, we would also be in trouble because they would become the national quality leader, and then we would have to change our mission because that is supposed to be our job.

Also, Meals' executives are frequently called upon to act as juries for the "Educational Excellence Award," a prize granted by the local government to outstanding educational institutions. Through his relationship with the district secretary of education, Meals' president became an advisor to the National Education Ministry.

Congresses constitute an additional exposure mechanism. In late 2002, the *Líderes* Program organized its second national congress to discuss school transformation experiences, with a turnout of almost 300. In regard to the forums organized by the CGH, General Médica's president says: "Hospital managers, administrators, and department heads drop by our stall, and we help them understand various technological aspects while we get to know what hospitals are doing and thinking; when are they buying, which resources do they have, what are their plans, and how are they growing. We are really eager to learn, to be there, to get them to know us."

Congresses involving several hundreds of participants in the health and education sectors have been made possible on account of the number of alliances within which each organization participates, along with their image in the sector, which guarantees adequate turnout. Thus, another virtuous circle arises: congresses provide greater exposure, more people get to know the organization and their attendance contributes to congress success, which in turn provides more exposure to organizing institutions.

Public Policies

Another alternative for value creation in multi-party alliances is the involvement of leaders in designing and transforming state agencies and influencing public policies. The size of alliances creates more of an appeal for state officials to monitor their progress and listen to their advice. Positive results from ten private schools made it possible for the Líderes Program to work with public schools; getting housing loans for traditionally excluded sectors has driven MD to be part of housing policy debates; working with different kinds of hospitals is a key asset for the CGH to participate in bids issued by the Colombian Health Ministry to develop its health system; and transforming community life through corporate policies has earned Indupalma a seat in national discussions on rural development.

Several practices, common within the private sector, have been adopted by the public sector to transform state agencies. Alberto Espinosa, Francisco Manrique and Carlos Alberto Leyva, participants in the *Líderes* Program have promoted the use of management indicators in the processes used by the secretary of education. Francisco Manrique explains:

> In 1994, I suggested that all company presidents should constitute a support board for public agencies, and we started out with the local administration. We began supporting José Luis Villaveces, secretary of education, through a fascinating process. Villaveces and his staff found it hard to accept our notions on management. We looked for management indicators and measurements, and they tried to collect the necessary information. At first it was a mess, and they were embarrassed every time we brought up the subject.

These organizations may also show governments a different way to go about politics. They start off with specific needs and provide effective local solutions that may later become more general solutions. This is very different from designing policies and programs from a central office in the capital city, only to await local transformations in a few years' time.

Based on the *Líderes*'s experience, Bogotá's secretary of education has designed a system of franchise schools that allows private schools to aid in public school management. Having the same resources, these private managerial teams will have to obtain better results. The CGH created a national award that, in 2002, was adjusted by Bogotá's Secretary of health to raise service standards at regional hospitals. The Secretary used the award as a mechanism to turn its demands into incentives, "less threats and more appeals." As Patricia Gómez put it, "Secretaries of health are starting to organize their own contests; they have taken our award to design improvement plans for their institutions. All of them are evaluating their operations, designing plans and implementing improvements with the support of their secretaries. It is being done in Quindío and Huila. Bogotá crafted its own award to set incentives. This is so much more than what secretaries usually do, which is to push from behind."

Institutionalization

The complexity of multilateral alliance management leads organizations to institutionalize their collaborations. Both of the coordinating companies in the sample, Indupalma and Meals, created a special area to manage their alliance portfolio. In turn, for both nonprofit organizations studied, MD and CGH, collaborative practices had been incorporated into their managerial style, and alliances were part of their organizational culture.

Indupalma has a department for community relations, as well as a consultant who looks for alternatives to consolidate alliances in order to support the company's four strategic axes. Additionally, its general manager devotes a great deal of his time to community activities, as well as interaction with state agencies and NGOs. Since 1995, the company's recovery after a general crisis has been associated with the development of what management calls a "business community," which includes not only "our workers and their families, but also the whole community surrounding the company and those who can be involved in the business." For Claudia Calero, Indupalma's consultant,

> It is not about social responsibility as it is usually understood: the identification of specific needs and implementation of a series of programs. Rather, we are trying to mobilize a whole productive chain and create a business community so that social development may be leveraged by means of income opportunities.

At Meals, the *Líderes* Program belongs to their Human Resources Department, which has two full-time employees assigned to the project. The performance evaluation of the department's manager includes a special indicator that measures her contribution to the community through the program. The general manager knows the program and regularly attends program events such as its annual congress. For his part, Alberto Espinoza, the organization's president, devotes part of his time to activities related to the program and other educational issues. For Adriana Hoyos,

> The job description for the Human Resources manager has always included an item for community work, but we only did scattered stuff. Once we entered the *Líderes* Program, my job description was reviewed, and I now have a key performance area called "community contribution." Obviously, it is hard to allocate percentages to something like this, for I devote much more time to the program than I should in terms of its share in my workload, but I don't care.

Meanwhile, at MD and CGH, alliances are an essential part of their operations; therefore, people and technical resources are allocated as needed. Father Camilo Bernal referred to Father García Herreros, MD's founder, as follows: "He got in touch with both the public and the private sectors. Then, he founded an organization [...] and what started with a single person has now become a community, and later a series of institutions, eight today, each with specific social goals. It became institutional."

In short, when an organization manages a large alliance portfolio, institutionalization becomes important for both the people and the processes involved. The high institutionalization degree usually attained by multilateral alliances facilitates communications, trust-building, and leadership. A description of these elements follows.

Communication

In the first two kinds of alliances, a single project replicated several times and a project involving many organizations, communications feature frequent interactions, agreed meeting schedules that are crucial for project operation, reports and specific information, and accountability mechanisms. Good communications are instrumental in these kinds of collaborations, since these alliances depend on projects: if projects fail, alliances are compromised as well.

The role of frequent communication seems to be less critical in partnerships of the third kind (i.e., alliances that do not depend on projects). MD does not contact Manuelita everyday; on the contrary, it handles its interactions with the company with extreme caution so as not to overwhelm it with messages. Rather, communications are based on Manuelita's participation in MD's board and in significant events. For example, the company never misses the Million Banquets organized by MD, and MD is always a guest of honor at the recognition ceremonies for the sugar company.

There are formal mechanisms, such as magazines, newsletters, reports, and documents (e.g., a social balance sheet) to communicate alliance progress both inside and outside of the organizations. In addition, these mechanisms may be supplemented by broad advertising campaigns. Indupalma has a communication strategy that has turned its experience into an interesting topic for different audiences. According to Rubén Darío Lizarralde, company general manager,

Throughout this process, we have had the support of an image and communications firm that has worked with us since 1992, and so we have been able to communicate clearly with our stakeholders. With this firm, we have carried out several surveys to investigate what the people, the workers, their wives, and San Alberto's store owners all thought. We got different pictures of what society was thinking. This information enabled us to issue statements that provided feedback to the region. These statements were large posters, printed in a very visible font, which we distributed and posted everywhere; on trees, on doors, at the square. Thus, we tried to set up a communication mechanism between the community and ourselves to break the barrier that totally distorted communications both ways. It was an extremely important process.

The CGH has recently worked on two major endeavors. First, a quarterly magazine published since 1997 that has approximately 1,300 subscribers; the other, the organization of an international forum since 1993 that involves approximately 600 representatives from 130 institutions. Finally, disseminating project results on radio and television is one of MD's key characteristics. Its daily minute on television, on the air since 1955, is the oldest time slot on Colombian networks, and in 2003, it was aired by seven channels.

Trust

As in bilateral alliances, specific results and commitment compliance also help build trust in multilateral partnerships. However, multiple alliances face an additional challenge associated with the ability of organizations to build trust among several partners. Image helps, according to Father Camilo Bernal. He explains: "Today, MD is a brand that everyone trusts: the government, businessmen, and the people. That's why we can get things done." This accomplishment, as their perceived ability to earn the trust of agents that become somewhat isolated, has led the government to request MD's involvement in certain areas of conflict, along with businessmen's interest in having MD initiate interactions for them with various communities. However, diversifying organizational attention in many areas may be a source of concern for partners. In order to overcome this difficulty, the MD has centralized communications with its partners, thus preventing the individual interaction of members with other organizations, which could ultimately serve to undermine their collaboration disposition.

Even more than in bilateral alliances, trust building in multilateral partnerships depends on having a "facilitator" and shared leadership. A mentor, with leadership and vision, can tighten a relationship that goes beyond a business deal; one that is based on a common goal that exceeds the individual interests of its partners. It is also essential to promote collective leadership so that each partner leads the processes associated with their respective strengths.

Leadership

Studying the common traits of leaders becomes relevant if we subscribe to the notion that their active involvement has a favorable effect on alliance results.[12] The leaders of all four sample alliances share some basic features like personal charm and flexibility, or better stated, the ability to adjust to changes in their immediate environment. The role of the people in coordinating organizations of multiple alliances should be noted. Sometimes, there is more than one "mentor" in each alliance; people who are deeply committed to the collaboration. However, these traits are not exclusive to multilateral alliance leaders, as they also apply to bilateral alliance leaders.

To understand the elements that shape leadership in multiple alliances, it is necessary to take a new approach to the concept itself and consider leadership as an element not necessarily related to people's behavior.[13] This contextual approach to leadership provides a perspective to understand, for instance, how multiple collaborations may respond to certain complex environmental demands.

This approach may be useful in analyzing what happens in multiparty alliances when certain organizations act as leaders. Systematic processes enabled the CGH to keep its institutional leadership (which it earned throughout ten years) after the replacement of its only director up until that point. At Meals, though there are still a lot of personal efforts involved, the company took over the alliance and all other collaboration agents view them as the alliance leader. Even though up until early 2003 there had been no management changes in the company (something that would have checked whether leadership depended more on the personality of the company's president or the company itself), factors such as learning systematization through textbooks led to the assumption that, in case of potential company management changes, multilateral alliances would still remain under Meals' leadership. Marymount School Principal Elisenda Recassen agreed, stating,

"Meals provided us with very significant feedback when we completed our process; we submitted all our analysis and our strategic planning, and they helped us to focus." Santa María School Principal Ana María de Samper stated: "We all envy the schools that have Meals as a partner. The company invests money in the program, does it without self-interest, and has two people leading it."

The importance of individuals during transitional times should not be underestimated. After Father García Herreros' death in 1992, MD underwent a change in leadership. When the general public expressed their desire for a new person to trust, the position was filled by another priest, who managed to uphold the image, leadership, and institutional recognition that resulted from 40 years of hard work. However, MD's organizational culture, which favors alliances, is the key factor in its operations. Ultimately, these cases seem to prove that organizational leadership is more important than personal leadership in multiple alliances.

Coda

Multilateral alliances constitute the alternative chosen by organizations that take advantage of the knowledge acquired in bilateral alliances to enhance the scope of their projects. Their knowledge of collaborative processes enables organizations to attract other partners, and their knowledge of value creation becomes a driving factor in this decision.

Multilateral and bilateral alliances are different phenomena. The comparison between the four Colombian cases of multilateral alliances and the many Latin American bilateral alliances in the SEKN study reveals several differences in initial contacts, degree of alignment, value creation, and institutionalization.

In the multilateral alliances studied, organizational leadership is as important as personal leadership. It is hard for these alliances to accomplish an alignment of mission, strategy, and values. The integrative stage that bilateral alliances may reach is almost impossible for multilateral partnerships. In spite of this difficulty, multiple alliances still manage to create great value for coordinating organizations on account of their exposure, while creating similar value for a larger number of end beneficiaries on account of their greater scale and influence on public policies. Also noteworthy is the institutionalization process undergone by the coordinating organizations of multiple alliances. The two private companies in the sample created new areas to manage alliances, while the two nonprofit organizations included alliances as part of their culture.

Multilateral alliances perform a very important task for the organizations coordinating them. If the coordinating organization is a business, alliances increase the company's contribution to society. If the coordinating institution is a nonprofit organization, alliances enhance its capability to deal with the complex social issues included in its mission. In either case, efforts put forth to confront those challenges associated with the coordination of a large number of partners are worth it.

Notes

1   Chris Huxham, "Collaboration and collaborative advantage," in *Creating Collaborative Advantage*, ed. Chris Huxham (Thousand Oaks, CA: Sage Publications, 1996), 4–6.

2   Diego Jaramillo, *Comentarios al artículo segundo de los estatutos de la Corporación El Minuto de Dios* (Corporación El Minuto de Dios, n.d. [cited June 29, 2003]); available from http://www.minutodedios.org/cmd/estahist.htm.

3   According to the 2002 report on the financial Colombian sector, the Davivienda bank ranked 5th among the 50 largest financial entities in the country. *Semana*, no. 1086 (2003): 59.

4   Eric Trist, "Referent Organizations and the Development of Inter-Organizational Domains," *Human Relations* 36 (1983).

5   James E. Austin, "Strategic Collaboration between Nonprofits and Business," *Nonprofit and Voluntary Sector Quarterly* 29 (supplemental 2000). Also in James E. Austin, *The Collaboration Challenge: How Nonprofits and Businesses Succeed through Strategic Alliances*, 1st ed. (San Francisco: Jossey-Bass Publishers, 2000).

6   The *increase* and *decrease* concepts, in their formal meaning, arise from the "law of requisite variety" formulated by W. Ross Ashby in 1956. These and other cybernetics concepts are useful in the study of organizations.

7   Austin, *The Collaboration Challenge: How Nonprofits and Businesses Succeed through Strategic Alliances* 141.

8   Ernst F. Schumacher referred to human beings' capability to find higher levels to dissolve contradictions found in lower levels as a great faculty. *A Guide for the Perplexed*, (New York: HarperCollins, 1978).

9   Adam Brandenburger and Barry Nalebuff, *Co-opetition*, 1st ed. (New York: Currency/Doubleday, 1996).

10 Michael E. Porter and Mark R. Kramer, "The Competitive Advantage of Corporate Philanthropy," *Harvard Business Review* 80, no. 12 (2002).

11 Augusto Solano Mejía, "Asocolflor-es hogar," *Asocolflores*, July-December 2001, 6.

12 Berger (1997), quoted in Chris Huxham and Siv Vangen, "Leadership in the Shaping and Implementation of Collaboration Agendas: How Things Happen in a (Not Quite) Joined-Up World," *Academy of Management Journal* 43, no. 8 (2000): 1161.

13 Refer to the quoted Huxham and Vangen work for other approaches and implications related to this notion of leadership; especially, within the context of inter-organizational collaborations between the public sector and communities.

11

Mexico: The Business Sense of Cross-Sector Alliances

Gerardo Lozano-Fernández

Introduction

Who draws larger benefits from cross-sector alliances, profit-oriented companies or Civil Society Organizations (CSOs)? There is a general tendency to believe that CSOs are the main beneficiaries in these types of partnerships; however, this belief is far from true. Our research in Mexico revealed that value created in cross-sector alliances develops both ways and is usually balanced.

This chapter explores the evidence of the joint management of social programs between companies and CSOs and the value created by these cross-sector alliances for the companies themselves. Although we cannot make definitive generalizations, given the limited number of cases in our sample, we do draw tentative conclusions to guide future research. At this time we will approach the topic through two specific case studies on collaboration partnerships between companies and CSOs in Mexico: H-E-B International Supermarkets (*Supermercados Internacionales H-E-B,* hence HEB) and the Monterrey Food Bank (*Banco de Alimentos de Monterrey,* hence BAM), and the Let's Build their Dreams (*Construyamos Sus Sueños*) campaign by Danone Mexico, S.A. and the Friendship Home (*Casa de la Amistad,* hence CdA). The collaborations presented are in different stages of the Collaboration Continuum presented in Chapter 1, and were created for different reasons. However, both have yielded positive results for the companies, thus demonstrating the business sense of cross-sector alliances.

After a brief contextualization of philanthropy in Mexico and a typology of collaboration, the first part of the chapter deals with value creation in collaboration partnerships basically arising from philanthropic objectives, and the benefits drawn throughout their development. Then, we approach value creation in partnerships predominantly resulting from commercial objectives. Finally, we draw conclusions and formulate general recommendations to enhance value creation in cross-sector alliances.

Philanthropy Evolution in Mexico

Although Mexican society tends to believe that the government and the Catholic Church are responsible for the solution of social problems,[1] it is a fact that some private companies have contributed to this task since they started operating. However, it was not until the 1960s that the private sector rose to a new awareness and started to adopt a stronger "socially responsible" attitude. Since then, more and more companies have gotten involved, in one way or another. A survey carried out by the Mexican magazine *Expansión* revealed that among the 20 most admired companies in Mexico half of them had their own philanthropic programs and the rest supported foundations, contributed donations, or allowed their personnel to participate in social activities.[2] In fact, if we take into account that more than two thirds of Mexican consumers believe that the profit-oriented sector has to share in the responsibility of solving social problems, and more than half of consumers believe that this responsibility has to be equally assumed by the government, CSOs, and companies, it could be said that the collaboration between the private sector and civil society is not only desirable but essential for companies.[3]

Many Mexican companies allocate part of their budgets to philanthropic activities. Results from an exploratory survey by CEMEFI and ITESM showed that 91 percent of 109 surveyed Mexican companies follow some kind of philanthropic activity, although the donations remain low compared to those in the U.S.[4]

However, increasingly competitive markets and severe financial pressures drive companies to seriously consider the possibility of reducing or eliminating their philanthropic budgets. In the search of alternatives to overcome this difficulty, some companies have reviewed the way in which they relate to civil society. Thus, the purely philanthropic activity of contributing a donation in response to a collaboration request—a common practice in past years—is giving way to a new notion of social responsibility that seeks to combine philanthropy and strategy in the hope that companies obtain a return on donations. This does not mean that companies or business people are no longer driven by altruism. Far from that, the upcoming sample cases will provide clear examples of mixed or blended motivations. What this really means is that the operationalization of social responsibility is focusing more and more on combining corporate strategy and philanthropy in search of gaining competitive advantages. Though this may be considered as a kind of "selfish altruism,"[5] it is a fact that, in times of financial difficulty, the strategic use of philanthropy prevents or, at least, deters companies from withdrawing their contributions. As a result, social organizations or causes supported are not impaired, and companies eventually go on contributing to the development of a better society.

Companies may undertake social responsibility in different ways; one of them is to handle their social projects internally, which calls for a commitment that goes beyond mere cash or in-kind donations to include their involvement in planning and implementing specific social projects. However, another alternative is the joint project planning and management between companies and CSOs. [6] In this respect a recent exploratory study revealed that 32 percent of the surveyed Mexican firms develop their social programs independently, whereas 63 percent do so in collaboration with an array of organizations (19 percent of them through mere philanthropic relationships). Interestingly, despite the finding that companies' motivation tends to be more related to strategic factors (e.g. fiscal benefits, legal requisites, clients' preferences) than altruism, the study also showed that the prevalence of strategy is incipient. Namely, only 11 percent of the firms with social programs had a corporate social strategy.[7] Along the same lines, a study conducted by Zimmat in 1998 shows that the profesionalisation of philanthropy (or 'new philanthropy') is still an uncommon practice in México. That is, 55 percent of surveyed firms suffered from the lack of any plan for allocating donations. Nevertheless, all of the surveyed companies supported welfare and development nonprofits rather than operationalizing their social activities internally.[8]

Different Types of Collaborative Relations between Companies and CSOs

There are many different types of cross-sector collaborations. At one end, there is corporate philanthropy, a basic donor-recipient relationship. At the other end stands the most complex type of collaboration, much in the way of a joint-venture, where both organizations involved combine their capabilities to create a completely new program.[9] These opposite ends correspond, respectively, to the philanthropic and integrative stages in the Collaboration Continuum, largely described in Chapter 1.[10]

Along these lines Wymer and Samu[11] offer the following description of collaborations between companies and CSOs:

- **Corporate Philanthropy.** Sporadic cash or in-kind donations to a CSO. It may include fund allocation to a philanthropic budget.

- **Corporate Foundations.** Nonprofit institutions created by companies to handle philanthropic objectives.

- **Franchising.** Agreements with CSOs to allow companies to use organizations' names or logos in exchange for a fee.

- **Sponsorships.** Companies pay CSOs for the use of their corporate name in advertising or other forms of external communication, usually in conjunction with some event or activity.

- **Transaction-Based Promotions.** Donation of a specific amount, whether in cash or in-kind, to a single or more CSOs, calculated as a fixed percentage of corporate sales. Cause Related Marketing (CRM, hereafter) is the clearest example of this type of collaboration.

- **Joint Promotions.** Promotions in which both CSOs and companies work together to support a cause. Instead of offering a monetary contribution, companies get directly involved in socially related activities.

- **Joint Operations.** Agreements through which CSOs and companies work in close collaboration to attain common goals and develop competitive advantages.

Whatever the type of collaboration between a CSO and a private company (whether collaboration objectives are philanthropic or profit-oriented, and whether relationships are in the philanthropic or the integrative stage), benefits rendered to the company will prove inter-sector collaboration to be a powerful corporate tool.

Discovering Value in Cross-Sector Alliances

In most cases, cross-sector collaborations arise from altruistic objectives and start off at the philanthropic stage. However, as the relationship deepens over time and moves on to a more integrative phase, combining partners' capabilities to create new value sources, top management will realize that collaboration partnerships and corporate business strategies may come together to develop unequalled competitive advantages. Such was the case of HEB, the Texan supermarket chain that started operating in the city of Monterrey, Mexico, in early 1997.

HEB and Its Social Strategy

When the company decided to enter the Mexican market, it also committed to adhering to the same social strategy it pursued in the United States. HEB remains a family-owned business, and the clear-cut philanthropic profile of its owners, the Butt family, is reflected in the company's mission: "To enhance life conditions of customers, partners, suppliers, and the community at large."[12] HEB's social programs in Mexico focused on feeding the needy, improving youth education in public schools and supporting charity institutions that provided direct assistance.

HEB had started its social activities in Mexico several years before it began operating in the country. However, this experience had not been very satisfactory. In response to a public agency request, the chain had been donating food to be delivered to needy sectors. Although the contributions did reach the targeted beneficiaries, the company realized that those were being used for political purposes. Thus, HEB became reluctant to carry out its social initiatives in partnership with public agencies and, instead, developed a willingness to collaborate with CSOs. In order to implement its social strategy in Mexico, the chain decided to create a nonprofit food bank— the first in the country. At the time, HEB did not take into consideration that BAM was already operating in the city.

HEB, under the company's Mexican name, *Supermercados Internacionales HEB,* started advertising its arrival to Monterrey more than a year before its first store opening. It was through an ad that Blanca Castillo, BAM director, found out about HEB's imminent arrival in the city and got in contact with the company to invite it to join the pool of BAM donors. At the time, she was not aware of HEB's close relationship with Texan food banks or of its intentions to collaborate with local food banks once it started operating in Mexico.

Food Bank Support to HEB's Social Strategy

Selling damaged goods[13] at discount prices in what is a known as second or third-class markets is a common practice in the supermarket industry. However, HEB's policy was not to profit from its damaged goods; instead, to pursue its mission, the company distributed them in needy areas. For this purpose, the company had to allocate special resources for an activity outside the company's core competencies. Therefore, an institution such as BAM could become an ideal partner for HEB to outsource this task, thus allowing the company to implement the same corporate social strategy it developed in the United States. The chain only had to make sure that food reached the bank, and the latter would take over the distribution process to the needy. It appeared as a relatively easy way to accomplish HEB's social strategy. Therefore, it could be argued that the motivation driving HEB to enter an alliance was triggered by profit-oriented reasons, since the chain *needed* someone to handle food distribution among the socially excluded. However, the significant funding provided by the company to refurbish BAM and the fact that it did not use its social strategy as an advertising asset or a sales incentive tool proved quite the contrary.

In fact, the owners' personal philanthropic values were reflected on almost all company operations. As Norma Treviño, HEB Mexico Public Relations Manager, put it, "We are not in this to increase our sales… nor to obtain profits. HEB's social commitment is such that contributing to society is part of its operating strategy in any city it operates in."

The Beginning of the Relationship and Its Value Creation Potential

As already mentioned, HEB's intention was to replicate in Mexico the social strategy it pursued in the United States. The *Feast of Sharing* was one of the activities carried out by the chain in Texas, and the company decided to start its social work in Mexico through a similar event. Since the decision was made in October, and the event was scheduled for December, little time was left to organize a large scale celebration to feed more than 10,000 low-income people. The first *Feast of Sharing* took place in December 1996, two months before the company opened its first store in the country. Since HEB was unable to coordinate the event on its own, it sought the assistance of BAM. It is to be noted that the first of these events was followed by subsequent yearly editions, combining both parties' efforts, and with increasing turnout. Moreover, the experience acquired in Monterrey enabled the company to replicate the event in other cities where the chain started operating.

BAM contributed to this first activity in several ways. It not only provided all its data bases to draw up a guest list, but it used its influence to invite other CSOs' members to volunteer and cooperate for this important event.

After this first undertaking in which both institutions committed their capabilities to a common purpose, they came to realize that joint collaboration was a potential value creation vehicle for both of them. This realization led to the development of a series of joint initiatives that resulted in a sound integrative collaboration.

The analysis of this alliance model leads to the conclusion that the collaboration significantly helped both partners meet their respective missions. In the initial stage BAM offered its distribution and event organizing capabilities, while HEB contributed its expertise derived from operating and managing food banks in the United States. However, it should be taken into account that both parties were willing not only to contribute their key capabilities since the beginning, but also to eventually adjust and combine them to create value jointly.

The Creation of New Food Banks

As we already explained, HEB's operations were closely linked to food banks. Therefore, its policy supported the opening of a food bank whenever it started operating in a new city, if one did not already exist. The creation of new food banks in five Northern Mexican cities jointly carried out by HEB and BAM was perhaps one of the greatest alliance accomplishments. Setting up the first food bank in any city is not an easy task. However, BAM facilitated the process by documenting start up procedures for new food banks. Norma considered Blanca's[14] documentation efforts as a key element in the opening of new banks. She elaborated on the topic: "When we were faced with the task of opening three food banks in three months, which was absolutely insane, Blanca showed up with her manual on 'steps to open a food bank'... It proved very helpful; we would have never managed it on our own."

BAM supplied the operation manuals, and both organizations set out to recruit individuals to join in the new food banks governing boards. They also embarked together on the process of approaching people and winning them over to the cause, "to make them fall in love with the project, thus selling the idea of creating new food banks." As a result, HEB managed, with the help of BAM's and its parent organization Caritas' credibility and extended social networks, to pursue its social strategy in these cities; it became a committed donating company to the new banks, making in-kind contributions and providing the necessary equipment for their operation.

Supporting Internal Operations

The administrative processes of both organizations gained in efficiency and efficacy through the collaboration; the dynamics of sharing and adjusting operation manuals (internal storage, regulations, job description manuals, etc.) were evidence of this. When HEB shared its proprietary operation manuals with BAM in a clear demonstration of trust, the latter designed an improved and simpler version that later contributed to nurturing its relationship with HEB. Hence, after assimilating, adapting, and applying the knowledge acquired from HEB, the food bank generated new value for the partnership by adding its own contribution. The first manual written by Blanca and HEB's first store manager in Monterrey was the "Damaged Goods Management Procedure Manual," which included a detailed training plan for HEB staff (managers and department heads) to optimize the delivery process of donated goods.

When describing the value created by BAM, HEB's Norma Treviño pointed out, "Blanca and her people go to our stores and detect improvement opportunities. For us, as a company, that is very valuable." She added, "Blanca and the BAM people know our warehouses better than many of our own people... They usually come up with some very positive suggestions for HEB." In monitoring and providing information related to HEB store operations, BAM was carrying out an internal operating function, a clear indicator of the integrative quality of the alliance. Also, at one point, HEB used BAM's warehouse to store goods before the inauguration of one of its Monterrey stores, paying rent and, thus, generating extra revenue for BAM from its excess warehousing capacity.

Third Party Involvement

As the alliance grew, new initiatives were developed. One of the joint activities carried out by HEB and BAM in the first six years of the collaboration was the *Golf Tournament*. It was a day-long event for top management executives of HEB supplier companies that donated cash sums going from $300 to $1,000. Although it was a new concept for BAM, this event had been carried out every year in Texas under the name, *Tournament of Champions*,[15] enabling HEB to involve its Mexican suppliers in social activities, thus achieving a desirable multiplier effect.

Another important step was engaging HEB's customers in the collaboration with the food bank through a CRM campaign. The *Thanks to You, I Will Eat* campaign was the result of Blanca's idea to replicate in Monterrey HEB's *Check Out Hunger* U.S. campaign. This activity proved very significant for both organizations. BAM not only raised funds through donations given directly by HEB customers, but it also gained more public exposure. Although HEB's policy was to keep a low profile regarding its social activities, this campaign was carried out inside the stores, supported by advertising, both at the cashiers and through a loudspeakers' announcement repeated over and over, thus creating an emotional bond with customers that would have otherwise been very hard to achieve.

The economic value created for HEB through the alliance has not been systematically quantified; in fact, measuring it is extremely complex, and, in an altruistic collaboration, it is probably unimportant. In this case, even economic losses were acceptable.[16] As Eddie García mentioned, qualitative measurements were taken, at least by HEB. He handled informal indicators, "Here in Monterrey, I see their distribution, their volume, and visit them to check on their progress." In addition, he expressed his belief that the large resources and work investment required to create BAM severely restricted its opportunity areas.

The Future

This alliance was born with predominantly altruistic ends, and, as the partnership evolved and mutual trust grew, new collaboration venues were discovered, thus creating competitive advantages. Future possibilities are enormous. For example, on account of its corporate policy, so far, HEB has not taken full advantage of its relationship with BAM for its public relations programs. In fact, most of its consumers are unaware of this partnership. However, now that competition in Monterrey's supermarket industry is fierce, and there is a price war going on,[17] differentiating their brand on attributes having emotional connotations for customers becomes a more relevant strategy. When HEB arrived in Monterrey, it changed the rules of the game and forced other supermarkets to raise the quality of their philanthropic offerings.[18] So, the question is whether, by exposing its social work, it will change the rules again and motivate other chains or retailers to join in the effort to develop a better society.

Alliances Founded for Utilitarian Purposes

The HEB-BAM case explores how collaborations developed for predominantly altruistic purposes at a philanthropic stage may evolve into integration and combine altruism with utility to benefit both organizations. The close collaboration built by these partners enabled them to create new opportunities to accomplish their missions. This joint value creation also allowed HEB to obtain hard-to-copy competitive advantages.

However, not all alliances are born for purely altruistic purposes. In 1983, American Express Company (AEC) launched a campaign in the United States to donate one cent out of every dollar[19] spent with its credit card, and one dollar for each new credit card issued during the last quarter of 1982. Donations were aimed at refurbishing the Statue of Liberty. Through this campaign, AEC proved that companies may simultaneously achieve both economic and social objectives. As regards its economic objective, the company experienced a 28 percent increase in the use of its credit card, and the number of new users rose by 45 percent as compared to the same period in 1981. From the social standpoint, AEC collected $1.7 million for the cause it supported.[20] This CRM campaign was a landmark in cross-sector collaborations, and has become one of the multiple ways in which companies can collaborate with CSOs to create social capital. Collaborations that match altruistic and utilitarian goals from the start are equally valid, as proven by the American Express Company project. Generally, these kinds of collaborations are related to company or brand marketing,[21] like the CRM campaign launched by Danone Mexico in association with several CSOs in 1997.

Danone and Its Social Strategy

Like HEB's, Danone's philanthropic disposition can be traced back to the company's founder, Antoine Riboud. His philanthropic philosophy is clearly reflected in the following excerpt from a speech he delivered for French employees: "I believe we can be efficient and humane at the same time, as long as we plan strategically (...) Let's run our business with our hearts as well as our minds, and let us remember that, while the planet's energy sources are limited, ours are unlimited when we are motivated." For Danone, humanitarianism is a corporate value, and decisions always take into account individuals—consumers, employees, or citizens. Moreover, this philanthropic conviction underlies what is internally known as the two-fold economic and social project: "Our culture is based on the belief that business success and a concern for people are inseparable. We are true to this two-fold project: we combine our commitment to business success with social responsibility. This is the founding principle in our business, and all our decisions—though sometimes hard—have been made on the basis of that belief."[22]

In all the countries where Danone operates, social responsibility starts inside the company, according to the guidelines set by the company founder in 1974. Employees are offered top working conditions so that they may reach their full potential within the company. Also, salaries are competitive for the market.[23] Similarly, the company has always been aware of its social responsibility, not only by offering excellent quality products, but also committing to several social development and environmental programs in each of those nations.

CSOs Supporting Danone's Brands and Social Strategy

In the mid 1990s, Danone realized that it had a weak public image in Mexico. "We were doing fine, but we were perceived as cold and detached from our consumers," explained Rafael Pamias, marketing director. After evaluating several alternatives, the company decided that a project associating it with nonprofit organizations could provide the means to change that image. Thus, inspired by Danone's philanthropic spirit and its two-fold mission, the company turned to assessing available venues. Though common at the time in several countries, these projects were new in Mexico. A survey would later prove that the Mexican public was willing to favor products supporting social causes.[24] Finally, the company settled for a CRM campaign to support specific projects submitted by organizations rather than the organizations themselves in order to serve its two-fold purpose more adequately (this will be explained in further detail later). In other words, Danone intended to reach out for consumers and, at the same time, contribute to solutions for social problems. Since it started operating in Mexico in 1973, its products were widely accepted for their top quality, thus turning the company into a market leader. However, its competitors were making some inroads; in less than six years, one of them had managed to position its yoghurt brand as second in the domestic market. Thus, in a highly competitive and slowly growing yoghurt market, Danone was under pressure to come up with novel initiatives to keep its leadership.[25]

In light of the situation the company was facing and its social philosophy, a CRM campaign seemed to be the most suitable solution, since these kinds of campaigns had been launched in other countries to accomplish a wide scope of objectives, such as: corporate image enhancement, sales volume increase, promoting repeated purchases, brand image improvements, and customer portfolio growth.[26]

For the campaign, which consisted of donating a percentage of the price of each yoghurt sold over a period of time, a strong promotional effort was deployed before, during and after the campaign, to raise awareness, thank the public and to show the results.

Throughout the campaign's first six years, Danone had supported several organizations targeting children. However, the closest and longest relationship had been built with the *Casa de la Amistad para Niños con Cáncer* (CdA—Friendship Home for Cancer-Afflicted Children). CdA was the only organization Danone had supported non-stop during all those years.

The Beginning of the Relationship

Chapter 2 has shown that prior personal relationships between leading individuals involved played a predominant role in the development of surveyed alliances. The Danone-CdA case was no exception. A prior relationship between participants reduces the risk perceived in long-term commitments. As we have said, Danone evaluated several social involvement alternatives to find a solution for its image problem. Among the possibilities initially assessed was creating the company's own foundation to handle social responsibility projects, which is a frequent corporate practice in Mexico. For this purpose, a company executive, who knew CdA's founder, Amalia García, decided to visit the organization to get a better picture of what a CSO was and how it worked. García remembered, "When the people from Danone came over, they told me 'we'd like to have our own foundation, and we want you to tell us how you do it.'" During the visit, the team from Danone noticed the professionalism displayed by CdA management and realized it would be better to support already established organizations, since it would not be wise to duplicate efforts. The company would therefore "outsource" its social responsibility projects by collaborating with organizations that had a solid image in the community.

Once Danone decided to enter into partnerships with CSOs, it set the criteria to choose potential partner organizations. Among other requisites, selected organizations would have to target children, display professional management, prove a background of transparency in resource allocation, and submit a specific project. The company contacted the Private Assistance Board (the association of Mexican private assistance institutions), which provided a list of organizations for the selection process. After coming up with a reduced number of organizations, the company invited them to submit their projects for evaluation. The CdA's proposal was selected, among others, because both the project and the organization complied with the selection criteria set by Danone. As a company executive put it, "This institution is very professional; it is legally incorporated. They are audited by Price Waterhouse, and they have an advertising agency working for them. They get everything for free; it's amazing, but they get everything for free."

Supporting Organizations through Specific Projects

An interesting development in the case is Danone's decision not to support organizations as such, but to specifically label its donations for individual projects. "We look for children-oriented institutions; we ask them to submit a project that is soundly designed for us to sponsor fully and, preferably short-term in order to show our results to the consumers." Supporting projects only, accounts for a series of advantages for the company: its social impact was easily quantifiable and, therefore, easy to communicate. The support is provided for a specific period of time during the year, and commitments are reviewed every year, thus preventing exit barriers and minimizing termination costs for campaigns and partnerships. In short, supported organizations have to ensure constant value renewal to secure collaboration continuity—which is what the CdA achieved through its proactivity and business awareness.

Value Creation for Danone

In many ways, CRM campaigns constitute a sales promotion campaign, as a company executive indicated. The basic difference lies in the fact that sales promotions offer an economic incentive for customers, while CRM campaigns offer philanthropic incentives instead.[27] As the cited authors have stated, CRM provides an advantage that is hard to obtain by means of other corporate activities: it links customers emotionally to a noble cause through their purchase of company products or services. As a Danone marketing executive elaborated,

We are building an emotional awareness of our brand in the

minds of our customers. That is far more powerful than any functional benefit, and, therefore, we are building brand loyalty. We are giving customers a reason to prefer our brands. We know this in Mexico; we have image surveys that have revealed that the first and second causes of preference for Danone yoghurts over the competition are more related to emotional closeness and quality than to functional reasons, such as nutritional value or flavor itself. Although, apparently, brand switching in yoghurt has to do with nutrition and flavor, the reasons for choosing Danone are based on emotional and quality factors—"it is a close company I trust and I like"—more than on price or functional attributes.

Through the campaign, Danone managed to get closer to consumers and projected an image of a socially committed company. In company awareness, Danone rose from the eighth to the second position in the top of mind ranking. During the campaign, which lasts four months every year, the company maintains its product prices, while, usually, the competition resorts to price discounts to promote their products. Interestingly, consumers still prefer Danone. In effect, the social cause insulates the company from price competition. Another significant campaign achievement has been Danone's image of a company strongly committed to society. For example, consumers assume the company is involved in the national fund-raising *Teletón*,[28] when, in fact, Danone has never participated in it.

In addition, the campaign has turned Danone into an attractive company to work for, allowing it to recruit highly skilled human resources, as indicated by one company executive:

> Many people answer Danone's call when we are hiring. They say they want to work for Danone because they think it is really cool! They are very specific about it, too, "I switched to Danone because... of course, the offer was good; we all need to make a living, but, also, I decided to change jobs or to join this company instead of another one because I think it is a good company," and then they mention the "Let's Build Their Dreams" campaign.

Throughout the campaigns, the CdA worked on constant value renewal for Danone and made sure the relationship was highly visible to the rest of society. At first, the company supported the treatment of CdA children in Mexico City, but, as time went by, its support expanded to other significant activities carried out by the organization, such as the creation of cancer-related medicine banks in other Mexican cities. The benefits were mutual: the CdA was able to grow geographically, while the campaign obtained nationwide exposure. Thus, both organizations' missions were accomplished at the same time.

As a token of the value Danone derived from the campaign, it should be noted that, by the time the case was written, the company had carried out the campaign during six consecutive years, under three different general managers. The main feature in the HEB-BAM collaboration is its high degree of integration, while the Danone-CdA partnership is mostly transactional. This difference does not mean that one relationship is better than the other; that depends on organizational objectives and how far organizations want to go in their alliance. However, it should also be noted that, although a transactional relationship may afford competitive advantages, it is highly probable that these advantages are short-lived, since activities of this kind are easily replicated by the competition. Differentiating brands on account of emotional attributes when other differentiating factors have been depleted has proven an effective strategy, as this case clearly illustrates. Still, as more companies get involved in similar programs, this differentiating effect for consumers will tend to disappear. Quite possibly in the future, association with social causes will become regular requirements to compete in any given market. Also, in transactional collaborations, where companies are free to choose the CSO they will support, the latter will also have the same freedom, once they have discovered their capabilities to create value for companies, to select the companies that best match their mission, values, and strategy and can provide the greatest value. The evidence shows that integrated collaborations provide partners with a greater capability to develop new sources of value for each partner, thus producing longer-lasting competitive advantages.

This case clearly describes an alliance that was born for mainly utilitarian purposes and, throughout its six campaigns, has proven to be a significant source of value both for the company and the CSO. After six years, the company finds no reasons to discontinue the campaign. In fact, company executives felt that "we will have a lot of explaining to do to our employees and the public in general if we don't have a campaign this year." The real challenge, both for the company and the organization, lies in keeping a constant value flow.

Lessons Learned

Our case studies reveal that benefits from cross-sector collaborations can be quite robust for both partners. The value flow not only goes from the company to the CSO, but also the other way around, and the gains appear to have been balanced. There is a great variety of value sources provided to companies by organizations, such as: brand and company image exposure, motivation for employees, support for internal operations, sales volume increases, strategic support, mission accomplishment, lobbying capabilities, and even testing new products in target segments, like in the case of Bimbo and its partnership with the Papalote Children's Museum in Mexico City.

As we have said, given our restricted sample, it is not the purpose of this chapter to be conclusive. However, some learning takeaways may be drawn to help companies or social purpose organizations interested in developing cross-sector collaborations.

Knowledgeable Candidates for Alliances

The company-CSO selection process to build alliances should not be random. It is necessary for a series of factors to be compatible, the most relevant ones generally being convergence between missions, fit between both target markets and between product and cause, and finally, complementariness of capabilities among the partners. In the HEB-BAM case, the desire to fight hunger and malnutrition in poverty-stricken populations was one of the common goals that triggered the partnership. Additionally, in this case there was also complementariness of capabilities between HEB, as resource and food supplier, and BAM, as food distributor to target markets. As to the Danone-CdA case, the fact that both organizations shared the same target—children—and a compatible philanthropic calling, made the partnership feasible. Also, CdA's capability to develop a positive image and Danone's capability to launch a CRM campaign were essential ingredients in the collaboration.

However, it must be understood that, even if they abide by these conditions, not all organizations are suitable candidates for collaborations. Both BAM and CdA were already consolidated organizations before these alliances developed; they were renowned and known to be professional and open to changes. Both organizations had extremely captivating leaders, who could communicate their causes to any audience. Thus, conditions were set for them to show their full potential once alliances were in place. Executives from both companies knew it: "From the very first time I visited BAM, I realized they had everything to turn it into something really big." "CdA leaders have the gift of seduction; they 'corner' you, and you can't say no to them."

When companies look for value in cross-sector alliances, either because their missions and strategies call for it (like in HEB's case) or because they are seeking marketing benefits, they should choose their partner organizations carefully. The conclusion drawn from the cases analyzed is that organizations to be considered as potential partners should have a reasonable degree of experience and stability. In addition, companies operating on a national level will probably seek organizations that have nationwide operations or are willing to grow to a national scale. BAM supported HEB in creating regional food banks as the supermarket chain expanded, while the CdA grew regionally through the creation of cancer treatment centers supported by Danone in other states.

The same question applies to companies: are all companies suitable candidates for cross-sector alliances? The answer is definitely negative. First, their missions must be compatible with those of the nonprofit organization. Also, capabilities should be complementary. Value creation in alliances should go both ways, and, for CSOs, value is not necessarily restricted to financial resources. Therefore, in order to choose a partner in the private sector, organizations should carefully consider whether the company image is compatible with the organization's cause, whether it has a non-controversial background, and whether it is willing to commit various kinds of resources to make the alliance work.

Finally, many companies launching corporate social responsibility programs face a tension between two fronts: the strategic front, where costs are absolutely relevant, and the altruistic front, where costs, though still relevant, are far less significant.[29] Once the decision has been made for the company to get involved in corporate social responsibility, the next step should be to determine whether projects will be undertaken internally or in collaboration with other parties. Both options have pros and cons, and both entail corporate risks and costs. This decision will depend on the company, its environment, and the objectives pursued by these programs. In many countries, collaborations between the private and the social sector have proven to be a very important source of value for companies. As a result, it is worthwhile to consider seriously joining a CSO to carry out strategic social responsibility projects. Cross-sector collaborations can make very good business sense.

Notes

1   *Mexico's Consumer Survey on Cause Related Marketing* (Promoting Public Causes, Inc., 2001 [cited February 18, 2002]); available from http:// publiccauses.com /resources/resource.mexico.htm.

2   Yolanda Ruiz, *Los ogros filantrópicos* (Expansión, August 1997 [cited May 22, 2003]); available from http://www.expansion.com.mx/2nivel. asp?cve=722_26.

3   *Mexico's Consumer Survey on Cause Related Marketing, Promoting Public Causes, Inc. (2001)* (cited). Available online http://publiccauses.com/ resources/resource.mexico.htm (accessed on Feb 18, 2002)

4   Patricia Greaves Lainé, *Empresas y empresarios. Tendencias actuales de la filantropía corporativa en México* (México: Procura, 2000).

5   Yolanda Ruiz, *Los ogros filantrópicos, Expansión* (cited).

6   Bryan Husted, *Making or Buying Corporate Social Responsibility* (EGADE Working Paper Series, 2001 [cited July 2003]); available from http://www. egade.sistema.itesm.mx/investigacion/documentos/index.html.

7   Bryan Husted and J. Salazar, "Un estudio exploratorio sobre la estrategia social de las empresas en México" (paper presented at the XXXI Congreso de Investigación y Extensión del Sistema ITESM, Monterrey, Mexico, 2001.)

8   Lainé, *Empresas y empresarios. Tendencias actuales de la filantropía corporativa en México.*

9   Walter W. Wymer Jr. and Sridhar Samu, "Dimensions of Business and Nonprofit Collaborative Relationships," *Journal of Nonprofit and Public Sector Marketing* 11, no. 1 (2003).

10 A more elaborated discussion of the continuum, and its phases, can be found in James E. Austin, *The Collaboration Challenge: How Nonprofits and Businesses Succeed through Strategic Alliances,* 1st ed. (San Francisco: Jossey-Bass Publishers, 2000).

11 W. Wymer Jr. and S. Samu, "Dimensions of Business and Nonprofit Collaborative Relationships." (cited)

12 "Partners" is the term used by HEB to refer to its employees.

13 Damaged goods are food products that, though in perfect condition for human consumption, are not suitable for store sale because their packaging is damaged or their due date is close to expiring.

14 She refers to Blanca Castillo, Cáritas de Monterrey, A.C. Food and Nutrition Service assistant manager and Food Bank director.

15 The Tournament of Champions is carried out in Texas every year to raise funds for the Special Olympics, not for the food banks.

16 P. Rajan Varadarajan and Anil Menon, "Cause Related Marketing: A Coalignment of Marketing Strategy and Corporate Philanthropy," *Journal of Marketing* 52, July, pp. 58–74 (1988).

17 Arturo Cantú, *Gane la guerra de los precios bajos* (November 3) (El Norte, 2002 [cited May 22, 2003]); available from http://www.elnorte.com/negocios/articulo/258231.

18 Ibid.

19 Throughout the case all references to monetary value are quoted in U.S. dollars.

20 Wendy L. Wall, "Companies Change the Ways They Make Charitable Donations," *Wall Street Journal*, June 21 1984, 1.

21 James E. Austin, "Marketing's Role in Cross-Sector Collaboration," *Journal of Nonprofit and Public Sector Marketing* 11, No. 1 (Spring 2003).

22 *Antoine RIBOUD Fondateur et ancien Président du Groupe DANONE 24 Décembre 1918–5 Mai 2002.* (Groupe Danone, May 2002 [cited April 17, 2002]); available from http://www.danone.fr/wps/portal/jump/DanoneCorporate.Presse.CommuniquesPresse.CommPresse050502.Edito3.

23 *Double project* (Danone, [cited April 17, 2002]); available from http://www.danone.com/dev_durable/img/double_project.doc.

24 *Mexico's Consumer Survey on Cause Related Marketing.*

25 *Boletín informativo FIRA* ([cited October 2002]); available from http://www.fira.gob.mx/Boletines/boletin009_06.pdf.

26 Varadarajan and Menon, "Cause Related Marketing: A Coalignment of Marketing Strategy and Corporate Philanthropy."

27 Ibid.

28 The *Teletón* is one of the most important and traditional fund-raising events in Mexico, involving a large number of companies that contribute to handicapped children rehab programs.

29 Husted, *Making or Buying Corporate Social Responsibility.*

12

Concluding Reflections

James Austin, Ezequiel Reficco, and SEKN Research Team

This final chapter derives from the rest of the book some final and brief reflections on three important questions:

- What are the key differences and similarities in cross-sector collaboration among Latin American countries and between Latin America and the United States?
- What conceptual advances have been made for the study of such collaborations?
- What important paths for additional research have been uncovered?

Comparative Analysis

Because each country is unique, there is an understandable tendency to believe that phenomena in one country will be different than in others. That expectation was even prevalent among the SEKN researchers as we initiated our study in each of the countries. What our research ultimately and importantly revealed, however, was that the cross-sector collaboration processes in the Latin American countries studied shared many more commonalities than differences. While differing, of course, in their specific operations, the collaborations were quite similar in terms of the factors that created strong alliances. Furthermore, these similarities meant that insights gleaned from collaborations in one country often enabled a greater understanding of collaboration processes in another country.

The chapters in Part II of the book did, however, identify some features that appeared particularly salient in some countries. First, in terms of the level of development of cross-sector collaboration markets, *Brazil* and *Colombia* appear relatively more sophisticated than in the **Central American** countries where the NGO sector appears relatively weaker and the corporations' collaborations tend to be more at the philanthropic end of the Collaboration Continuum.

Mexico, Chile, and Argentina appear to fall more in the middle of the Continuum.

Across Countries

Brazil appears to have vigorous cross-sector collaboration activity. The ideas associated with Corporate Social Responsibility (CSR) occupy center stage in mainstream thinking, attracting the attention of higher education institutions, think tanks, government, business chambers and the media. This solid consensus makes ignoring the social implications of private business a costly proposition. Not surprisingly, leading firms in the private sector seem to be well aware of their responsibilities toward the well-being of society, and to be constantly exploring ways of leveraging their considerable resources to that end. Perhaps more so than in other countries reviewed, CSR in Brazil is not only approached from an altruistic/charitable perspective, but is becoming an increasingly integral part of corporate strategy. As such, business engagement in the social sector is subject to the same rationality applied to other functional areas, and expected to be efficient and effective.

To implement their CSR, Brazilian companies find a mature third sector with which to collaborate. CSOs carry out roles that do not differ substantially from familiar patterns identified in analogous organizations in the developed world. These organizations possess technical expertise, professional management and sophisticated governance structures. Faced with the challenge of becoming self-sustainable while serving clients who cannot pay for the benefits received, in the last decade these organizations opened themselves to the ideas of competitive differentiation, accountability and cost-effectiveness. They are perceived by the private sector and government as valued potential partners. Thus, they are frequently sought after, much in the same way that companies approach other suppliers, or strategic partners, depending on the case. Stemming from the previous point, relations across sectors tend to be egalitarian and balanced.

In part, this apparent higher level of alliance development may be a "Big Country" phenomenon, in that the absolute numbers of companies and NGOs are greater. But it also appears that cultural and political forces have converged to nurture these emerging trends.

Colombia demonstrated vigorous engagement by corporations in social sector activities, often through corporate foundations that tend to operate somewhat independently of the companies' commercial agendas. Our collective review of this country revealed an intense interaction across sectors, with many sophisticated CSOs professionally managed, a private sector that actively seeks their cooperation, and a public sector that actively follows those experiences, learns from them, and seeks to enter collaborative schemes as an equal partner. Another prominent feature was the substantial wealth of aggregated experience in cross-sector partnering, perhaps best exemplified by the *Minuto de Dios* Corporation. This is a nonprofit group formally established in 1958, which from the very beginning embraced cross-sector partnering as the backbone of its strategy. After almost five decades, it has diversified into different industries, including higher education, construction, and radio and TV stations which also produce content.

Colombia's chapter stresses that their cases show that one of the byproducts of partnering across sectors was the mastering of the process itself, which encouraged the emergence of new partnerships, particularly multi-party collaborations. That could help explain why all four Colombian cases engaged various parties, even when they started (with only one exception) as bilateral schemes. The analysis of the Colombian cases shows that the virtuous snowballing effect of previous learning fosters the process of engaging in multilateral schemes:

- The institutional memory of successful cross-sector partnering creates incentives to scale up, so as to maximize value creation for participants and the community.
- Going up the learning curve diminishes uncertainty, and thus creates incentives to join new collaboration schemes.

In **Argentina**, cross sector partnering was energized by a burst of entrepreneurial energy in the 1990s, which placed this country among the most entrepreneurial nations in the world. A portion of those were social entrepreneurs, who channeled their efforts into cross-sector partnerships. The process came about as the result of two contradictory trends, which nonetheless contributed to the same outcome:

- In the early portion of the decade, the Argentine economy expanded substantially, particularly in the service sector, and those companies launched a number of social initiatives. The relative abundance of funds bred the emergence of *opportunity-based entrepreneurs,* some of which founded NGOs and engaged in cross-sector collaborations.
- In the latter portion of the 1990s, the Argentine economy con-

tracted dramatically, bringing about a severe deterioration of all social indicators. Massive unemployment and exclusion facilitated the emergence of a different class of social leader: *need-based entrepreneurs*, those who saw in social initiatives an opportunity to help others while helping themselves overcome some of the hurdles they were suffering. A good portion of these entrepreneurs carried out their activities through cross-sector partnerships.

Chile's social context stood out for its relatively high level of collaborative efforts displayed between people who were already familiar with each other. Its cases highlighted how in such a tightly knit society, social networks and family relations among leaders serve as trust-building bridges across sectors. Those networks can be seen as a competitive advantage in lowering barriers of entry into cross-sector partnering—direct relationships emerged as key in three out of their four cases. The central role played by the Catholic Church—which in that country appears to command a legitimacy spanning across the ideological spectrum, from left to right, and across social classes—may also have performed a similar role, lowering the barriers of entry into cross-sector partnering. The Catholic Church emerged as relevant in all four Chilean cases. Of course, the absence of these trusted connections can also represent a serious barrier to those seeking partners.

Mexico's cases particularly illuminated the effects of the globalizing economy—which played a direct role in three of their four cases—and the distinctive role of multinational corporations as a source of cross-sector collaborations. Of particular interest was how multinational corporations bring a more utilitarian and strategic perspective to their collaborations than local enterprises. There is a transfer of their philanthropic frameworks, strategies, and techniques deployed elsewhere into the Latin American countries. Furthermore, their philanthropic approaches provide an additional competitive stimulus to local firms to rethink their level and approach to collaborating with NGOs. This is a particularly interesting and positive attribute of globalization.

Central America revealed a paucity of highly developed collaborations. The analysis carried out by INCAE researchers depicts a private sector engaged with the solution of social problems, although the business community tends to see their CSR more linked to their charitable drives than to the competitive needs of their organizations. This outlook pervades cross-sector relationships in the form of what is sometimes called the "charitable syndrome," where roles become petrified in bipolar fashion, with one side "giving" and the other "receiving," as opposed to a more bilateral and balanced relationship. Instead of partnering with the third sector, businesses often undertake social activities on their own; when they do collaborate, they tend to restrict their efforts to traditional philanthropic engagements with the NGOs. This trend limits their contributions to donations of financial or in-kind resources, as opposed to a more strategic leveraging of core assets. Here again, the comparison between the initiatives sponsored by AMCHAM and the *Foro de Presidentes,* as it was discussed on p. 163, seems illustrative. The most important consequence of this view is that it hinders the discovery of connections between competitive strength and social initiatives.

In part this may be a "Small Country" phenomenon, the opposite of Brazil: fewer and smaller companies and NGOs that are more resource constrained. If unchecked, this dynamic might become self-perpetuating: weak NGOs do not attract the interest of the private sector, and thus remain relatively marginalized and institutionally underdeveloped—witness the different role that CSOs played in otherwise similar initiatives in Nicaragua and Colombia referred to in the previous paragraph. INCAE's analysis brings our attention to the fact that the region's third sector historically emerged closely linked to the work of international cooperation agencies. These organizations still play a substantial role in the social sector nowadays, as revealed in their cases, where NGOs received critical support from development agencies such as the United States Agency for International Development or the Peruvian-Canada Fund. This dependency on external funding may have impeded the search for collaboration opportunities with the business sector.

Our INCAE partners tentatively linked the scarcity of cross-sector partnerships, among other factors, to consumer characteristics, insofar as people tend to base their buying choices exclusively on price with the social value engrained in products of cross-sector partnerships not being factored into their purchasing decisions. This weakens the incentive for companies to support social causes from a utilitarian perspective. In contrast, consider the case of *Posada Amazonas,* the only one in INCAE's sample that reached the integrative stage—which took place not in Central America, but in Peru. That alliance would not have come about without the intervention of an international cooperation agency, which made funding conditional to the creation of a cross-sector scheme. Moreover, the partnership targeted a segment of highly educated customers from developed countries, who did treasure the social component of the "product" created by the cross-sector partnership. Furthermore, the business entrepreneur saw corporate social responsibility as its primary competitive advantage.

From a comparative perspective, other cases studied seem to confirm that point. In Brazil, as commented earlier, the social responsibility of the business sector is widely shared across different sectors of society—and by consumers in particular. Thus, companies have strong incentives to engage in cross-sector partnerships, both carrots (*"what's in it for me?"*) and sticks (*"do it, or else…"*). The case of the Forest Stewardship Council (FSC) mentioned earlier,[1] also points in the same direction. The experience of this global NGO in partnering with companies confirms that educating demand is absolutely vital to the success of a cross-sector collaboration. To a large extent, FSC's efforts in bringing in more companies to its sustainable forestry certification scheme will depend on the education of demand: the difference between a commodity and "good wood" is not evident to the uneducated customer.

Latin America and the United States

The second cross-country comparison of interest was collaborations in Latin America relative to those in the United States. While we again found many similarities in the partnering processes and principles, particularly in building alignment and generating value, there were clear differences in motivations and barriers, which derive primarily from different contexts.

Our research suggested that the frequency of business-NGO alliances was lower in Latin America than in the U.S. as was the level of development of those alliances, with more being toward the philanthropic or transactional rather than integrative stages of the Collaboration Continuum. In part, these differences are a reflection of contextual differences. Country contexts can be systematically analyzed in terms of their economic, social, and political dimensions and there are significant differences between developed and developing nations.[2] The relatively lower levels of development of the alliance marketplace reflect scarcer economic resources; individual and corporate philanthropy is constrained by lower affluence. Social differences also impinge on corporate involvement in philanthropy. There is not the same degree of tradition or social norms favoring corporate philanthropy in Latin America as in the U.S. Charitable functions have tended to be seen more as the responsibility of churches and the government rather than business. Political and legislative differences regarding philanthropic engagements by companies also create distinct incentives for partnering. Tax deductibility for charitable donations in the U.S. positively induces corporate giving. Such incentives are not so prevalent in Latin America but do exist in various forms. For example, in Colombia special legislation in the health and education areas was instrumental in enabling the cross-sector alliances there. While our research explicitly excluded the study of partnerships with government, the influence or incursion of the governments in alliances seemed greater in Latin America.

There is a notable increase in interest of Latin American companies in CSR that has sparked growing engagement in philanthropy. One clear distinction, however, is that the motivations of the Latin American firms compared to the U.S. companies tend to be more altruistic than utilitarian, and are sometimes rooted in leaders' religious beliefs. For many managers and others, gaining commercial benefit from social sector activities is seen as socially inappropriate or even morally wrong. However, there are many local firms that are rethinking their traditional charitable giving and formulating more strategic engagements with NGOs. These efforts are propelled by utilitarian motivations and have closer links to the companies' business operations. Thus, we are witnessing an emerging trend that is similar to but lagging behind that of U.S. companies. As indicated above the presence of multinational companies that bring this strategic philanthropy approach to their international operations is also stimulating this trend.

These findings are consistent with those emerging from recent research on cultural differences among business managers in different parts of the world. In a comparison of 61 countries, the Anglo-Saxon culture emerged as performance-oriented and individualistic, as opposed to the approach prevalent among Latin American societies, more oriented towards their primary groups, such as family, and more "humane."[3] While both cultures do care about "giving back to community," they seem to understand it in different terms. The Anglo-Saxon culture expects individual performance to result in the general well-being of society. Alternatively, the culture prevalent in Latin America leans toward primary group collectivism, coupled with a strong priority given to the strengthening of public institutions.

The findings are also in line with recent studies on cross-cultural negotiation, which found that Anglo Saxon societies have an approach that can be characterized as impersonal, pragmatic and utilitarian.[4] On the other hand, the approach to negotiation prevalent in Latin America is marked by the importance of close personal relations, mistrust toward strangers, and a tendency to see negotiations in zero-sum terms. Those differentiating characteristics have implications for cross-sector partnerships in the Americas, and may help explain the difficulty of going beyond traditional philanthropy in Latin America. If relations across sectors were indeed zero-sum, every time a company wins, the partnering NGO or society at large should loose. In contrast, the Anglo-Saxon pragmatic approach, which pays attention to net results after a cost-benefit analysis, would facilitate transition towards transactional or integrative partnerships, which aim at creating win-win situations.

One of the social context barriers that Latin American firms face is the lower level of development of the third sector compared to that of the U.S. While companies in the U.S. have many more and organizationally stronger NGOs to pick from as possible partners, companies in Latin America often need to engage in institutional strengthening of their partners in order for them to realize their full potential. In Chapter 2 we constructed a typology to classify the NGOs covered in our sample, which ranked them according to their institutional capacity, from 1 (low) to 5 (high).[5] It is interesting to note that while in our Latin American sample the NGOs in the 5 category were a relatively rare exception, the opposite was true in the sample of U.S.-based cross-partnerships[6] where all of the NGOs studied belonged to that category, defined as "mature organizations, with strong executive leadership and highly specialized staff." This helps us to understand why the need to invest in building institutional capacity in the third sector partner emerged with higher frequency in our sample of Latin American cases. This implies greater transaction costs and is another explanatory factor for the lower development of the alliance marketplace in Latin America.

Because of this institutional underdevelopment and because of the cultural attitudes toward trust mentioned earlier, it also appears that in the Latin American context social networks that provide some personal or intermediated validation of the nonprofit organization are particularly important in establishing and developing the initial contacts.

Conceptual Advances

The research also produced some advances in the conceptual and analytical framework for studying cross-sector collaborations. These discoveries were propelled precisely because of the need to understand and explain some of the differences that emerged from the comparative analyses. There were new discoveries and advances in each of the four components of the partnering process.

- **Building the Cross-Sector Bridge.** There were three important advances in this first component of the partnering process:

  - *Motivational Spectrum.* In order to understand more fully the motivational underpinnings of partnerships, we conceptualized the motivational spectrum that allows partners to assess their own and their collaborator's motivations along the altruistic and utilitarian dimensions in terms of motivational type, intensity, and mix. It is very important to have a clear understanding of why partners are collaborating; unless expectations are understood, confusion and conflict can easily arise.

  - *Preexisting Relationships.* In the Latin American context of personalistic cultures, relationships emerged as more significant to starting a collaboration. These connections were vital to mobilizing the necessary level of trust essential to opening the door to partnering. Our research elaborated crucial types of relationships: personal and professional, direct and indirect third party validators.

  - *Institutional Capacity.* As indicated above, our research revealed that the institutional capacity of NGOs was a significant barrier in Latin America whereas it was not so in the initial stages in the U.S. collaborations. Different levels of institutional capacity were identified, each creating distinct impediments to collaboration and calling for varied responses by both partners to overcome these.

- **Achieving Alignment.** While the concept of fit existed in the prevailing conceptual framework, this work elaborated and refined that to deal with degrees of both breadth and depth of alignment of mission, values, and strategy. The greater the alignment, the stronger the alliance. Our new framing allows one to understand and assess more precisely the extent and strength of alignment. Thus, one can have a very narrow alignment with only one of the three variables, say values, but if that is very deep, the collaboration can have considerable strength. However, it is also vulnerable because if anything happens to reduce that intensity for that single variable, there is no other connection to draw on. Breadth of alignment across multiple variables provides sustainability through multiple connections, but the strength will be determined by the depth of that alignment with each of those variables. If the connection is very superficial, then that too makes the collaboration vulnerable. Finally, this study identified the fact that different points of alignment operate in distinct ways. The range of alignment can vary from being compatible to convergent to congruent, which can carry important implications for the evolution of the partnership.

- **Creating Value.** While our research confirmed the importance of deploying and combining core competencies and key assets as a source of generating value, we also advanced our understanding of the dynamics of the value generation process. From this we conceptualized the Virtuous Circle of Value Creation wherein recognition of partner's needs and proactive responses to them leads to reciprocal and reinforcing reactions that benefits both partners at ever-higher levels.

- **Managing the Alliance.** The research identified additional key elements contributing to the effective management of partner relationships, and it deepened our understanding of the processes that build the critical intangible asset of trust. Furthermore, it extended the framework to encompass the management of multi-party alliances, which have additional complexities due to scale and diversity. The multi-party dynamics also affect the value creation process. It appears that value depreciates more slowly than in bilateral relationships because the same resources can be redeployed to new partners instead of being used again and again with the same partner with declining value each time. Furthermore, bilateral value imbalance can be tolerated more because a partner is also drawing value from the other members in the multi-party alliance.

It is also important to note again that collaborations are not panaceas in the U.S.A. or Latin America. There are clear risks and costs to partnering, as revealed throughout the book. Some of the problem areas that were uncovered in the research both in Latin America and the United States that warrant keeping in mind include the following:

- *Unclear Motivations and Expectations.* This points to the importance of understanding one's own and one's partner's reasons and goals for partnering. Not only is this important in the initial stages of starting a relationship but also as part of an on-going process of periodic review and introspection.

- *Weak Alignment.* Where either partners' connections to values, strategy, or mission are either narrow or shallow, the relationship is fragile. Abandonment of the collaboration can readily occur due to any modest disruption. Consequently, it is vital for partners to scrutinize explicitly these connections and to search out ways to either create additional points of alignment, i.e., greater breadth, or deepen the intensity of the variable for which there is a connection.

- *Low Value.* There is no such thing as a free collaboration. Partnering costs. When the benefits do not exceed those costs, the partnership is not sustainable. Nor should it be continued. Partnering for the sake of partnering is not a good use of scarce resources from an institutional or societal perspective. In addition, to have clarity about what your partner needs and values, special attention can be focused on how to bring into play any of your key assets and competencies that are not being used to the benefit of your partner.

- *Mismanagement.* Problems arise because inadequate attention is given to managing the partner relationship. Insufficient communication or miscommunication appear to be particulary problematic. One would be well advised to have clearly established and intensively used channels of communication between the partners. In addition, jointly formulating external communication strategies is wise, particularly as it relates to giving credit for the partnership. This area involves the mutual use of partners' brands and reputations, which are key intangible assets that require careful management.

Future Research Avenues

While our research has certainly advanced the empirical knowledge of cross-sector collaborations between businesses and nonprofit organizations, more would be better. Studying this phenomenon in different countries than those we examined would further test the validity of the findings in this book and undoubtedly shed new light on the partnering process.

Among the aspects of the partnering process that seem particularly worthy of further exploration is the motivational dimension. The apparent ambivalence that some business people and others feel about companies capturing commercial benefits while also producing social benefits calls for further investigation. There appears to be a trend toward businesses thinking about philanthropic engagements in more strategic terms, and that managerial issue merits further scrutiny.

The phenomena of multi-party alliances spotlighted by this research revealed distinct dynamics and managerial challenges. This merits additional study, particularly in terms of the management of partner relations and the value creation process.

There is also a productive avenue to pursue by studying alliances with governments, both by businesses and NGOs. This would lend itself to comparative analysis with the business-NGO alliances to ascertain what findings and principles hold and which are different. Our hypothesis is that many of the findings will be applicable but differences will arise because of the organizational and political characteristics of government. In the same vein, it would be fruitful to explore three-sector collaborations involving business, NGO, and government entities.

Beyond research on the partnering process, there is a major need to probe more deeply those factors that enable NGOs and businesses independently engaged in social purpose activities to achieve high performance. And it is precisely that path of inquiry that the Social Enterprise Knowledge Network has selected for its next research activity.

It is clear to the SEKN researchers that collaboration across sectors represents an emerging source of value to the Latin American societies. It is our fervent hope that this book on collaboration has enriched and

stimulated scholars and practitioners toward building stronger partnerships between CSOs and businesses. It is our aspiration to continue
our contribution to the well-being of the region's people through our
ongoing journey of knowledge generation.

Notes

1 James E. Austin and Ezequiel A. Reficco, "Forest Stewardship Council,"
   HBS Case No. 9-303-047 (Boston: Harvard Business School Publishing,
   2002).

2 James E. Austin, *Managing in Developing Countries: Strategic Analysis and
   Operating Techniques* (New York: Free Press, 1990).

3 The characteristics of Anglo-Saxon culture were reported on Edwin
   Trevor-Roberts Neal M. Ashkanasy, Louise Earnshaw, "The Anglo Cluster:
   Legacy of the British Empire," *Journal of World Business* 37, no. 1 (2002).
   See also R.J. House et al., "Cultural Influences on Leadership and Orga-
   nization: Project Globe," in *Advances in Global Leadership, Volume 1*, ed.
   Val Arnold (Stamford, CT: JAI Press, 1999). On the main traits of Latin
   American culture, see Enrique Ogliastri et al., "Cultura y liderazgo orga-
   nizacional en 10 países de América Latina, el estudio Globe," *Academia.
   Revista Latinoamericana de Administración* 22 (1999).

4 A comparative study highlighting the main traits of the negotiation culture prevalent in Latin America can be found in Enrique Ogliastri, *El
   sistema japonés de negociación. La experiencia de América Latina* (Bogotá:
   McGraw Hill Uniandes, 1992). See also Enrique Ogliastri, "Una introduc-
   ción a la negociación internacional. La cultura latinoamericana frente a la
   angloamericana, japonesa, francesa y del Medio Oriente," *Monografías de
   Administración* 49 (1997).

5 Refer to "Imbalances in Partners' Institutional Capabilities" (p. 56).

6 City Year and Timberland, CARE and Starbucks, Bidwell and Bayer, The
   Nature Conservancy and Georgia-Pacific, Jumpstart and American Eagle
   Outfitters.

Epilogue

Partnering: An Additional Perspective

James Austin, Ezequiel Reficco, and SEKN Research Team

This book on partnering was produced by a partnership. The Social Enterprise Knowledge Network (SEKN) was created as a research and institutional development collaboration among leading business schools in Latin America, and the Harvard Business School (HBS). In the past two years, not only have we learned a good deal about the organizations studied but SEKN's activity has also proved to be a rich laboratory on the process of collaborative knowledge creation on a continental scale. As a way of providing an additional perspective on the partnering principles that we have been exploring in the previous chapters, we conclude this collective effort by sharing some reflections on our own partnering experience. The SEKN collaboration differs from those studied in the book because it is a partnership among NGOs rather than between NGOs and businesses. Therefore, examining it offers an opportunity to explore the extent to which the collaboration process and principles found in building cross-sector partnerships applies to an intra-sector alliance. We will revisit our experience through the basic components of the partnering process set forth in Chapter 1 and elaborated in the rest of the book: Crossing the Bridge, Achieving Alignment, Creating Value, and Managing the Relationship. We will also take a forward look at the Growth and Innovation dimension of the alliance.

Crossing the Bridge

Collaborations emerge to meet needs perceived by potential partners. In the case of SEKN, the original perception of an unmet need emerged from conversations between the chair of HBS' Initiative on Social Enterprise (ISE) and colleagues at other business schools in Latin America as well as with Latin American business and NGO leaders. This dialogue identified a pressing need in Latin America for enriched management education that increases the inclination and capabilities of current and future business leaders to engage effectively in the social sector so as to foster sustainable development. There is a parallel and equally urgent need to strengthen the managerial capacity of leaders of non-governmental organizations that are key implementers of socioeconomic change and betterment. Societies will achieve meaningful progress when there is a dynamic and responsible business sector and a vigorous and capable civil society. Furthermore, development possibilities are even greater if these two sectors are able to join forces in collaborative undertakings. Schools of management were seen as potentially playing a critical role generating the knowledge and providing the managerial training required to meet these human resource development needs. To respond to this need on a hemispheric scale there emerged the vision of a collaborative undertaking among leading business schools, with the purpose of not just conducting research together, but actually producing teaching materials that would allow each institution to fulfill its educational mission.

Because the collaboration was within a single subsector, higher education in management, there was greater industry knowledge, social and professional connections, common academic language, and similar cultures. Thus, many of the barriers present in the cross-sector collaborations studied in the book were either not present or reduced in importance. Nonetheless, the founding members of SEKN did have to overcome geographical, cultural, economic, and institutional differences. As in the creation of most alliances, there is an initiating entrepreneur, in this case the Chairperson of the Harvard Business School Initiative on Social Enterprise. The task of connecting with other business schools was facilitated by his long-standing personal and professional relationships with professors at several Latin American schools. In many instances there was a reasonable amount of knowledge about potential partner schools and a high enough level of mutual respect and trust to have frank conversations with colleagues at these schools about the desirability and feasibility of creating a network. In countries where the ISE Chair did not have preexisting relationships, the Director of the HBS Latin America Research Center (LARC) used his relationship network to create the connection.

While personal connections provide access and a point of contact to engage in dialogue, the prospect of entering an inter-institutional alliance, be it cross-sector or intra-sector, elevates the organizational stakes. SEKN was not simply a possible research project involving a couple of professorial colleagues, but rather a more ambitious undertaking involving significant institutional commitment. In a higher stakes collaboration situation, institutional rather than just personal credibility becomes essential. The Harvard Business School's internationally recognized role in management education coupled with the physical presence it established in the region through the HBS Latin America Research Center[1] provided this additional dimension. Another asset more specifically related to the collaboration was HBS's experience and intellectual capital in mounting its Initiative on Social Enterprise begun in 1993. HBS was offering to share that knowledge and teaching materials with its potential partners to enable them to engage more deeply in this arena. Analogously, the potential Latin American partner schools had credibility through their reputations as leading management education institutions in their countries. A few also had considerable experience in research and training of NGO leaders. The resources of the SEKN member schools were greater than NGOs in general, thereby further facilitating the collaboration process.

The fact that all participating institutions came to the table preceded by their individual reputation as centers of academic excellence made possible the emergence of a collegial environment, characterized by mutual respect, which facilitated the early discussions leading to a shared vision. Also, several of the leaders from the different schools had worked together previously in various undertakings and these personal relationships fostered the coming together. Among the barriers identified in this early stage, however, were the institutional differences. Although being similar facilitated the collaboration, some of the SEKN members were exclusively business schools and others were part of larger universities private and public, which required time to understand each other's organizational context. An additional difference was the fact that while some schools were experienced in the case study approach to teaching and research, others had little experience. As the network had embraced the case method as its methodology of choice, a decision was made early on to make an up-front investment to level the field and equip all parties with the capabilities that would be required to pursue the network's mission. To that end, SEKN faculty were invited to participate in an HBS teacher training program, the Colloquium on Participant Centered Learning in Boston, together with other professors from outside the United States. Additional training on case writing was carried out in the SEKN research workshops held approximately every six months. This process is analogous to the institutional strengthening that we saw was sometimes necessary in the business-NGO alliances we studied.

In designing all types of partnerships, it is important for partners to clearly communicate their needs. In the dialogue with the Latin American schools, it became evident that in order to mount a serious research and training effort in social enterprise, substantial financial resources would be needed to support faculty and administrative research teams. To meet this need HBS began a dialogue with AVINA, which partners with leaders of civil society and business in their initiatives for sustainable development in Ibero America. AVINA saw SEKN as a new approach to strengthening the social contributions of both business and social sector leaders and thus agreed to enter as a full partner to provide matching grants to each of the schools that entered into SEKN. The partnership was envisioned as six years in duration consisting of three two-year research cycles, with additional schools joining SEKN for each cycle. The AVINA funds provided a critical enabling resource, and the foundation's matching requirement increased each school's institutional commitment to the undertaking. AVINA also offered its experience and network of contacts with business and NGO leaders as additional assets relevant to the work of the Network.

In the emergence of NGO-business alliances discussed in this book we saw that underlying motivations were often a mixture of altruism and utilitarianism. In the creation of SEKN all of the partners were NGOs and so the altruistic motivation of strengthening the capacity of nonprofit and business leaders to create social value and better society was predominant. Additionally, however, from a utilitarian perspective, the schools saw the Network as a vehicle for enhancing their institutional capabilities, developing new programs, and strengthening ties with social and business leaders. For some it was also seen as another way to differentiate further their school and create some competitive advantage.

Achieving Alignment

We have seen from the previous chapters that achieving an alignment of partners' mission, values, and strategy with the collaboration is essential to creating a strong strategic alliance. The strength of the alignment can come from breadth of connection across mission, values, and strategy, and also from depth of connection through profound congruency on one or more of these three dimensions.

Mission

In general, intra-sector collaborations have a greater chance of mission compatibility than cross-sector alliances because they all are engaged in the same basic activity, in this instance higher management education. But not all business schools have the same mission. The founding members of SEKN, however, shared a strong alignment with the Network's mission because seeing social enterprise as an integral dimension of the school's mission was a prerequisite to entering SEKN. Confirmation of this mission fit was ratified in conversations with the top leadership of each school. The premise was that social enterprise must be seen as central to a school's core purpose if it is to receive the level of organizational support required to achieve meaningful impact.

SEKN's experience constitutes an example of the dynamics of cross-fertilization, where deep and intimate interaction sometimes lead partners to redefine their organizational identity, becoming more alike to each other and building a deeper alignment. Moved by the experience of working in a closely integrated network devoted to social enterprise, at least one of the participating institutions is considering reformulating its mission, so as to give the social component a more prominent place.

Building on the commitment from each institution's top leadership, SEKN teams and team members collectively shaped the following mission statement, which captured and formalized the alignment of missions between all participants:

> *To advance the frontiers of knowledge and practice in social enterprise through collaborative research, shared learning, case-based teaching, and the strengthening of management education institutions' capabilities to serve their communities.*

Values

Although the core values of each institution varied, there was sufficient congruency in several important ones: professionalism, high academic standards, practitioner-orientation, integrity, and social responsibility. It is probably easier to find values congruency in intra-sector alliances than in cross-sector collaborations because of the relatively greater institutional homogeneity. However, it is worth noting that in the business-NGO alliances we studied in this book, alignment of values was quite common.

Strategy

The alignment of SEKN with each individual school's existing strategy varied. For some the fit was close because they were already engaged in social enterprise research and training. For others the field was nearly virgin territory and represented the opening up of an entirely new domain. Yet for others, there was depth in some dimensions of social enterprise, e.g., corporate social responsibility but not in nonprofit management, or vice versa. Overall, however, and despite the uniqueness of each individual fit, some common traits emerged. Chapter 3 showed that a partnership can help an organization by strengthening its connection with its stakeholders, internal and external, or by adding value to its products. SEKN has motivated and empowered the faculty and staff of member organizations interested in working in the creation of social value. SEKN's work also responds to an increasing demand by current and future leaders in each of those nations to understand the interplay of the business and social sectors. Finally, through the creation of a critical mass of cases studies, SEKN members have added a strong social dimension to their MBA and Executive Education curricula. In the particular case of HBS, the mounting of SEKN was consistent with the school's and the ISE's globalization strategy, which focused on engaging in important field-based research beyond the United States to generate new intellectual capital relevant to the school's global constituencies.

A fundamental strategic organizational issue facing each of the member schools was whether or not to enter into a collaborative production undertaking. While each of the schools had some cooperative bilateral arrangements with other institutions and affiliations with industry associations, none, including HBS, had an alliance that had SEKN's aspiration to engage in joint production of new knowledge in a tightly coordinated hemispheric organization with other schools. While most of the schools operated in different markets, thereby reducing potential competitive conflict, in various respects, some members considered others as competitors in the larger Latin American MBA industry. As Chapter 10 showed, even competitors can come together aligning the social dimension of their individual missions, putting the common good over the particular interests, in this case, the creation of practice-oriented knowledge that would contribute to more sustainable societies. SEKN shows the dynamics of *co-opetition* at play, where competitors come together to *make* and expand the market for social enterprise education. The win-win opportunities from collaboration were seen as substantial.

Joining the Network constituted a significant strategic risk for all parties, given its novelty, ambitious agenda, organizational and task complexity, and scale. The willingness to assume the risk was based on the perceived value that could accrue from this novel collaboration.

Creating Value

As we have seen throughout the book, the strongest social purpose alliances are those that combine their resources and deploy their core competencies so as to generate significant benefits for the partners as well as for society. One of the valuable attributes of cross-sector collaborations between businesses and NGOs is the diverse nature of their assets and competencies, which tend to be greater than that existing in collaborations within the same sector. SEKN's value generating potential is based on complementarity, scale, and scope. The Network's member schools, while similar in many aspects, are diverse in many regards. This creates value-generating opportunities by combining their distinctive competencies; weaknesses of some are compensated for by the strengths of the others. Part of SEKN's learning process has been discovering these differences and leveraging respective institutional and individual strengths. For example, one school's superior technological competency and infrastructure was used to create the Network's internet-based communication system and webpage, www.SEKN.org. At the heart of capturing the potential value emanating from diversity is the willingness to engage in lateral learning from partners whether these are from a different sector or the same sector. The opportunity to interact with colleagues outside of one's own institutional setting creates access to additional and different perspectives and competencies. This mutual learning has been evident from the beginning of the interactions of the SEKN researchers and has been a powerful motivating force for members. The learning has not simply been on the substantive research issues being pursued but also on how to build and institutionalize Social Enterprise activities within each school. Ideas have been gleaned from the practices instituted by other partners.

The second source of value generation comes from the scale of the network. As we saw in Chapter 10, multiparty collaborations—in that case multiple businesses and NGOs coming together in Colombia—can create greater social impact because of the greater scale. In the case of SEKN the combined efforts of multiple educational NGOs reach many more students and practitioners than a single or bilateral relationship could. Furthermore, there are learning economies of scale because multiple cases are examined and more peer teachers are involved, thereby accelerating the collective journey along the learning curve. The fact that there are more cases and more data points increases the robustness of the findings. Additionally, because each school produced a set of four cases, collectively twenty-four cases were produced, thereby making available a much larger body of teaching materials than individual schools could have produced on their own. This enables the creation of entire courses or programs more quickly.

The third source of value generation comes from the geographical scope of the Network. By having members from multiple countries in the hemisphere, SEKN is able to engage in cross-country comparative research on the same topic using a common methodology. Such multi-country studies are rare because of their complexity and resource requirements and are therefore particularly valuable in shedding greater light on phenomena in terms of differences and similarities across countries, as was highlighted in Chapter 12. Additionally, the Network can study simultaneously the multi-country operations of a company or an NGO, which in fact is being planned for the next research cycle. Another value generator emerging from scale was the interaction between partners—a case in point was the exchange of students between Argentina's POSFL and Brazil's CEATS.

Managing the Relationship

We have seen from the cross-sector alliances studied in this book that their effectiveness is greatly determined by how the partner relationship is managed. Focused attention on the relationship is an important element. In every SEKN school there is a faculty member designated as the institution's leader for its social enterprise effort. Within their institutions these individuals play the critical role of social entrepreneur in building their organization's social enterprise activities and linking them to SEKN. Each leader in turn has assembled a research team and these are the groups and individuals that interact across the schools in the Network. Top leadership support is an essential component of focused attention. So the backing of each school's top leader, which was elicited at the moment of entering SEKN, continues to be cultivated, including instances when there have been changes of leaders.

But important as it is, we know that top leadership commitment is not enough to sustain vibrant alliances. The collaboration has been institutionalized within each school in different forms. While the specifics varied, in every case SEKN-related activities were made an important part of the portfolio of responsibilities of faculty and staff involved—even to the point of being a full-time responsibility, in some individual cases—and was fully integrated into their incentives.

We also know that clear and frequent communication is the lifeline of any collaboration. For starters, good communication between partners is vital to the building of the personal relationships from which trust emanates. The communication challenge facing SEKN was significant given the members' geographical dispersion. This was met by a two-pronged approach. First, we created an internet communication channel using a Yahoo discussion group. This instantaneous e-mail channel has proven quite effective and efficient as a communication vehicle, although we had to learn how to not overuse it and to not send every message to everyone but only to the subgroup for which it was most relevant. We also created our own webpage that enabled us to have common files and other communication vehicles. We tried to migrate our e-mail communication from Yahoo to our web-based intranet platform but discovered that doing this significantly reduced rather than facilitated our communications. Consequently, we returned to the dual system. In order to provide a more systematic process of reporting progress and sharing lessons, we instituted a monthly report from each school that is consolidated by an HBS administrator and distributed as the SEKN monthly newsletter. The group reviewed whether the benefit of this communication outweighed its assembly costs and concluded that it did, with the main benefit being the capture by partners of good ideas generated by others. The reporting also created a discipline in self-reflection that was seen as helpful to the reporters themselves. The SEKN Coordinator role, played by HBS and its LARC during the first two-year cycle, also involved a major responsibility for communicating on common tasks.

The second form of communication was face-to-face, through workshops about every six months. While the electronic communication is vital, its effectiveness has been greatly enhanced by the personal interactions enabled through these group meetings. The depth of the relationships increases through the spontaneity and informal conversations that take place in the meetings. An electronic *abrazo* simply does not create the emotional connections that come from direct contact.

Equally important is communication within each participating school and towards their external constituencies. This has been carried out through a number of dissemination articles and activities. For example, SEKN has been recently featured in the *HBS Bulletin*—a publication by which the school remains in touch with alumni all over the world—and the *ReVista*—a magazine freely distributed and published by Harvard University's David Rockefeller Center for Latin American Studies, which focuses on Latin America, the U.S.-based Latino community, and the Iberian Peninsula. Additionally the SEKN team at the Universidad de Los Andes publishes bimonthly a virtual social-enterprise bulletin called *Makruma*, to connect various stakeholder groups to its social enterprise efforts. More broadly, in 2002 SEKN was prominent in the 1st Americas Conference on Corporate Social Responsibility, "Alliances for Development," organized by the Inter-American Development Bank, which focused precisely in cross-sector partnerships. Business, NGO, and government leaders from the hemisphere participated. HBS' team leader presented a preliminary version of the Network's research in the plenary session, and other SEKN team leaders moderated subsequent panel discussions. SEKN has again been invited to participate in the 2003 Conference, which will focus on "Corporate Social Responsibility as a Tool for Competitiveness." Given that SEKN's mission is to generate and disseminate knowledge, the group is engaged in a very proactive and coordinated process of making presentations in 2003–04 based on our research findings in a multitude of international and national professional association conferences and leadership meetings. In addition to the publication of this book and the distribution of the cases and teaching notes as a special SEKN Collection by Harvard Business School Publishing, SEKN scholars are also publishing additional articles based on the research in various academic and trade journals.

While the form of communication is important, the nature and content is even more so. SEKN developed norms in this regard. First, we had a shared commitment to producing very high quality research. Honoring this mutual accountability was more a function of peer pressure and respect, i.e., social control, than the formal contractual obligations to the funder. From this emerged the norm of valuing frank and constructive feedback. Good criticism is hard to come by and yet is absolutely essential to achieving superior quality. This type of communication has become an important benefit accruing to the SEKN members. That same norm has been applied not only to our substantive work but also to our group processes. We have a companion norm that explicitly encourages self-reflection on our own processes. Given that this network building process involves a great deal of learning by doing, we inevitably make mistakes, so we allocate time in each meeting for reflection on what is and is not working as well as it should. Giving and accepting criticism individually or collectively is not easy. It takes courage, maturity, and trust, but is nurtured by the underlying understanding that it is aimed at the commonly held goal of continuous improvement. It is our perception that these processes for accountability, along with frank and constructive mutual feedback, are equally important to the vitality of cross-sector and intra-sector collaborations.

Each school manages its portfolio of collaborations with other institutions independently and differently. However, they seem to be aware of the need to keep focus and balance in their alliances. Considering the magnitude of institutional resources that an undertaking such as SEKN requires to operate, this network tends to stand out as a strategic initiative in the portfolio of all members involved. That is certainly the case for HBS' Initiative on Social Enterprise, for which SEKN has a clearly cardinal dimension, as the backbone of its strategy of internationalization and field building.

Chapter 5 made clear that collaborations cannot come about nor operate without trust. In SEKN's case, almost the entire list of resources enumerated in that section were deployed to good results. Mutual trust was built by refraining from creating unreasonable expectations, by delivering on promises and showing results, by ensuring transparency in every step of the way, by institutionalizing a routine of joint work, by mutual respect and recognition, by jointly overcoming tough challenges, by walking your talk, by showing a long-term commitment, by building strong inter-personal relationships, and by the credibility that came attached to well-known institutional brands. In effect, the mechanisms for trust building hold for both cross-sector and intra-sector collaborations.

Another important element for a healthy partnering relationship is clear and shared responsibilities. In SEKN there has emerged a process by which all the tasks that need to be done get shared, with the division of labor striving for a sense of equitable workloads, recognizing comparative competencies, and creating learning opportunities. For example, different schools have served as hosts for the periodic research workshops or volunteered to take on specific tasks such as serving as treasurer for the Network. Each of the sessions in the workshops is led by different faculty. Delivering fully on these assumed responsibilities builds credibility and trust among the partners. This in turn has created a performance expectation that is a constructive form of peer pressure. The governance system is one of shared decision-making and a network coordinator role that rotates among the members.

It is important to note that the role that AVINA has played within the Network has not been that of a passive funder. From the beginning AVINA was seen as full partner in realizing the SEKN mission. Accordingly, AVINA representatives have been participants in the workshops and worked closely with the schools. Just as the SEKN schools have gone through and continue to go through a process of learning how to work together effectively, so too has there been a discovery process in the relationship with AVINA. The scope and nature of SEKN led AVINA to adjust some of its procedures and approaches to fit the requisites of the SEKN process and structure. There was sufficient congruency in goals and personal trust that these adjustments could take place as part of the ongoing collective learning process.

The organization is a coalition and the idea of formally incorporating as a distinct nonprofit entity was rejected, primarily because such a form might reduce the prevailing sense among the members of direct and collective responsibility for the existence and vitality of the Network. A separate formal organization risked becoming an entity "run by others" rather than existing only through the continuing direct inputs of the alliance members. We can think of the evolution of SEKN in terms of the Collaboration Continuum. The schools came together initially in what could appropriately be categorized as a transactional relationship: a research project that had a two year cycle, defined activities, and specified outputs. This book and the accompanying 24 teaching case studies[2] represent the completion of that cycle. In the process, however, SEKN has evolved more toward an ongoing integrative relationship. The Network has become a distinct identity in terms of its name, logo, outputs, external recognition, organizational structure and culture. It is worth noting that the members engaged in considerable dialogue around the name and the logo. There emerged a variety of linguistic differences for the same terms across countries. As a result, the members agreed that each country would use the wording that best represented the Social Enterprise Knowledge Network in their local language, but preserve the English name and SEKN acronym and a collectively designed logo as a common identity for all countries. SEKN is now more a joint venture, a collective undertaking, than a transactional project.

Growth and Innovation

Vital collaborations face the ongoing challenge of growth and continual innovation. SEKN is early on in its life cycle but is moving forward systematically. It entered into its second two-year research cycle beginning September 2003. Joining seven SEKN founding schools were four additional schools bringing in three new countries, including Spain, thus making the network Ibero-American. One of the founding schools withdrew because there was mutual agreement that it was not possible to mobilize sufficient faculty resources committed to the undertaking to deliver the expected outputs. This reinforced the Network's quality and output standards. For Cycle II the SEKN members selected a new research topic: "Key Performance Determinants for NGOs and for Corporate Engagement in the Social Sector." In contrast to the Cycle I research focus presented in this book that examined collaborations between NGOs and businesses, the new research will look at successful NGOs and corporations separately and will identify and analyze the key factors that have led to their superior social performance. The process by which SEKN selected this new intellectual agenda also illuminates the dynamics of the partnership. The basic selection criteria were that the topic would fill an important knowledge gap, would serve the needs of the member schools, and would be feasible. Many interesting and important research topics were suggested in a process of collective dialogue, but distinct preferences emerged because of different felt needs among the schools. A subsequent iterative process produced consensus around the aforementioned topic. An important additional norm manifested itself again in this process, namely, a willingness to continue to search for consensus solutions and to compromise rather than create destructive impasses. Constructive collaboration is not about winning, but rather winning together.

A final dimension of the SEKN growth strategy has been to create a multiplier effect within each country. One does not want to over-expand the SEKN membership because the Network could become organizationally unwieldy. There can be diseconomies of scale that should be avoided. However, to fulfill its mission SEKN does want to magnify its impact. This is achieved in part through the dissemination of the book and the teaching case studies as discussed above. Beside the creation of intellectual capital, an additional approach is for each SEKN member to create networks of schools and other social purpose organizations in their respective countries. These national networks aim to capture collaboration synergies and expand the knowledge generation and dissemination channels.

The need for strengthening the capabilities of NGO and business managers to generate social value remains acute. The potential for societal betterment through such efforts is enormous. It is a journey that SEKN is embarked upon. We hope that this book has moved us closer to that goal and that this Epilogue proves useful to others interested in harnessing the power of institutional networks to produce value for the greater good of society.

Notes

1   The Latin America Research Center (LARC) was one of five research centers established outside of Boston since 1997. The LARC was inaugurated in Buenos Aires, Argentina, in August 2000. It also maintains a presence in São Paulo, Brazil, and works in the other countries in the region.

3   Available through Harvard Business School Publishing as the SEKN Collection, http://www.hbsp.harvard.edu.

INDEX

INDEX